THE NATIONAL INSTITUTE OF
ECONOMIC AND SOCIAL RESEARCH

Economic and Social Studies
XXVII

THE FRAMEWORK OF REGIONAL
ECONOMICS IN THE UNITED KINGDOM

THE NATIONAL INSTITUTE OF ECONOMIC AND
SOCIAL RESEARCH

OFFICERS OF THE INSTITUTE

PRESIDENT
SIR ERIC ROLL, K.C.M.G., C.B.

COUNCIL OF MANAGEMENT
SIR HUGH WEEKS* (*CHAIRMAN*)

S. BRITTAN*	PROFESSOR W. B. REDDAWAY*
DUNCAN BURN	G. B. RICHARDSON*
SIR ALEC CAIRNCROSS	THE RT. HON. LORD ROBERTHALL
SIR PAUL CHAMBERS	PROFESSOR E. A. G. ROBINSON
THE RT. HON. LORD FRANKS	SIR ERIC ROLL*
PROFESSOR SIR JOHN HICKS	T. M. RYBCZYNSKI*
E. F. JACKSON*	PROFESSOR SIR ROBERT SHONE*
A. A. JARRATT*	THE HON. MAXWELL STAMP*
PROFESSOR HARRY JOHNSON*	PROFESSOR RICHARD STONE
PROFESSOR J. JOHNSTON*	D. TYERMAN
PROFESSOR R. G. LIPSEY	PROFESSOR T. WILSON*

G. D. N. WORSWICK*

Members of the Executive Committee

DIRECTOR
G. D. N. WORSWICK

SECRETARY
MRS K. JONES

2 DEAN TRENCH STREET, SMITH SQUARE
LONDON, SW1P 3HE

The National Institute of Economic and Social Research is an independent, non-profit-making body, founded in 1938. It has as its aim the promotion of realistic research, particularly in the field of economics. It conducts research by its own research staff and in co-operation with the universities and other academic bodies. The results of the work done under the Institute's auspices are published in several series, and a list of its publications up to the present time will be found at the end of this volume.

THE FRAMEWORK OF
REGIONAL ECONOMICS
IN THE
UNITED KINGDOM

A. J. BROWN

CAMBRIDGE
AT THE UNIVERSITY PRESS
1972

Published by the Syndics of the Cambridge University Press
Bentley House, 200 Euston Road, London NW1 2DB
American Branch: 32 East 57th Street, New York, N.Y.10022

© The National Institute of Economic and Social Research 1972

Library of Congress Catalogue Card Number: 72-83665

ISBN: 0 521 08743 0

Printed in Great Britain
at the University Printing House, Cambridge
(Brooke Crutchley, University Printer)

CONTENTS

List of Tables	*page* ix
List of Charts	xi
Preface	xiii
Conventions and Symbols	xvi

1	REGIONAL POLICY AND THEORY	1
	The basis of theory	1
	The long term	3
	The medium term	12
	The short term	16
	The chances of instability	20
	Moving people or moving jobs?	23
	A summary	25
2	THE REGIONS	27
	What is a region?	27
	The planning regions	31
	Physical differences	37
	Industrial structure	38
	Social differences	44
3	PRODUCTION, EXPENDITURE, INTERREGIONAL FLOWS AND REAL INCOME DIFFERENCES	52
	Gross domestic product	52
	Interregional transfers	61
	Regional current balances	67
	Interregional trade	68
	The 'openness' of regional economies	72
	Regional expenditure	76
	Price differences and real consumption	78
	How much does interregional inequality matter?	81
4	REGIONAL GROWTH: A THEORETICAL FRAMEWORK	85
	Lines of approach	85
	A start from factor supplies	86
	Demand and structure	89

The analysis of growth and its interpretation   page 93
A summary   98
Appendix 1. The basic neo-classical growth model   99
Appendix 2. Comparative cost and growth rates of
  industries   99
  (*a*) Change in terms of trade   99
  (*b*) Change in productivity   101

5 A LONG VIEW OF REGIONAL GROWTH   103
  The changing shares of population   103
  Autonomous versus induced population growth   108
  The sources of regional labour demand   116

6 STRUCTURE AND GROWTH IN RECENT DECADES   124
  The long-run employment multiplier   125
  Regional growth   131
  Effects of structure on growth rates   141
  Some elements in structure and growth components 143
  A recapitulation   145

7 DIVERSIFICATION, CONCENTRATION AND
  LOCATION   147
  Diversification and concentration   147
  Industrial advantages of scale   151
  Comparative advantage   158
  'Potential' and growth   160
  Optimal size of aggregation   164

8 DYNAMIC CONSIDERATIONS   176
  Regional multipliers   176
  The size of the input multiplier   179
  The size of the Keynesian multiplier in the short run 180
  The 'investment' and 'export' multipliers   188
  The longer run and the economic base multiplier   190
  Capital stock adjustment: the long run   192
  The short run: stability problems   198
  Other dynamic mechanisms   201
  Appendix. Proportions from other regions of the
    'mobile United Kingdom content' of regional
    consumption   202

9 THE LABOUR MARKET	page 205
The significance of labour-market discrepancies	205
Activity rates	205
The 'reserve' of female labour	213
Unemployment	215
The price of labour	232
The loss of income through mislocation of factors of production	245
10 FACTOR MOVEMENTS	250
Movements of capital	250
Movements of population and labour mobility	252
Types of factor movement: 'colonisation'	263
Mutual adjustment between capital and labour supplies and job-mobility	268
The role of multipliers	274
Costs of movement	278
11 EFFECTS OF POLICY	281
The earlier phases	281
The recent phases	288
The effectiveness of recent policy	292
The instruments of policy	305
Financial incentives	305
'Real' assistance	314
Industrial development certificates	315
Conclusion	317
12 THE SETTING FOR POLICY	319
The mislocation of population and industry	320
The concentration and dispersion of industry and population	322
Maladjustment between the growth patterns of population and jobs	325
Wage and income differences	326
The perverse working of market forces	332
Is regional policy necessary?	334
What policy?	338
Changes after 1970	344
Conclusion	346
List of works cited	348
Index	351

LIST OF TABLES

2.1	Distribution of regional employment by industry and regional coefficients of specialisation, 1966	*page* 40
2.2	Numbers in socio-economic groups as proportions of totals economically active in regions, 1966	45
2.3	Numbers in service occupations as proportions of totals economically active in regions, 1966	46
3.1	Factor incomes per head, 1961	53
3.2	Gross domestic product by industry per head of total population, 1961	55
3.3	Gross domestic product per head at factor cost, 1961	56
3.4	Occupational distribution of regional populations, 1961	56
3.5	Gross domestic product per occupied person, 1961	58
3.6	Earnings per employee, 1961	60
3.7	Gross regional product per head of population, 1961	62
3.8	Public sector current receipts per head, 1964	63
3.9	Public sector expenditure per head, 1964	64
3.10	Public sector net beneficial expenditure per head, 1964: deviations from national average	66
3.11	Financing regional net export balances per head, 1961	68
3.12	Interregional and intra-regional flows of goods, 1967	75
3.13	Domestic expenditure per head at factor cost, 1964	77
3.14	Interregional price indices and real consumption, 1964	79
6.1	The long-term multiplier, 1921–61: increases in occupied population at work	125
6.2	The long-term multiplier, 1953–66: increases in employees in employment	130
6.3	Regional and national growth rates in total employment: composition and growth components of the differences	134
6.4	Regional and national growth rates in non-service employment: composition and growth components of the differences	139
7.1	Coefficients of specialisation by region, 1953 and 1966	148
7.2	Coefficients of localisation by industry, 1953 and 1966	150

7.3	Levels of net output per head (Industrial Orders) explained by scale, size of plant and region, 1954	page 154
7.4	Levels of net output per head (all census trades) explained by scale, size of plant and region, 1954	155
7.5	Industrial structure and comparative advantage, 1954	159
9.1	Variations in male activity and inactivity rates, 1961: deviations from England and Wales average	206
9.2	Variations in female activity and inactivity rates, 1961: deviations from England and Wales average	208
9.3	'Deficiencies' of economically active women below those in the region with the highest age-specific activity rate, 1966	214
9.4	Total and partial unemployment rates, 1958–67	219
9.5	Structural changes in employment, 1959–63	225
9.6	Proportions of unskilled in unemployed adult males and economically active males, 1961	229
10.1	Movements of manufacturing jobs and capital	251
10.2	Gross migration between regions, 1961–6	253
10.3	Internal migration between standard subregions, 1961–6	254
10.4	Net migration between regions and from overseas, 1961–6	258

LIST OF CHARTS

2.1	Old and new Standard Regions of England and Wales	*page* 30
3.1	The 'openness' and size of various regional and national economies, 1967	73
4.1	Production possibilities for two commodities: change in terms of trade between regions	100
4.2	Production possibilities in two regions: change in productivity in one industry	101
5.1	Population by region, 1801–1966	104
5.2	Regional distribution of population, 1701–1966	105
6.1	Relation between increases in total and non-service employment, 1921–61	127
6.2	Relation between increases in total and non-service employment, 1953–66	129
7.1	'Potential' in Great Britain	161
7.2	Gross benefits of aggregation	165
7.3	Gross costs of aggregation	165
7.4	Net benefits of a single aggregation	166
7.5	Maximising net benefits of a single aggregation	166
7.6	Net advantages of two aggregations (unstable equilibrium – case 1)	168
7.7	Net advantages of two aggregations (unstable equilibrium – case 2)	168
7.8	Net advantages of two aggregations (stable equilibrium)	170
7.9	Net advantages of one aggregation and many small centres	170
7.10	Net advantages of one aggregation and several others all of optimal size	171
8.1	The flow of regional income and expenditure as a basis for estimating regional income multipliers	181
9.1	Hourly earnings relatives weighted by United Kingdom structure (male manual workers, all industries)	235

9.2	Loss of real income through inequality of marginal products	*page* 246
10.1	Net migration, 1961–6	257
11.1	The assisted areas, 1971	291
11.2	Moves to peripheral areas, 1945–65	293
11.3	Industrial development certificates, approvals in Development Areas and Great Britain, 1956–70	295
11.4	Industrial development certificates, floor areas approved in Development Areas and Great Britain, 1956–70	297
11.5	Industrial development certificates, estimated additional employment in Development Areas and Great Britain, 1956–70	298
11.6	Numbers of moves in the United Kingdom, 1945–65	299

PREFACE

In 1965 the Department of Economic Affairs invited the National Institute of Economic and Social Research

'to build up a theoretical and empirical framework for the analysis of regional economic development and the consideration of regional policy in the United Kingdom, especially in relation to problems of national economic development'.

A substantial grant was made for a four-year period which the National Institute gratefully acknowledges. The Institute in turn invited the present writer to direct the study, starting in the summer of 1966. It was a challenging, indeed a daunting assignment, which could be interpreted only as giving the research workers a most generous measure of freedom to seek out problems and to select those most likely to prove rewarding in a very wide area – subject always to the obligation to provide at the end a general view of the wood as well as studies of some of its more picturesque trees. This book, along with a number of monographs published or to be published as Regional Papers, sets out the result.

The study as a whole, including this book, has been the work of many hands. In some ways it would have been fitting for a number of names to appear on the title page, but the question is – what number? There is a continuous gradation, which it would be invidious to break too sharply, between long-term, major contributors to the work at one end of the spectrum, and those, at the other end, whose membership of the team was relatively brief. In the event, I have thought it best to take responsibility for telling the story in my own way, as well as the responsibility for those mistakes from which not even my colleagues have managed to save me.

This having been said, I must nevertheless select some members of the team, and others outside it, for special thanks. First, not only in the alphabet, comes John Bowers, the only member of the team for virtually the whole duration of the project, whose important contributions on most of the major topics we have touched are far from being fully represented by the Regional Paper on which his name appears. Next, Paul Cheshire, whose work on unemployment is to appear in a Regional Paper; Harold Lind, who in his early work on migration discovered one of the oddest errors ever to have crept into official statistics; Ed Webb, who has worked not only on earnings–unemployment and other labour market relationships, but, *inter alia*, on a regional index of industrial production which makes only a brief appearance in this book; Robert Weeden, who, besides his work on the analysis of structure and growth, and on migration, has given us a great deal of general econometric help; and Vivian Woodward, whose pioneering work on regional social accounts has already appeared as a Regional Paper. Among the briefer memberships of the team which have left their mark I must mention those of Agu Anyanwu and David Steele. As consultants to the team, Bernard Corry, Kenneth Gwilliam and Peter Hart – all of whom were elevated to professorial chairs during the period of the study, so fortunate were we in our selection – gave us valuable advice at particular stages. Others who worked on the project at one time or another were Mrs Jennifer Clarke, O. E. Essien, David McKee and Hugh Wenban-Smith. Miss Judith Williams was secretary to the team in the early stages. She was followed by Miss Marion Whitmell who, together with Mrs Evelyn McInulty, typed the manuscript.

From the officials of the Department of Economic Affairs and those who took over from it responsibility for regional economics, as well as other relevant departments, we have had unfailing help, as well as great patience with a project that took much longer than had been intended. And, while civil servants in their official capacities must remain anonymous, I hope I may make grateful acknowledgement of much expert advice and comment given in their personal capacities by Humphrey Cole, Robert Howard and Roger Thatcher. Among many academic friends outside the project to whom I am indebted for advice on particular parts of the work, I should like to mention especially Rodney Crossley of the University of Leeds.

I am deeply grateful to the University of Leeds for giving me leave of absence for the academic year 1966/7, without which I could not have launched myself effectively into the work. I am grateful, also, to whatever fates ordained my membership of the Committee on Intermediate Areas (the Hunt Committee) in the years 1967–9. Although the preoccupations it brought have delayed the completion of this book, only I am to blame if my participation in such a wide-ranging investigation of a major regional problem has not made it better.

This long (though very incomplete) catalogue of acknowledgements must end, where the study has both begun and ended, at the National Institute of Economic and Social Research itself. I am personally most grateful to it for presenting me with a most exciting opportunity, to which I cannot claim to have done justice. On behalf of the whole team of research workers on the project, I must express the warmest appreciation of the help given by all our colleagues outside our own circle; most particularly to the Director, who has given us every possible encouragement, but also to members of the staff, and indeed of the Council, who have in many cases shown a practical interest in our work well beyond whatever might reasonably be regarded as the call of duty. Whatever they, and others, may think of the results of our labours, it may comfort them to know that they have contributed enormously towards making those labours a pleasure.

NATIONAL INSTITUTE OF ECONOMIC A. J. BROWN
AND SOCIAL RESEARCH

April 1972

CONVENTIONS AND SYMBOLS

Note on conventions

Anyone working on United Kingdom regional data for any considerable number of recent years encounters the changes in the definitions of the Standard Regions introduced in 1966, as well as various earlier changes in the Ministry of Labour regions. The general practice in this book is to refer to regions by the names they had at the relevant time, though the old Midland region, which subsequently, in 1966, became the West Midland region without change of boundary, is referred to as the '(West) Midlands' to avoid possible confusion, and the term 'South East England' is used to mean either the new South Eastern region plus East Anglia, or the old Standard Regions London and the South East, Eastern and Southern, which cover nearly the same area. The differences between the old and new Standard Regions are shown in the map which occurs as chart 2.1.

The study is, in principle, of the United Kingdom, but lack of statistical comparability with Northern Ireland causes some parts of the discussion to be confined to the regions of Great Britain. References to 'the country as a whole' should be interpreted in context.

Finally, government departments as well as regions have changed their names and jurisdictions during the period to which the study refers, and while it was in progress. In general again, the practice in the book is to refer to departments by the names they went under at the time of any activity or publication in connection with which they are mentioned.

Symbols in tables

— nil or negligible
.. not applicable
n.a. not available

The following abbreviations are used for the new Standard Regions:

N	North
Y & H	Yorkshire and Humberside
NW	North West
EM	East Midlands
WM	West Midlands
EA	East Anglia ⎫ SEE South East England
SE	South East ⎭

SW   South West
Wa. Wales
Sc. Scotland
NI   Northern Ireland

and for the old Standard Regions where they differ:

EWR East and West Ridings
NM   North Midlands
S   South ⎫
LSE London and South East ⎬ SEE   South East England
E   East ⎭

CHAPTER I

REGIONAL POLICY AND THEORY

THE BASIS OF THEORY

Concern with most branches of economics starts with complaints from sections of the community with a grievance, or with conflicts of interest about the course of policy. From there it leads on to diagnosis – an elucidation of the workings of the economic system that are the sources of grievance or of conflict; thence to a systematic account of the constraints that the nature of the economy imposes on policy choices in regard to the matter in hand and, with luck, to the formulation of some criteria that may help in choosing between the available options. It may eventually even take one as far as a theory of how, in principle, an optimal choice might be made.

Regional economics starts from the existence of grievances that are identified with particular parts of the country, and from conflicts of economic interest between the predominant parts at least of different regional communities. Progress into the higher stages of analysis which have just been mentioned has been irregular and uncertain. This may spring partly from the great variety of the kinds of economic grievance or conflict from which discussion starts, partly from the implausibility in this field of some of the simplifying assumptions that are useful in either international or much of national economics, partly from the lack of relevant empirical information, and partly from the close and unavoidable involvement of the discussion with many values which resist economic measurement, such as the stability of communities, the pride that people take in them, or the political unity of the country as a whole.

It is useful for a start, however, to reverse this order of development, and to ask what the general form of a theory of regional policy would be and what sort of information one would want to make it useful. If some of this information seems to be hopelessly out of reach, we can then look at the possibility of valid approaches that somehow manage without it. In starting from this end of the subject, it is hard to think of a better beginning than Pigou's three famous *desiderata* of economic policy in general:

(i) to achieve the highest possible level of social real income (which we ought presumably to interpret as the highest present value of social income prospects),

(ii) to promote a socially desirable (presumably egalitarian) pattern of income distribution, and

(iii) to promote the steadiness and security of the prospective income-stream – in particular to avoid serious falls, or the reasonable apprehension of serious falls, in the incomes of individual households.

Because there are three *desiderata*, there is in principle a problem of how to combine them, to trade off equality against the average level of affluence, or security against either. This, however, is a general problem of welfare economics, and for the present we can leave it aside and proceed to the matters that are more specifically regional or spatial.

Assuming, then, that one can somehow assess any given outcome in terms of the three criteria, what is ideally required is a knowledge of all the possible courses of development of the economy that could be followed as the result of adopting the various possible programmes of policy – programmes stretching out into the remote future. Although the present discussion is concerned with regional policy, it would presumably be necessary to take into account the effects on the spatial pattern of economic development of various measures of policy outside the specifically regional field (of general social policy, for instance), except in so far as the lines of non-regional policy could be taken as given.

Even assuming policy in other fields to be given, however, and with all possible simplifications, it is plain that this is asking far more than we have any chance of getting. It is bad enough to ask that one should be able to estimate the effects of specific policy measures on the development of the economy in a given state of technology and of demand patterns, though the assumption that something can usefully be said about such effects is implicit in all policy choices. What is utterly unrealistic is the requirement that one should have knowledge of changing patterns of technology and demand stretching into the remote future. Intelligent guesses can be made for a little time ahead, but their reliability falls off rapidly as the time is extended from a decade to a generation and beyond. The identity, even the existence, of the natural resources, and the costs and related characteristics of the transport systems that will bear upon industrial location decisions fifty years hence must be regarded as very largely unknown. Our ignorance of the preferences people will have for different places a generation or two hence is perhaps less disabling, but this too must be borne in mind.

This would not matter if resources were highly mobile geographically; one could then switch without high cost from the configuration that suits today's conditions to that which suits tomorrow's before much of tomorrow had passed. On the other hand, if resources were geographically entirely immobile the problem would not arise; changed conditions of demand and technology would have to be met by changed specialisations within each region suitable to its particular endowment of factors of production in the way discussed in the conventional theory of international trade. The question would then be whether industrial structure could be changed rapidly enough within regions to avoid a serious lag behind the needs of the market; there might sometimes be a question whether policy should be directed towards catching up with the requirements and opportunities of the market as they are now, or trying to anticipate what they will be in (say) ten years. These are, however, the problems normally faced by national governments in their endeavours to help in adjusting national economic structure to changing world conditions. The peculiar problems of regional policy arise largely because resources of many kinds are neither perfectly mobile nor perfectly immobile between regions, but have a finite degree of mobility which, while it cannot be ignored, is not large in relation to the rate at which patterns of demand and of technology change. New or enlarged communities depend upon accumulations of physical capital which are expensive, fairly slow to grow and physically durable. Once established, communities tend to show a tenacity of life which can extend far beyond the normal physical life of their initial capital. In seeking to operate on the location of population and industry, policy is dealing not with quicksilver, but with treacle.

Economic theorists have generally simplified their approach to problems of this kind by using two analyses, one for the long run in which the treacle is assumed to have had time to respond to the forces operating upon it and to reach a static equilibrium, the other for the short run in which the distribution of the treacle has to be taken as given, though some account can be taken of the consequences, for the time being, of the fact that it is not in static equilibrium. This is a useful approach so long as one remembers that ultimately a more comprehensive view must be taken, in which the relation between the short and the long-run analyses is seen. With this proviso one may approach problems of regional policy in this way; indeed, it may be useful to insert a third set of 'medium-run' considerations. Let us see what questions fall to be discussed under each of these three heads.

THE LONG TERM

The long-run approach amounts to looking at the advantages to be gained by shifting to some optimal disposition of population and industry, no account being taken of the problems of transition. It has already been seen that it may be impossible to do this meaningfully. We may not be able to take a sufficiently confident view into the future to say what is the optimal disposition of our resources to which, or towards which, it is worth trying to move. The continuance of the foreseeable trends in requirements and conditions may be so uncertain that, in view of the limited speed at which the economy can be moved in the indicated direction, and the impossibility of subsequently making rapid adjustments for changed requirements, it is not worth initiating any considerable long-run programme of change at all. In that case the evolution of the geographical shape of the economy, in so far as it was influenced by policy, would be influenced by successive policies pursued for short-term or medium-term reasons. This, it should be emphasised, could be a perfectly rational way of doing things. 'One step enough for me' is a doctrine that may be defensible on grounds of reason as well as piety. There is no point in having a long-term programme unless one can see what it ought to be. Whether, for the time being, a sufficiently convincing long-term objective presents itself is an empirical question.

Such programmes have been enunciated, in general terms at least, in the past. The Barlow Commission reporting in 1939,[1] apart from declaring in favour of well planned satellite towns as means of relieving congestion in the existing badly planned, perhaps too large, and in most cases unhealthy conurbations – a recommendation more relevant to intra-regional arrangements than to the broad, nationwide pattern of location – stated firmly that growth in London and its immediate surroundings was excessive and should be diverted elsewhere. Its first reason for this conclusion was the vulnerability of the south eastern corner of England to aerial attack from the Continent; the second, the vulnerability of London by virtue of the concentration in it of so high a proportion of the national resources; the third, the special size and severity of congestion (of traffic especially) in London; and the fourth, the undesirable extent to which London acted 'as a continual drain on the rest of the country both for industry and population'.

The archaic sound in the nuclear missile age of the first, and to some extent the second, of these reasons may be regarded as a warning of the speed and unpredictability of change in technological conditions to which attention has already been drawn. The question is, however, whether thirty years after the Barlow Report one can state a new set of presumptions about the proper, long-term changes in distribution of population and industry that carries conviction.

Such a statement would, presumably, have to be concerned with some or all of four matters:

(i) the disposition of industry in relation to the natural resources and features of the country,

[1] Royal Commission on the Distribution of Industrial Population, *Report*, Cmd 6153, London, HMSO, 1939.

(ii) the disposition of the population in regard to those natural resources and features that have some relevance to their health and welfare,
(iii) the disposition of industry with regard to other industry – that is to say, its pattern of aggregation or dispersion, and
(iv) the aggregation or dispersion (and the form of aggregations) of the population, again considered in its relevance to their health and welfare.

A good deal that has some relevance to these matters will fall to be discussed later in the book. We need, however, a preliminary canter over the course to see more clearly what the issues are.

The first point that emerges about the siting of industry in relation to natural resources and features is that, prima facie, it has been growing less important, and it would be plausible to expect a continuation of this trend for some time. The extractive industries and those in which transport costs form a high proportion of total costs – principally those which handle large physical quantities of materials per unit of labour (and in some cases capital) employed, such as iron-smelting, steelmaking, brickmaking, electricity generating, heavy chemicals, or oil-refining – and those otherwise tied down geographically like shipbuilding are, in aggregate, employing decreasing proportions of the total labour force. On a very rough count such industries occupied about a fifth of the labour force in 1921, but occupy only about a ninth of it today. The great and increasing majority is in those manufacturing industries where transport costs of materials are not very important, or in the service and construction trades or the professions and public services, where the location of employment is, more often than not, determined by the location of the general population.

The siting of populations, on the other hand, is tending to become more important. Whether people live in the place they prefer has always been a factor in their welfare, though not capable of being taken into account in statistics of consumption. They seem, however, to be becoming more particular about the physical surroundings, both natural and artificial, in which they live; a result, no doubt, of rising real income, increased leisure, better education and wider interests. An increasing proportion of the population wants, and can in varying degrees and forms afford, what most of the wealthy have always aspired to – ample house-room, private gardens, private transport, and access to both the countryside and the facilities associated with large towns. Public housing schemes reflect the results of increased affluence and sophistication in broadly the same ways as private housing.

The main locational results of this are, of course, intra-regional changes – the accelerated spread of suburbs, and the increasing range and scale of daily commuting to work from rural areas not yet strictly suburban. The rise of weekend motoring and (still for a minority, but an increasingly important one) the weekend cottage involve longer-range movements and affect the prosperity of remoter rural areas, but their main significance in relation to the general distribution of population and industry is probably that, like rising expectations generally, they give people new reasons for preferring one part of the country to another. Since entrepreneurs and their management staffs and key workers are among those who can afford to have strong preferences for a pleasant environment, it would not be surprising if amenity was found to play an increasing part in determining industrial and commercial location also. We shall have to see whether such influences as these are detectable both when we examine the movements of factors of production between regions, and when we look at changes in the location of industry.

The productive benefits of industrial agglomeration constitute the third of the locational considerations that have been set out. The operation of economies of scale external to the firm, some of them connected with pools of specialised skills and knowledge, some with commercial outlets for the products, some with ancillary and otherwise linked industries, has been evident for a very long time. In the eighteenth and nineteenth centuries (to go no further back) it produced very high, and for a long time increasing, localisation of pottery, wool, linen and cotton textiles, factory-made clothing, cutlery, and many of the lighter metal and engineering trades, far beyond anything that could be explained by the neighbourhood of natural resources or by transport costs.

The forces that made for these advantages of aggregation have no doubt changed. In some respects they are probably weaker than they used to be. The average size of the establishment has risen; so, still more, has the average size of the firm, which makes for greater ability to train labour, and greater independence, therefore, of an existing pool of the required skills, as well as for greater ability to undertake ancillary services. The increasing importance of semi-skilled labour which can be trained on the job may work to the same end. Telecommunications, better trade publications and speed of personal travel have made for some independence from the ties of proximity on which personal business contacts formerly depended more strongly. The typical process by which a new establishment was founded in (say) the worsted manufacturing industry a hundred years ago was a skilled operative renting a few looms and setting up in business on his own. The typical way in most industries now is an established, often multi-plant firm setting up a new branch, sometimes to work a process hitherto outside its range. The degrees in which these two modes of growth depend upon the precise industrial environment of the new establishment are obviously different.

On the other hand, products and production have become more complex. A higher proportion of manufacture consists of the assembly of components processed by a number of different specialist subcontractors – often more than one for a single component. The variety of necessary skills (many of them mental rather than manual) has increased, and access to large aggregates of population where such special skills may be found is probably of increasing importance, while the availability of a large pool of trainable (rather than already trained) manual or clerical labour remains a prime advantage. Consultant and similar services are assuming increasing importance. The number of necessary contacts has increased and will no doubt continue to do so, especially as concentration of ownership raises the number of contacts between headquarters and branches. Although improvement of telecommunications has coped with much of the need, it seems that manufacturing production and the associated commercial operations as a whole have, for some time, been becoming more dependent upon personal visits and meetings, and that this trend will not be drastically reversed at an early date. The business lunch will die hard.

In manufacturing production one might expect to find that the advantages of industrial aggregation are rather less strong and specific than they used to be, but that there is still advantage in being located, not so much with other establishments of the same kind, as with a wide variety of subcontractors, suppliers and customers within a moderate range, and with reasonable access to the central services and agencies that usually operate from national or regional capitals. The important costs that are reduced by this are those of communication rather than of transport of goods – the imputed costs of managerial time rather than the cash expenses of travel or telecommunication being the principal item. There is perhaps a presumption that it is the large and varied industrial area rather than the compact, specialised one that is coming to confer advantages of aggregation, and with improved means of transport and communication the area over which industry and (to some extent) population can be scattered without losing these advantages is increasing. In the service trades (other than those tied down to local markets), and in head office activities of all kinds, improved communications might be expected to make for centralisation on a national scale, and these activities are, on the whole, growing relatively to others. But whether changes in the location of economic activity are consistent with these presumptions we shall see.

Against this, the geographical concentration of industry and population may spell congestion, which is the enemy of easy communication, or at least of easy personal travel, as well as adding time-costs to the movement of goods, which may offset, or more than offset, the advantages of short distances. Ultimately, of course, in so far as its burden falls on industry itself, congestion is self-limiting; when it gets bad enough it drives establishments out of the congested area as fast as others come in. This, however, is likely to happen only when the advantages of being in the area are roughly offset for its industry as a whole by the disadvantages. The optimal position with regard to production (to which we are still limiting the discussion) is one in which the greatest possible balance of advantage over disadvantage of aggregation is preserved for the country's industry as a whole. This is clearly achieved if all industry is disposed in one or more aggregations each of an optimal size. The optimal size for an aggregation is reached when an extra establishment entering it harms those already there by the extra congestion and the like that it causes to just the same extent that it benefits them through enlarging the labour market, encouraging common services, cheapening local supplies of components, or otherwise producing external economies. Choice of policy, in this connection, clearly depends largely upon the possibility of assessing, in very general terms, the size of the optimal industrial aggregate in relation to the total size of the country's industrial economy. To make matters harder, this optimal size will presumably be different for the different kinds of industrial aggregate. The external economies created for each other and for other kinds of activity by the departments of central government may, for instance, make the optimal size for the national capital bigger than that for other concentrations of industry.

Before looking at this, however, it is necessary to pass on to the last of the four matters we have listed as bearing upon the optimal long-term location policy – the direct significance of aggregation or dispersion for the welfare of the population. Since the locations of population and industry are closely related to each other, we have, in the end, to consider both the physical location and the optimal state of aggregation or dispersion, not of industry and population separately, but of both together, with qualifications about daily travel to work which are likely to be minor in relation to the interregional pattern, though they are clearly important in relation to town planning and intra-regional distribution.

The direct advantages to people of living in large aggregations arise from the power of such aggregations to provide a wide variety of choice. Living in a large labour market means that one has a wide choice of different kinds of work and different employers, and that members of a family or of a group of friends who want to stay together have good chances of finding jobs that suit them without leaving the home or the group. Living in a large community of consumers means that one has access to a wide variety of goods and (still more) of services, some of them catering for uncommon needs and tastes. These advantages are summed up by the Benthamite principle 'aggregation for the purpose of segregation'. Associated with this variety and the high concentration of activity in, at any rate, the main centres of a big population aggregate, there is a generally stimulating quality which provides on balance a powerful attraction to many people during some part of their lives, and to some throughout their lives. Some but not all kinds of large aggregation also provide the possibility of anonymity, which, again, some people like for some of the time.

On the other side of the account there come, most obviously, the opposites of the attributes which are prized in the life of large cities: the absence of quiet, of really open country, of small, settled communities, often of visual harmony. How heavily these faults weigh in the balance is largely a matter of taste, though probably a great many people who are not disposed to regard them as important in comparison with the urban virtues, nevertheless regret them for some part of the time. The more easily assessed disadvantages, however, are those related to congestion in its various forms.

Congestion has several senses, loosely connected with one another, but all associated in various degrees with existing large aggregations of population; how far the association is inevitable will have to be discussed. Shortage of house-room, lack of privacy and the often attendant easy communication of disease have not been by any means exclusively urban phenomena; rural housing is probably, on the whole, worse than urban. This, however, is no doubt the case mainly because, with an absolutely or relatively declining rural population, rural housing is on average older than urban, and because, outside the commuting areas of the towns, rural incomes are lower. Aggregations of population make land locally scarce and, *ceteris paribus*, make for smaller dwellings. The effect of land scarcity on the open space available for recreation is, however, a good deal more drastic. The congestion of rural slums has always been mitigated, in comparison with that of urban slums, by the open countryside on their doorstep.

For people with jobs in large urban areas, the alternative to living where scarcity of land tends to produce the kind of congestion that is simply lack of living-space is, of course, to live a long way from work (and perhaps also from central shopping and cultural facilities) and incur heavier travel costs, in money, time and discomfort. This is a true cost of aggregation in as much as the forces of the market, arising from the search of enterprises and institutions for the most profitable or convenient locations, tend to segregate workplaces from residential areas in such a way that the average separation grows with the size of the aggregation. In so far as the greater amount of regular travel in a larger place arises from the fact that it offers a wider choice of work, education, shopping and entertainment, spread over a wider area, the greater travel cost is a further cost of aggregation, to be set off against the corresponding advantages. With more travel, other things being equal, would come more traffic congestion, the most conspicuous kind of congestion in modern urban areas, which makes the costs of travel, including the imputed costs of the time it occupies, rise faster than the average distances covered. As aggregations grow other things do not stay equal. Bigger aggregations can support public transport systems better than smaller ones, and this economy of scale postpones or mitigates the onset of rising real costs. But eventually the costs seem likely to rise faster than the benefits.

To throw light upon the proper objectives of long-term location policy, these advantages and disadvantages which large aggregations of population and industry confer directly on their inhabitants have to be added to those, already referred to, which they confer upon productive enterprises situated in them. If this can be done, one can in principle see how total social advantage varies with size, estimate the optimal size, and draw conclusions about the optimal number of separate aggregations for the country as a whole – still bearing in mind the presumption that aggregations with different productive functions are likely to have different optimal sizes.

One very important qualification has to be noted, however. Both the advantages and the disadvantages of aggregation depend upon the physical shape that the aggregation takes. For considering what would be an optimal arrangement of the country's population and industry in the very long run, one should no doubt assume that each single aggregation (if there is to be more than one) is optimally planned in detail – whatever that may imply. But all our experience is of aggregations that are far from optimal in their physical form; cities and groups of cities that were shaped mainly by the market forces of the railway age and by road frameworks gradually accumulated over at least a century. If one looks so far ahead that location of industry, commerce, residence and open spaces, and the network of transport and communication can be considered perfectly flexible (within the constraints of physical geography), one is no doubt dealing with advantages and disadvantages of size that are different from those we know now.

The planned cluster of settlements or the linear conurbation will no doubt have a different optimal size from the centralised unplanned sprawl growing on the London model, or the more diffuse unplanned sprawl growing on the pattern of south Lancashire or the West Riding.

It may be that the *long-run* optimal size of an aggregation, assuming perfect planning of its whole infrastructure, is very large indeed, though here we are looking so far into the future (because of the time it would take to build up an aggregation answering to this description) that the fog of technological uncertainty becomes very thick. In practice, decisions of policy have to take into account a short or medium run in which congestion arises from the persistence of a physical infrastructure that is obsolete already, and a long run in which anything that can be planned now is likely to have become obsolete.

The fact that the form of the infrastructure of large (and therefore not very new) aggregations is never likely to be ideal in the light of existing needs and knowledge probably strengthens the presumption that there are congestion costs that do not enter into the private calculations of residents or enterprises, and that the sizes of these aggregations, if left to market forces, may diverge greatly from the social optima. We shall have to explore this matter rather more systematically later on, even though we lack most of the empirical data that would be needed to give the discussion solid content.

One substantial question at least has been begged, however, in what we have already said. Is there a possibility worth considering that industrial establishments will, in general, think the advantages of one agglomeration superior, while population shows a net preference, for reasons arising from size, for another one? There is no *a priori* reason why the size of aggregation that provides the best facilities for industry should be such as to make it, in the general view, the best to live in.

When this question is stated, however, the answer soon emerges. If population and industry are drawn in different directions, the price mechanism ought to come to the rescue. The area sought by entrepreneurs and shunned by residents will become one of dearer labour, so that the divergent movements will be checked and eventually only a net flow of both industry and labour either in or out, produced by the resultant of the two initial preferences, will remain. We may provisionally take this as representing the net balance of average advantages offered by the two areas to all concerned. The same reasoning can be applied when one is seeking to superimpose on the shifts of location attributable to advantages and disadvantages of scale of agglomeration those (to which we have referred earlier) that arise from preferences related to physical features and climate: the preference of industrialists (in their professional capacity) for flat land on deep-water estuaries at the crossroads of world trade, and that of all the human beings concerned, in their private capacities, for a good climate and interesting scenery.

There is one further consideration that it seems worth adding to this painfully abstract review of long-run matters affecting welfare. It concerns the value of variety. The differences between British regions, in scenery, general social and intellectual character, and to a minor extent in physical climate, are important though often subtle. Many (perhaps most) people acquire a preference for the region in which they were brought up – a point to which we must return presently – but very many at some point in their lives find it stimulating to move to somewhere with a different general character, and may come to prefer something other than their original home ground. If a substantial majority of the employment opportunities in any given line of work are concentrated in a single industrial aggregation, then freedom to combine that line of work with residence in the region one prefers, or with a change in one's region of residence, may be significantly limited. This kind of limitation has existed for a very long time; indeed it is to some extent inevitable. Anyone who wants to make a career in national government, for instance, is at a disadvantage if he does not like London or the scenery of the south east. But a United Kingdom in which choice of an important range of careers automatically confined one to a specific region to live and work in would clearly, in this respect, offer less than one in which some choice of region was left open. There would be some losses, other than those that might be associated with scale and congestion, if the whole of the industrial population, other than the minority tied to natural resources elsewhere, drifted to the midlands and the south of England.

THE MEDIUM TERM

These, then, are the most obvious considerations that might be held to govern the directions in which location of industry and population ought to be guided for the long run, in which all of us now living are dead and all existing personal attachments to particular regions are accordingly dissolved. Strictly, what has been said so far has assumed the dissolution also of those attachments to particular regions that are traditional – handed on from one generation to another. That the substantial part of them does in fact dissolve in time, leaving a more or less tenuous residue of sentiment, is a general fact of experience among immigrant communities. 'In dreams beholding the Hebrides' is a first generation phenomenon; after that it does not seem to be very common to regret the separation from the old home to an extent that seriously weakens satisfaction in the new one, though ancestral ties may continue for a long time to be good for the tourist trade.

In relation to the welfare economics of relocating population therefore, the attachments (including traditional attachments) of people to particular parts of the country must be regarded as medium-term rather than long-term forces. In this context they are obviously important, though they require to be looked at rather closely. On the face of it, the people who declare themselves willing to move to another part of the country for a good reason (most often career prospects or good housing) though a minority (43 per cent according to the Labour Mobility Survey[1]) are a sufficiently large minority to produce much higher rates of migration than are ever actually observed. Even allowing for the fact that quite a high proportion of migrants – internal or international – return after, presumably, finding the promised land overrated, one is still left with a fairly high level of effective willingness to move.

Two points, however, deserve note. The first is that a majority of those who are impelled by some misfortune such as unemployment towards considering a move from their home region, like the majority of the population as a whole, will be unwilling movers to whom the move if they make it is likely to be a matter of immediate, if not of lasting, regret. Those who are positively willing to move in response to some moderate incentive tend to be the younger, better educated, more highly skilled, who are likely to do relatively well even if they do not leave home. Migration in response to a push is far more likely to involve psychic costs than that which takes place in response to a pull.

The second point, which needs rather more discussion, is that the cost to those who are called upon to move in the course of any change in the pattern of population may be very far from the whole cost. This is most obvious when an area is actually declining in population, not, let us say, because of an absolute decline in employment opportunities which forces people to leave, but simply because the more ambitious, who find better opportunities elsewhere, exceed in number both those who for any reason are drawn in and the natural increase of the resident population. In these circumstances, there are very likely to be loud protests and strong pressure for policy changes designed to stop the decline. (This may also happen to a smaller extent where there is a noticeable net outward migration, even if it is not sufficient to bring about a decline in total population.)

These protests signify genuine hardship, or social costs, of various kinds and to various degrees. Local authorities are sure to protest at anything that lowers their revenues, though with rate support grants from the central government and with diminished local responsibility for welfare services their situation is, of course, vastly better than before the war or, still more, in the twenties. The vicious circle of reduced rate income, increased need and poorer services, which was one of the

[1] Government Social Survey, *Labour Mobility in Great Britain 1953–63*, by A. I. Harris and R. Clausen, London, 1966.

most notable mechanisms of interregional destabilisation, is now greatly weakened. Local traders and, indeed, all who serve the local market have perhaps a more obvious reason to complain at any reduction in the rate of growth of population and income; their ground for complaint becomes especially strong when there is an absolute reduction in the real purchasing power of that market below the size on which their expectations have been based, so that some of them face commercial failure and perhaps unwilling departure to another part of the country.

The selective nature of migration – the greater responsiveness of the younger, more enterprising, better educated and more skilled to the pull of opportunity elsewhere (and perhaps also to the push of poor opportunity at home) – may mean that, other things being equal, places with sizeable rates of net emigration are felt by many to be less interesting and stimulating to live in than those with substantial net immigration. This fact reflects back adversely, of course, upon their prospects of growth; bright people are glad to leave (and not anxious to go to) places believed to be dull. Dullness of another sort – the drabness of an industrial area with a high proportion of old and perhaps derelict buildings, and a low proportion of new – tends to be produced by relatively slow growth, and even more by actual decline, of total population, and this too tends to make the areas poor in growth still poorer. The old, unspoilt nineteenth-century industrial area has not yet acquired the glamour which already gives the prospect of early aesthetic spoliation, but of at least temporary commercial salvation, to the old, unspoilt eighteenth-century agricultural village.

There are thus good reasons why many people in communities suffering from net outward migration or decline in absolute numbers, or even just slow growth, should wish matters otherwise. Some of the reasons they adduce may not bear close scrutiny. The 'brain drain' argument, mainly used at the national level but to be encountered also at the regional, tends in its usual form to ignore the fact that the contribution to the local product that is lost when a person emigrates is largely offset by the transfer elsewhere of the obligation to pay him. At regional level it is clearly wrong to complain about the burden of educating people who then emigrate to other parts of the country and pay back nothing directly to the local community, without taking account of the extent to which costs of education are met from the central government. For good reasons as well as bad, however, various complaints arise from slow growing, declining, or emigrant-losing communities, which may combine to produce a generalised sense of grievance or a poor state of morale, rather like that of football fans whose team is not doing well. The extent to which this happens depends very largely upon the selfconsciousness of the community – the extent to which its members tend to identify themselves with it – a characteristic which itself depends at any time upon the course of the community's past (including its remote) history, but which current grievances tend to sharpen.

For the national policy-maker, of course, it is necessary to ask whether the medium-term woes of communities that are the victims of economic change are offset by the medium-term euphoria of communities that are receiving immigrants and growing fast. To a great extent the two are symmetrical; just as emigration and population decline make for a dull community, a depressing environment and perhaps generally low morale, their opposites make for liveliness, newness and a boom-town mentality. There are two respects in which the symmetry may fail to hold. First, the influx of strangers into an established community produces strains as well as benefits; the disturbance caused by incomers may be at least as great as that caused by their departure from the communities they left. Second, where some areas are declining in population at a considerable rate, there may be waste of social capital – a possibility of which a good deal was made in the 1930s. To this we shall have to return in due course to see what it amounts to in modern conditions.

Even though, to a very large extent, the medium-term costs of location change to some areas are matched by corresponding advantages to others, that does not entirely dispose of them for the policy-maker, who has to pay some attention to equity as well as to the sum of the advantages and disadvantages to individuals (if he can assess them) from any line of policy. It may be that the degree of inequality of welfare introduced into the country by a policy which makes some areas rather depressed and others rather prosperous is not great in comparison with the inequalities in economic welfare between individuals within this or any other country, or even with the inequalities (in morale as well as cash income) between people engaged in, say, cotton-weaving and electronics, or between occupational groups such as engine drivers and airline pilots – all of which are more or less organised and coherent interests, capable in varying degrees of making demands and protests collectively. This can perhaps be better considered when we have seen how big interregional differences are. In relation to their size however, regional inequalities – for some regions at least – may well be less acceptable than industrial or occupational ones. Perhaps this arises from a feeling that interregional differences are less inevitable, more easily subject to policy than the great inter-occupational and inter-industrial ones; perhaps it is a by-product of the fact that local or regional views lend themselves more to electoral representation in a democracy than do industrial or occupational views; perhaps it arises from the peculiar selfconsciousness that can grow in a community with a territorial basis, of which modern nationalism is largely an example. At all events, this is clearly a matter that policy has to take into account, though the extent to which welfare economics can help it in doing so is small.

THE SHORT TERM

We come now to what we may call the short-term factors in regional policy. The line between short and medium-term factors is necessarily a rather arbitrary one. Both have close connections with the difficulties of economic and social adaptation but, whereas what we have called the medium-term factors are concerned with the disutilities people suffer (possibly for the rest of their lives) on account of movements of themselves or others away from surroundings to which they are attached, or with the creation of surplus capacity that may outlast the population movement to which it is due by quite a long time, the most obvious short-term factors arise from frictions of movement and, in the first analysis, can be expected to persist for only a little longer than the operation of the forces which are making for the movements in question. Later one can introduce some dynamic considerations, again short-term in themselves, which may point to the possibility of self-sustaining chains of consequences persisting for a considerable time after the initial forces have ceased to work.

The simplest example of the operation of short-term, frictional factors in regional affairs might be something like the following. Suppose that in a part of the country which we shall call 'the north' the labour force is largely engaged in industries whose demand for labour is rising only slowly, whether because of automation, or foreign competition, or a shift of world demand away from the products concerned. In the rest of the country, 'the south', the industrial structure is specialised towards industries in which demand for labour is rising fast. Suppose that the rate of natural increase of the population of working age is the same in both regions and, moreover, that the level and growth of effective demand are so managed as to keep the demand for labour in the country as a whole equal to the number of people available for employment. Then there will clearly be a rising excess of jobs over people seeking them in the south and an equal excess of people seeking jobs over jobs available in the north.

Perhaps one may pause here to reflect that the result just stated could be produced by any – or any combination – of a number of mechanisms. We have arbitrarily chosen as the source of maladjustment difference between industrial structures, coupled with different rates of growth of industries' demands for labour. One could, however, equally well have assumed similar regional structures of industry and a higher rate of natural increase of population in the north than in the south. Or, with similar industrial structures, one could have supposed higher growth rates of all (or some) industries in the south, because (say) the locations it offers are more convenient, so that southern establishments make bigger profits and grow faster *in situ* than northern ones, and/or newly created establishments which have a sufficiently wide choice of site tend to locate themselves preferentially in the south. Some combinations of causes are particularly plausible; for instance, if there are economies of scale external to the establishments in the expanding industries and if (reverting to our first assumption) the south has tended to specialise on them, then it will be able to realise greater economies of scale in them than the north can and will add intra-industry advantages to its structural advantage. It is true that, if there are also economies of scale in the industries of declining manpower demand, the north will have an advantage over the south in those industries, but then both sets of scale effects together will tend to push the north further towards specialisation on industries of shrinking manpower demand and the south further towards specialisation on industries of rising manpower demand. Later we must look in some detail at what can be found about the ways in which differences of regional employment growth in this country have been produced.

Whatever the reasons for differences of this kind, however, it is clear that if they occur then, in the hypothetical conditions we have described, unemployment piles up in the slow growing region (the one we have called the north) and unfilled vacancies to a similar number (if they are all recorded) pile up in the south. These developments may be expected to affect movements of people, movements of establishments, relative prices of labour, growth of establishments *in situ* and no doubt much else. The simplest plausible supposition, however, is that the main effects are on movements. As unemployment in the north increases, fewer southerners will be drawn in and more northerners will be disposed to seek their fortunes in the south (though the evidence is that those actually unemployed are not very mobile). As unfilled vacancies increase in the south, the opposite will happen there. At the same time, increasing labour shortage in the south will tend to make firms based there think of meeting their plans for expansion by opening branches in the north, or in some cases of moving there bodily in order to have a better supply of labour. There will thus be a southward net flow of people seeking work and a northward flow of entrepreneurship seeking labour, both of them presumably varying as increasing functions of the level of northern unemployment (or southern unfilled vacancies). When the sum of the two flows equals the excess of natural increase over job-creation in the existing industries of the north (which we have assumed equal to the excess of job-creation by establishments in or emanating from the south over southern natural increase), then supply of and demand for labour are equalised in both regions and what looks so far like a neutral equilibrium is established.

In this equilibrium, the amount of unemployment in the north and the equal amount of unsatisfied demand for labour in the south clearly depend upon the mobility of labour and of jobs between the two regions. If one makes the further simplifying assumption that annual net flows of people and of jobs between the regions are both *proportional* to the number of unemployed in the north, being equal respectively to a and b times that number, then the equilibrium number of unemployed is easily seen to be $D/(a+b)$, where D is the annual discrepancy between natural increase and indigenous job-creation in either region. It obviously approaches zero as the mobility of either people or jobs approaches infinity. It follows, too, that if some policy measure speeds up the flow of labour, or that of jobs, in the direction that reduces unemployment, the equilibrium number of unemployed in the north and of unfilled vacancies in the south are each reduced by $1/(a+b)$ for every man (or job) per year by which the sum of the flows is increased. If the annual value of what a hitherto unemployed man will produce in a hitherto unfilled job can be computed, then, as a first approximation, a limit can be set on the annual cost of the measures it is worth using to increase the flow of people or jobs by one per year. (The estimates become unrealistic for very low values of the mobilities, a and b, because if they are low a new equilibrium level of unemployment is slow to establish itself and, where one is making the assessment for periods of more than (say) ten years or so, one cannot properly treat the natural increase of the population of working age as being independent of the inflow or outflow of migrants. These migrants are mostly in the early adult age group; they do not begin to fall out of the labour force at a substantial rate until about 25 or 30 years after an influx, but their children start entering the labour force a good while before that.)

Once again, as has already been hinted, there are a number of possible variations on the equilibrating mechanism just sketched. First, labour surplus in the north may lower the relative price of labour there, labour scarcity in the south may raise it. If there were a sufficiently strong tendency for regional labour markets to be cleared through the price mechanism, the maladjustments of supply and demand with which we started would be resolved without the help of differences in unemployment rates and the equilibrating mechanism would be the same as before, except that labour net migration would be geared to differences of earnings rather than of unemployment or vacancies, and firms would have to be regarded as moving in search, not just of labour, but of cheap labour.

It might be objected that the notorious existence of interregional unemployment differences puts this suggestion out of court. A modification of it, however, looks a little more viable. It might be that regional labour markets have strong tendencies to clear themselves through the price mechanism, leaving out of account frictional and structural unemployment – labour which cannot find employment even at a reduced rate of earnings because it has the wrong skills or is in the wrong place within the region for the industries capable of expanding. This would mean that there is little or no difference between regions in 'Keynesian' or demand-deficiency unemployment, the observed differences being due to the different regional rates of change in the industrial and occupational structure and intra-regional location of their labour demand. This is, at all events, a hypothesis that will have to be examined in a later chapter.

But suppose that the price mechanism plays at least some part in the adjustment. In that case, so long as factors are not perfectly mobile, there will be some differences in their prices in different regions, and this signifies a cost, since it indicates that national output would be greater if factors were moved from places where their prices (and presumably marginal products) are lower to others where they are higher until no differences remain. Costs of this sort, arising from the mislocation of employed factors in relation to each other, will naturally be smaller than those that would arise if the same factors were unemployed. Beyond this they are hard to estimate with confidence, but something more can be said on this question, and it will be convenient to say it when we come to consider the labour market in detail.

It can, of course, be objected to this that, if there is a shortage of labour in the south and a surplus in the north, and if one assumes that there is time for the economy to adjust itself to the difference without interregional factor movements, it will do so not by making each industry more capital-intensive in the south than in the north, but by developing the more capital-intensive industries selectively there. In this way, as is well known, it is possible for full employment of factors to be attained without any interregional movement of them, and without any interregional differences of marginal productivity – regional specialisation and flows of goods having taken the place of interregional flows of factors. The only cost – the only loss of real product in comparison with a situation where the initial maldistribution of labour in relation to the demand for it never arose – will then be the cost of the extra (mostly interregional) transport of goods that follows from increased regional specialisation.

The fact is, of course, that we are talking about continuing processes of adaptation to continuing pressures of change. There are several possible channels of adaptation, but all of them present frictions. The continuous build-up of unemployed manpower in the north will be opposed by emigration and inflow of new industry (both dependent upon either unemployment differences or wage differences), by adoption of more labour-intensive methods in existing industries and a shift to a more labour-intensive structure (both dependent upon wage differences, or possibly labour availability) and by a longer life for capital assets. The south will show the opposite adjustments. The processes of labour intensification in the north and the corresponding ones of capital intensification in the south should be thought of as depending on the rise and the fall, respectively, of the ratio of manpower employed to capital employed as old capital assets are replaced or new ones added. How much the ratios are raised or lowered is, presumably, a function of the price or the availability of labour – just as rates of labour migration and transfer of jobs are. Equilibrium is attained when wage and/or unemployment differences are such as to promote a combined rate of adjustment through all of the channels we have mentioned that just balances the rates of increase of demand for and supply of labour in the two regions.

This is, of course, a short-run equilibrium. In the longer run, the forces that are generating the adjustment run down; if they arise from the worldwide or national decline of industries initially localised in the north, then the process of adjustment gradually replaces these industries with others, which, with luck, will not go into decline for a long time. If the north is a poor location for modern industry generally, that fact will be reflected in the form of the adjustment – a big outflow of people and little if any inflow of industry, so that the whole economy of the region shrinks at least relatively; high outward migration will, in addition, lower the rate of natural increase not only through the diminished size of the population but also through a change in its age composition. There is a movement towards long-term equilibrium as well as a short-term equilibrium of the adjustment process, but it is relatively slow. It can be argued that the United Kingdom has been making a single long-term adjustment for the last fifty years.

THE CHANCES OF INSTABILITY

All that we have said about adjustments so far assumes that these adjustments are stabilising, in the sense that they tend to some degree to offset the locational effects of the forces initiating change, although some mention has been made in passing of factors that could make for instability. In what was said about the long-term optimal location of population and industry for instance, the possibility was mentioned that there are economies of aggregation operating on a sufficiently large scale to draw the whole population and industry of the country that is not tied down by natural resources like agricultural land or minerals into a single conglomeration, even though it did not follow that such a result was in the general interest. If that were the case, any external force operating in the direction of aggregation, instead of evoking opposing responses from the economy, might start a self-reinforcing process, even though a slow one. Again, in discussing medium-term problems of locational change, we noted that, since migration tends to be selective and stagnation or decline often makes for an unattractive environment, net outward migration from a community may have a certain self-reinforcing quality, as too may net inward migration for corresponding reasons. If this is so, then local or regional prosperity contains an element of inherent instability.

So far as the short-term processes of adjustment are concerned, the most obvious and general destabilising mechanism is the multiplier, whether applied to income or to employment. The way in which the multiplier mechanism adds a secondary element to any autonomous primary increase or decrease of income or employment in an economy is familiar, as is the rather more complicated working of the mechanism in international economics, where a change of income in one country spills over into others and starts an infinite series of converging international repercussions. What has to be added in applying these ideas to regional economics is the interregional mobility of factors of production. Interregional migration has multiplier effects which we shall have to consider in due course.

The multiplier effects, including those of migration, on local income and employment, and through them on migration itself, are obviously important in principle, but in considering them one has to remember that in the short-run local or regional multipliers are presumably small, because the import leakages are heavy. (In the longer run, in which local services adjust fully to local population and income, they may be larger.) Moreover, no multiplier by itself can lead to a divergent process of growth or decay. To achieve that we have to invoke some other mechanism.

The mechanism that immediately comes to mind is capital stock adjustment. It is well known that when this is combined with the multiplier impressive possibilities of instability are opened up, and it is probably the thought of some combined mechanism of this sort, including effects of migration, that has most frequently led economists to doubt the validity of the kind of short-term analysis of adjustment that we have discussed a littler earlier. Once a region has suffered a blow to (say) its external sales, has higher than average unemployment and has begun to suffer net emigration, will not these circumstances depress local investment spending by its existing industry and spending on its social capital to an extent that offsets any tendency of external industry to be tempted in, and which starts a further cycle of secondary income reduction, increased emigration and lowered investment? Whether this is so, and, if it is, to what extent, are matters that clearly need some empirical investigation, which we shall attempt later.

In this preliminary survey, however, we may mention a further question that inevitably arises from our line of argument. If we are asserting that depressed regions are suffering from 'Keynesian' unemployment, is it likely that this should continue, in some degree, for decades? What is to be said about the 'real balances effect' in its various forms as an automatic adjuster? Will not the pressure of relatively high unemployment tend to damp down price and wage inflation and to stimulate spending through the effect of this in raising the real value of cash balances and other assets of fixed money value?

In part this is easily answered. First, even if these mechanisms operate at regional level, they will not dispose of the troubles of a depressed region if, as we have suggested, those troubles come in the first place from the continuous (or for that matter the intermittently repeated) operation of unfavourable exogenous forces. Adjusting mechanisms – like the effect of relatively reduced prices of labour on either the value of real balances, or (more convincingly) the region's general competitiveness and attractiveness to incoming industry which we have already discussed, may work in the right direction but they cannot produce instantaneous adjustment; they would enable the region (after a simple time-lag) to adjust to a *fallen* demand for its products but they can never quite catch up with a *falling* one. Secondly, it is not very likely that the real balances effect has much chance to work in a regional setting; the scope for a region's price level of consumable goods and services (which is presumably what matters) to fall relatively to that of the rest of the country is slight, since a high proportion of the goods and services in question come from the rest of the country. Even the scope for unemployment to produce a relative fall of the price of labour in a region in relation to that of the rest of the country is almost certain to be small compared with the scope for it to produce a fall in the national price of labour in relation to prices abroad – and experience has not shown even this to be a simple matter. Thirdly, given some measure of interregional labour mobility, the very reduction in regional earnings that increases competitiveness (and perhaps works marginally towards a favourable real balances effect) helps to produce emigration with unfavourable effects on the regional pressure of demand and the regional environment which we have discussed.

MOVING PEOPLE OR MOVING JOBS?

Our discussion of short-term problems so far has been concerned with their diagnosis and analysis rather than with policy. All that has emerged about the latter is that there should be a trade-off between reduction of unemployment and the cost of such policy measures as may be taken to hasten adjustment by augmenting either the movements of workers to areas of relative labour shortage, or those of jobs to areas of unemployment. (In the conditions we have assumed for simplicity of exposition – with the total demand for labour equal to the total supply in the country as a whole – unemployment and unfilled vacancies are, of course, equal and are reduced equally by these measures.) We have not considered any criterion for deciding whether it is better to operate on movements of labour or of jobs, or how much on one and how much on the other.

There are several considerations of obvious relevance to this. First, there is the question whether taking the workers to the work or vice versa is more nearly in accordance with the long-term redistribution of industry and the industrial population that is thought desirable. If London is the area of labour shortage and London is too big (as the Barlow Commission thought), then there is clearly more to be said for resolving the relative misallocation of people and jobs by moving jobs out of London than by moving people in. Similarly, if a particular area of labour surplus is thought to suffer from permanent locational disadvantages as a site for a major industrial concentration, it is better to move people out than to move jobs in, other things being equal.

Secondly, there is the question of relative cost; moving people involves costs which, in a free society, have to be borne largely by the rest of the community in the form of inducements to overcome personal unwillingness and inertia, but which also include those costs of disturbance to the communities both of emigration and of immigration that we have noted earlier. Moving jobs involves costs in the form of inefficient production during a settling-down period, or rather the excess of such costs when an establishment is persuaded to set up in some distant region to which it is diverted over what they would have been if it had set up in the region of its first choice. The costs of additional social capital made necessary by the movement of the man or the job have to be included too. The minimum-cost policy will presumably be the one that equalises the marginal cost of moving an extra man in one direction to that of moving an extra job in the opposite one.

Thirdly, the issue is complicated by the multiplier and by the consequence of capital stock adjustment. Both moving people and moving jobs involve moving the impact of effective demand from one area to another: any policy-induced movement of people produces some parallel movement of jobs and any policy-induced movement of jobs produces an additional job-movement. These secondary job-movements ought to be taken into account when one is considering the effects of policy, as should the further complications due to capital stock adjustment. Moving jobs is, for this reason, a more efficient way of reducing a discrepancy between the distributions of jobs and of people than moving people, other things being equal.

To put it another way, moving workers to the work generally means pumping additional effective demand into a region that has an excess of it already; moving jobs to workers generally means moving effective demand to regions where it is deficient. With sufficiently high values of the multiplier and the capital–output ratio, the movement of people might be entirely self-defeating as a measure for equalising supply of and demand for labour within each region, though, as we have seen, this outcome is by no means to be taken for granted.

There is a matter of interregional equity here which has already been discussed. The more tangible issue, however, is connected with inflation. If excess demand for labour is exactly as productive of wage and price inflation as an equal deficiency of demand is of deflation, then clearly the national rate of inflation depends only on the amount of excess demand in the country as a whole, not on its distribution. If, however, there is more resistance to wage and price decrease than to their increase, zero total excess demand will still be inflationary provided that there is not zero excess in every single sector of the economy, whether regional or industrial. (In the present discussion it is, of course, with geographical sectors, rather than industrial ones as such that we are concerned.)

So far as wage inflation is concerned at least, it seems very likely that the suggested asymmetry exists – that the resistance to reduction is substantially greater than that to increase, and indeed, it is easy to believe that a given increase in excess demand is more inflationary the higher the excess already is. If this is so it follows that, for a minimum of internally generated inflation with any given level of excess demand in the economy as a whole, excess demand (positive or negative) should be so divided between regions that the marginal responsiveness of inflation to an increase of excess demand is everywhere the same. If that marginal rate of responsiveness varies in exactly the same way with the level of excess demand in different regions, this of course means equalising pressure of excess demand between regions.

Whether this is the same thing as equalising unemployment, or vacancies, or the ratio of the two between regions is another matter; it depends on the answer to the question we have already raised in another connection, whether the degrees of efficiency of the labour market are the same in different regions. Like most lines of theorising, this one brings one quickly to the point where it is possible to reach conclusions of practical interest only after a difficult scrutiny of the real world.

A SUMMARY

What conclusions then emerge from this preliminary survey of regional problems, in which we have tried to sort out the long-term, medium-term and short-term considerations relevant to policy with only a minimal appeal to the particular facts of the British case? The factors bearing on the optimal long-term distribution of industry and population are necessarily obscure, because the time-scale with which we are dealing here is long and our capacity to foresee, in particular, the relevant technological conditions a generation or two ahead is inadequate. Prima facie, the current trend, which seems reasonably likely to continue for some time, is towards a loosening of the bonds that tie industry to particular natural resources, an enlargement of the geographical range within which economies of aggregation are effective, an increasing importance of the quality of the environment in which people live, of their access to varied amenities and of their freedom from the various kinds of congestion that limit their space and movement. In the long-term also, the values – the opportunities for choice – inherent in the environmental and human differences between the main regional centres of population create a presumption against development of the national population distribution towards a single megalopolis.

The medium-term considerations are concerned with the costs and the equitable aspects of change in the regional distribution of population and prosperity. Heavy migration entails some medium-term psychic costs, not only for reluctant migrants, but for those communities that it deprives of enterprise and interest on the one hand, or of quiet, open space and valued elements of stability on the other. In selfconscious communities, either of the extremes of stagnation and growth (but particularly the former) can build up senses of grievance that have to be taken seriously as setting limits to the possible – and the desirable – rate of change, especially as both economic success and its opposite have some tendency to be self-reinforcing. More obvious economic loss through redundancy of social capital in a declining area is also a possibility of which account must be taken.

The short-term considerations are concerned with much more tangible losses arising from the frictions of interregional factor movement – losses which are most tangible when they are manifested in unemployment on the one hand and labour shortage on the other. How far existing unemployment arises from interregional immobility of factors, and how far from inter-industry immobility, or from other circumstances that render labour markets imperfect, is, however, a question that cannot be answered *a priori*. Another important question that cannot be answered in advance is how far multiplier and capital stock adjustment effects cause the movement of labour between regions to be destabilising, so that it is inefficient, or even completely self-frustrating, as a remover of interregional discrepancies between increases in the labour force and those in the demand for its services. A third question – or group of questions – which cannot be answered *a priori* concerns the extent to which uneven distribution of effective demand between regions is inflationary and, if it is, whether usable criteria of even distribution of demand in the relevant sense can be found.

Predictably, therefore, a preliminary review of the theoretical considerations that should be relevant to regional policy produces some distinctions that seem useful, some initial presumptions arising from the known orders of the relevant magnitudes, but a far larger number of questions that can be answered, if at all, only when further light is thrown on the nature of the mechanisms at work and something of the strength and sensitivity with which they operate. The following chapters are designed to provide some such light, though in this subject, where so many considerations are imponderable, so many systems of causation complex beyond hope of early disentanglement and so many desirable data lacking, much of the darkness is sure to remain.

CHAPTER 2

THE REGIONS

WHAT IS A REGION?

How one delimits regions should depend on the purpose for which one does it. In fact, practically all organisations, public, semi-public, or private, that provide goods or services on large scales to all parts of the country choose to divide their administrations on some regional pattern, and these patterns differ from one another, always in detail and often radically, according to the constraints of the particular case. British Rail's five regions are naturally divided by boundaries that run between rather than across main lines, so that four out of the five notionally meet at a point in London. The twenty Hospital Regions of Great Britain conform to the catchment areas (governed by capacity, distance and ease of transport) of the major hospital and teaching centres, which, in turn, are the major urban centres, though again with the important qualification, unusual among regional arrangements, that the London area is divided into four. The BBC operates with seven regions to cover the United Kingdom (four of them in England), for reasons which may have (or may have had) something to do with convenient ranges of transmission, but which appear to owe more to supposed differences of culture and interest. The Central Electricity Generating Board, presumably because of factors that determine economic location of power-stations, operates with a set of regions quite different from those of the Electricity Boards which sell electrical energy to consumers. Anyone working on the regional statistics of government departments and public corporations will become acquainted with at least a dozen different systems of regional division.

These functional differences in regional boundaries intended for different specific purposes are understandable enough. What criteria of regional division should one seek to apply (if there were scope for choice) in delimiting areas for a general economic analysis, such as that with which we are concerned here? On the face of it, there are two rival economic principles of division. One can try to divide the country either into areas of which each is internally homogeneous as to the problems it presents and the effect on it of particular measures of policy, or into areas that have some claim to be to the maximum extent self-contained. The two principles are largely antithetic, but by no means entirely so. The first – homogeneity – is in any case ambiguous. One could, for instance, select areas in accordance with it on the basis of their dependence upon a particular product or group of products (agricultural areas, mining areas, textile areas, areas of heavy industry), or one could classify by degrees of prosperity (areas of unemployment, areas of labour shortage) or some other criterion (old industrial areas, new industrial areas, areas of slow or of rapid growth). Some of these criteria may give broadly similar regional patterns; in general they will give different ones. For purposes of study, one would like to be able to try out a number of different criteria. For purposes of policy involving discrimination between different areas, central governments will tend to choose appropriate criteria (high unemployment, high dependence on obsolescent coalmines) *ad hoc*.

The second principle of division – complementarity or self-sufficiency – is the one that would occur most naturally to anyone delimiting areas within which some measure of local autonomy or some planning functions are to be exercised. Planning is more effective where more, rather than fewer, of the factors bearing on the economic fortunes of the area in question are within the ambit of the planning authority. Local financial responsibility is easier to achieve if people both live and work in the administrative area in which they vote and pay local taxes.

The first principle, then, leads one to put together areas that are economically alike, the second leads one to combine some that are complementary and therefore unlike. But the contrast is not quite so stark as this suggests. The interpretation of either principle depends on the scale on which one is working. If one is concerned to define and perhaps combine relatively small areas of the demographic and economic dimensions of (say) Parliamentary constituencies, or still more parishes, then many of the most homogeneous will be working-class housing estates, middle-class suburbs, or specialised working areas such as Trafford Park or the City of London. The internal homogeneity goes with extreme 'openness' of their economies – almost complete dependence upon what happens elsewhere. On this scale one can find other areas of much greater (though limited) internal diversity and complementarity such as small towns, but in large cities and conurbations one could achieve internal diversity only by a sort of 'gerrymandering' – selecting odd-shaped areas running from the centre of the built-up area to its periphery. Even so one would not find much internal complementarity, because it is of the nature of large cities that people from a particular suburb work and shop in all parts of the central area, and some may be found at work also in many, if not all, parts of the industrial belt.

But in a discussion of regional economics one is not thinking on this parochial scale. Although British central government policy sometimes operates on single employment-exchange areas (as under the Local Employment Act of 1960 and more recently in designating Special Development Areas), regional policy and economics are broadly concerned with the layer of problems immediately below those that affect the whole country; problems which involve distinguishing, at any given time, anything from two to not more than (say) a dozen spatial divisions of the economy. On this scale it is areas of great economic, occupational, or social homogeneity that could be defined only by gerrymandering. Such is the 'grain-size' of the British economy that any spatially coherent area with a population of more than $1\frac{1}{2}$ million (the population of the smallest United Kingdom planning region) possesses very considerable industrial and social diversity. That being so, if one is looking for homogeneity on this scale, one is likely to be looking for the homogeneity of high or low prosperity, or of fast or slow growth, rather than for a particular kind of industrial or occupational specialisation; though one may very well be looking for closely connected systems of complementary industries that take their prosperity (or lack of it) from the fortunes of a single leading export. In other words, at the regional level one is quite likely to want to distinguish closely integrated, internally complementary sub-economies, even if one's motive is to select for treatment the sections of the country that have particular problems, rather than to find those to which planning functions can most appropriately be delegated. Some local problems require national action at subregional levels, but for dividing the country into a dozen regions (as opposed to sixty subregions), internal complementarity or self-sufficiency seems likely to be the appropriate principle.

In any case, the present (or new) Standard Regions with which we now have to manage, because they are the ones for which data are available, are described (sometimes) as 'economic planning regions', and they are no doubt designed as such; they are the bailiwicks of the Regional Economic Planning Councils and Economic Planning Boards.[1] With modifications that cannot be regarded as more than minor, the English members of the family have been blessed by the Redcliffe-Maud Commission, in the words, '...we believe that the economic and geographical composition of the country falls broadly into the pattern of the eight economic planning regions'.[2]

---

[1] These regions bear a strong resemblance to their predecessors, the old Standard Regions. The most important difference between the two is the treatment of the South East: under the present scheme it includes in a single region virtually the whole of the London commuting area, with a fringe stretching beyond it in parts, whereas the older scheme divided this area, along with East Anglia, into three regions – London and the South East, Eastern and Southern (see chart 2.1).

[2] Royal Commission on Local Government in England, *Local Government Reform*, Cmnd 4039, London, HMSO, 1969.

Chart 2.1. *Old and new Standard Regions of England and Wales*

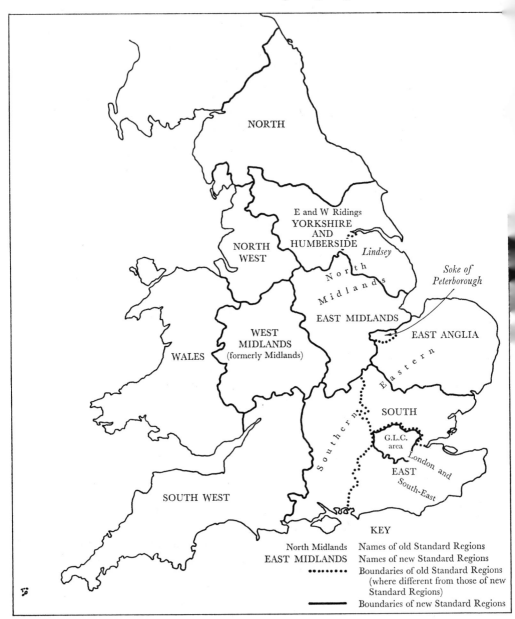

SOURCE: Department of Trade and Industry.

Note: The boundaries of the North, the North West, Wales, the West Midlands (formerly called the Midlands) and the South West were not changed.

This judgment should perhaps be scrutinised a little, and the question to which it relates should be asked also about the non-English regions. What, on a first examination, are the claims of the various United Kingdom regions as now delimited to possess the kind of internal economic cohesion that should make them good planning units, and what signs are there that they possess other economic, social, or political qualities that mark them off from each other in respects that are relevant to this? Some interregional differences, of course, will emerge only from our later, more searching, discussion of the regional economies, but a look at the more manifest characteristics of the conventional boundaries seems to be in order for a start.

THE PLANNING REGIONS

Politically and historically the regions of the United Kingdom are a mixed bag: one kingdom that had enjoyed seven centuries of more or less effective unity before its union with England; one principality with little history of political unity outside English control, but with a largely separate culture, including a language spoken by a quarter of the present population; one province, geographically separate from the rest of the United Kingdom, established in 1921 in the vain hope that Southern Ireland would be persuaded to accept a similar federal status under the Crown; and the eight English regions, with no direct political ancestry except the Civil Defence Regions of the second world war – a sort of augmented reincarnation of the Heptarchy.

The separate identities of Northern Ireland, Scotland and Wales clearly rest on political and cultural bases rather than on considerations of internal economic cohesion or any other economic criteria at all. Nevertheless, both Northern Ireland and Scotland could make strong claims for planning region status within something like their present boundaries on the strength of economic geography alone. Northern Ireland is unique in being separated by a sea channel from the rest of the United Kingdom, while the extent to which Belfast, with 60 per cent of all its non-agricultural workers, dominates its economy, amply qualifies it as the Belfast 'city region', subject to a doubt as to exactly where its rural boundaries would run if politics had not settled the issue. Three-quarters of the Scottish population is in the compact industrial belt of central Scotland, a hundred miles from the nearest major centre of English industry and population. This belt lies a good deal further from its nearest comparable neighbour than do any of the major English centres, and it is separated from England by a considerably emptier tract of country than lies between any pair of neighbouring centres south of the border. The border itself cuts across only small daily flows of commuting to Berwick and Carlisle, and the Scottish border counties are mainly served by their own cultural and distributive centres.

It is harder to make a case for Wales as an ideal planning region on economic grounds. Like some other mountainous countries, it has tended to enjoy growth of industry and population at points around its edges with better natural communications overseas or with the adjacent lowlands than with each other. It is true that over two-thirds of its population lives in the industrial belt of the south coast and the mining valleys behind it, and that this belt is separated from the neighbouring English centres by the Severn estuary and the rural belt of eastern Monmouthshire. Even there, however, better communications (especially the Severn bridge) are probably tending to produce greater geographical continuity of development and greater interchange of populations for work, shopping and recreation with, at least, Bristol and Gloucester, apart from the future possibility of a nationally sponsored, major development on Severnside. Further north, not only are the rural areas of central Wales served largely by towns across the border (a fact of little importance in so far as the population concerned is small), but the industrial area of north east Wales is continuous with that of Cheshire, and there is considerable overlap of commuting areas through which the boundary runs. But even apart from these boundary problems, one has to admit that Wales is far from being an integrated economic region; its main industrial area has relatively little connection with the other notable Welsh centres of population, and some of these have relatively little connection with each other.

Cultural and political ties, however, bind Wales together in defiance of economic geography. The Welsh-speaking population, constituting a majority only in central and north Wales, has transmitted something of its character and values to the bigger population of the south, which does not for the most part share either its language or its religious denominations. The southern majority, largely descended from nineteenth-century immigrants, has itself developed a sense of community identified with Wales as a whole, which is probably stronger than the sense of community to be found in English regions, though the major English coalmining areas show something of the same sort, stopping short of the Welsh sense of separate nationality.

The English regions are naturally less distinctive in economic character, less marked by communal selfconsciousness and, in general, less definitely bounded than Scotland, Northern Ireland, or Wales. The whole central part of England, from the north of London through the midlands to the skirts of the southern Pennines, is a zone of fairly high industrialisation and urbanisation, within which daily movements of people to and from neighbouring centres tend to overlap and economic connections are complex. The areas within which one would wish to draw some of the boundaries of the regions centred on London, Birmingham, Leicester–Nottingham, south Lancashire and west Yorkshire fall within this zone; moreover, its limits are creeping over the southern boundary of East Anglia and have reached or are reaching the Bristol–Gloucester area, which is the main industrial centre of the South West. This leaves only the Northern region entirely free from the ambiguity of boundary that comes from being connected with the main trunk or tree of English industrialisation.

The heart of the North is, of course, the industrial and mining area of the Tees, Wear and Tyne – an area of strong individuality second only to central Scotland in the distances (and the emptiness of the country) that separate it from its nearest comparable neighbours. Only one question arises seriously about the boundaries of the region which this industrial area dominates – namely, whether it extends only to the Pennines, or takes in Cumberland and Westmorland, which are at present included in the region. The Redcliffe-Maud Commission is almost certainly right in declaring that the area west of the Pennines has feebler links with the north east than with Lancashire.[1] Granted that the small industrial area of west Cumberland is somewhat isolated, it is nevertheless clear that the lines of communication to it, both before and after the building of the M6 motorway, are from the North West – in which the neighbouring and similar area of Furness is already included.

The North Western region is essentially Lancashire and the adjoining parts of Cheshire and Derbyshire that depend on the twin conurbations centred on Manchester and Liverpool. It has the unity of character and the particular flavour that come from its compactness and the strong internal connections of its industrial complex – a complex in which the cotton industry originally played a leading part, both in its spectacular growth and in its no less spectacular decline. As in south Wales and the north east, the awareness of great economic achievement, still in part within living memory, and of great economic misfortune endured in the last two generations, has produced a particular sense of community, different from and probably stronger than that in parts of the country with less dramatic recent histories.

Outside its core, the North Western region properly includes the Calder valley towns, which grew on cotton-weaving, and the more varied areas to the north, and it should, as has just been mentioned, probably include Westmorland and Cumberland, on the ground that they have closer connections with it than with anywhere else. With these counties included, the region's boundary would present no prob-

[1] Royal Commission on Local Government, *Local Government Reform*.

lems. To the south, there is no line that can be drawn between the North West on the one hand and the West Midlands and Wales on the other without cutting across some journeys to work and some spheres of urban influence, though there are a number of solutions (including the existing one) that create only small anomalies. The Pennines provide for the most part a very satisfactory boundary with Yorkshire and Humberside. That the M62 motorway will modify the effectiveness of this barrier any more than the railway lines of the last century did is unlikely. The Pennine moorland still cannot be comfortably lived on, and few people would opt to cross it daily or weekly (in winter at least) who did not have to.

Yorkshire and Humberside is a more artificial creation, as is suggested by the tangled history of regional delimitations in this area. The west Yorkshire conurbation is clearly the nucleus of an area of influence and internal complementarity stretching some way north and from the Pennine watershed towards (if not to) the east coast. The conurbation has a very distinct character, evinced rather than denied by the separatism of its constituent towns, which are apt to behave like Greek city states. Wool has been to it what cotton has been to the North West, but the greater gradualness of the rise and, more notably, of the decline of the wool textile industry has left a stronger sense of permanence, a nearer approach to complacency, than is to be found west of the hills.

The boundary between the area dominated by this conurbation and that dominated by the north eastern industrial area presents few difficulties, though the present boundary cuts York off from much of its commuting area and shopping customers, and a line further north in the rural North Riding, *à la* Redcliffe-Maud, would be better. The real problems arise on the south, where high industrialisation and interdependence of neighbouring areas continue with little natural break as far as Nottingham, if not Leicester or Birmingham. One could travel through this belt as far as Nottingham or Derby without passing through any rural district from which less than 60 per cent of its active resident population went to work in a town. In this continuum of industrial areas, Sheffield stands out as a major city of substantially different industrial character from the rest, its products different from but not really complementary with theirs, which invites the drawing of the boundary immediately either to the north or to the south of it. The latter solution is, of course, adopted, though in a way that cuts across important lines of travel to work and of urban expansion.

Further to the east, the inclusion of Lindsey in the region is a planning decision, based less on the present position than on the ground that future development south of the Humber should rely on the established urban facilities of Hull, given adequate communications. To the south of Scunthorpe and Grimsby, however, there is considerable freedom to draw a boundary in a number of different ways with few anomalies.

The West Midland region has its obvious centre in Birmingham and the Black Country, and runs off into the empty (and still emptying) country of the Welsh borders on the west. Its northern and southern boundaries present few problems, though both of them cross what might be regarded as likely 'corridors of growth', and Stoke on Trent has a distinctive industrial character and few links with either the Black Country on the one hand or Lancashire on the other. The eastern boundary presents difficulties, because it necessarily lies in the main trunk of industrial England. Coventry stands clear of the conurbation, but has strong industrial links with it; Rugby's connections are slighter, though probably stronger than such as it has with Northampton or Leicester. The Redcliffe-Maud Commission recommends a boundary extension to bring in the Northamptonshire part of its commuting area.[1] The Commission would transfer Burton on Trent, the other town that stands awkwardly against the regional border, to join its neighbour Derby in the East Midlands.

Industrial structure helps. There is a more or less clear industrial difference between Birmingham and Coventry in the metalworking and vehicle complex, and Nottingham, Leicester, or Northampton, traditionally specialising in pharmaceuticals, tobacco, textiles, clothing and footwear. But the tradition is changing, and the borders between the different industrial complexes (in so far as they are different) cannot be precisely drawn. Derby is, after all, a metalworking town and Burton a national brewing centre.

The English regions whose bounds we have so far beaten, as well as the South Eastern region, which is so clearly the London region as to require no discussion in this context, are all essentially the spheres of influence of conurbations – of twin conurbations in the case of the North West. In the case of Sheffield, the validity of this basis of regional division raises serious problems, and less serious questions of delimitation are raised by smaller free-standing towns of some consequence, like Rugby or Carlisle. Broadly, however, the system can be made to work.

In the remaining regions there are no conurbations and the basis must be rather different. The East Midlands however delimited is an area of many free-standing towns, shading off from Nottingham and Leicester, which perform some of the economic functions of regional capitals, to Lincoln, which might be described as a subregional capital, and so to what were originally small agricultural market towns, now with accretions of industry. A region of this kind can operate as a plan-

[1] Ibid.

ning region just as a 'conurbation region' can, but it is a different kind of region, with limits less sharply defined by the nature of the case, and perhaps with a lower urgency of planning problems than appears when the needs of a conurbation set the pace.

The East Midlands (and its predecessor the North Midland region) can be, and have been, delimited in various ways. The problems of the western and northern boundaries have been discussed; to the south east the drawing of a boundary with East Anglia leaves room for choice, because East Anglia, even more than the East Midlands, lacks the definition that comes from domination by an urban core. To the south it is the logic of the South Eastern region rather than any internal East Midland logic that is bound to fix the limits; the Redcliffe-Maud Commission recommended the transfer of most of Northamptonshire to the South East on the ground that projected new city development there is related to the needs of London.[1]

The same is true of the southern limit of East Anglia. The spread of London presses against it and is bound to reduce the appropriateness of the present boundary – indeed it might well, in time, destroy the case for a separate East Anglian region. For the time being however, Norfolk, Suffolk, Cambridge and Huntingdon retain a distinctive character and a pattern of settlement belonging to an older England – a country of agricultural villages, small towns with some industry and occasional larger towns, but no major industrial cities. The pattern is changing fast as the villages decline and the larger towns grow.

Finally, the South West presents a more complex picture. It possesses a strong and growing industrial nucleus in Bristol (or the wider area including Bristol, Cheltenham and Gloucester), but the nucleus can hardly be described as a 'core', lying as it does at one extreme tip of a region two hundred miles long. Bristol performs a metropolitan function for Gloucestershire and much, if not all, of Wiltshire, Dorset and Somerset, but the south western peninsula proper, like East Anglia, attained some wealth and urban development before the Industrial Revolution and, having escaped that revolution in the form in which it came to the Midlands or the North, retains a pattern of economic life in which the large industrial city still plays little part.

Given, however, that the south western peninsula is not to be treated like East Anglia, but is to be grouped with Bristol, on the ground that there is, at any rate, no other major centre to which it looks, the problem of defining a South Western region becomes relatively simple, resolving itself largely into the question – so variously and unconfidently answered – of what to do with Bournemouth and Poole. This region then becomes (as a former Chairman of its Economic Planning Council used to say)

[1] Ibid.

a small model of Great Britain, with its fast growing metropolitan area at one end and its more problem-ridden Celtic fringe at the other.

To sum up then, there is no principle of division into regions that works uniformly for all parts of the United Kingdom. Because what is being sought is a system of relatively large economic planning regions with some internal cohesion and self-sufficiency, the 'conurbation region' offers a good solution where it exists. It happens too that, of Scotland, Northern Ireland and Wales whose boundaries are predetermined on political and cultural grounds, at least the first two answer quite well to the conurbation region criterion. But this criterion becomes of little use in the East Midlands, a little strained in the South West and perhaps in south Yorkshire, and completely inapplicable in East Anglia. In such a field as this however, any principle that scores as many as six complete and two qualified successes out of eleven cases is worthy of some respect.

So much then for the criteria that can be used to justify, or to criticise, the regions' boundaries. If we take them as they are – as indeed we must – what are their relevant differences of character?

PHYSICAL DIFFERENCES

First, there are some obvious physical differences, most conspicuously those related to the geographers' distinction between 'highland' and 'lowland' Britain – conventionally divided by a line from the Exe to the Humber, preferably drawn convex to the north west so that it leaves Birmingham to its south east. This line approximates only very partially to regional boundaries; it cuts seriously across the South West and Yorkshire and Humberside, at the least. But it leaves to its north west virtually all the hill country that, for reasons mainly of climate, is difficult to inhabit and is, indeed, largely uninhabited – the rough grazing that occupies 60 per cent of the area of Scotland, about 30 per cent of that of the North and of Wales, but less than 3 per cent of the Midlands, East Anglia and the South East. The existence of this, for the most part beautiful, near-empty space is responsible for a good deal of the dispersion of the regional population densities, which run from 341 people per hundred acres in the North West to 27 in Scotland. If rough grazing is excluded, all the regional densities lie between 52 and 161 people per hundred acres, except those of the South East (260) and, again, the North West (397). These two last are, on this showing, the regions shortest of habitable open space; at the other end of the scale lie East Anglia and the South West (52 and 69 respectively), which, as we shall note later, are also the two that are filling up fastest. But even in the regions where the density is highest, by far the greater part of the land is in agricultural use (including rough grazing) – 65 per cent of it in the South East and 70 per cent in the North West. No region is predominantly given over to land-use of urban kinds.

The Exe–Humber 'highland line' has also a general significance with regard to rainfall, but this is much reduced if one excludes the land that is in practice sparsely inhabited because it is high. Indeed, it is altitude that produces the cloud, the rain and the exposure to wind that make British hills better for a summer holiday than for a permanent home. The lowland parts of the west do, of course, suffer extra rainfall and wind in comparison with the east, but they enjoy a winter mildness that may compensate for it. Perhaps the biggest climatic difference that remains, apart from effects of height, is the summer temperature difference between north and south, with the largely consequent difference in the growing season which any gardener with both northern and southern experience knows, and the pervasive difference in the lushness of the countryside which any traveller sees. Spring starts on the southern coasts and is said to move inland and northwards over the lowlands at 2 miles an hour. It sometimes seems slower.

But, since the main centres of population are mostly in the more clement areas within their respective regions, the climatic differences between them are not really very great. There are, moreover, sometimes compensations in the form of scenery. The highland zone has all the national parks, while, however much the lowland zone may resemble a garden (as is sometimes claimed for it), it is a garden that only the Almighty could find much scope for walking in. The environmental differences that affect the great mass of the inhabitants of the various regions are man-made rather than natural.

INDUSTRIAL STRUCTURE

Apart from the variations in degree of urbanisation, and in the amount of virtually empty country the regions contain, the main interregional differences obvious to the eye, and the most important economically, are those of industrial structure, as described most conveniently by the percentage distribution between industries of the whole occupied populations including the self-employed. It is useful for a start to measure the differences of structure between each region and the United Kingdom as a whole by means of the so-called coefficient of concentration (really a coefficient of specialisation), which can best be interpreted as the minimum percentage of the region's occupied population that would have to change from one industrial classification heading to another in order to make the percentage distribution of the region's population coincide with the initial one (before this was done) of the whole country.

A nearly corresponding measure can be calculated of the difference in structure between any two regions – the proportion of either region's population that would have to be shifted between industries to make its distribution between them like that of the other region.

The distribution between the Standard Industrial Classification Orders and the coefficients of specialisation calculated from the 1966 Census of Population are given in table 2.1. Two regions – the West Midlands and Northern Ireland – prove to be equally specialised, and substantially more so than any others; the measure of their difference from the country as a whole is 20 per cent. They are, of course, specialised in very different directions; the corresponding measure of the difference between them works out at 35 per cent.

This is a big difference. In modern British conditions, the minimum percentage of a region's occupied population that is required for essentially local services is apparently about 45. It seems from this that the highest coefficient of specialisation one can readily imagine as measuring the difference in structure between two regions is unlikely to exceed 50 per cent. At subregional level, differences of a little over 40 per cent can be found, but none much higher. The more extreme differences between the regions of the United Kingdom must, therefore, be taken as showing fairly high degrees of specialisation in relation to the highest degree that is reasonably possible.

At the other end of the scale, Scotland and the North West (with coefficients, in round figures, of 9 and 10 per cent respectively) show the lowest degrees of specialisation in comparison with the country as a whole. Half way between the extremes come Wales, the South West, East Anglia and the East Midlands, with coefficients of 14 or 15 per cent; the remaining regions – the North, Yorkshire and Humberside, and the South East – fall a little below the middle of the range at about 12 per cent. The differences between these regions are, however, in some cases very considerable. While the structural gap between Yorkshire and Humberside and the North is fairly small (14 per cent), that between the North and the South East is over 19 per cent; they diverge from the national structure in different directions.

It may be argued that specialisation measured in the way adopted here is likely to be affected by the size of the region. Suppose that a given industry consisted of establishments of uniform size scattered at random among other establishments which, for simplicity of exposition, we might suppose to be of the same size also. Then, if one examined regions of various sizes – that is containing different total numbers of establishments – the standard deviations of the proportions of establishments found to be in the chosen industry among regions of a given size should vary approximately in inverse relation to the square

Table 2.1. *Distribution of regional employment by industry and regional coefficients of specialisation, 1966*

Percentages

	North	Yorks. and H'side	North West	East Mid-lands	West Mid-lands	East Anglia	South East	South West	Wales	Scot-land	Great Britain	Northern Ireland	United King-dom
Agriculture, forestry and fishing	3·62	2·83	1·42	3·73	2·49	10·95	1·77	6·47	5·31	5·22	3·16	9·90	3·31
Mining and quarrying	7·61	5·06	1·13	6·75	1·74	0·22	0·18	0·92	7·21	2·57	2·33	0·31	2·28
Manufacturing													
Food, drink, tobacco	2·43	3·47	3·84	2·82	2·61	5·08	2·51	3·89	2·20	4·10	3·08	4·81	3·12
Chemicals etc.	4·04	2·06	3·83	1·50	0·98	1·33	1·89	0·77	2·20	1·45	2·04	0·59	2·01
Metal manufacturing	3·86	5·10	1·22	3·12	5·82	0·69	0·58	0·38	8·25	2·34	2·44	0·12	2·39
Engineering and electrical goods	8·82	7·46	9·67	9·19	12·30	7·81	9·75	6·86	5·29	7·66	9·06	4·81	8·97
Shipbuilding	3·04	0·33	0·91	0·09	0·04	0·52	0·40	0·78	0·33	2·14	0·74	2·29	0·77
Vehicles	0·89	2·07	3·58	3·46	8·47	2·00	3·08	4·06	2·03	1·84	3·36	1·86	3·32
Metal goods n.e.s.	1·07	3·23	1·98	1·44	8·20	0·56	1·64	0·82	2·12	1·21	2·33	0·70	2·30
Textiles	1·36	8·11	6·58	8·03	1·54	0·58	0·45	1·02	1·54	4·17	2·99	8·89	3·12
Leather and fur	0·12	0·26	0·32	0·31	0·27	0·16	0·25	0·23	0·17	0·16	0·24	0·16	0·24
Clothing and footwear	2·39	2·58	2·97	4·99	0·92	2·01	1·86	1·85	1·43	1·33	2·14	4·22	2·18
Bricks, pottery, glass	1·20	1·47	1·54	1·51	3·25	1·13	0·98	0·77	1·08	0·99	1·36	0·79	1·35
Timber and furniture	1·01	1·33	1·08	1·07	0·97	1·33	1·52	1·19	0·74	1·20	1·24	0·84	1·41
Paper, printing, publishing	1·32	1·77	2·78	1·66	1·36	2·14	3·67	2·44	1·04	2·65	2·56	1·27	2·52
Other	0·88	0·70	1·92	1·12	2·01	1·16	1·48	1·07	1·41	0·78	1·36	0·76	1·34
Construction	8·20	7·02	6·70	7·40	6·79	9·32	7·84	8·80	8·76	9·00	7·80	9·58	7·84
Gas, electricity, water	1·61	1·76	1·64	1·66	1·48	1·59	1·79	1·94	2·04	1·50	1·71	1·47	1·70
Transport and communication	5·98	5·89	7·15	4·92	4·42	5·58	7·99	5·83	6·73	6·97	6·67	5·04	6·63
Distribution	13·33	13·22	14·20	12·07	11·36	13·40	14·05	14·02	12·66	13·92	13·46	14·06	13·48
Insurance, banking and finance	1·69	1·90	2·24	1·57	1·73	2·20	4·28	2·20	1·74	2·07	2·72	1·79	2·70
Professional and scientific services	9·64	9·06	9·51	8·30	8·71	10·18	11·60	11·22	10·17	11·64	10·37	10·52	10·37
Miscellaneous services	10·01	9·20	9·59	8·84	8·63	12·88	13·31	12·76	9·46	9·89	10·99	9·22	10·95
Public administration and defence	5·89	4·12	3·91	4·49	3·93	7·20	7·15	9·72	6·10	5·21	5·84	6·16	5·85
Coefficient of specialisation	12·0	12·5	10·2	13·9	20·4	14·4	11·7	14·0	14·7	8·9	—	20·4	—

SOURCE: General Register Office, *Sample Census 1966. Great Britain. Economic Activity Tables*, Parts I and II, London, HMSO, 1968, tables 16 and 20.

Notes: (i) Census definition includes self-employed as well as employed but excludes unemployed; (ii) 66,380 persons of the Great Britain total of 24,168,820 are in the category 'industry inadequately described' and are therefore excluded.

root of the size. Our coefficient of specialisation, which is the sum of deviations of such proportions from the national proportion for a number of industries, would presumably vary with size of region in a somewhat similar way.

The real world is, of course, much more complex than this. The fact that regions are not random collections of industrial establishments but continuous areas defined so as to have some organic unity reduces the dependence on size of region of the deviation of structure from the national norm, because the organic unity of the region implies some considerable degree of variety and complementarity among its industries. In fact, if coefficients of specialisation are plotted against regional population, it looks as if there is some general tendency of the kind one would expect from this; specialisation falls with increase of size, though less steeply than an inverse square-root law would demand. But it is the outstanding deviations that are interesting. The West Midlands region is much more highly specialised than any of the half-dozen smaller ones – even slightly more so than Northern Ireland. The South East, likewise, is very much more specialised than its large size would lead one to expect; it is more specialised than either the North West or Scotland. Its specialisation on the service trades (balanced by its small shares of the extractive and most of the manufacturing industries) sets it apart. East Anglia, much less specialised than Northern Ireland, and about as much so as the bigger regions, Wales, the East Midlands and the South West, must be reckoned rather highly diversified for its size.

The directions of specialisation emerge clearly from the table. The North shows the highest concentration of any region on mining, chemicals and shipbuilding, which with the addition of metal manufacture (in which it ranks fourth in degree of specialisation) employ some 19 per cent of its occupied population. The most notably under-represented group is the vehicle industries. Yorkshire and Humberside spreads its specialisation rather more widely, and is not the most highly specialised of the regions in any one industry-group, though it comes near to this in textiles, which, with metal manufacture and mining, account for 18 per cent of its employment. Its deficiencies in comparison with the national industrial composition are fairly widely spread over the metal-working industries and the service trades.

The North West, the second largest of the regions in population, now shows a very decidedly lower degree of specialisation. It is only in its leading traditional speciality, textiles, and in chemicals, that it specialises to a degree that involves any substantial parts of its population, and in textiles it falls below Northern Ireland, Yorkshire and Humberside, and the East Midlands in degree of specialisation, though it is worth noting that the characteristic textile products of these four regions are markedly different from each other. The long-standing strength of the North West as a leading centre of the metalworking industries emerges from the table, as does its strength in the clothing and footwear group; in fact, it shows (inevitably relatively small) degrees of specialisation in comparison with the national structure on a larger number of manufacturing industries than any other region, besides having more than the general proportion of its population in transport and the distributive trades. On the other side of the account, it shows the smallest proportions of all the regions not only in agriculture, but, at the time of the 1966 Census, in construction – a reflection of its slow growth and its large stock of redundant factory buildings.

The East Midlands at this level of disaggregation of industries has a structure very like that of Yorkshire and Humberside, specialising on mining, metal manufacture, textiles and the clothing and footwear group. In detail there are differences; the textile industry is based on knitting instead of weaving, and footwear is relatively more important than clothing in comparison with Yorkshire. The East Midlands region, too, is notable for having smaller proportions of its population in the industrial categories of insurance, banking and finance, and professional and scientific services than any other region has. Nevertheless, the general similarity of structure with Yorkshire and Humberside – the coefficient of difference between them is only 9 per cent – adds point to the observation, made earlier, that the geographical boundary between these two regions is more than usually unsatisfactory; they really consist of a series of industrial areas of subregional size, each with a quite strong industrial speciality, and with partly overlapping rural dependencies which, in the East Midlands, bring the degree of specialisation on agriculture above the national average.

Structurally, the West Midlands has a much clearer character; it is the most highly specialised British region, with higher proportions of its population than any other region in no less than five Industrial Orders, the large engineering and electrical group, vehicles, miscellaneous metal trades, bricks, pottery and glass, and the miscellaneous industries group (of which the rubber industry is an important constituent). It has, moreover, the second highest specialisation in metal manufacture. Correspondingly, it has the lowest proportions of any region in clothing and footwear, and, perhaps more notably, in some of the important service groups – transport, distribution (partly, no doubt, because it has no seaport) and the miscellaneous services group. In professional and scientific services and public administration and defence it has the lowest proportion but one. It is the manufacturing region *par excellence* and, with the exception of the Potteries, which it seems half inclined to disown, pre-eminently the metalworking region.

East Anglia has an almost equally definite character as the pre-eminent agricultural region, with nearly 11 per cent of its occupied population in agriculture, forestry and fishing, and another 5 per cent in the food, drink and tobacco group. Its catering and holiday trades help to make it second only to the South East in concentration on the miscellaneous services group, and to Northern Ireland in concentration on construction – a reflection of its very rapid growth.

The South West's composite character is reflected in its general industrial structure. It has the highest degree of specialisation among regions only in public administration and defence, and stands third in its specialisation on agriculture. Its holiday trades (as in East Anglia) give it some bias towards the miscellaneous service group, and its rapid growth is reflected in a higher than national proportion of its population in the construction industry. Its manufacturing industry gives it an appreciably greater than average degree of specialisation in only two groups – food, drink and tobacco, and vehicles (mainly aircraft) – though its proportion in shipbuilding is a little above the national average. Mainly through its concentration on agriculture and the two service groups mentioned, however, it ranks among the more specialised regions.

Wales is a little more specialised still, though perhaps only to an extent that its smaller population could explain. Most of its specialisation is accounted for by metal manufacture, on which it concentrates more than any other region, and mining, in which its specialisation is exceeded only by that of the North. Agriculture, however, also makes a considerable contribution to its departure from the national pattern. It falls below the United Kingdom level of concentration in all the orders of manufacturing industry except metal manufacture, chemicals and the miscellaneous group 'other manufactures'.

Scotland, as has already been noted, is the least specialised region. It ranks as the most specialised in only one industry-group – rather surprisingly, professional and scientific services – though it has notably more than its share also of agriculture, the food, drink and tobacco group, shipbuilding, textiles and (in 1966) construction. Northern Ireland stands near the other extreme, though with certain similarities of structure: heavy concentration on agriculture and textiles (the heaviest of any region on the latter), on the food, drink and tobacco group, shipbuilding and construction, with the addition of a specialisation on clothing which Scotland does not share. It has corresponding heavy deficiencies in comparison with the United Kingdom structure in chemicals, metal manufacture and most of the lighter metalworking industries.

Lastly, the South East, heavily specialised for its size, owes that specialisation mainly to concentration on the service industries (most notably, the miscellaneous services and financial groups), though it is also heavily biased towards transport (largely because of its ports) and, among the manufacturing industries, towards paper and printing and the large engineering and electrical group, as well as the smaller timber and furniture industry. The extractive industries, metal manufacture and textiles are heavily under-represented in it. In most, though not all, of these specialisations it is complementary with that pre-eminently manufacturing region the West Midlands (the measure of structural difference between them being 26 per cent), or mining and manufacturing regions like Yorkshire and Humberside and the North (measures of difference 22 per cent and 19 per cent respectively). It is a long time since the London region was unique in being 'town' as opposed to 'country', and even its status as the centre of national government does not give it the highest specialisation in the field of public administration and defence (taken together); but its head office, commercial, financial, entertainment and governmental functions combined set it apart from all other regions.

Such then are the differences of industrial structure between the regions; some of them are large – considerably more than half the maximum differences of structure that are reasonably possible between such considerable areas, given the range of essentially local services that all such areas with anything like our present standard of living must have. But there are also very substantial occupational differences, which carry perhaps greater social significance than the diversities of industrial classification.

SOCIAL DIFFERENCES

In fact, the Census of Population makes two classifications other than the industrial one, though neither succeeds in being wholly independent of it. The classification by socio-economic groups concentrates on status within organisations, degree of independence and level of skill, but distinguishes also the largely industrial categories of professional workers, personal service workers, and those in agriculture and the armed forces. Since the distinctions between industries (providers of different kinds of goods or services) are largely removed, however, it is not surprising that the structural differences between regions become much smaller than when industry is the basis. People differ less between regions in the kinds of work they do than in the kinds of output for the sake of which they do it.

The position is shown in table 2.2. The most conspicuous fact that

Table 2.2. *Numbers in socio-economic groups[a] as proportions of totals economically active in regions, 1966*

Percentages

	N	Y & H	NW	EM	WM	EA	SE	SW	Wa.	Sc.	GB
Employers and managers (large establishments)	2·3	2·5	2·6	2·5	2·6	2·3	3·5	2·5	2·3	2·5	2·8
Employers and managers (small establishments)	4·0	4·7	4·7	4·2	4·3	4·7	5·8	5·4	4·5	4·0	4·9
Professional workers – self-employed	0·4	0·4	0·4	0·4	0·4	0·5	0·6	0·6	0·5	0·5	0·5
Professional workers – employees	2·2	2·1	2·5	2·2	2·6	2·2	3·5	2·4	2·2	2·1	2·7
Intermediate non-manual workers	5·8	5·4	6·0	5·4	5·2	5·6	7·2	6·7	6·0	6·3	6·3
Junior non-manual workers	19·2	18·2	20·7	17·8	19·3	18·1	25·7	20·2	17·8	20·8	21·5
Personal service workers	5·7	4·9	4·8	4·4	4·6	6·2	6·0	6·8	5·1	5·6	5·4
Foremen and supervisors – manual	2·8	2·9	2·6	2·8	2·6	2·2	2·3	2·1	2·8	2·4	2·5
Skilled manual workers	25·0	25·9	23·7	28·5	26·9	21·1	19·3	20·8	22·9	23·9	22·9
Semi-skilled manual workers	15·9	17·9	17·2	17·0	17·7	12·2	12·3	11·8	16·4	14·8	14·9
Unskilled manual workers	9·6	8·7	9·2	7·0	7·7	7·6	7·0	7·3	9·2	9·8	8·1
Own account workers (excl. professional)	2·2	2·9	3·5	3·0	2·7	3·2	3·4	3·9	3·5	1·7	3·1
Farmers – employers and managers	0·7	0·5	0·3	0·7	0·5	1·7	0·3	1·3	0·8	1·0	0·6
Farmers – own account workers	1·0	0·6	0·4	0·8	0·6	1·4	0·2	1·7	2·6	0·7	0·7
Agricultural workers	1·7	1·4	0·6	2·0	1·2	7·0	1·0	3·0	1·7	2·6	1·6
Armed forces	0·9	0·5	0·1	0·8	0·5	3·6	1·2	2·9	0·9	0·8	1·0

SOURCE: *Sample Census 1966. Great Britain. Economic Activity Tables*, Part III, table 30.
[a] Excluding those classified as 'indefinite'.

emerges is the difference between the South East and all, or nearly all, of the other regions. It is outstanding in the proportions of its active population that are employers or managers in large establishments, employees in professional work and junior non-manual workers. In all of these categories, it contains about 40 per cent of the total for Great Britain, whereas it has only about a third of the total of economically active people. This reflects, of course, the office (especially head office) and public service functions of London. The South East region also has more than the national average proportion of employers and managers in small establishments, of self-employed professional workers

Table 2.3. *Numbers in service occupations as proportions of totals economically active in regions, 1966*

Percentages

	N	Y & H	NW	EM	WM	EA	SE	SW	Wa.	Sc.	GB
Transport and communications workers	6·2	5·9	6·2	5·3	4·7	5·8	6·3	6·0	6·4	6·4	6·0
Warehousemen, storekeepers, packers, etc.	2·6	3·8	4·1	4·1	3·9	3·0	3·4	3·0	2·6	3·1	3·5
Clerical workers	10·8	11·1	13·2	10·9	12·1	10·6	17·7	12·0	10·3	11·8	13·7
Sales workers	9·6	9·3	9·6	8·8	8·6	9·8	9·8	10·4	9·9	9·9	9·6
Service, sport and recreation workers	12·4	11·5	11·7	10·2	10·4	11·9	12·8	13·4	11·3	12·4	12·0
Administrators and managers	2·1	2·8	2·8	2·8	3·1	2·4	4·0	2·6	2·2	2·1	3·1
Professional, technical workers and artists	8·5	7·9	8·9	8·2	8·6	8·4	11·3	9·9	8·7	8·9	9·6
Armed forces	0·9	0·5	0·1	0·8	0·5	3·6	1·2	2·9	0·9	0·8	1·0

SOURCE: *Sample Census 1966. Great Britain. Economic Activity Tables*, Part I, table 13.

and of intermediate non-manual workers, but this distinction is shared by the South West and, though it has also more than its share of personal service workers, the South West exceeds it in this respect, while the other tourist and holiday regions, East Anglia, Scotland and the North, show some bias in this direction. If one sets the South East against the rest of Great Britain, it turns out that one or the other would have to shift over 12 per cent of its active population from one to another of the seventeen main occupational categories to give both areas the same occupational composition. Only East Anglia is as widely different from the rest of the country as this – largely because of its agricultural specialisation and the treatment of agricultural workers as a separate occupational category.

The South East's bias is towards non-manual workers; the essentially, manufacturing and mining regions – both Midlands regions, Yorkshire, the North and, to rather smaller extents, the North West, Wales and Scotland – show the opposite bias, and with it a bias away from the professions, employers and managers. In short, a cloth-cap bias.

The specifically occupational (as opposed to the socio-economic) classification (table 2.3) tells broadly the same tale. The South East has 43 per cent of the total for Great Britain both of administrative and managerial workers and of clerks. It also has 39 per cent of the national total in the professional, technical and artistic group. Some

33 per cent of its active population is in these three groups; in the rest of the country the proportion is 23 per cent.

We shall return to regional income differences of various kinds in considering regional social accounts, but differences in average size and in distribution of personal income must be mentioned here, since they play important parts in forming interregional social differences. It can be shown that there are no two arithmetic means of taxable incomes either for Standard Regions, or for the rather smaller areas that the Inland Revenue Surveys distinguish (conurbations and regional remainders), that do not differ significantly from each other. The average for the old Standard Region, London and the South East, stood in 1959–60 about 8 per cent above its nearest rival, the (West) Midlands average, and 36 per cent above the figure for Northern Ireland.

These differences arise, of course, partly from variations in the regional average levels of particular categories of income (profits, wages, salaries and so on); partly from the different proportions of taxpayers who have incomes in these categories. London and the South East shows lower average wage incomes than the (West) Midlands, but the highest average salary income of any region; it also has the highest proportion of salary earners and the lowest of wage earners among its tax cases, while salary incomes are generally about 40 per cent bigger than those from wages. London and the South East's incomes from profits (Schedule D), from interest and dividends and from other property are bigger than those in any other region, but there are proportionately fewer of them than in several others—the South West, the old Southern region and Wales have the highest proportions of property owners, Scotland (with its small private ownership of house-property) the lowest. But, in aggregate, the southern regions – South East England and the South West – have some 57 per cent of United Kingdom rent, dividend and net interest income, against 41 per cent of population and 43 per cent of personal income from all other sources. That is where the weight of property ownership is concentrated.

Educational differences to some extent correspond. South East England and the South West stand somewhat apart from the rest of England and Wales in the low proportion of their children who leave school with no 'O' level passes in GCE examinations and in the high proportion with two or more 'A' level passes. They stand apart from the rest of England (though not Wales, and probably not Scotland for which comparable data are not available) in the higher proportion of school-leavers who proceed to full-time further or higher education. In the resident population as a whole something of the same kind is to be seen. The proportion of the male population aged over 15 that had undergone full-time education to the age of 20 or more was, according to the 1961 Census, some 57 per cent higher in South East England and the South West than in the rest of England (about 4·4 per cent against 2·8), though Scotland and Wales were in intermediate positions in this respect. In the female population, where the differences were otherwise similar, Scotland and Wales matched the southern English standard.

To some extent these differences in the concentration of the more highly educated in the population can be explained by differences of occupational structure. Among occupied men the percentage with education to age 20 plus varies from a fraction of 1 per cent among labourers, construction workers and decorators to over a third among professional and technical workers, and the proportion in the occupied (or indeed the total adult) population depends greatly upon the geographical distribution of the last named class. The explanation, however, is only a partial one. The percentage excess of the incidence of the highly educated in London and the South East, the South and the South West (but not the old Eastern region) in 1961 was very much larger than occupation, at least on a broad classification, would explain; the deficiency in the rest of England was also bigger. But Wales and Scotland attained the high concentrations of such men to which we have referred, despite occupational structures weighted against this result. That the more highly trained members of many occupational classes should congregate around the national capital is not surprising; that they should also be found in Scotland, Wales and (to some extent) the South West perhaps requires more explanation. Regional traditions differ; so do (and still more did) regional opportunities. Higher education is a great mobiliser; to a lately much increased extent it takes people away from home, and in any case it introduces them to markets for their services that are national or international. But where facilities traditionally geared to the local population are locally plentiful, as in Scotland and Wales, we may expect to see (as we do) a high proportion of their products in the regional populations, as well as a net export of the highly educated. At all events, the curious dual concentration of educated manpower, at the administrative centre of the British economy and at the periphery, is an interesting fact. It does not follow that the *kinds* of training, or use of training, to be found at these two locations are similar.

The economic and social differences that are implied in these figures carry with them some differences in expenditure and in provision of services. Car ownership in relation to population stands 10 or 15 per cent higher in South East England and the South West than in the midlands, 20 per cent higher than in Wales and 40 or 50 per cent higher than in other regions. (*Ceteris paribus,* the more rural regions show higher ownership than the more urban ones.) Average household expenditure on housing is, of course, particularly heavy in the South East; it stands some 60 per cent higher than in all the other British regions except East Anglia, the South West and the West Midlands, where it occupies an intermediate position. But this is mainly a matter of price difference rather than amount or quality of accommodation. The housing stock is rather newer in southern England and the midlands than elsewhere (38 per cent of dwellings built before 1919, against 44 in the rest of Great Britain), but the average number of persons per room is only marginally lower, either in the South Eastern region itself, or in the south and midlands generally, than in the rest of the country except for the Northern region and Scotland. On the other hand, purchase prices of houses in Greater London seem to be 25 or 30 per cent higher than in the rest of southern England and 70 to 90 per cent higher than in Wales, the midlands and the northern half of England, though only some 50 per cent higher than in Scotland. Moreover, weekly unrebated rents of modern local authority dwellings of a given description follow a similar pattern of variation between London and the English regions, though Wales seems to be rather dearer in this respect than the northern half of England. Housing provides by far the most important instance of an interregional difference in prices. In spite of dearer housing, however, households in the South East are more frequently equipped with central heating, refrigerators and (most strikingly) telephones than those in other regions. But the north of England is the land of the domestic washing machine.

In mentioning housing we have touched on the most important part of the artificial environment, but there are, of course, others. However its housing situation is rated, South East England enjoys an environmental advantage in having by far the lowest regional incidence of derelict land; the benefit mainly of having never been a significant mining area, though brickfields and gravel-pits are not inconspicuous there. This has to be set against the relatively poor access to recreational open space already referred to.

As one might expect from what has been said about income distribution, southern England has advantages in such matters as incidence of recommended eating places and of theatre seats, while the concentration of shopping facilities in London – indicated by the South East region's considerable lead in retail turnover per head of population – provides a further advantage to those who live within easy visiting distance. These are aspects of the concentration of high demand and of national facilities in the capital, for which those who live or work in it pay a penalty, not only in the high housing cost just mentioned, but in long journeys to work and other aspects of the urban congestion that London exemplifies on a scale so much larger than anywhere else in the country.

Many, if not all, of these interregional differences are relevant to health. On the face of it, interregional health differences are large. Mortality rates give one indication of this. In most age groups and in both sexes deaths per thousand in that group are (or were in 1961–3) lowest in either South East England or the South West and highest in Scotland. On average, weighted for the age composition of the United Kingdom population, male mortality rates in Scotland were some 27 per cent higher than those of South East England. For women the difference was slightly smaller. The North West and Wales also stand out as high-mortality regions.

There are, however, big differences in standardised mortality between social classes (as distinguished by the Registrar General) and between town and country. For England in the years 1948–53, data are available classified in this way, as well as by three broad regional areas – the North, the Midlands and East, and the South. On analysis, it seems that the specifically regional element is significant (mainly to the disadvantage of the North), though less so than either differences of social class or those between urban and rural areas. The two latter classifications, however, appear to go with differences so nearly parallel to each other that their effects cannot be clearly distinguished.

Data on illness are also to the point. National Health consulting rates for England and Wales are available by broad regional group – North, Midlands and Wales, South – and by three types of area – urban, semi-urban and rural. Analysis of these data suggest that type of area has some degree of significance, but that region has none.

Data of much more direct relevance, however, are those relating to days of incapacity per thousand men, standardised for age. They have been analysed for nine occupational groups: agricultural workers, coalminers, furnace, forge and foundry workers, engineering workers, woodworkers, textile workers, clerks, shopworkers, and administrative and managerial workers.[1] Between these groups the figures vary enormously, from about twenty days a year for coalminers to three in the managerial category. A simple analysis of variance suggests that interregional differences are significant, though responsible for only about 7 per cent of the total variance of the data (against 83 per cent for which occupation is responsible). The only regional average that approaches significant departure from the mean, however, is that for Wales, which is high.

[1] Ministry of Social Security, *Report of an Inquiry into the Incidence of Incapacity for Work*, Part II (*Incidence of Incapacity for Work in Different Areas and Occupations*), London, HMSO, 1966.

Apart from the different occupational influences on health there are, of course, diverse environmental influences on the population at large that stem from industrial activity – notably atmospheric pollution. The correlation between incidence of bronchitis and the atmospheric sulphur dioxide concentration, for instance, is a reasonably close one, though the rate in south Wales is much higher than can be explained by this influence alone. Probably natural conditions (humidity, for instance), occupational hazards (exposure to dust) and general atmospheric pollution interact to produce more drastic results than can be explained by adding the specific effects of each of them in isolation. At all events the total interregional differences in health are very considerable, though, as we have seen, by far the greater part of them seems to derive not from where the people in question live but from what they do.

What does all this amount to? The United Kingdom regions do not possess homogeneous characters either of natural or built environment, or of industrial or social structure. Each is a mixture, but they are mixtures differing significantly from one another in composition, and yielding for very many people flavours of life which differ, as a rule subtly, but occasionally more decidedly, and which can evoke strong preferences. How far they are so integrated together economically as to share their prosperity or adversity and how far they go their separate ways we shall see more clearly as our investigation proceeds. But we should remind ourselves that in one respect, not immediately an economic one, they differ from one another very widely – the extent to which they are communities with political and cultural selfconsciousness; from Northern Ireland, Scotland and Wales at one end of the scale to (say) the East Midland region at the other. That some of them – not only those outside England – do possess at least significantly widespread senses of their identity, history and culture as communities, of the value of their peculiar flavour of life, and of their claims as major components of the nation, is a fact to be reckoned with in considering regional policy. It is, indeed, one of the main reasons why one has to consider regional policy at all.

CHAPTER 3

PRODUCTION, EXPENDITURE, INTERREGIONAL FLOWS AND REAL INCOME DIFFERENCES[1]

To form a clearer impression of the economic performances and interrelations of the regions, we require a set of regional social accounts; that is to say accounts of production in the regions, net transfers between them, and final absorption of goods and services in them, for some recent year or years. To this we may add whatever can be discovered about the *gross* flows of goods, if not of services, between them. It is convenient to start with gross domestic product – the value of goods and services produced within the regions – and to work our way from there to the final absorptions by regions of goods and services, which give the best single basis for judging their relative economic welfare.

GROSS DOMESTIC PRODUCT

There is broadly adequate information about personal incomes received by those whose workplaces (or, in some cases, residences) are in the various regions, about earnings of employees resident in the regions and about household incomes in them. None of these sources, however, tells us directly about the production of income in the regions, since income produced includes some elements (mostly of dividends and interest) that are paid to residents in other regions, as well as undistributed profits which do not enter into personal or household income at all, while personal or household incomes correspondingly contain elements not originating in the regions in which they are received. Reasonably good estimates of the gross domestic products produced in the various regions can, however, be made by starting with the earnings of employees and the self-employed, and adding estimates of profits, interest and rent generated regionally. A large part of profits – those in industries covered by the Census of Production – can be assigned to regions of origin on the basis of the census data on gross value of output and expenditure on labour, materials and power by industrial establishments situated in the regions, and for the remainder various other sources, including the accounts of the nationalised industries, agricul-

[1] The discussion of social accounts in this chapter is derived almost entirely from the work of Mr Vivian Woodward: see V. H. Woodward, *Regional Social Accounts for the United Kingdom*, NIESR Regional Papers I, Cambridge University Press, 1970.

Table 3.1. *Factor incomes per head, 1961*

	Employment income		Self-employment income		Company profits[a]		Public enterprise surpluses[b]		Rent		GDP at factor cost[c]	
	(£)	(Index)	(£)	(Index)	(£)	(Index)	(£)	(Index)	(£)	(Index)	(£)	(Index)
North	271	88	36	90	69	99	15	112	21	84	410	90
E & W Ridings	302	98	34	85	78	111	19	142	21	82	452	100
North West	300	98	33	84	86	122	11	80	22	87	449	99
North Midlands	303	99	42	106	76	108	22	163	23	92	463	102
(West) Midlands	341	111	36	90	78	112	13	92	23	91	489	108
SE England	349	114	41	104	69	98	13	95	33	128	503	111
South West	261	85	53	136	52	74	10	74	25	97	400	88
Wales	258	84	43	107	67	95	14	105	22	87	401	88
Scotland	258	84	42	105	62	88	12	89	20	77	392	86
N Ireland	190	62	46	116	29	42	8	61	16	63	289	64
United Kingdom	307	100	40	100	70	100	14	100	25	100	454	100

SOURCE: Woodward, *Regional Social Accounts*, table 4.
[a] Gross trading profits.   [b] Gross trading surpluses.
[c] Including stock appreciation and residual error.

tural statistics, the Census of Distribution and, in the last resort, the industry tables of the Census of Population, provide bases of estimation. Income generation can thus be reasonably well assigned to the regions where the activity in question is carried on, irrespective of where the income is subsequently received, or where head offices happen to be.

Table 3.1 shows the results of such an estimate for the year 1961, the regions in question being the old Standard Regions, with London and the South East combined with the old Southern and Eastern regions under the title South East England (not very different from the new South Eastern and East Anglian regions combined). The estimates are all shown per head of the total regional population, the main classes of factor income being shown separately. The production of each kind of factor income and the total per head of regional population are also shown as percentages of the corresponding United Kingdom figures. Very similar relative outputs per head of total regional populations are obtained by calculations for 1964, except that the Northern region stands rather lower in the latter year.

It is at once clear that output per head of total population is highest in the South East and the (West) Midlands, and falls fairly steadily as one moves north or west from there. South East England and the (West) Midlands stand (in round figures) 10 per cent above the national average; the North Midlands, Yorkshire and the North West are virtually on the average; the South West, Wales and the North are 10 to 12 per cent below it, and Scotland a few points lower. Northern Ireland is in a class of its own, 36 per cent below the United Kingdom average. Most of these differences, of course, spring from employment income (which is two-thirds of the total in the country as a whole), but it is noteworthy that self-employment income is especially important in the South West and Northern Ireland, that gross trading profits make relatively large contributions in the four regions most specialised on manufacturing (the two Midlands regions, Yorkshire and the North West), that public enterprise surpluses are most important in the regions of coalmining and electricity generation, and that the contribution of rent in the South East is higher by a third than in any other region.

A division can be made, which is rough in parts but still useful, of the gross domestic product of each region between its industries of origin. Such a division, expressed per head of total population in each region, is shown in table 3.2. This division reproduces to some extent the picture of industrial structure which has already been discussed on the basis of the industrial classification of the population, but the two pictures naturally differ in so far as productivities vary between industries and regions, and the present one, based on output, is especially valuable where the census statistics of numbers engaged in an industry are difficult to interpret, as in agriculture where farmers' wives and other family workers present a problem both as to how they are recorded and as to what they actually contribute. Thus, agriculture, forestry and fishing, which contributed in 1961 just under 4 per cent of the United Kingdom gross domestic product, were responsible for about 13 per cent of that of Northern Ireland. Manufacturing contributed less than 27 per cent of gross domestic product in the South West, but 48 per cent in the (West) Midlands. The heavy dependence of South East England on transport, distribution, finance, ownership of dwellings, public administration and defence, and the miscellaneous 'other services' group is also clear; they provide it with 54 per cent of its gross domestic product, whereas the corresponding national proportion is 44 per cent and that for the Northern region only 37 per cent. This particular contrast is probably understated by these figures, since the conventions of national accounting lead to understatement of the product of insurance, banking and finance.

The figures of total regional production so far quoted refer to income generated per head of the *total* regional population. Part of the inter-regional differences they show can be accounted for by the fact that different regions have different proportions of their populations actively engaged in production. Table 3.3 shows the effects of this and table 3.4 gives a further account of the way in which it arises. In the first place, age structures differ. The proportion of the total population that is of

Table 3.2. *Gross domestic product by industry per head of total population, 1961*

£ per annum

	N	EWR	NW	NM	(W)M	SEE	SW	Wa.	Sc.	NI	UK
Manufacturing											
Engineering, electrical goods	27	31	40	37	55	42	20	16	28	13	36
Shipbuilding, etc.	14	2	5	1	—	2	5	1	10	11	4
Vehicles	4	10	16	18	42	15	21	6	6	5	15
Metal goods n.e.s.	3	14	7	4	37	6	1	7	5	—	9
Sub-total[a]	*48*	*57*	*68*	*60*	*134*	*65*	*47*	*30*	*49*	*29*	*64*
Food, drink, tobacco	10	18	24	19	18	18	24	7	23	22	19
Chemicals, etc.	35	14	30	10	7	13	4	13	11	—	15
Metal manufacturing	25	29	7	26	33	3	1	51	13	—	15
Textiles	5	39	25	28	7	2	5	11	14	20	13
Leather, clothing	5	9	9	15	3	7	5	3	3	8	7
Bricks, pottery, glass	6	8	8	7	13	5	3	5	4	3	6
Timber, furniture, etc.	3	4	4	4	4	6	4	2	3	1	4
Paper, printing, publishing	4	8	13	6	6	19	9	4	10	3	12
Other manufacturing	2	2	10	3	9	5	5	4	3	4	5
Total	*143*	*188*	*198*	*178*	*234*	*143*	*107*	*130*	*133*	*90*	*160*
Agriculture, forestry, fishing	18	12	8	27	16	14	35	23	29	37	18
Mining and quarrying	42	33	6	38	11	1	5	32	13	2	13
Construction	25	25	26	26	27	32	29	28	30	22	29
Gas, electricity, water	12	15	12	15	14	13	11	13	11	9	13
Transport and communication	31	34	40	30	27	49	32	35	36	17	38
Distribution[b]	42	50	54	52	51	69	49	39	45	33	54
Insurance, banking, finance	8	10	11	10	12	24	10	9	10	7	15
Ownership of dwellings	16	16	17	16	16	23	18	16	14	12	18
Forces (pay and allowances)	5	2	1	6	4	8	19	5	4	5	6
Public administration and defence	16	14	15	13	15	23	17	16	14	13	17
Health and education	16	17	17	16	17	20	20	19	19	17	18
Other services	37	40	47	38	47	83	51	38	42	24	56
TOTAL GDP[c]	410	452	449	463	489	503	400	401	392	289	454

SOURCE: Woodward, *Regional Social Accounts*, table 9.

[a] GDP per employee in each of the constituent industries of this sub-total was assumed uniform by region because the Census of Production does not provide separate data.

[b] Wholesale and retail.

[c] Including stock appreciation and residual error.

Table 3.3. *Gross domestic product per head at factor cost, 1961*

	GDP per head		Variations explained by:		
			Working age/total population	Labour force at work/working population	Productivity of labour force at work[a]
	(£)	(*Index*)	(%)	(%)	(%)
North	410	*90*	99·4	92·0	98·9
E & W Ridings	452	*100*	100·9	100·7	98·1
North West	449	*99*	100·3	102·6	95·9
North Midlands	463	*102*	100·3	98·0	104·1
(West) Midlands	489	*108*	101·5	104·0	101·8
SE England	503	*111*	100·5	104·3	105·5
South West	400	*88*	98·5	93·1	96·0
Wales	401	*88*	100·3	88·4	99·4
Scotland	392	*86*	97·8	96·0	90·7
N Ireland	289	*64*	94·0	88·7	77·0
United Kingdom	454	*100*	100·0	100·0	100·0

SOURCE: Woodward, *Regional Social Accounts*, table 3.

[a] Part-time workers adjusted as far as possible to full-time equivalents.

Table 3.4. *Occupational distribution of regional populations, 1961*

Percentages

	Economically active					Economically inactive		
	Self-employed	Married women	Pensionable age	Out of employment	All	Under 15 years	Retired	All
North	2·8	5·6	9·1	1·6	43·3	25·1	4·5	56·7
E & W Ridings	3·0	8·4	9·7	1·2	47·2	23·3	4·8	52·8
North West	3·2	9·3	9·7	1·7	48·1	23·6	5·1	51·9
North Midlands	3·3	7·8	9·7	0·9	46·8	23·7	4·4	53·2
(West) Midlands	3·0	8·9	8·9	1·1	49·2	23·7	3·8	50·8
SE England	3·3	8·1	10·5	1·1	47·6	21·9	4·9	52·4
South West	4·7	5·9	11·1	1·0	43·2	22·5	5·9	56·8
Wales	4·3	4·9	10·0	1·8	42·4	23·1	5·0	57·6
Scotland	3·1	5·3	9·3	2·0	44·8	25·3	4·2	55·2
N Ireland	5·7	3·6	8·0	4·0	42·2	29·0	4·6	57·8

SOURCE: Woodward, *Regional Social Accounts*, table 2.

working age varies little from the national proportion in most of the English regions and in Wales, but it is 1½ per cent above the national figure in the (West) Midlands, 1½ per cent below in the South West, 2 below in Scotland and 6 below in Northern Ireland. These differences tend to account for at least some of the more extreme variations from the average in income produced per head of total population. The variation in activity rates – the proportions of the population of working age that are actually in work – are, however, much greater. In the South East and the (West) Midlands, the rate stands 4 per cent above the national average, in the North 8 per cent below, in Wales and Northern Ireland some 12 per cent below. Again, these variations help to account for the extremes of output per head of the total population, though the correlation of activity rates with income level is far from perfect.

The consequence of adjusting for variations in age structure and in activity rates is thus that the range of average incomes produced per occupied person in work (which can be referred to as 'productivity') is a good deal narrower than that of incomes produced per head of the *total* population. At one end of the scale, South East England stands 5 or 6 per cent above the national average of productivity; at the other end, Northern Ireland stands 23 per cent below. The North and Wales come up nearly to the national average – their low levels of income produced per head of total population are almost entirely attributable to low activity rates. The (West) Midlands, with a high activity rate, comes down to less than 2 per cent above the national productivity level, and the North West, also with a high one, to 4 per cent below average. The North Midlands, with a low activity rate, is seen to be almost up to the South Eastern level of productivity. It will be necessary to return to interregional differences in activity rates in a later chapter; they clearly play an important part in determining the pattern of average household incomes.

From average productivity per person in work in a region as a whole, the next step is to look at average productivity per person occupied within each industry in each region. Unfortunately we have reliable estimates of this only for the manufacturing industries and for coal-mining and agriculture, for which the basic data are reasonably adequate. The figures for the twelve industry-groups in question, and for the British regions (comparable figures for Northern Ireland not being available) are given in table 3.5. When an analysis of variance is performed on the data in this table to determine whether there can be said to be significant differences in productivity between different industries extending across all regions, or between that in different regions extending across all industries, the answer is, fairly unam-

Table 3.5. *Gross domestic product per occupied person, 1961*

£ per annum

	N	EWR	NW	NM	(W)M	SEE	SW	Wa.	Sc.	GB
Agriculture	1040	1112	1167	1219	1151	1147	1063	852	1069	1099
Coalmining	1080	1159	960	1415	1107	913	784	907	896	1091
Food, drink, tobacco	1180	1155	1403	1408	1377	1425	1614	1131	1449	1391
Chemicals, etc.	2078	1541	1929	1610	1496	1890	1518	1560	1683	1814
Metal manufacturing	1234	1094	1125	1366	1097	1249	924	1562	1131	1219
Engineering, shipbuilding, vehicles, metal goods	970	973	975	990	973	1041	930	945	945	991
Textiles	872	898	706	874	931	995	1083	1718	774	844
Leather and clothing	572	568	569	687	628	742	631	589	586	650
Bricks, pottery, glass	1015	1192	1278	1132	775	1315	984	1095	1091	1093
Timber, furniture, etc.	813	820	851	843	878	1048	824	687	822	928
Paper, printing, publishing	990	936	1055	932	950	1222	992	1029	981	1109
Other manufacturing	838	833	1158	1028	1033	946	1429	1054	959	1030

SOURCE: Woodward, *Regional Social Accounts*, table 10.

biguously, that interregional differences are not statistically significant, while inter-industry differences probably are. (The issue is, however, somewhat fogged by a lack of independence between the two 'variables' – there is a considerable tendency for the averages for both a region and an industry to owe their high or low levels largely to the same high or low figure.) A simple inspection of the table throws some light on the absence of significant interregional differences that can be regarded as general – applying to all (or most) industries. There is, for instance, no region in which all industries show productivities below the average for Great Britain; Scotland, which comes nearest to this, is above average in the food, drink and tobacco group. Similarly, no region is uniformly above, though the South East fails to be so only in coalmining (which is of very little importance there) and in the 'other manufacturing' group, which is notoriously of varying composition between regions. The North and the South West are both below average in nine out of the twelve groups, but the only simple statement to be made about the remaining five regions is that they stand above the national average of productivity in some industries, below it in others.

Thus, *generally* high or low levels of productivity make some contribution to interregional differences in aggregate output per head in the extreme cases. Composition obviously affects the outcome, too. One would expect general productivity in the North, for instance, to be pulled up by its specialisation on chemicals and metal manufacture, which are among the most 'productive' industry groups (in this sense), and by the relative absence from the region of the generally low-productivity clothing, timber and textile groups; and this is indeed so, though it is also important that labour in metal manufacture and chemicals (especially the latter) tends to be more productive in the North than elsewhere. There is some tendency (which will be discussed in a later chapter) for regions to specialise on those industries which show higher labour productivities in them than elsewhere, but this in itself does not, of course, help to explain the differences in average productivity between regions; it is the *extent* of the comparative advantage that matters here. The North is helped by specialising on the chemical group in which its output per head is particularly high, but Wales is handicapped by specialising to some extent on agriculture in which its output per head is particularly low.

One should, however, be careful not to misinterpret interregional differences in productivity, either on the average across all industries, or within what is classified as a single industry-group. The product in question is the total net output of all the factors of production involved, and to relate it to the number of units of a single factor – labour – which take part directly in producing it is necessarily arbitrary. The big differences of productivity between industries are largely due to their different capital-intensities or, more generally, the differing extents to which factors other than labour have a claim on output. One cannot, unfortunately, assess interregional differences in the efficiency of production in the proper sense – differences in levels of output per unit of *all* inputs – because of lack of data and conceptual difficulties in measurement of inputs other than labour. What can be related to labour inputs without these difficulties are, of course, labour earnings. Earnings per employee in the various regions and industry groups are shown in table 3.6.

From this it is clear that the range of variation is much smaller than with productivity – especially between industries. The inter-industry variation, however, is still large in comparison with that between regions, though analysis of variance shows that, within industries, there is a significant general tendency for earnings to vary from one region to another. The South East in particular shows a high level, and the Midlands regions also to a smaller extent, but no region shows earnings above the national average in all industry-groups, nor does any show earnings below the relevant average in all. The picture is again clouded, of course, by differences in the kinds of activity covered by the same industry-group classification in different regions.

The sex-composition of the labour force is important here, since women, broadly, earn only half as much as men. This is responsible

Table 3.6. *Earnings per employee, 1961*

£ per annum

	N	EWR	NW	NM	(W)M	SEE	SW	Wa.	Sc.	GB
Agriculture	470	462	457	497	493	475	476	452	480	477
Coalmining	856	842	832	920	834	913	784	784	805	845
Food, drink, tobacco	567	587	628	641	653	665	662	575	603	635
Chemicals, etc.	844	715	845	732	747	834	758	842	804	815
Metal manufacturing	761	736	699	770	731	781	727	845	699	753
Engineering, ship-building, vehicles, metal goods	737	684	715	727	727	754	719	664	718	729
Textiles	523	572	525	570	624	600	753	737	506	559
Leather and clothing	424	443	441	517	434	532	490	452	462	484
Bricks, pottery, glass	722	736	749	709	578	782	672	697	680	698
Timber, furniture, etc.	655	640	653	651	660	778	647	624	644	706
Paper, printing, publishing	643	633	721	616	655	820	674	635	661	746
Other manufacturing	524	562	756	615	705	631	687	634	680	670
Construction	714	707	697	707	734	730	662	708	688	726
Other services	544	579	566	622	648	685	605	588	526	625

SOURCE: Woodward, *Regional Social Accounts*, table 11.

for a great deal of the differences in average earnings per head of the total numbers occupied in different industries; it is responsible for less (though still for some) of the differences in average earnings within a single industry between regions, since there are considerable inter-regional differences in the sex-composition of the labour force in some industries such as textiles. This factor can, of course, be avoided by looking at data for men only. Analysis of male manual earnings more finely classified as to industry shows that levels within industries in the South East and the Midlands are significantly above the national average, those in Scotland and the South West significantly below. There are to some extent generally high-earnings and low-earnings regions. Moreover, the general averages of earnings within regions are appreciably (though not very greatly) affected by their specialising on high-earnings or low-earnings industries: Wales and the North on coalmining, steel and chemicals, or the (West) Midlands on motor vehicles and, at the other end of the scale, East Anglia on agriculture, or the North West and Yorkshire on textiles and clothing. But by no means all interregional variations can be explained in such simple terms.

INTERREGIONAL TRANSFERS

What income is consumed or in some other way absorbed in the regions differs from what is produced in them because of two factors: payments of property income (interest, rent, dividends) and occupational pensions to persons resident in regions other than those from which the payments come; and transfers through the channels of public finance – taxation on the one hand, grants and State pensions, subsidies, and State purchases of goods and services on the other. There is also the discrepancy which arises because undistributed profits and personal savings are passed between regions in ways that cannot in practice be traced except by the most general kind of inference.

Personal receipts of rent, dividends, interest and occupational pensions are easily traced, but their sources (especially those of dividends and interest) are more problematic. It is easiest to assume that the sums distributed by industry and commerce arise from the various regions in proportion to the corresponding gross profits. On this assumption, in 1961 South East England and the South West both received net transfers of property income and occupational pensions from the rest of the country or the outside world to the amount of about £20–£25 a head of their total populations – some 4 or 5 per cent of their gross domestic products, or about £450 million altogether. Scotland roughly broke even with regard to payments of this kind and Northern Ireland enjoyed a small net receipt, but all the other regions – the two Midlands regions, the North, the North West, the East and West Ridings, and Wales – made net payments of between £16 and £21 a head of population, or again about 4 or 5 per cent of their gross domestic products.

This transfer, of course, reflects the differences in distribution between property owners and the retired on the one hand (with their marked tendency to seek the capital region or the south coast) and the high concentrations of (especially corporately owned) industry and commerce on the other. The pattern is probably a fairly stable one from year to year. There is a net transfer of property and similar incomes into the two southernmost regions from the rest of the country equal to some 2 per cent of the whole gross national product.

Gross domestic product *plus* net receipts of personal property incomes get us near to estimates of gross regional income or product. Non-personal (corporate) receipts have to be ignored for lack of information and because the location of corporations, in any sense other than that of their establishments, has been taken to be unimportant in the scheme of regional accounting we have adopted. Our present figures also include personal receipts of national debt interest, which are not strictly

Table 3.7. *Gross regional product per head of population, 1961*

	Gross domestic product		Net internal transfers[a]	Gross regional product	
	(£)	(Index)	(£)	(£)	(Index)
North	410	90	−20	390	86
E & W Ridings	452	100	−17	435	96
North West	449	99	−21	428	94
North Midlands	463	102	−17	446	98
(West) Midlands	489	108	−20	469	103
SE England	503	111	+20	523	115
South West	400	88	+25	425	94
Wales	401	88	−16	385	85
Scotland	392	86	+1	393	87
N Ireland	289	64	+6	295	65
United Kingdom	454	100	—	454	100

SOURCES: Woodward, *Regional Social Accounts*, tables 1 and 20.

[a] Property incomes and pensions.

part of gross regional product, but are, of course, taxable. The ways in which the distribution of this approximation to gross regional product differs from that of gross *domestic* product are implicit in what has been said about transfers of factor incomes. The two are shown in table 3.7. The predominance of South East England is reinforced; in income per head it stands some 15 per cent above the national average. At the other end of the range, Scotland and Northern Ireland are at less disadvantage than in regard to domestic product, but, while the South West comes up to within 6 or 7 per cent of the national average, Wales and manufacturing regions of England go down. In particular the Northern region stands 14 per cent below the average. On a calculation for 1964 it stands 17 or 18 per cent below average, which would make it the poorest, in this important sense, of all the regions except Northern Ireland.

Along with transfers of factor incomes, the State is the other big interregional income distributor. Part of its redistributive function arises, of course, from the varying incidence of taxation. Its operations for 1964 are summarised in table 3.8. Leaving aside capital taxes (which in any case yield only a relatively small revenue), tax and State insurance revenue of the central government and local authorities in 1964 ranged from £220 a head in South East England to £151 a head in Wales and £118 a head in Northern Ireland. The tax bases to which these revenues should be related cannot be estimated precisely, but taking our approximation to gross regional product (gross domestic product of each region plus net receipts by persons in it of property incomes and

Table 3.8. *Public sector current receipts per head, 1964*

£ per annum

	Income and surtax	Taxes on expenditure	Company tax	NI and health contributions	Rates	Total receipts Amount	Index
North	34·7	65·7	12·3	21·5	17·1	151·3	83
Yorks. and Humberside	43·0	66·2	15·2	25·6	17·2	167·2	91
North West	42·4	70·6	16·2	24·9	18·5	172·6	94
E Midlands	41·4	67·3	14·4	24·1	17·5	164·7	90
W Midlands	51·1	77·3	16·7	29·0	20·6	194·7	106
SE England	70·3	78·1	14·8	30·5	26·6	220·3	120
South West	47·3	64·3	10·3	21·1	18·6	161·6	88
Wales	35·9	64·9	11·2	21·7	17·3	151·0	82
Scotland	42·5	69·2	12·0	21·9	21·1	166·7	91
N Ireland	26·3	57·6	7·5	15·8	11·2	118·4	65
United Kingdom	51·8	71·7	13·5	25·9	20·3	183·2	100

SOURCE: Woodward, *Regional Social Accounts*, table 24.

occupational pensions), and regressing tax revenue against it, one finds that in 1964 about 38 per cent of differences in regional product per head between regions was offset by differences in *per capita* taxation. Or, looking instead at the proportionate differences in taxation, one finds that a 1 per cent difference in *per capita* regional product went with a difference in *per capita* tax payments of about 1·1 per cent. Between richer and poorer regions the tax system was mildly progressive.

In looking at the other side of the account – what goes back into the regions from the public purse – there are three separate questions to be asked. First, what goes back in the form of money transfers? Second, what goes back in all forms of expenditure that may be regarded as specifically beneficial to residents in the region? Third, what goes back in all forms of expenditure – how is the total outflow of purchasing power from public authorities divided between regions? These questions are dealt with in table 3.9.

To the first question the answer seems to be that absolute *per capita* receipts of current grants and subsidies from public authorities and personal receipts of public debt interest do not differ much between regions by comparison with tax payments, though their proportionate variation is wide. They were in 1964 highest in Scotland, Northern Ireland, the South West and probably East Anglia, lowest in the West Midlands, the East Midlands and the North West. The high level in Northern Ireland and East Anglia was mainly due to agricultural sub-

Table 3.9. *Public sector expenditure per head, 1964*

£ per annum

	N	Y&H	NW	EM	WM	SEE	SW	Wa.	Sc.	NI	UK
Money transfers											
Agricultural grants	5	4	2	6	4	3	8	6	7	19	4
Other grants and subsidies	51	50	49	46	43	47	49	54	57	47	49
Debt interest[a]	6	9	8	8	8	16	16	6	10	6	11
Total	62	63	59	60	55	66	73	66	74	72	64
Beneficial expenditure on goods and services											
Current[b]	51	52	52	49	50	57	54	58	56	50	54
Capital[c]	13	12	12	15	13	13	14	16	16	22	14
Total (inc. money transfers)	126	127	123	124	118	136	141	140	146	144	132
Current defence and central administration	25	19	23	22	28	52	68	24	24	25	36
Trading services and dwellings[d]	27	40	25	42	31	35	31	49	41	19	33
Total expenditure	178	186	171	188	177	223	240	213	211	188	201
Excess of receipts over:											
Money transfers	89	104	114	105	140	154	89	85	93	46	119
Beneficial expenditure	25	40	50	41	77	84	21	11	21	−26	51
Total expenditure	−27	−19	2	−23	18	−3	−78	−62	−44	−70	−18

SOURCE: Adapted from Woodward, *Regional Social Accounts*, table 24.

[a] To persons.   [b] Excluding defence and central administration.
[c] Excluding trading services and dwellings.   [d] Capital expenditure.

sidies; that in Scotland was largely made up by subsidies on housing; that in the South West was mainly due to agricultural subsidies and debt interest. These estimates somewhat understate the degree of assistance to the peripheral regions in as much as the method of distributing the rail subsidy has almost certainly underestimated their share, but the general impression is not invalidated by this. It is more to the point that, from the autumn of 1967 onwards, Northern Ireland, Scotland, Wales and the Northern region must have fared £10 a head better than in 1964, because of the Regional Employment Premium. Their *per capita* receipts under the present head must also have been some £5 higher in relation to those elsewhere because of investment grant benefits.

In addition to these transfers there is much public expenditure on goods and services that may be regarded as conferring a benefit on specific regions; most obviously expenditure (both current and capital) on public services and facilities for which the public makes no payment, such as health, education, roads, sewerage, police, local administration and (rather less certainly) water supply. In fact, one may put into this category all central and local expenditure on goods and services except that on central government administration, defence and capital formation related to trading services – with which one must include the public provision of dwellings, the cost of which is covered by rent except in so far as there are subsidies which have already been taken into account. Neither the current nor the capital component of this 'beneficial' expenditure on goods and services shows great absolute *per capita* variation between regions, except that the capital component in 1964 was high in Northern Ireland and fairly high in both Scotland and Wales.

Total 'beneficial' expenditure, including both grants and expenditure on goods and services, showed only a range from £118 *per capita* in the West Midlands to £146 in Scotland. The gap between it and public revenue, however, varied over a range of £110 a head. In the country as a whole, some £50 a head more was paid in taxation and State insurance contributions than was received in grants of locally 'beneficial' services – the difference being mainly the cost of defence, central government administration and capital expenditure on trading services met from current revenue, and public debt interest not paid to persons. Only two regions – South East England and the West Midlands – showed less favourable balances than this with the public sector; they fared worse than the national average by about £32 and £25 a head respectively. On the assumption that the remainder of expenditure paid for from taxation – expenditure the benefits of which are not specific to regions – yields equal *per capita* benefits everywhere, one can say that these two regions provided a balance of taxation over benefits received of some £800–£900 million, of which £200 million went to Scotland and something like £100 million each to Northern Ireland, Wales, the Northern and the South Western regions. These transfers as proportions of gross regional products are shown in table 3.10. The South East and the West Midlands transferred outwards more than 5 per cent of their combined gross domestic product through these channels; Northern Ireland (to quote the extreme case) had its gross domestic product supplemented by nearly 25 per cent.

If the *per capita* net balances (benefits minus taxation) are plotted against *per capita* gross regional product (or the nearest approximation to it that we can get), the correlation is strongly negative. In the context of the broad relationship that emerges, Wales, Scotland and the South West seem to do rather well, the North West, the North and the West Midlands rather badly. For this differences of income distribution and consumption habits are presumably responsible, along with peculiarities

Table 3.10. *Public sector net beneficial expenditure per head, 1964:[a] deviations from national average[b]*

Percentages

N	Y & H	NW	EM	WM	SEE	SW	Wa.	Sc.	NI
+6·0	+1·5	+0·7	+1·0	−4·0	−5·8	+7·3	+8·3	+7·2	+24·2

SOURCE: Adapted from Woodward, *Regional Social Accounts*, table 25.

[a] Includes trading surpluses or deficits of public corporations.
[b] Expressed as percentages of gross regional products: a positive sign indicates net receipt.

of the public expenditure pattern. The general implication of the relation between income per head and net benefit received (or given) by a region, however, is that in 1964 net transfers of benefit offset differences in *per capita* regional product to the extent of about 47 per cent. Increases in taxation and in benefits directed to the Development Areas since then must have brought this proportion to over a half. In this important financial respect we have indeed a United Kingdom.

The total transfers of purchasing power through public authorities present greater difficulties. For reasons connected with interregional differences in the pressure of demand one would like to know where the funds abstracted from income-flows in the form of taxation are fed back to create demand for factors of production. In so far as they are used to pay for services the answer is in principle easy to get, but in so far as they are used to pay for goods (plant and equipment for instance), one can generally discover where the equipment was installed but not where it came from – and indeed the sources of the various inputs that go into it will usually have been numerous and scattered. There is, however, some value, though a limited one, in knowing in what region in the first instance the money can be regarded as having been spent, subject to the qualification that much of it will usually have been spent on imports into the region in question from unknown sources.

When one balances the immediate destination of total public expenditure against its sources, three regions – South East England, the West Midlands and the North West – emerge as net providers of funds; the two former, however, on different scales from those on which they are net providers of 'beneficial' expenditure to other regions. The main difference is that the South East with its large receipts of payments for central administration and defence is a net source of funds to only a small extent in relation to its size, while the West Midlands, with few central or defence establishments, is a relatively bigger source. It is perhaps surprising that the North West is a source at all, but this seems to be

PRODUCTION, EXPENDITURE, FLOWS AND INCOME 67

so. Together the three regions provided net outflows through public channels to the extent of £600–£650 million in 1964 – about 4 per cent of their combined gross domestic product. Among the net receivers, the South West with its defence establishments took something approaching £60 a head, and Wales, Scotland and Northern Ireland were also large net recipients, though less strikingly so in this matter of public expenditure than in their receipt of benefits. The remaining regions – the North, Yorkshire and Humberside, and the East Midlands – came near to breaking even in their transactions with the public sector. Thus, the tendency is clearly for the combined public authorities to shift purchasing power equal to something over 2 per cent of gross national product towards the peripheral regions, with the South West as a net receiver to the extent of something like 12 per cent of its regional product. The very broad tendency is to move purchasing-power towards regions where the pressure of demand is relatively slack, but in this regard the North West, as a far from prosperous net provider, seems to have been an exception in recent years.

REGIONAL CURRENT BALANCES

The two sets of transfers that have been considered – transfers of factor incomes and transfers through public finance – must play large parts in financing the regional current balances, the differences between the regions' gross domestic products and their respective expenditures on, or absorptions of, goods and services. Regional expenditure may be estimated independently of, though rather less reliably than, gross domestic product; interregional variations in it and its components are, of course, interesting in themselves and we shall return to them presently, but first the relation between regional current balances and the identified means of financing them are worth a glance. They are shown for 1961 (with personal receipts of public debt interest excluded from the balances of transactions with the public sector since they are already included in transfers of factor incomes) in table 3.11. All the figures, especially those of regional current balances, are subject to wide margins of error, but they display a pattern which is reassuring; estimated inflows of funds from factor incomes and the public sector generally go with estimated net imports of goods and services. One is at least encouraged to believe, as estimates for 1964 also confirm, that the big manufacturing regions – the North, the North West, Yorkshire and both Midlands regions – produced substantial net exports; that South East England nearly breaks even, and that the peripheral regions – though this is less true of Scotland than of the others – are net importers. The difference between inflows of factor incomes and public funds and the

Table 3.11. *Financing regional net export balances per head, 1961*

£ per annum

	Transfers			Net exports of goods and services[b]	Financed by: capital imports, errors and omissions
	Net public sector expenditure[a]	Net receipts: property income and pensions	Total identified items		
North	+7	−20	−13	+13	—
E & W Ridings	−9	−17	−26	+46	−20
North West	−11	−21	−32	+21	+11
N Midlands	+6	−17	−11	+34	−23
(W) Midlands	−19	−20	−39	+19	+20
SE England	−10	+20	+10	—	−10
South West	+40	+25	+65	−74	+9
Wales	+28	−16	+12	−54	+42
Scotland	+13	+1	+14	−9	−5
N Ireland	+43	+6	+49	−65	+16

SOURCE: Woodward, *Regional Social Accounts*, table 20.

[a] Excluding debt interest.   [b] GDP minus expenditure.

regional import surplus is, in principle, the net inflow of private capital, but it would be presumptuous to draw any conclusion from figures that must largely reflect errors and omissions, though the implied heavy capital inflow into Wales is confirmed by other evidence.

INTERREGIONAL TRADE

The social accounts which have just been discussed give a partial view of the working of regional economies in terms of income and expenditure flows within regions and net transfers between regions. These net transfers are, of course, the result of imbalances between much greater gross flows in opposite directions of goods and services, and of payments for them. These, if we knew about them, would provide a further insight into the regional economies and their interactions. Confining the question, for a start, to flows of goods, what evidence have we that bears on this?

There is only one region of the United Kingdom for which there are reasonably reliable statistics of external trade with other regions – namely, Northern Ireland. There, regional imports in 1967 for instance amounted to £552 million, of which £411 million came from other regions of the United Kingdom. Regional imports were thus equal to nearly 90 per cent of the region's gross domestic product, the extra-

United Kingdom portion of them being about 23 per cent of gross domestic product, which is not very different from the corresponding figure (about 18½ per cent) for the United Kingdom as a whole.

For other regions we have no comparable evidence, but only what is provided by surveys of the physical movements of goods – the Road Goods Surveys of 1962 and 1967,[1] and the Rail Wagon Load Survey of 1964.[2] These are sample surveys based on questionnaires completed by carriers. For particular classes of goods, if not for the total tonnages of goods carried, they are subject to considerable sampling errors, but the major problem they present is that of valuation – the goods carried are recorded in tons weight and for our present purpose we need figures of value.

The 1962 road survey data were scaled up by the Ministry of Transport to make them applicable to 1964 and combined with the rail survey figures of that year for the purpose of a calculation of the Ministry's own. They were thus classified on a system approximating to the rail classification, which meant that a very large part of the total value – apparently about half – was concentrated in a single miscellaneous class of 'manufactures'. It was in this form, distinguishing a large number of areas of origin and destination, that the data were kindly supplied to us. For 1967 we received the road survey data classified into 171 commodity groups, which should make valuation rather more practicable. On the other hand, at the date of our calculation, the 1967 data were available for only one quarter of the year, so that the sampling and grossing-up errors might be expected to be larger than those in the 1962 figures.[3]

The method of valuation we used – the best that seemed to be available for a start at least – was to multiply the tonnages in the various commodity-classes by the average values per ton for the most closely comparable classes of goods in British exports, or occasionally the exports of other countries where the classification appeared to fit better.[4] Some classes were valued at different rates according to the regions of origin – making use of the fact that 'vehicles', for instance, is a label covering different kinds of product in different areas. This yields totals of goods carried by inland transport in Great Britain, including intraregional as well as interregional journeys, of a little over £200,000 million

[1] Ministry of Transport, *Survey of Road Goods Transport 1962. Final Commodity Analysis*, London, HMSO, 1964 and Department of the Environment, *Survey of the Transport of Goods by Road 1967–1968. Report and Tables, Great Britain*, London, HMSO, 1972.

[2] British Railways Board, *Rail Wagon Load Survey, 1964* (unpublished).

[3] Certain apparent errors in order of magnitude appeared in the 1967 data and were eliminated by rough adjustments in our calculations.

[4] This valuation of the flows was part of a study carried out in connection with our investigations by Mr David Steele.

both in 1964 and in 1967. Since the gross domestic product increased by about 18 per cent between the two years, this suggests that the valuation is excessive in the former year in comparison with the later one. Since the goods classification on which the valuation is based is so much coarser for 1964 than for 1967, it seems likely that it is the 1964 valuation which is more at fault.

Whether the 1967 valuation is itself greatly at fault in the magnitude it gives for total intra- and interregional trade in Great Britain it is not possible to check with precision, though there are some considerations that throw light on it. We know from the 1963 Input–Output tables[1] scaled up for the increase in national income between 1963 and 1967 that the total sales of the goods-producing industries in the latter year to other industries and to final purchasers, along with transactions between establishments within each industry-group, must have been about £41,000 million. There is a further transaction whenever a middleman intervenes between two stages of production, or between a producer and either his foreign supplier or a final buyer. We should therefore add the total turnover of wholesale traders, which from a scaling-up of the 1959 figure can be put at about £20,000 million. Sales by retailers to final consumers do not add a further set of transactions likely to be reflected in movements of goods unless the goods are delivered in a commercial vehicle, and one may guess that such deliveries are worth perhaps £2,000–£4,000 million at most. Altogether, therefore, there are transactions involving possible movements of goods to the extent of something like £65,000 million. This figure is consistent with estimates that put total payments for goods *and services* at nearly four times gross domestic product (say £125,000–£130,000 million in 1967), which in turn are roughly confirmed by bank clearing statistics, if the purely financial part of the latter is excluded and allowances made for payments between customers of the same bank which involve no clearing.[2]

Some of the transactions that we have reckoned as possibly corresponding to a physical movement of goods may not in fact do so. Much more important, however, are likely to be physical movements which do not correspond to any transaction. These will take place whenever intermediate goods are processed on commission. The textile finishing industry, for instance, is not shown in the input–output tables as purchasing the textiles it processes, though obviously they are physically delivered to it and carried away from it. Many specialised operations in engineering are done on the same basis. Moreover, a multiple retailer or a wholesale distributor may move goods more than once while

---

[1] Central Statistical Office, *Input–Output Tables for the United Kingdom 1963*, London, HMSO, 1970.
[2] See P. J. Welham, *Monetary Circulation in the United Kingdom*, Oxford, Blackwell, 1969.

they are in his possession, from a central depot to a regional one, for instance, as well as from there to the retail shop or final buyer. Many passages between one owner and another must take place in more than one physical stage; in particular, a movement by rail is rarely 'door-to-door' except for minerals – it is likely to be combined, as part of a single journey, with one or more movements by road.

What all these 'non-transaction' movements amount to one can only guess, apart from such evidence as the transport surveys provide. The total movements of textiles and metal products, in particular, are so large in relation to the weight of materials used in producing them as to suggest that non-transaction movements are substantial. The physical substance of an article of clothing has probably made a score of journeys inside the country by the time the consumer buys it, and that of a metal product half a dozen or more. It is not impossible that goods in general move twice, on average, for every time they change ownership, though this might be thought rather surprising.

On the other hand, there are *a priori* reasons for thinking that the reckoning of goods moving by inland transport at the foreign trade valuations of the most nearly comparable – and still very broad – classes will result in a substantial overestimate. Exports will normally have been carried further and perhaps handled more by the time they are delivered free on board than goods of the same description at the moments when they move inside the country. What is more important, in a predominantly manufacturing country especially, the goods exported will normally belong to the more highly finished and probably the higher quality subdivisions of the class in which they are listed as compared with the members of the class that move about inside the country; the latter will probably consist to a greater extent of inputs for further processing, and the fact that they move only intra-nationally not internationally may be due to their being of relatively low value in relation to bulk or weight. The wider the classes, the more this will be so. That the valuation of the 1962–4 flows, divided into only fourteen classes, is higher than expected by about 18 per cent in relation to the valuation of the 1967 flows, which are divided into 171 classes, perhaps gives some indication of the extent to which this is the case. The classification used for the 1967 road movements is still very wide; everything from vehicle parts and containers to finished vehicles comes into the single class of 'transport equipment'; everything from ingot-moulds to gas-turbines into the single class of 'other non-electrical machinery and parts'; everything from clogs to furs into the single class of 'travel goods, handbags, clothing, hosiery and footwear'. At a guess one might suppose that these considerations warrant the reduction of the 1967 goods valuation by (say) one-third. It would perhaps be better to take account also of the corresponding probability that the higher valued goods in each class tend to be the ones that are traded interregionally rather than intra-regionally, and to suppose that the intra-regional movements are overvalued by a higher factor – that they should be reduced by (say) half from the international trade valuations. This would reduce the total value of all inland movements to £100,000–£110,000 million, which would involve a perhaps more credible estimate of some £35,000–£45,000 million for movements not corresponding to internal transactions. With overseas and coastal sea movements added, one would get a total of something over £120,000 million, of which £40,000 (in round figures) would be interregional or overseas.

THE 'OPENNESS' OF REGIONAL ECONOMIES

All this is rather wild guesswork. There is, however, a consistency check of a sort that we can apply to it. The transport data yield estimates of the external trade of the regions[1] which can be plotted against the corresponding regional gross domestic products, and the resulting relationships can be viewed in comparison with those obtained for Northern Ireland and any other 'regions' or comparable territories for which the external trade is directly recorded. The results (when the valuations of British interregional movements have been reduced by a third below the international trade unit values in the way described) are shown in chart 3.1.

It will be seen that the relationships have a certain plausibility. The points for those regions which occupy more or less central geographical positions – the South East, the two Midlands regions, Yorkshire and Humberside, the North West and perhaps East Anglia – lie reasonably close to a downward sloping curve. Wales, the South West and the Northern region yield points that lie close together at a decidedly lower level of 'openness'. The points for Scotland and Northern Ireland – the latter based upon 'hard' statistics of external trade – are in a plausible relation to each other at a lower level still, as seems to befit the still more peripheral positions of these two regions.

It is interesting to plot for comparison the external trade and gross domestic products of sovereign countries. Luxemburg, the Netherlands and Belgium, which enjoy free trade with each other and incipient free trade within the European Economic Community, seem to belong to the same family-group as regards the relation between size and 'openness' as Scotland and Northern Ireland. Perhaps, if anything, they are a little less 'open' for the sizes of their gross domestic products.

[1] Taken here as the average of their import and export estimates because of the wide margin of error on either.

Chart 3.1. *The 'openness' and size of various regional and national economies, 1967*

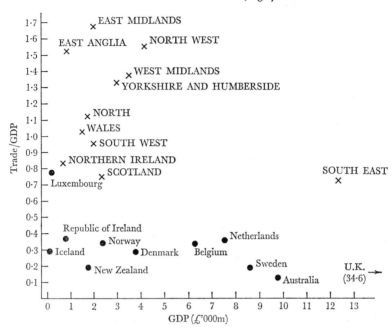

SOURCES: table 3.12; United Nations Statistical Office, *Yearbook of National Accounts Statistics 1967*, New York, 1968.

Making allowance for the different sizes of the economies concerned, it looks as if Northern Ireland and Scotland were in 1967 about as 'open' as, or a little more 'open' than, the Benelux countries, and these in turn seem to be somewhat more 'open' than Norway, Sweden, or Denmark. The Republic of Ireland, with a gross domestic product not much more than a third of that of Scotland, seems, having regard to its size, to fall into a lower category of 'openness' still – a result perhaps of peripheral position combined with absence of free trade arrangements. It is noteworthy that the very small economy of Iceland – even smaller in gross domestic product than Luxemburg – has a far smaller ratio of trade to gross domestic product than any British region; primarily, no doubt, the result of remoteness. The same result of remoteness (and protection) can be seen in such highly developed and generally trade-oriented economies as those of New Zealand or Australia.

The 'openness' of regional economies in the United Kingdom, unsatisfactory though the evidence about it is, thus seems to be very high in comparison with that of sovereign states with comparable sizes of domestic product, and degrees of 'openness' seem also to vary very widely between regions, dividing them into three main groups – the central regions, constituting what economic geographers used to call the 'coffin', the neighbours of these central regions, and the further periphery composed of Scotland and Northern Ireland. It is tempting to speculate on the extent to which the differences in 'openness' are connected with the different incidences of movements not associated with change of ownership – though pure transit movements which do not involve trans-shipment or storage in a region are, of course, excluded by the terms of the transport surveys. On this, however, we have no evidence.

Assuming that the very tenuous evidence just discussed establishes a prima facie case for scaling down the international trade valuations of interregional flows and intra-regional flows in the ways that have been mentioned, table 3.12 may be set out, very tentatively, for the year 1967. The interregional flows are supposed to include both road and rail traffic; those labelled 'coastal and overseas exports' (and 'imports') notionally include traffic entering or leaving the regions' ports in coastwise as well as foreign trade – the information about coastwise trade being scanty and failing in particular to specify port of origin of imports or port of destination of exports. It must be emphasised that these figures cannot be claimed to do more than indicate orders of magnitude. In particular they are far too imprecise to throw light on regional balances of trade; the regional balances given by straightforward valuations of the 1962 and 1967 surveys are almost perfectly uncorrelated with each other and, where they agree, their indication is sometimes (as for the South West) at variance with what is suggested by the social accounts.

At the bottom of the table, certain of the magnitudes in it are shown related to the gross domestic products of the regions, roughly up-dated to the year 1967 from our 1964 estimates. First, the ratio of interregional trade (that is to say, the average of the movements into and out of the region from and to other regions and the outside world) to gross domestic product is shown. These are the figures that are plotted against gross domestic product in chart 3.1. Next, partly as a check of consistency, the ratios of intra-regional trade to regional gross domestic product are shown. These ratios lie between just under 2 and just over 3. Finally, the ratio of flows originating in each region to its gross domestic product is shown. The range here is between 4·5 (East Anglia) and 2·7 (the South East).

Some of this variation can be explained by the varying extents to which regions' products consist of goods as opposed to services. The low value of the ratio for the South East might be rationally explained in large part if not wholly in this way; so perhaps can the moderately

Table 3.12. Interregional and intra-regional flows of goods,[a] 1967

To: From:	N	Y & H	NW	EM	WM	EA	SE	SW	Wa.	Sc.	Total intra-regional	Coastal and overseas exports[b]	Total inter-regional	Total trade originating
						(£ thousand millions)								
North	(5·1)	0·4	0·4	0·2	0·1	—	0·3	—	—	0·3	5·1	0·2	1·9	7·0
Yorks. and Humberside	0·5	(8·8)	1·0	0·8	0·5	0·1	0·6	—	0·1	0·1	8·8	0·6	4·3	13·1
North West	0·4	1·0	(11·7)	0·5	0·9	0·1	0·9	0·1	0·4	0·3	11·7	1·7	6·3	18·0
East Midlands	0·2	0·6	0·6	(4·4)	0·6	0·2	1·0	0·1	—	0·1	4·4	0·1	3·5	7·9
West Midlands	0·2	0·4	0·9	0·4	(6·6)	0·1	1·1	0·3	0·4	0·1	6·6	—	3·9	10·5
East Anglia	—	0·1	0·1	0·3	0·2	(2·6)	0·6	—	—	—	2·6	0·1	1·4	4·0
South East	0·2	0·5	0·6	0·6	1·0	0·7	(25·3)	0·7	0·3	0·2	25·3	2·7	7·5	32·8
South West	—	—	0·1	0·1	0·5	—	1·0	(5·1)	0·2	—	5·1	0·2	2·1	7·2
Wales	—	0·1	0·3	0·1	0·4	—	0·4	0·2	(3·1)	—	3·1	0·1	1·6	4·7
Scotland	0·5	0·1	0·3	0·1	0·2	0·1	0·1	—	—	(8·8)	8·8	0·7	2·0	10·8
Total intra-regional	5·1	8·8	11·7	4·4	6·6	2·6	25·3	5·1	3·1	8·8	81·5			
Coastal and overseas imports	0·1	0·5	2·2	0·1	—	0·1	2·9	0·3	—	1·1		7·3		
Total interregional	2·1	3·7	6·5	3·2	4·4	1·3	8·9	1·7	1·4	2·2		6·4	41·8	
Total flow														123·3
GDP estimates	1·8	3·0	4·2	2·0	3·4	0·9	12·4	2·0	1·5	2·8				
Ratios of trade to GDP						(Ratios)								
Interregional[c]	1·1	1·3	1·5	1·7	1·2	1·5	0·7	1·0	1·0	0·8				
Intra-regional	2·9	2·9	2·9	2·2	1·9	3·0	2·1	2·6	2·1	3·1				
Total originating	3·9	4·4	4·3	4·0	3·1	4·5	2·7	3·6	3·2	3·7				

SOURCES: Department of the Environment, *Survey of the Transport of Goods by Road 1967–1968*; NIESR estimates.

[a] Movements are those made continuously without unloading, but 'pure' transit trade in which goods pass through a region without unloading is excluded.
[b] Movements of goods overseas are credited to the region of the port of shipment.
[c] Average of interregional exports and imports, including overseas movements.

low value for the South West. The low figures for Wales and the West Midlands, however, suggest that the arbitrary corrections applied to the valuations of flows (internal flows in particular) have been excessive for these regions in relation to their suitability for the others. It may be that the manufactures that circulate in these regions come nearer in average value per ton to the export goods similarly classed than is the case elsewhere. Subject to this, the comparison with regional gross domestic products seems, very broadly, to support the credibility of the *relative* magnitude of the estimated internal regional flows of goods, just as the comparison with Northern Ireland suggests that the general level of our tentative valuation of interregional flows is roughly right.

One further aspect of the estimated interregional flows deserves mention. It is possible to attempt an explanation of the patterns of such flows (or the flows of particular commodities) by means of a 'gravity model' – that is to say, by the hypothesis that the flow from region A to region B is a function of the production of the relevant commodity in A, the total absorption of it in B and the distance between the two regions. Models of this kind were attempted for twelve of the thirteen classes of goods distinguished in the 1962 surveys.[1] For most of them the extent to which the pattern was 'explained' was reasonably satisfactory. The point of greatest general interest, however, was that the exponent of distance in the resulting formula changed from one commodity-group to another, and that the extent to which distance was apparently an obstacle to movement varied in roughly the way one would expect. For coal flow varies inversely as the cube of distance; for petroleum products it falls off even more sharply; but for raw materials (so classified), building materials and foodstuffs it falls not quite as the square of distance; and for iron and steel, chemicals, transport equipment and 'other manufactures' flow falls off only a little more rapidly than in proportion to the distance concerned. This is not surprising and, in a mild way, perhaps adds credibility to the relative sizes of interregional flows as revealed by the evidence. Used with more finely classified data, however, such an analysis might throw useful light on the inherent transportability that various classes of products possess, and the extent to which the minimising of their movements has, in fact, been an effective factor in determining the location of economic activity.

REGIONAL EXPENDITURE

After this rather long consideration of interregional flows, we may now come to regional expenditures, which are related to production in each region and the net flows into or out of it. The interregional differences

[1] By Mr David Steele.

Table 3.13. *Domestic expenditure per head at factor cost, 1964*

Indices, UK = 100

	Consumers' expenditure	Public authorities' current expenditure	Capital formation			Total domestic expenditure[a]
			Public	Private	Total	
North	86	84	82	95	90	86
Yorks. & H'side	91	77	109	105	107	92
North West	95	82	73	100	89	93
E Midlands	91	79	122	93	106	92
W Midlands	105	86	91	103	99	101
SE England	114	122	100	109	105	113
South West	92	140	93	97	95	101
Wales	90	91	138	88	110	94
Scotland	93	89	122	72	95	93
N Ireland	78	96	85	91	88	82

SOURCE: Woodward, *Regional Social Accounts*, table 13.

[a] Including value of physical increase in stocks.

in *per capita* expenditure, in aggregate and in its main categories, are shown in table 3.13.

Mainly as a result of the transfers which have been described, total *per capita* expenditure varies much less between regions than *per capita* production. In particular, expenditures in Northern Ireland and Scotland in 1964 seem to have been only 18 and 7 per cent respectively below the national average, whereas the corresponding gross domestic products per head were 36 and 14 per cent below. The South West had expenditure of about the national average, in spite of its gross domestic product being 12 per cent below. At the other end of the range, South East England stood about as high above the national average in expenditure as in domestic product, because its net receipts of factor income from other regions roughly balanced its net lending and outward transfers through public finance, but the Midlands regions, the North West and Yorkshire stood markedly lower in relation to the national average in expenditure than in domestic product, mainly because of their outward factor payments. Much the same generalisation may be made about levels of consumers' expenditure per head: in the poorer regions they stood better in relation to the national average than did production, in the richer regions worse, but with the important exception of the richest region of all, South East England, where consumption was at least as high in relation to the national average as production – a result, once more, of its property income from outside.

Of public authorities' current expenditure per head of the population there is little to be said except that it stands high in South East and the South West (perhaps surprisingly highest in the latter). Capital formation (public and private), however, perhaps deserves more attention, though its year-to-year variation enjoins caution about any generalisation from the figures of one year. In 1964 it was highest (10 per cent above the national average) in Wales, lowest (12 per cent below average) in Northern Ireland, with the North and the North West also notably low, Yorkshire and Humberside, the East Midlands and the South East notably high. The pre-eminence of Wales was due to high expenditure in the public sector, mainly on plant and machinery and non-residential building, so was the eminence of Yorkshire and the East Midlands, while the South East rose above average mainly in private sector investment. Scotland showed the lowest *per capita* level of private investment; it stood below average in every category, but most notably in housing – a deficiency more than compensated for by the public provision of dwellings. The North and the North West owed their sub-average position mainly (in the North West entirely) to deficiencies in public spending in all categories except the small class of ships, vehicles and aircraft.

The caution about drawing conclusions from one year's figures must be repeated, but some indication of events over longer periods is given by statistics of new buildings and works in the public sector since 1962/3, and (rather less reliably) in the private sector since 1964. From these indicators, it seems that the North West has indeed had a low rate of *per capita* capital formation (mainly in the public sector) over a five or six year period, that Wales may not have done as well as the 1964 figures alone would suggest, but that Scotland has maintained a high level both in the public sector and in total. The South East seems to have maintained a high level in the private sector and in total, and East Anglia a very high one. The other region of rapid growth, the South West, has shown a high level of private capital formation, but a consistently low one in the public sector, and the same is true to a smaller extent of the West Midlands. There is a general tendency for the less prosperous areas to do relatively better in public than in private capital formation, but the North West, and in a smaller degree the North, stand out as exceptions to this.

PRICE DIFFERENCES AND REAL CONSUMPTION

Finally, we should perhaps return to the estimates of consumers' expenditure as the basis from which to derive an impression of relative average levels of welfare. To get such an impression, one presumably has to make at least two adjustments. First, some account ought to be

Table 3.14. *Interregional price indices and real consumption, 1964*

Indices

	N	Y & H	NW	EM	WM	SEE	SW	Wa.	Sc.
Price indices (GB = 100)									
Food	99	101	98	100	102	99	99	104	105
Housing[a]	82	85	92	79	89	129	88	80	89
Fuel & light	95	96	98	93	96	109	112	102	101
Travel to work	80	89	96	90	92	119	78	104	89
All goods & services	96	97	99	97	98	106	97	98	99
Consumers' expenditure (UK = 100)	86	91	95	91	105	114	92	90	93
Consumers' expenditure valued at GB prices	90	94	96	94	107	108	95	92	94
Consumer's expenditure plus beneficial current public expenditure[b]	90	94	97	94	105	107	95	94	95

SOURCES: Central Statistical Office, *National Income and Expenditure 1964*, London, HMSO, 1964; Ministry of Labour, *Family Expenditure Survey 1966*, London, HMSO, 1967; Ministry of Agriculture, *Household Food Consumption and Expenditure 1964*, London, HMSO, 1965; Ministry of Power, *Statistical Digest 1966*, London, HMSO, 1967; Government Social Survey, *Labour Mobility in Great Britain 1953–63*.

[a] Including maintenance.   [b] On goods and services.

taken of interregional differences in the price levels of the goods and services on which consumers' money is spent, and, secondly, account ought to be taken of the provision of public goods and services which, properly speaking, enter into regional consumption.

Comprehensive statistics of interregional price differences are lacking, but data exist in detail on food prices and the prices of fuel and light, and something can be said about variation in the price of accommodation, which certainly contributes most of the interregional variation in the price of consumers' goods and services, and about the costs of travel to work. The regional price indices calculated for these items, and the results of incorporating them into the official index of retail prices on the assumption that all other prices are uniform throughout the country, are shown in table 3.14.

Food is relatively cheap in the south of England, dear in Scotland and Wales, but the range between British regions (the price data were not obtainable for Northern Ireland) is only about 7 per cent. Coal, gas and electricity together are cheapest in the Midlands regions, Yorkshire and the North, dearest in the South West and in London, the range between the extreme regions being almost 20 per cent. Housing presents great difficulties; what has been used for the present purpose is a calculation of average rent (or imputed rent) per room, with no allowance for interregional differences in the average room-size, age or condition of the property, or the quality of its surroundings. This method probably leads to an overstatement of price differences, because the regions with the highest rents per room seem, on the whole, to be those with the highest proportions of new and the lowest proportions of substandard housing. The range it shows is very large, from 50 per cent above the national average in London (45 per cent above in the old London and the South East region) to 20 per cent below in Wales.

Cost of travel to work may be regarded as a supplement to cost of housing, since there is often a measure of choice between living in more expensive property nearer to work and in cheaper property further off, though a complication is introduced by the fact that the quality of housing and its surroundings often improves as one moves further away from the places where most people work. To some extent a high expenditure on travel to work is a mark of ability to afford pleasant surburban surroundings rather than of inability to afford high urban rents. The greater part of the higher cost of travel to work in big cities (especially London) as compared with smaller places, however, is certainly a genuine cost of living in a conurbation rather than a measure of the superior attractions of the conurbation's residential districts. Expenditure on travel to work, therefore, may not unreasonably be treated as if it was an unavoidable addition to the cost of living; moreover, to take account of differences in *time* spent in this travelling, its imputed cost (reckoned at about half the average rate of hourly earnings) may reasonably be added. If this is done, costs of travel to work vary over a range from about 30 per cent above the national average in London and the South East to about 22 per cent below it in the South West.

The result of taking account of these interregional differences and assuming that there are no others (or that if they exist they cancel each other out) is that the retail price index for London and the South East stands some $8\frac{1}{2}$ per cent above national average, that for South East England 6 per cent above, and that for the Northern region, at the other end of the scale, somewhat more than 4 per cent below. Apart from South East England there is little interregional variation; the dearest region (Scotland) is less than 4 per cent above the cheapest. The real contrast is between London and the rest of the country. The result of correcting *per capita* consumer's expenditure for price differences is thus to narrow the range of variation; the level in South East England comes down almost to equality with that in the West Midlands – 7 or 8 per cent above the national average. The lowest region in Great Britain in 1964 turns out to be the North, 10 per cent below average, with Wales 2 points higher, though there are indications that the North did relatively better in other years both before and after. Scotland and the other English regions lie in a narrow band between 4 and 6 per cent below average.

Adding public current expenditure on goods and services for purposes other than those connected with central government administration and defence, so as to include regional consumption of public goods and services, makes a little difference; it tends to narrow the interregional gaps. At the end of the story South East England and the West Midlands stand near together at the top of the range, 10 or 11 per cent lower come Scotland, Wales and all the remaining English regions except the North, with only such gaps between them as are within the margins of error of the estimates, and 4 or 5 per cent lower still comes the Northern region, again perhaps understated a little by the results of this single year.

This is, on the whole, a picture of remarkable uniformity in regional levels of material welfare, so far as statistics of this kind enable them to be measured. With all the evident differences between the regions in such matters as industrial structure, the proportions of the population gainfully employed and the impression of prosperity they convey to the visitor, the real levels of consumption of goods and services per head of the populations – with the notable exception of Northern Ireland – fall within a range of plus or minus 9 per cent of the national average. And, in so far as there are interregional differences, the main contrast is between the South East and the West Midlands on one hand and the rest of the country on the other, with Northern Ireland below the rest of the country in a class of its own. The pattern of interregional differences in material welfare so assessed is essentially the same as that of differences in *per capita* regional products measured in money terms, but it is a far less bold pattern – the range of variation is not much more than half as great. The responsibility for reducing this range lies mainly with the centralised, progressive taxation system and central financing of the social services, though the high London cost of living contributes substantially to the result too. Both of these factors, in very different ways, spring from a common cause – the highly integrated nature of the United Kingdom economy, developed through many generations of political union in a compact country.

HOW MUCH DOES INTERREGIONAL INEQUALITY MATTER?

Now that we have given some consideration to the degrees of inequality both between regional average incomes and between average real consumptions of goods and services, it may be appropriate to conclude this chapter by dealing with a question that was posed in chapter 1 – how far do these inequalities matter? It may be remembered that we noted two simple reasons for being concerned about inequality of incomes. First, in so far as there are different rewards for comparable units of factors of production in different regions, the implication may be that those factors are imperfectly distributed and that the volume of national production is therefore smaller than it might be given total national resources. This is a matter to which we can best return when we consider costs of factor immobility between regions. For the present we will confine ourselves to the second ground for concern. This is the presumption that, with a given volume of output, the satisfaction that it provides is capable of being increased so long as there is scope for reducing the inequality of distribution between consumers. If inequality of average incomes between regions were eliminated without changing the total volume of production, how far would that reduce inter-personal inequality of income generally, and what would be the effect of this on material welfare?

The first part of this question cannot be answered unambiguously because we have no uniquely correct measure of degrees of inequality; the second part cannot be answered at all without some bold assumptions about the relation between income and welfare. Let us make some bold assumptions and see whether they yield decisive answers; we can try afterwards to assess the probability and the implications of the assumptions being wrong.

The first assumption, common in welfare economics, is that an income receiver's material welfare depends only on his income, not on anyone else's. The second is that welfare varies with the logarithm of income; increasing a man's income by (say) 10 per cent makes the same absolute addition to his welfare no matter what his income was to start with. The third assumption is that, while the relation between income and welfare may not be by any means the same for different income receivers, individual or collective (family), it will be the same on average as between the large groups of people with whom we are concerned for policy purposes, including the populations of different regions and (though more dubiously) different income groups as distinguished in the Inland Revenue Reports.

The simplest procedure after this is to compare two magnitudes:
(i) the percentage gain in welfare if two communities of equal population, one with the present after-tax distribution of income found in the United Kingdom, the other with the distribution that would be produced by raising each of these individual incomes by (say) 20 per cent, shared their incomes without altering the form of the distribution – that is to say, formed a single community in which, for every individual income in the first community, there were now two incomes each 10 per cent bigger, and

(ii) the percentage gain in welfare if a community with the present income distribution of the United Kingdom shared its incomes completely, so that all income receivers came to have incomes equal to the arithmetic average.

If we can do this, we can get some idea of how important interregional differences rather like the present ones are in relation to the general inequality of personal incomes after tax, both in the country as a whole and (what amounts to the same thing in very broad terms) within each region.

Our hypothetical utility function is of the form $U = k \log_x Y$, where U is utility (or material welfare) of the income receiver, Y is after-tax income, and k a constant. Now, the proportional gain in U consequent upon any sort of sharing is independent of the constant k and, by the same token, also of the base x chosen for the logarithms of income. Logarithms to any base can be converted to any other by an appropriate manipulation of k, and k cancels out. What these proportional changes are *not* independent of is the choice of units in which to measure income.

Ideally we should choose as our unit some kind of 'subsistence income', austerely interpreted as the level at which utility was zero, since zero is the logarithm of unity to any base. (Presumably this is the level of income at which the victim does not care whether he lives or not.) It is difficult to quantify this unit for groups of the British population in (say) the year 1968/9, but it would be reasonable to suppose that it lay somewhere between (say) £1 and £500. One can try the calculation using both of these units, and indeed intermediate ones if required.

In a rough calculation based on the Inland Revenue Report for 1968/9,[1] it emerges that the proportionate gain from the equalisation between two communities – originally with incomes in the one 20 per cent higher than those in the other, as in (i) above – is only about 2 per cent of the gain from a complete equalisation of personal incomes even if one takes £1 as the unit of income, and this percentage falls as the unit is increased. It vanishes as that size of unit ('subsistence income') is approached at which our figure for the material welfare of the whole United Kingdom population in 1968/9 becomes zero – a unit of a little under £900.

On this showing therefore, the benefits of interregional equalisation are small in comparison with the benefits of complete equalisation of incomes, or, to put it in the way more appropriate to our purpose, the real disadvantages of interregional inequality on the sort of scale on which we experience it in this country are small compared with those of the general inequality of personal after-tax incomes in the country or,

---

[1] *112th Report of the Commissioners of Inland Revenue*, 1968/9, Cmnd 4262, London, HMSO, 1970.

presumably, within single regions. The whole calculation, of course, is hypothetical. There is no empirical evidence that the utility function is logarithmic. The result suggests, however, that a low relative importance of interregional inequalities as we have them now might be inferred on a wide variety of assumptions about the function that fulfilled the usually postulated condition of diminishing marginal utility.

It seems likely that the broad conclusion is vulnerable more by virtue of another of our assumptions – the assumption that personal material welfare is a function of personal incomes only. It is vulnerable to attack from either side. First, in so far as communities develop pride and selfconsciousness, the awareness of their members that incomes in them are lower than elsewhere can probably become a source of discontent, additional to any disadvantage in actual material position of which the people in question are conscious on their own behalf. If the poor in (say) Scotland or Wales, or the general masses of the people in those countries, are known to be worse off than corresponding people in England, politically conscious Scots and Welshmen are likely to express dissatisfaction, even if they personally are under no similar disadvantage. Levels of real income can become status symbols for a whole community, or at least for important and vocal parts of it.

Against this we have to set the conflicting possibility that (as Duesenberry long ago suggested) the individual's sense of well-being is dependent upon his position in the income hierarchy of his immediate community as well as on his absolute income level, so that the individual members of a relatively poor community feel better off than they would if, with the same incomes, they were set to compete with the richer Joneses of a more affluent one.

There is no obvious way of balancing out these opposing considerations. One may perhaps guess that, though the latter one is likely to be widely relevant, its strength is limited, while the former one (collective sense of grievance) might in rather special cases become considerably more powerful. But this is conjecture. What can be said with rather more confidence is that, apart from the more extreme possibilities of common grievance about the general income status in a region, the diminution of material welfare arising from the inequalities between the British regions is rather slight in relation to that implied by the huge general interpersonal inequalities to which most people have become reconciled. The consequences of the high degree of integration of the United Kingdom economy are further emphasised by these considerations.

CHAPTER 4

REGIONAL GROWTH: A THEORETICAL FRAMEWORK

LINES OF APPROACH

Why, in the most general terms, can it be that one region grows in total output over longish periods of time faster than another? The question is a difficult one, since economies are complex organisms, and answers to such a fundamental question about them are bound, if the matter is pursued at all vigorously, to involve the interaction of a great many forces and considerations. Nevertheless, it is helpful to sort out the possible lines of attack according to the angles from which they approach the problem.

First, one can seek to explain a superior rate of growth from the side of supply, leaving demand, initially at least, to look after itself. Perhaps the best developed approach of the kind is the one that starts from the neo-classical production function – the relation between the amounts of factors of production used and the quantity of product – and considers what conditions are necessary to bring about sustained differences in rates of growth of output, assuming that demand is adequate to keep the available resources fully employed. Demand, however, inevitably begins to play a more active part in the game as soon as one advances beyond the sweet simplicity of assuming that there is only a single kind of product.

The complementary (or at least diametrically opposed) approach is that which makes the different rates of increase of demand for different goods or services the key to events. The simplest version of this takes the industrial structures of the regions as given and different from each other, and traces relative regional fortunes to the different rates of increase or decline of national or world demand for the products on which the various regions are specialised. The simplest assumption to make in this connection is that a given industry tends to grow or decline at the same rate in every region. Pursuit of this line of attack, however, soon brings one up against a more explicit concern with supply factors, since a region specialising on rapidly expanding industries will presumably have more difficulty in meeting the derived demand for inputs than one specialising on slowly growing or declining ones.

Third, a macro-economic approach is sometimes essayed, based essentially on the Harrod–Domar analysis of the conditions of steady growth in a closed economy, but this is not by itself very helpful. What remain from a scrutiny of it are certain dynamic mechanisms that have to be taken into account along with the supply and demand considerations to which we have referred.[1]

There is thus no single approach that can usefully be made to retain its original simplicity for very long, and to some extent it does not matter how one starts. Rather arbitrarily, we shall begin with the neo-classical production function approach, and elaborate it with elements derived from external demand forces and internal macro-economic interactions as the argument seems to require.

A START FROM FACTOR SUPPLIES

The simplest production function of the sort we need as a starting point is that which formed the basis of J. E. Meade's single-product growth model[2] and was also used by Borts and Stein as the foundation for their analysis of regional growth differences in the United States.[3] If, like Borts and Stein, we assume that we can manage with only two factors of production – capital and labour – and that all other influences on production can be compounded into a single element, technical improvement, which progresses at a constant rate through time, then the rate of growth of total output can be represented as the sum of three terms: the growth of the stock of capital, weighted by a coefficient which, in fact, expresses the proportion of the product that will accrue to capital under conditions of perfect competition and constant returns to scale; the growth of the labour force weighted by a corresponding coefficient; and the rate of technical progress. Assuming constant returns to scale implies that the coefficients of capital and labour add up to unity.

If (still following Borts and Stein) we assume that capital is perfectly mobile between regions, and that it moves so as to maintain in all regions a given rate of return related, presumably, to the national (or perhaps the world) interest rate, we find that this requires the stock of capital to grow at the same rate as total income, and that in our two-factor world the rate of growth of income *per head* and of labour earnings per head is entirely dependent upon the rate of technical progress. If there is no progress, there will be no *per capita* income growth. If progress is the same everywhere, *per capita* incomes will change at the same rates everywhere.

---

[1] See for instance H. W. Richardson, *Regional Economics*, London, Weidenfeld and Nicolson, 1969, pp. 323–31, and the same author's *Elements of Regional Economics*, London, Penguin Books, 1969, pp. 47–50.

[2] J. E. Meade, *A Neo-Classical Theory of Economic Growth*, London, Allen and Unwin, 1961.

[3] G. H. Borts and J. L. Stein, *Economic Growth in a Free Market*, New York, Columbia University Press, 1964.

In these conditions therefore, mobility of capital means that labour earnings in different regions will not diverge and that, in so far as interregional movements of labour are motivated by differences in earnings, none will take place. The relative growth of *total* (as opposed to *per capita*) regional incomes will depend entirely upon the growth rates of regional labour forces, and these in turn will depend on differences in natural increase (which for a start we can take as given) plus any interregional migration *not* motivated by earnings differences, such as tendencies for net migration to take place towards the regions where the physical surroundings are preferred.

The two-factor model may well be thought unrealistic. If, of two regions that are similarly endowed by nature, one has a markedly higher rate of natural increase of population than the other, this surely will mean that relative shortage of immobile natural resources – of land in the usual sense – will, at some point, begin to hamper production in the one region in comparison with the other. To express this one can introduce 'resources' or 'land' as a third factor of production, and put the rate of increase in the supply of it at zero. In this case, still with technical improvement running at the same rate everywhere and perfectly mobile capital, the more congested region will experience a slower rate of growth of *per capita* income than the less congested one. If labour is mobile between regions at all, we may suppose that net migration from the more congested region will begin and will increase as a function of the *per capita* income difference. Eventually it will offset the initial difference in the rates of increase of population in the regions, and the relative change between *per capita* incomes will then cease, the income gap being stabilised at the size necessary to bring about the required migration.

Against this possibility of the influence of some absolutely scarce factor one may, of course, set a possibility of economies of scale, which, up to a point, would work the other way. It is not hard to see that such economies have the effect of adding to the technical improvement factor a supplementary effect which rises with the population of the region. (The argument so far is set out more formally in section 1 of the appendix to this chapter, see page 99 below.)

Another modification in the direction of greater realism is to abandon the assumption that capital is perfectly mobile between regions, and to suppose that it is only partly so, in the sense that (as we have taken to be the case with labour) the flow of it between regions is an increasing function of differences between them in its marginal product. Again, as with labour, this introduces a modification which is not fundamental; interregional differences in the yield of capital will diverge only up to a point and will then settle down. With both capital and labour in this condition of imperfect mobility, the result will be counterflows of them between the relatively capital-rich and the relatively labour-rich regions, and the fastest growth will take place in the region that has the relatively fastest growing indigenous supply of the less mobile factor. If labour is less mobile interregionally than capital, then the fastest growers (as concerns total output) will be regions of high population growth (probably high natural increase). In them, labour incomes will be relatively low and profits relatively high, and they will show net outflows of labour and net inflows of capital. If labour is the more mobile factor, the fastest growing regions will be those with relatively high savings, high wages and low returns to capital, and they will tend to show net outflow of capital and net immigration of labour.

So far then we have encountered only the possibility of equilibrium systems, in which regional growth rates cannot diverge by more than the finite amounts corresponding to the interregional immobilities of the factors labour and capital, and interregional flows of these factors too are limited. More spectacular possibilities open up when one considers interregional differences in rates of technical improvement. Take the case where capital is perfectly mobile interregionally and labour partly so. If one region has a faster rate of technical improvement than others, it will have, as we have seen, a faster rate of growth of *per capita* income. This will induce an increasing flow of labour into it up to the point where the flow is adequate to prevent further widening of the wage gap, and this flow of labour will be accompanied by the appropriate flow of perfectly mobile capital. The region of fastest technical improvement will, therefore, tend to absorb both population and capital from the rest of the country. It will eventually absorb the whole supply of these factors, unless increasing shortage of some fixed factor – land – makes itself felt.

If capital is not perfectly but only imperfectly mobile between regions the result is broadly unaltered, except that the region of rapid technical improvement will show an increasing superiority over its neighbours up to a point, not only in *per capita* labour income, but in the rate of return on capital as well, and the process of sweeping the board of mobile resources will, of course, be slowed down in comparison with the situation where capital flows in with perfect freedom.

Differences in rates of technical advance in production are, therefore, great destabilisers of equilibrium relations between regional growth rates, and it follows from what has been said earlier that they may be assisted in this by economies of scale. It is tempting to try applying these doctrines to the history of economic development, but one should perhaps resist the temptation for the time being on the ground that we are so far operating with the extremely unrealistic assumption that there is only one kind of output from economic activity. This defect we must remedy. Before doing so, however, we should note another complication that we have so far shunned. It has been assumed that natural increase of population is given, though we have allowed that it can be supplemented (or offset) by migration, which can plausibly be assumed to respond to real income differences. More realistically, the possibility has to be contemplated that natural increase too depends to some extent on real income, though which way the connection will work is not so obvious. Almost certainly natural increase will respond to migration, which alters the age structure of the population, usually through the fact that migrants tend to be young adults with higher fertility and lower mortality rates than the population as a whole. The bearing of these complications on the argument can be reserved for discussion when we come to concrete applications of our growth theory; here we need only give a preliminary warning of them. We pass now to the more drastic complications that arise from multiplicity of products.

DEMAND AND STRUCTURE

When one allows more than one product, two important changes in the argument ensue. One concerns the effects of interregionally differing rates of growth of factor supplies coupled with incomplete factor mobility. The other is concerned with the effects of differing rates of change of demand for the different products. If either factor of production (supposing there are two) is perfectly mobile, then there is no reason to modify the argument about differential rates of growth of indigenous factor supplies as we have already encountered it in the case of a single product – relative regional growth rates will be determined by the growth rates in the indigenous supplies of the immobile factor. If the factor not perfectly immobile – capital, say – is only partially mobile, then there will be a tendency for the region where capital supply is growing more slowly in relation to that of labour to start specialising on labour-intensive products. In practice it will take some finite difference in factor prices to bring this about, and such differences will tend to produce some interregional movement of capital; the region where the indigenous supply of labour is growing relatively faster will tend *both* to specialise increasingly upon labour-intensive goods *and* to import some capital. If this goes on until complete specialisation is attained on the most capital-intensive of the goods for which there is a sufficient market, further specialisation will have to cease, and the interregional differences in factor prices will rise further, until they bring capital into the region of more rapid population growth at such a rate as to prevent further divergence. The only new element is progressive specialisation – so far as that is possible – as an additional means of interregional adjustment supplementing factor mobility.

Given the fact of some regional specialisation, however, the relative prices of the different products become potentially important. In discussing the affairs of regions, one can for a start regard their industries as producing for national or world markets in which they have little effect on prices – the prices can be taken as externally determined. Allowing this, what happens if the price of one product begins to rise in relation to that of others? If one region were completely specialised on that product, its terms of trade with regions specialised on other products would improve, indeed this would be the case so long as it was in any degree more highly specialised than other regions on the good that was rising in price. The effect upon growth of income would be exactly analogous to that of its acquiring a superior rate of technical advance. The region concerned would show a rise (in relation to other regions) in the prices of factors of production not perfectly mobile interregionally, would draw in all factors not perfectly immobile at increasing rates and would embark on a process of growth at the expense of other regions. This process might be checked by the cessation of its external cause – the relative rise in the price of the product on which the region specialised – or by increasing shortage in it of some immobile factor.

There is, however, another set of considerations that may bear on it. An improvement in the price of a particular product will cause resources to be diverted to its production in all regions where comparative advantage is not too strongly in other directions. It is *possible* to envisage a situation in which comparative advantages are very clearcut, so that, even when the market situation moves continuously in favour of (say) the electronics industry, production in it continues for a long time to be concentrated in a single region which has specialised on that industry and in consequence enjoys rapid growth in the circumstances described. This, however, is not invariably or perhaps even usually the case – especially in the absence of economies of scale within an industry situated in a region. It is more common in a developed country for an industry to be represented in a number of regions, or at least not to be entirely excluded by local conditions from several regions besides the one or more that specialise heavily upon it. In this case, when the market moves in its favour it will tend to show a more rapid percentage rate of growth in the regions where it has been relatively lightly represented than in those that have specialised heavily upon it, and also to spring up in others where it has not been represented at all. It can be shown that, on some not implausible assumptions, roughly similar proportions of the various regions' resources will be transferred to an industry whose product rises in price, provided that the industry exists on some scale in the region to start with, and excluding any effects of interregional movement of factors (see appendix 2 (*a*), page 99). In general, where an industry already occupies a large proportion of the available resources its prosperity will make the factors of production scarcer than elsewhere, and it will be dependent for its growth largely upon interregional mobility of factors. In regions where the growing industry is less important, it has more chance of drawing factors from other locally established industries, as well as a chance of attracting them from other regions.

Where a product, instead of rising in price, becomes easier to produce in relation to others to an extent not offset by a decline in its relative price, there is a presumption that broadly the same result will follow (see appendix 2 (*b*), page 101). Thus, whenever a particular product enjoys an increasing advantage either of price or of cost of production in relation to price, there is a presumption that output of it will grow *proportionately* most rapidly in the regions that specialise upon it least.

This, however, should not obscure the fact that, over any given period of time, the region that specialises most heavily on products that are in this sense 'winners' will have an advantage in growth of income over other regions. It could be prevented from enjoying this only by perfect mobility of resources in other regions into the 'winning' industry, or, as one might say, on to the bandwagon; but this (if it happened throughout the world at least) would effectively prevent the very rise in the relative price of the good in question, in relation to its cost of production, that we are postulating. And, so long as resources have at least some mobility between regions, the region that has backed the winner most heavily will grow at the expense of others by drawing factors of production out of them. All that prevents its doing so more or less indefinitely is the mobility (*any* finite degree of mobility) of the other regions' resources into the winning industry. Because of this the advantages of this kind of structural success are necessarily self-extinguishing, but the process of extinguishing them is a long one and they are real and important while they last.

The disadvantages of having backed a loser are no less real. A region more specialised than others on industries suffering either from relative falls in the prices of their products uncompensated by relative rises in factor productivity, or from relative falls in factor productivity uncompensated by relative rises in price, will, so long as this situation persists, suffer a tendency towards declining *per capita* employment income and returns to capital in comparison with other regions. This being so, it will tend to lose both labour and capital. If, however, it possesses, or is naturally not ill-suited for, some of the industries whose products are rising relatively in price, or falling relatively in cost of production, then their percentage rate of growth in it may be high, and this should eventually remedy its unfortunate industrial structure – always supposing that the interregional mobility of factors, and/or the existence of regional economies of scale in the prosperous industries, are not such as to enable the regions specialising originally most strongly on those industries to claim all the national growth in them.

Starting then with a theoretical scrutiny of the regional differences in rate of growth of supply of goods and services as determined by rates of growth of factor inputs, one arrives at a position from which differences in industrial structure, coupled with different rates of change in the market situations of different products, seem likely to be very important, especially in the short and medium terms. This does not mean that we have capitulated to the crude 'structural hypothesis' which lies behind some analyses of regional fortunes. That hypothesis (usually implicit rather than explicit) may be taken as stating that, if we start from spatial equilibrium, meaning a spatial pattern of industry which would not change if supply and demand conditions for factors and products did not change, we may expect any industry to grow at its national rate – in general different for each industry – in every region. This *could* happen if the factors of production were all perfectly mobile between regions; otherwise it could not. Our implied model is rather more subtle than this. It too assumes that we start from spatial equilibrium in the sense we have just defined (unless notice is given to the contrary) and postulates different national or world rates of growth of demand for (or of factor efficiency in producing) different products. But it accepts zero interregional mobility of some factors, finite mobility of others, coupled with different rates of growth in the indigenous regional supplies of, at any rate, labour and capital, and this leads to a fairly complex set of expectations.

First, one would still expect that a region specialising on nationally fast growing industries will show faster growth than others, and that it will show net inward migration of labour, and probably of capital, with somewhat higher rates of return to these factors than other regions. But the rates of growth of individual industries in such a region may well be generally below the national rates for the same industries because of the pressure on factor supplies. There is a general presumption that the percentage rate of growth (or decline) of any industry will be high where relatively little of the region's resources are in it to start with, low where relatively much of them are. The region with a high specialisation on a nationally growing industry and only a little of its resources in a declining one will therefore tend to show a low rate of growth (in relation to the national record of the industry) in the growing one, a relatively high rate of shrinkage in the one that is in decline, though this will be modified in a favourable direction – higher growth rate for nationally growing industry, perhaps slower decline for nationally declining one – by the inward mobility of factors.

Correspondingly, the region that specialises on nationally declining industries will be likely to show slow total growth and net outward migration of factors, but growth in individual industries rather better than the national average rate for those industries despite the adverse effect of net loss of resources. The declining industries will probably shrink rather less fast proportionately than in regions where they are proportionately less important, the growing industries will probably do better than where they bulk larger in the total regional scene.

THE ANALYSIS OF GROWTH AND ITS INTERPRETATION

Perhaps this statement should be put a little more formally. It is plain that a region can grow faster (say) than the country as a whole, or than another region taken as a standard of reference, for any or all of three immediate reasons. First, it may specialise on industries that grow faster than others, though each particular industry grows at the same rate regionally as nationally. Second, it may show better growth in some or all of its industries than the same industries show nationally, though it has the same industrial composition as the country as a whole. Third, it may specialise on industries that show better growth in it than they do in the country as a whole, though there are other industries that grow less fast in it than they do elsewhere. These simple statements of possibilities hide some complexities; in comparing the average growth rate of industries in the region with that in the country, it matters a good deal how we weight the averages, and likewise, in defining what we mean by the regional industrial structure being biased towards fast growing industries, it matters a good deal whether we take national or regional growth rates as our criteria. In spite of these ambiguities, the three components of deviation between regional and national growth rates seem to be worth distinguishing for their economic significance, and the separation of them is simply done by a 'standardisation analysis', if one uses national industry growth rates in measuring the effects of difference in composition and national industrial composition in measuring the effects of difference in industry growth rates. It will be convenient to postpone further explanation of this until chapter 6, in which we apply our analysis to data for recent decades. We shall see there, too, that there is an alternative technique of analysis, which maximises the amount of the growth differences that is 'explained' as due solely to composition differences on the one hand, and to general regional tendencies towards fast or slow industry growth on the other.

What we have been saying, when put in terms of the three components of relative regional growth distinguished by the standardisation analysis, is that regions with a positive structural component are likely to have a negative growth component because of the finite elasticity of supply of factors. The growth component will also be affected by interregional variations in the rate of growth of factor supply – by differences in natural increase of population, for instance. The third logically possible source of divergence – systematic connection between direction of specialisation and the comparative performance of the industries specialised on – seems, on the face of it, capable of bearing more than one economic interpretation.

The first interpretation that leaps to mind is comparative advantage. In the present connection, however, a *progressive* increase of the degree of regional specialisation can mean either of two things. It can mean that we are not starting from a situation of equilibrium in the distribution of industry and that the potential advantages of regional specialisation are only gradually being realised, or it can mean that the differences of factor endowment on which specialisation is based are increasing – that the relatively labour-rich regions, for instance, are further increasing their ratios of labour to other factors, perhaps because of high rates of natural increase, so that specialisation on labour-intensive industries is becoming steadily more appropriate for them.

An alternative interpretation that suggests itself is one depending on economies of scale, and here again there are at least two ways in which the result might be produced. Either, starting from disequilibrium, the benefits of large scale might be only gradually asserting themselves, or, in a state of equilibrium, technical change might be operating in a way that continually opens up further opportunities for scale economies. In either case, however, the effect would be to increase regional specialisation only if regions (regarded as aggregations of industry) were sufficiently similar in size for there to be a significant correlation between degrees of specialisation on industry X in the regions and the absolute amounts of industry X which they contain. An outsized region (such as the South East) could contain larger concentrations of several (or even of all) industries than ordinary-sized regions without in fact specialising on any of them, and it would presumably gain the competitive advantages of large scale in those industries. Given the existing disparities of effective regional size therefore, scale effects might produce only a loose correlation between specialisation on an industry and its local relative performance, but they could not be ruled out as factors contributing to a correlation if one were found. There would simply be superimposed upon them an additional tendency for the effectively biggest regions to have superior growth rates in those industries, or complexes of industries, where economies of scale are most in evidence.

In addition to all this we have various dynamic factors to contend with – they will be further discussed in chapter 8. The simplest of these is the multiplier, by which demand spreads from any growing industry both to other industries supplying it with intermediate goods and, through the expenditure of consumers' incomes, to the suppliers of finished goods and services. The regional operation of the former of these multiplier mechanisms – the 'input multiplier' – depends heavily upon the considerations with which discussions of the location of industry have been traditionally concerned. How far does an industrial establishment tend, because of the various costs of transport and communication, to rely upon sources of supply that lie in the same region? Where this tendency is strong, the tendency is for spatially closely knit industrial complexes to grow, and for the numerical value of the input multiplier to be high. The increase in (say) external demand for the gross product of an industry may be reflected in something approaching an equal increase in the net output of industry in the region – local establishments supplying most of the required increase in inputs, as well as the value added by the industry on which the increased external demand immediately falls. If, on the other hand, considerations of transport and communication are less important, the increase in demand, impinging first upon establishments in a particular region, will stimulate a complex of industries which may be much more widely dispersed geographically, so that several regions share the total increase in activity that is required. On the extent to which the complex of industrial establishments bound together by an especially thick web of mutual transactions benefits from being concentrated spatially, depends, among other things, the tendency of growth to polarise geographically. In an economy as compact as that of the United Kingdom, the tendency for such polarisation to happen, or to be advantageous, within the confines of single regions must be regarded as, prima facie, an open question.

Superimposed upon the input multiplier one has the ordinary income multiplier. A large part, though by no means all, of the income generated by an increase in economic activity goes to residents within the region where the activity occurs, and some part of that income is necessarily spent in such ways as to generate further income within the region. The provision of many services and some goods is inevitably local or regional, and for that reason the provision of house-room, most personal and many public services, retailing and a good deal of wholesale distribution at least tend to grow within a region in more or less fixed proportions to total income. Employment in them, therefore, grows in more or less fixed proportion to that in the remaining industries, the so-called 'basic' industries, which cater for national or world markets, or perhaps for the local market in competition with similar goods from elsewhere. This relation of employment in industries necessarily geared to the local market to that in the 'basic' industries yields the 'economic base multiplier', which we shall have to examine also in connection with the growth of recent decades.

A direct stimulus from outside to some of a region's 'basic' industries will thus give a stimulus to growth not only in its local-market industries, but also, through the input multiplier, to some of its other basic industries – but probably not all of them. The stronger the pressure on the resources of the region, the more likely is it that those industries that are not closely tied either to its rapidly expanding trades or to the satisfaction of local consumers' demands will be squeezed and will show lower growth than the same industries display nationally. To the extent that the aggregate growth rate of all the basic industries is stimulated, however, the local-market industries will also be pulled ahead. Fast growth in a region engendered by rapidly expanding external demand for the products on which it specialises will therefore to some extent – though by no means completely – be generalised into rapid growth of its industries in general, but along with this may go a tendency towards a higher degree of specialisation on, at any rate, a broad group of industries.

Apart from these multiplier effects of particular stimuli, there is a class of dynamic effects which depend on the self-reinforcing character of either specially rapid or specially slow growth. Reference has already been made in chapter 1 to some of the mechanisms by which this occurs: the tendency of a rapidly growing region to become attractive to immigrants (including immigrant enterprises) because its physical capital is new and it has the air of presenting rich opportunities; the longer-run manifestations of interaction between the multiplier and the adjustment of capital stock; the destabilising effect (now much modified by central government subventions) of interregional prosperity differences on the standards of local public services, and of these in turn on the movements of population and industry. The obvious tendency of these mechanisms is towards augmenting and generalising prosperity or its opposite within a region; but here, too, in so far as interregional movements of the factors of production are inelastic, one would expect pressure of resources in the prosperous regions to divert elsewhere the growth of industries least tied to the local industrial complexes or the local consumers' markets.

Finally a word should be said about the systematic, Harrod–Domar, approach to the dynamics of regional growth, to which reference was made at the beginning of this chapter. The key to this approach is the simple proposition that growth of income depends on growth of capital stock. In a closed economy the latter depends on saving, which can plausibly be taken as related to income. It follows that, for the economy to be in equilibrium at any given level of income, the level must be rising at the rate required to absorb the accompanying savings into increases in the stock of capital. There is, in short, an equilibrium path of growth, and the rate of growth will be greater the higher is the proportion of income saved.

In an open economy, such as that of a region, everything becomes more complicated. First, the condition of equilibrium is not that savings should be absorbed into domestic capital formation, but that savings minus exports plus imports – that is the part of savings not used to finance net export of goods and services – should be thus absorbed. It is tempting to argue that imports are a function of the region's own income and its exports functions of that of the rest of the economy (or rest of the world).[1] From this basis one can argue further that a slowly growing region will find its export surplus growing in relation to its income and savings, and that its domestic capital formation will therefore fall and with it its rate of income growth. Equilibrium growth rates are unstable; the region that gets ahead acquires the means of increasing its growth rate further and the laggard falls ever further behind.

But this is too simple on at least two counts. First, it is wrong to suppose that region A's imports from region B are a function of A's income and that B's imports from A depend only on the income of B. Trade depends on supply as well as demand and, if a region's productive capacity is falling behind because its capital stock is growing slowly, then its exports will fall behind too, and booming regions will find their demand for its goods diverted (through the price mechanism, or delays in delivery, or perhaps changes in relative quality) to their own production or that of third parties. The only plausible simple assumption about trade between A and B is that usually made in gravity models – that it is proportionate to the product of their incomes. And that applies to trade in either direction.

Secondly, in an interregional (as in an international) economic system, there are movements of capital that are autonomous in the sense that they are not merely the results of predetermined trade-flows. The Borts and Stein assumption that capital moves interregionally so as to equalise rates of return is an example of a plausible supposition about such movements.[2] It remains true, of course, that, for the level of income to be maintained, saving minus domestic capital formation has to equal net exports of goods and services, but autonomous move-

[1] As in Richardson, *Regional Economics*.   [2] *Economic Growth in a Free Market*.

ments of capital will affect all the other variables – the levels of income and saving, and the level of imports if not of exports. They also, of course, affect equilibrium rates of growth. Without a firm assumption about them, there is no convincing conclusion about the stability or instability of regional growth rates.

A SUMMARY

To summarise then, one may say that autonomous rapid growth of supplies of one factor – say labour – will tend to raise the growth rate of a region's total income, though it will tend to reduce the regional unit earnings of the rapidly increasing factor, raise those of other factors, and bring about net outflow of the former, net inflow of the latter, so far as that is possible. So far as forces on the supply side are concerned, the region with the fastest growing domestic supply of the least mobile factors will tend to grow most rapidly. It is, however, differences between regions in rates of technical advance, or analogous matters, that seem likely to produce the most drastic tendencies towards divergence between regional fortunes. In the short or medium run, 'differences in rates of technical advance, or analogous matters' are most likely to take the form of differences in the fortunes of the industries on which the respective regions are predominantly specialised – differences in the trends of demand for their products in relation to trends of factor productivity in their supply. Either a 'favourable' or an 'unfavourable' structure of industry tends to correct itself (or to be corrected) not only through the superior national growth of the most rapidly expanding industries, but through the local effects of imperfect factor mobility on the growth rates of all industries; nevertheless, at any given time structural differences seem capable of being important. Multiplier relationships will to some extent tend to generalise the high or low rates of growth among the industries of a region, though they may also produce opposite effects on the growth of industries that have weak linkages with others in the region. Dynamic mechanisms, depending on rates of growth and on economies of scale that operate at the regional level, tend to oppose the equilibrating properties of the system.

With this simple theoretical framework in mind, one may usefully look at the development of the United Kingdom regions in the past two or three centuries. After that it will be profitable to examine more closely developments in the last few decades, about which we have better quantitative information.

APPENDICES

1. *The basic neo-classical growth model*

If the single product which we suppose to exist is produced under conditions described by a linear homogeneous production function from two factors, labour and capital, but with a constant proportionate rate of increase in production over time as a result of technical progress, the growth of total income can be described by $y = ak + bn + g$, where y is proportionate rate of growth of income per unit time, k that of capital stock, n that of labour, and g the technical improvement factor. Since the function is of the first degree (implying constant returns to scale), $b = 1 - a$. If we suppose that the marginal product of capital is fixed (the interest rate is constant), it follows, since the factors receive fixed proportions a and b of their average products, that the rate of growth of capital must equal that of income; that is, $k = y$. From these conditions, it follows that $y = n + g/(1-a)$, or $y - n = g/(1-a)$.

With three factors, that is to say with resources added, the growth of total income becomes $y = ak + bn + cr + g$, where r is the proportionate rate of growth of resources, from which, on the same arguments as before, $y - n = [c(r-n) + g]/(1-a)$. If the rate of increase of resources, r, is zero, this becomes $(g - cn)/(1-a)$.

If there are increasing returns to scale, so that the production function is of degree $1 + x$, and if the marginal product of capital is still held equal to a fixed rate of interest, then the equilibrium rate of growth of output per head is $[c(r-n) + nx + g]/(1-a)$, or, with the supply of resources fixed, $[g + n(x-c)]/(1-a)$.

2. *Comparative cost and growth rates of industries*

(a) *Change in terms of trade*

The curves C and C' in chart 4.1 represent production possibility curves of commodities X and Y in regions 1 and 2 respectively. Since both regions produce both commodities in equilibrium, it has been assumed that these curves are convex outwards from their origins, and they have in fact been drawn as arcs of circles with equal radii. The different positions of the centres of these circles with respect to the origins O and O' however, give production possibility curves ensuring that region 1 has a comparative advantage in the production of Y and region 2 in the production of X. If the number of units of Y that exchange for a unit of X in the national market is that given by the (equal) slopes of the market lines M_1 and M'_1, then regions 1 and 2 will produce at the points represented by A and A' respectively where the market lines are tangential to their respective production possibility curves.

Chart 4.1. *Production possibilities for two commodities: change in terms of trade between regions*

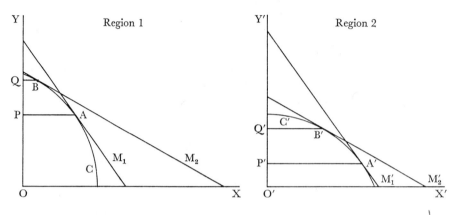

Suppose now that there is an increase in demand for Y relative to that for X, so that the market lines change their inclination to that shown by M_2 and M'_2. The equilibrium points of production now shift to B and B' where the new market lines are tangential to the production possibility curves. Since the initial relative price, the change of relative price and the curvature of the production possibility curves are all the same in both regions, the absolute changes in production represented by the shift from A' to B' are equal to those represented by the shift from A to B. In particular, the absolute increases in output of Y (namely, PQ and P'Q') are equal. Since region 1 specialises on Y much more than region 2 does, its *percentage* increase in output of Y will be much smaller than that shown by region 2.

Drawing the two production possibility curves with constant radii throughout their lengths is, of course, an arbitrary procedure; it implies (to put it rather loosely) that the X and Y industries are subject to diminishing returns to similar extents. (Drawing them with the same radii for both regions is also arbitrary, but does not affect the generality of this discussion.) For Q'P' to be much less than QP, so that it should be no bigger in relation to O'P' than QP is in relation to OP, would require region 2's production possibility curve to be more sharply convex in the segment A' B' than region 1's curve is in the segment AB. But if the terms of trade were to change back again, the X industry for which they were then improving could expand equiproportionately in both regions only if the segment AB was more sharply convex than A' B'. With static production possibility curves there is bound to be a tendency for shifts of equilibrium to involve smaller

Chart 4.2. *Production possibilities in two regions: change in productivity in one industry*

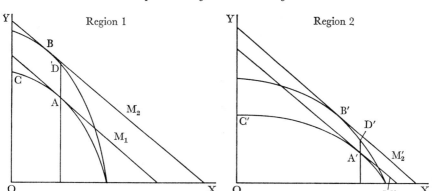

proportionate changes (in either direction) in regional outputs of products where they are being heavily specialised upon than where they are not.

(b) *Change in productivity*

In chart 4.2 we again start with the production possibility curves C and C', but what now happens is an increase in factor productivities in both regions in industry Y, so that the vertical ordinates of the production possibility curves are increased by a uniform factor, which we can call p. Assuming that relative market prices of X and Y do not change, so that the new market lines M_2 and M'_2 are parallel with the old ones M_1 and M'_1 (which, of course, are parallel to each other), the new equilibrium outputs are at B and B'.

The shifts from the old positions to the new are made up of two parts, increases in production of Y (AD and A'D'), which are proportional to the previous levels of production, and shifts (DB and D'B') along the new production possibility curves. Given, as we have assumed, that the original production possibility curves for the two regions are identical over segments which start from points of equal inclination, the new curves will also be identical over such segments – they have the property that their slopes are in both cases greater than those of the respective original curves at corresponding values of X in the ratio p in which productivity in the Y industry has increased. The segments DB and D'B' are therefore identical on our assumptions. It follows:
(i) that the absolute reductions in output of X are equal in the two regions,

(ii) that the proportionate reduction is greater in region 1, which is less highly specialised on X,

(iii) that the absolute increase in output of Y is greater in region 1, which specialises more heavily on that product, and

(iv) that the *proportionate* increase in output of Y is smaller in region 1, since the increases in the two regions are made up of amounts proportional to their original outputs plus amounts that are *absolutely* equal, and therefore *proportionately* smaller, in region 1.

CHAPTER 5

A LONG VIEW OF REGIONAL GROWTH[1]

THE CHANGING SHARES OF POPULATION

For the United Kingdom as a whole, the last two or three centuries have brought an experience of economic expansion, repeated with many variations elsewhere in the world and compounded of four main elements – population growth, urbanisation, technological advance and a rising general standard of living. The elements were combined in different proportions at different times and in different regions; our knowledge of them is uneven and diminishes rapidly as we move backwards in time. It is, however, of population growth that we have the best quantitative knowledge, imperfect though it is, extending over the longest period, and it is from this that one can most conveniently start. It may be useful to summarise the course of growth in regional populations before attempting any further analysis of regional fortunes.

Since the year 1701 the total population of what is now the United Kingdom has increased roughly sevenfold. The distribution of growth between the two halves of the eighteenth century is uncertain. It has, however, been widely believed that in the first half of that century total population was increasing slowly. There may well have been absolute decline of total regional population in the East Midlands and East Anglia and decline in many separate counties elsewhere. Thereafter however, there was almost certainly a general though uneven increase, in which no region showed any absolute decrease of population for a century (chart 5.1). Indeed, instances of absolute population decrease in a whole region at any time since about 1740 are probably confined to one major and three minor cases. The major case is, of course, Northern Ireland. The six counties shared with the rest of Ireland the catastrophic potato famine of the 1840s, and their population fell by a quarter by the end of the century before resuming a slow increase. (The population of the remaining twenty-six counties

---

[1] The chief sources from which this chapter has been drawn are: B. R. Mitchell and Phyllis Deane, *Abstract of British Historical Statistics*, Cambridge University Press, 1962; Phyllis Deane and W. A. Cole, *British Economic Growth 1688–1959*, Cambridge University Press, 1962; Wilfred Smith, *An Economic Geography of Great Britain*, London, Methuen, 1949; Edwin Hammond, *An Analysis of Regional Economic and Social Statistics*, Durham University Press, 1968; M. W. Flinn, *British Population Growth 1700–1850*, London, Macmillan, 1970; and, by the courtesy of the author, who made the manuscript available before publication, C. H. Lee, *Regional Economic Growth in the United Kingdom since the 1880's*, Maidenhead, McGraw Hill, 1971.

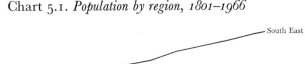

Chart 5.1. *Population by region, 1801–1966*

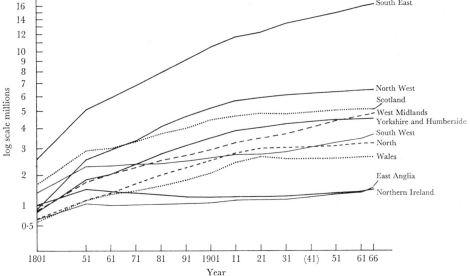

SOURCES: Hammond, *An Analysis of Regional Economic and Social Statistics*; Lee, *Regional Economic Growth in the United Kingdom since the 1880s*; Mitchell and Deane, *Abstract of British Historical Statistics*.

of Ireland fared worse; it halved by the end of the century and continued to fall until the 1950s.) The minor cases of regional population decline are East Anglia in the 1850s, Wales in the thirty years after 1921, and Scotland in the 1920s and a few isolated subsequent years. Otherwise, all British regions have grown in population continuously at least since the mid-eighteenth century.

The unevenness of regional population growth, however, has been no less striking than its extent and pervasiveness. Perhaps the best indicator of the consequent changes in the balance of population between regions is a set of regional population statistics for successive dates expressed as percentages of the national total, as in chart 5.2. Because of the greater uncertainty of the earlier history of Irish in comparison with British population, this chart has been confined to the British regions.

Viewed as a whole, the pattern of change in shares of total population shows a certain rough regularity. One aspect of this is the uninterrupted divergence since the mid-eighteenth century of the interregional distribution of population from that of habitable area – that is to say, broadly, the acreage of agricultural or potentially agricultural land.

Chart 5.2. *Regional distribution of population, 1701–1966*

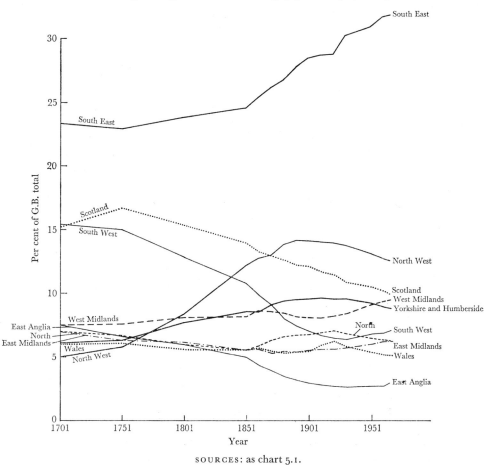

SOURCES: as chart 5.1.

(The difference between the two distributions can be measured by the minimum proportion of the population that would have to change regions to make population per square mile of habitable area the same in all regions.) The *rate* of divergence per half-century increased from the later eighteenth century to a peak in the later nineteenth and has since declined. The clustering of population in certain regions rather than in others thus appears, when viewed against this time-scale, to have been a continuous process that took a century to reach its most rapid rate and has continued at a declining speed for another century.

A related aspect of locational change is the rate of change of the interregional population distribution itself analogously measured. It also increased regularly from the early eighteenth century to a peak in the second half of the nineteenth. On a finer inspection of the last hundred years, it seems that the rate of change per decade in population distribution was highest in the 1870s, low in the nineties and the first two decades of this century, then jumped in the 1920s to a fairly high value from which it has been slowly falling ever since. We seem to have been passing through a second burst of locational change, distinct from and less drastic than the one that reached its peak a hundred years ago.

When one looks at the shares of the individual regions in total British population, the main features that at once emerge are the continually growing predominance, since about 1750, of the South East; the falling share, since about the same date, of Scotland and, from 1700 until very recently, of the South West and East Anglia; and the meteoric rise to an apex at the beginning of this century of the North West. Other changes are less striking. Yorkshire and Humberside's performance was a muted version of that of the North West, with a somewhat later culmination (about 1930 instead of 1890–1900). The Northern region shows a somewhat similar pattern, except that growth at more than the average rate began quite sharply from the 1850s after a century or more of gentle relative decline. The two Midlands regions show almost mirror-image trends until this century; the West Midlands increased its share of national population gently – mostly in fact in the late eighteenth century – while the East Midlands shows a fairly steady decline, levelling off from about 1870. From the first generation of the twentieth century they both gained. Wales kept a remarkably constant share of British population throughout, nearly always between 5 and 6 per cent, but with some relative loss in the late eighteenth and mid-nineteenth centuries, and a sharp temporary gain in the first two decades of the twentieth.

The South East's relative growth is particularly striking, reflecting as it does the fact that the growth of London relative to the rest of the country is not new but old. Indeed the relative decline of the South East in the early eighteenth century, if it really occurred, may well have been only an intermission in this process, since the growth of London from Elizabethan times to the Great Plague seems to have been particularly vigorous. The economic expansion of Britain was, emphatically, marked as much by urbanisation as by industrialisation. London was not only the biggest town, but the *only* notable town by modern standards in the country – in 1701 a giant the size of modern Edinburgh or Leeds, with no English rival bigger than modern Canterbury. It is not surprising that it claimed the greater part of total urban growth.

It is true that in the 'classical' Industrial Revolution period, from 1750 to 1850, both Yorkshire and Humberside and the North West increased more in population than the South East, but even then the South East grew proportionately faster than the country as a whole. And in the second half of the nineteenth century, the South East gained nearly as much in percentage of the national population as all the other gaining regions put together. From the beginning of the present century it has gained considerably more than all the other gaining regions together, but the rate of change in the interregional distribution of the population has been only half of what it was in the preceding fifty years, and the rate at which the South East has increased its share of the total population has fallen.

The other great gainers over the last two centuries as a whole are, of course, the manufacturing regions with which the events of the Industrial Revolution are most strongly associated. What is most striking about them is the predominance of the North West, which in two hundred years grew from the smallest in population of the British regions, with 5 per cent of the national population, to the second largest, with nearly 15 per cent of the total. No other region approached this feat of relative (or indeed of absolute) growth. Against this trebling of the North West's share of national population, Yorkshire and Humberside in the same period achieved an increase of a little over half, the West Midlands one of a quarter. The North raised its share by a quarter or a little more in the seventy years after 1850, and the Welsh relative expansion of the early twentieth century was both a briefer and a smaller episode. Taking these five industrial regions together, they raised their share of the British population total from something under a third in 1701 to about 45 per cent in 1921, when as a total it was at its maximum, though the Welsh contribution to this increase in share was zero in as much as Wales accounted for about 6 per cent of the national population at both dates.

Among the remaining regions which have been the relative losers, the South West is the most conspicuous. Indeed, the course followed by its share of national population since 1701 is almost a mirror-image of that of the North West – from more than 15 per cent at the beginning to a minimum of under $6\frac{1}{2}$ per cent in 1931. East Anglia followed a very similar course, from $7\frac{1}{2}$ per cent of national population to a minimum of under 3. These are the regions on which the urbanisation and industrialisation of the nineteenth century made the smallest mark. Scotland, on the other hand, presents at first sight a degree of paradox, in that it combined a distinguished part in the development of modern industrialism with an almost uniformly falling share of the national population total ever since the mid-eighteenth century.

On the strength of the distribution of population between regions, therefore, one may perhaps tentatively distinguish, in the last two and a half centuries, four periods characterised by different trends of relative regional fortune. First, in the earlier half of the eighteenth century, the relative advance of the North West and Yorkshire and Humberside was beginning at the expense most notably of the South West and East Anglia, but the South East was probably in a temporary phase of less than national average growth, and Scotland may have been growing in population faster than England and Wales. Second, from the mid-eighteenth to the mid-nineteenth century came what may be thought of as the 'classic' Industrial Revolution period, with above average growth of population in the North West, Yorkshire and Humberside, the South East, and the West Midlands – the last named apparently making its gain in the first half of the period and thereafter merely holding its own. All other regions suffered relative losses fairly uniformly in proportion to their original percentages of the national total, except that the South West's relative loss was somewhat greater than this. Northern Ireland, if it were included in the picture, would also be seen to be suffering a relative and, at the very end of the period an absolute, population loss.

From the middle of the nineteenth century until a rather shadowy dividing line which may be placed somewhere between 1911 and 1931, a new set of trends can be seen. The relative growth of the North West and Yorkshire and Humberside gradually diminished to zero, the North gained as, at the end of the period, did Wales, and the rate of relative gain of the South East was greatly increased. Until near the end of the period the two least urbanised of the English regions – the South West and East Anglia – were falling behind faster than ever before, though they were not (as Northern Ireland was) losing population absolutely.

Finally, from about the time of the first world war (though some of the trends in question are clear only from 1931) the now familiar pattern emerged. The South East continued its rapid gain; the West Midlands and, more modestly, the East Midlands joined it. The South West and East Anglia turned the corner and began to be relative gainers. The North West, Yorkshire and Humberside, the North and Wales – all the regions outside the Midlands and the South East that had ever shown relative gains since the beginning of the eighteenth century – have been in substantial relative decline, along with Scotland and Northern Ireland.

AUTONOMOUS VERSUS INDUCED POPULATION GROWTH

It goes without saying that the pattern of population distribution and its changes corresponded roughly with the pattern and shifts of economic activity. The causal relation between the two is another matter; two questions immediately arise. First, taking interregional variations in the balance of demand for labour as given, by what mechanism did they operate on the distribution of labour and population? Second, did changes occur independently in the supply of labour (not merely in response to demand), which may be supposed to have played a part in modifying the interregional distribution of population? Improved technology, or otherwise enhanced opportunities for production, might well lead to increase of regional population by stimulating immigration into the region, but might also either raise regional birth rates (by making possible earlier marriage, for instance), or, in a Malthusian situation with population pressing on the means of subsistence, they might reduce death rates. An 'autonomous' change in the rate of natural increase of population in a region – that is to say, one not induced by changes in production of goods and services in it – might well affect the rate of growth of regional production through its effect on the supply of labour. Can causal connections of any of these kinds be traced in practice?

Broadly speaking, throughout the last two centuries there has been a tendency for net immigration into the regions where production was growing fastest. In the first half of the eighteenth century Middlesex and Surrey had received massive immigration, which more than offset the natural decrease of their populations. Nearly every other county (with Lancashire and Warwickshire as probably the most significant exceptions), as well as Wales and Scotland taken as wholes, were sources of net emigration. This was probably the traditional demographic pattern of 'town' (meaning London) and 'country', though much of the emigration from Scotland was already directed overseas rather than to England in general or London in particular. In the second half of the eighteenth century and first part of the nineteenth the London counties continued to attract heavy net immigration, but Lancashire had begun to attract it on a similar scale in proportion to its population (that is to say, something like 1 per cent of its population per year) and the immigration spread to Cheshire. Monmouthshire began to increase its population by immigration at a comparable rate; Warwickshire continued to do so at a smaller one. Nearly all other English counties continued to lose by migration, the loss being heaviest in the neighbours of the big gainers – Lancashire and London – a fact consistent with the general proposition (for which there is independent evidence) that much of the movement was short-range. In Scotland there was much movement into the central belt, but for that country as a whole net emigration had become heavy.

The immediate suggestion of these facts is that migration responded to changes in demand for labour, and that in the outstanding cases of increasing demand it was responsible for satisfying a large part of it –

indeed all of it in early eighteenth century London, where the contribution of local natural increase was negative. It might still be that migration was 'autonomous' and served to promote growth, but such scraps of evidence about wages as are available militate against this. London wages were higher than those in Kent or Oxfordshire throughout the eighteenth century, and Lancashire wages advanced in the course of the century decisively faster than those in the south of England, though that is not where most of the immigrant labour came from. The flow of labour to London and the increasing flow to Lancashire apparently responded to economic inducements. The pattern of events is what one would expect from a rapid increase of factors of production other than labour, or a rapid rate of technical improvement in the growing regions.

As for natural increase, it seems (though on dubious evidence) that the great growth it showed in the middle of the eighteenth century was not uniform in its origin. In London and most of the south east, it was due to falling death rates. The causes of this are obscure; suggestions (none of them generally accepted) have ranged from the effectiveness of late eighteenth-century medical and hygienic improvements to the decline of the earlier passion for gin drinking. But it is not likely that rising demand for labour was responsible for much of it. On the same evidence it seems that, up to the end of the century, the rise in natural increase in the midlands and the north owed more to rise in birth rates than to fall in death rates, and for this the rising demand for labour may have been at least in part responsible – improved income prospects would promote earlier marriage, as would the decay of apprenticeship which was apparent at this time. In the early part of the nineteenth century, however, the further rise in natural increase in the north and midlands, as in the south, was seemingly due directly to falling death rates rather than rising birth rates. How far this change may have been induced by demand for labour or by rising real income is problematic. Natural increase in the first three decades of the nineteenth century, however, does not seem to reflect interregional differences of labour demand (or growth of it) very closely. Indeed there do not seem to have been any considerable broad differences of natural increase between regions, except that its level in London remained lower than elsewhere.

The interregional variations of natural increase and the amounts of net migration into or out of various kinds of area in England and Wales in the seventy years following 1841 were tabulated by Welton[1] and have been analysed by Cairncross.[2] Broadly, Cairncross's conclusions

[1] T. A. Welton, *England's Recent Progress*, London, Chapman and Hall, 1911.
[2] A. K. Cairncross, *Home and Foreign Investment, 1870–1913*, Cambridge University Press, 1953, ch. IV.

are as follows. The most rapid growth of population – a quadrupling in the seventy years – took place in what are classified as 'the colliery districts'. Next, with more than a trebling, comes the aggregate growth of eight big provincial towns – Manchester, Liverpool, Birmingham, Leeds, Sheffield, Leicester, Hull and Nottingham. London is not far behind, nor are the smaller northern industrial towns; these also trebled in population. The 'rural residues', outside both the towns and the colliery districts, grew by only about 18 per cent in the north and 9 per cent in the south. In total, the population of the northern half of England along with Wales increased by about 150 per cent, that of the southern half by 100 per cent.

Migration obviously played a big part in causing at least some of these differences in growth. Net migration to London, for instance, over the seventy years was about 55 per cent of the initial population; to the eight big northern towns named above it was (proportionately) rather higher. To the colliery districts, it was nearly 50 per cent of their initial population total. At the other extreme, the net emigration from the 'rural residues' was some 73 per cent of the population they started with. But Cairncross points out that the gains by migration were generally substantially smaller than the changes due to natural increase within the areas concerned – in London and the big northern towns only about a third of it, in the colliery districts only a fifth – though the emigration loss of the 'rural residues' was equal to some 85 per cent of their natural increase. And, on the larger scale, the difference in growth between the south and the north of the country seems at first sight to owe much more to difference in natural increase than to migration. The north's net migration balance with the rest of the country and the outside world was in any case negligible in this period. The south had a net loss of 1·2 million, but this was equal to less than 6 per cent of its net balance of births over deaths. Can the conclusion be that, apart perhaps from the relative decline in population of the rural residues, the changes in population balance between different kinds of area in the country (and presumably between regions) were mainly due to differences in their balances between fertility and mortality? If that were so, it would appear to be harder to attribute them to differences of demand for manpower than would be the case if migration was the main agent.

The problem of dividing responsibility for growth differences between migration and natural increase is, of course, too crudely stated. Demographic growth ideally requires to be divided for this purpose into three parts: first, the natural increase of the original population (what it would have been in the absence of migration); second, the actual net influx or efflux of migrants; and third, the balance between the sum of these two parts and the actual increase, which can be regarded as being the natural increase gained because of net immigration or lost because of net emigration.

Performing this division in practice is by no means easy. In a straightforward approach, one has to choose a convincing value for the rate at which the original population of the area in question would have increased in the absence of net migration. Alternatively, one can try to estimate the extra natural increase likely to have been produced in the period concerned by the immigrant population – an estimate which should take account of the time-shape of the net inflow, and of the fact that migrants are more likely than others to be young adults subject to high fertility and low mortality rates. Data on which to base systematic calculations of this sort are lacking, but it is possible by rough estimates based on both approaches to form an idea of the order of magnitude of the contributions that extra natural increase due to net immigration is likely to have made, and the rates of increase that might have ruled in the various communities in question in the absence of net migration. If one does this, it seems that perhaps as much as half of the difference in population growth between the south and the north of England and Wales may be attributed to difference in net migration. At first sight it is reasonable to suppose that this difference was due largely to more buoyant demand for labour in the north. Certainly the supply side of the relationship cannot be ignored – the north was nearer for the incoming Irish and Scots. However, although general comparisons of earnings between regions in this period are very difficult, agricultural wages, which may perhaps serve as very broad indicators of the level of labour demand in relation to supply, seem to have remained substantially higher in the north than in the south right up to the first world war. Once again, therefore, it looks as if the north's better record of net migration in comparison with the south was the result rather of a more active demand for labour than of an autonomous inflow of it.

As for the remaining growth difference, due to the north's superior balance of fertility over mortality, this seems to have been mainly due to the high natural increase in the coalfields. Even after allowing for the extent to which this may be attributed to the age structure of their largely immigrant population, they probably displayed a high fertility (in the technical sense), which may be credited to relatively high wages, absence of employment for women and absence of amusement for men. In some degree this constitutes a positive response of population to labour demand, but the relatively low fertility in the textile towns, where there was also strong demand for labour, but directed in that case largely towards female labour, shows that simple generalisations on this subject are dangerous.

From the 1870s there began the general fall in fertility rates that was so dominant a feature of the demographic scene from then until shortly before the second world war. In its first forty years up to 1911, it was most marked in the south of England with the important exception of London, and in the West Riding, Lancashire and Cheshire; least pronounced in London, the north east, Scotland and south Wales. One is tempted to associate these two groups of areas with low or slackening and high or rising pressures of labour demand respectively, though the classification is not entirely convincing, and there are some other features – the motives for family limitation in the textile areas and the relative absence of such motives in the mining areas, for instance – that provide perhaps more plausible partial explanations. But (apart from the maintenance of fertility in Scotland, where population was continuing to decline in relation to the British total) these fertility changes did, in general, work in such directions as to assist the changes in trend of interregional population distribution that occurred between 1871 and 1911. In the following twenty years, London, south Wales, the north east, the East Midlands and (again) west Yorkshire led the further fall in fertility. The south of England (excluding London) and Scotland were oddly grouped as the main areas where the fall was less than the national average. It is harder to associate these relative changes with differing levels of prosperity. It looks more like a spread of family limitation to regions that, for various reasons, had been slow to adopt it earlier, with Scotland still lagging behind; though the two most depressed areas of the thirties – the north east and south Wales – were certainly among the leaders in this phase.

Mortality generally began to decline substantially at about the same time as fertility, though ultimately it decreased less quickly than the latter. The fall accelerated in the nineties, when for the first time infant mortality began to decline fast. The decline was uneven; there was most scope for improvement in the big cities. London improved in relation to the industrial cities of the north and Scotland, and the latter improved in relation to the smaller industrial communities, especially mining communities in almost all coalfields. By the 1930s, standardised mortality rates in Scotland, Wales, the north east, and the North West were about 30 per cent above those of the best region in this respect, the South East. There can be no doubt that a good deal of this interregional difference was the result of differences in income levels (of both families and local authorities), which were exacerbated by the altered trend of relative regional fortunes in the twentieth century, though the general pattern of difference was established before the alteration in trends took place. The Scottish death rate deteriorated in relation to that for England and Wales from the beginning of the twentieth century. The changes in relative mortality in the late nineteenth and early twentieth centuries certainly contributed positively towards the changes in relative regional population growth which we have discussed.

Interregional migration, however, has played by far the major part in the redistribution of population in the present century, the more so as rates of natural increase have declined. Between 1921 and 1937, London and the Home Counties, which were responsible for well over half the total increase in the population of Great Britain in that period, showed a net immigration of over a million, against a natural increase of about three-quarters of a million. Wales lost by migration nearly half a million, which was substantially in excess of her natural increase. Scotland also lost by migration in excess of her natural increase in the twenties, but not in the thirties, when there was a heavy return of former emigrants from abroad.

Since the second world war migration has continued to dominate. To take the extremes, Scotland in the fifteen years 1951–66 had the highest percentage natural increase of any British region (10·2 per cent) and the South West the lowest (5·2 per cent). Scotland, however, lost by net emigration numbers equal to most of this natural increase (about $8\frac{1}{2}$ per cent of total initial population), while the South West, which was the region of heaviest percentage net immigration, made a gain of about 6·3 per cent of its initial population by this means. The difference in net gain by migration between these extreme cases was thus nearly three times as great as the difference in natural increase. More generally, the regions that suffered net loss by migration, Wales and the north of Great Britain, had nearly the same rate of natural increase as the rest that gained. In both cases the rate was between $7\frac{1}{2}$ and 8 per cent over the fifteen years. But in the former case there was a net loss of over $3\frac{1}{2}$ per cent, in the latter a net gain of over $4\frac{1}{2}$ per cent, by net migration. Net migration differences were responsible for the whole of the difference between the 4 per cent increase of resident population in the north and Wales, and the 12 per cent increase in the south and the midlands – in fact, they also offset a slight excess of natural increase in the north.

Perhaps the relationship between natural increase, net migration and total increase should be stated more formally. Across all the United Kingdom regions in the period 1951–69, the correlation between percentage total increase and natural increase of population is virtually zero. The range of rates of natural increase (as we have seen) was relatively small within Great Britain; the regions with the higher rates (the two Midlands regions, the North and Scotland) included instances of both high and low total growth, as did also the regions of lower natural increase (the South West on the one hand, Wales and the North West on the other). Northern Ireland, with a much higher rate of natural increase than any British region, achieved only a moderate rate of total growth. Net immigration was negatively correlated with natural increase, but not to a significant extent; most of the correlation was due to the high natural increase and heavy outward migration shown by Northern Ireland. Total increase, however, was quite well positively correlated with net migration; only Northern Ireland marred the relationship by showing a total increase much higher than that of Scotland in spite of a similar rate of net outward migration.

Migration has, of course, affected natural increase. A calculation by Hammond suggests that, of the increase in births due to rise in fertility of women of childbearing age between 1955–7 and 1961–3, something like a quarter in Wales and the north may have been offset by the fall in the number of women in that age range, whereas in the midlands and the south the relevant number of women rose, adding perhaps 5 or 10 per cent to the increase in births attributable to increased fertility.[1] Migration differences were presumably responsible for much of the interregional variations in age structure concerned.

In recent years it has continued to be generally true that fertility and mortality are both greater in the north than in the south. Whatever may have happened in earlier times, it is not very plausible to suggest of the last two decades that differences in pressure of demand for labour between regions have been visibly reflected in differences of fertility, though so many social differences enter into the picture that positive statements are, in any case, out of place. Certainly migration has been the main factor governing shifts in relative numbers, and it is reasonable to suppose that migration has been strongly influenced by differences of labour demand – though this matter too is full of complexity, as will be shown later.

Looking back over the last two and a half centuries as a whole, one cannot be entirely confident about the relative roles of 'autonomous' population growth and demand growth in altering the distribution of population. However, even for the country as a whole net migration seems to have been fairly responsive to demand pressure – or rather, to relative demand pressures here and in the other countries concerned – and to have played a not inconsiderable part in altering the growth rate of the resident population. For regions, and still more for single counties or cities, the sensitivity of migration to relative demand, and its relative importance as compared with differences of natural increase in causing changes in the general population distribution, were greater, and in the extreme cases dominant. The superior fertility of the north

[1] Hammond, *An Analysis of Regional Economic and Social Statistics*.

in the nineteenth century may be represented either as an autonomous demographic difference, or as a response of birth rate to labour demand; it is very hard to distinguish between the two. But if the miners had not been so prolific, would there not simply have been more net migration to the coalfields, and a net migration to the north taken as a whole? Looking at the apparent sensitivity of migration to demand, one suspects that there would. The very general impression so far seems to be that pressure of demand has been at any rate much the senior partner in bringing about the major shifts in the balance of population between regions that we have briefly examined.

THE SOURCES OF REGIONAL LABOUR DEMAND

The next question, then, is how differences in pressure of demand were generated. Our earlier theoretical discussion suggests that there are three main possibilities: higher pressure of demand for labour can arise from a superior rate of technical advance, a superior rate of increase in demand for the region's products, or a superior rate of increase in the supply of one or more of its factors of production other than labour. The first and third of these, in particular, are not easy to disentangle, but to understand changes in regional fortunes one should clearly try.

At the beginning of the eighteenth century, the main determinant of the location of population and production, in the broadest sense, was still agricultural land; agriculture was still probably responsible for more than half the national product. The textile industries (especially wool textiles, by far the most important branch of manufacture) were widespread, though with especially large concentrations in East Anglia, the West Country and the valleys of the southern Pennines. The iron industry was less widespread, being limited by the availability of ore and charcoal mainly to the Weald and a broad belt from south Wales and Gloucestershire to the West Riding, but could hardly rank as highly localised. For high localisation of a whole industry (as opposed to the existence of locally specialised varieties of product), one must look to coalmining with its fairly heavy concentration in Northumberland and Durham and, on smaller scales, the non-ferrous mining of Cornwall and Derbyshire, the associated smelting industries in Swansea and elsewhere, the brass industry of Birmingham, and perhaps the Hampshire shipbuilding industry. But these were relatively minor exceptions to the generalisation that population distribution was related to agricultural land; the only major exception was London.

The subsequent expansion was, of course, very much more in manufacturing industry and commerce than in agriculture, the growing output of the main manufacturing industries going largely to export markets. In value terms the textile industries dominated the first part of the expansion. By the 1820s they are estimated to have contributed about a seventh of the total gross national product, and to have been responsible for nearly two-thirds of total exports – more than half the output of the cotton industry and a quarter of that of wool textiles being sold abroad. So far as wool textiles were concerned, by far the greatest part of the expansion of production was in the West Riding; some other centres (such as the Scottish woollen area) also grew, but by comparison the west of England industry stagnated and the East Anglian industry withered. The main factors in this localisation of the expanding industry seem to have been availability of soft water, water-power and (increasingly important as time went on) coal. The cotton industry had a more spectacular rise, partly because the new spinning machinery originated in it and was more easily applied to it than to wool, partly because the invention of the cotton gin at a crucial moment when wool was becoming dearer vastly increased the supply of its raw material, and partly because there were enormous tropical markets to be won by cheap machine-made products. The industry grew rapidly on both sides of the southern Pennines and in Scotland – wherever there was a textile tradition along with adequate sources of power – but Lancashire was its main seat and gradually increased its predominance. The rise of these industries in this period should therefore, presumably, be put down to superior technical advance supported by elastic product markets. That particular regions grew on the basis of them can be ascribed to their possessing elastic and low-cost supplies of the factors needed for the new techniques – notably sources of power – besides being to a substantial extent seats of the textile industries to start with.

Economies of scale within the region also probably played a part. The tendency of originally widespread industries to become geographically concentrated was a strong one in the nineteenth century; it applied not only to wool and cotton, but also to linen – the Yorkshire branch of the industry declined sharply after the mid-century, the Scottish (though less drastically) a little later, leaving Northern Ireland finally dominant. Similarly, most of the quite numerous local potteries declined during the nineteenth century, leaving north Staffordshire supreme.

The metal-manufacturing and metalworking industries present a basically similar picture of technical advance, growing markets and localisation determined largely by natural resources. In their case technical advance was important not only directly in improving efficiency of production of the basic products, but also indirectly in developing entirely new products and thus opening new markets. The iron industry was a fast grower in the late eighteenth century; by that time coal had mainly replaced charcoal as a smelting material, and it was almost entirely confined to the coalfields, in most of which deposits of ore are conveniently to be found. The West Midlands owed its growth at that time largely to this industry, along with copper and brass, which received a strong fillip from the improved working (helped by steam pumps) of the Cornish mines and the discovery of ores in Anglesey. Early in the nineteenth century, south Wales moved into the lead in iron production. In the metal-producing industries as a whole growth continued to be faster than that of the gross national product (apart from a setback after the Napoleonic wars), and the metal-using industries, for which comprehensive data are lacking, almost certainly grew at a faster rate still, especially with the development of railways from the 1830s onwards.

It was this group of industries – likewise depending heavily and increasingly on exports – that took over from textiles as the chief leaders of growth sometime before the middle of the nineteenth century. This, however, did not immediately check the relative growth of the primarily textile regions, the North West and Yorkshire. These regions, as we have noted, were still increasing their shares of the national output in their main textile industries, though they sustained some losses of industries in process of concentrating elsewhere. But they also contained major growth points of the metal-manufacturing and the metal-using trades, notably textile engineering, one of the biggest branches of the engineering industry. In spite of their high specialisation on textiles, they were to a large extent microcosms of the new industrial economy. In Scotland (which up to the early nineteenth century had a strong textile bias), iron and the metalworking industries began to take the leading place from about the 1830s.

The strong relative growth from the mid-nineteenth century of the Northern region, which is evident from the population data, is also connected with the relative advance of the metal-producing and metal-working industries, but even more with a shift in their location. The increasing difficulty of mining the iron-ores on or adjoining the coal-measures, where they mostly occur in thin and scattered veins, put Lancashire, the West Riding, Wales and the West Midlands (and later on, Scotland) at a disadvantage as sites for the large-scale expansion of iron-smelting. The convenient combination of Durham coking-coal and the Jurassic ores of Cleveland (and on a smaller scale of coal and haematite in west Cumberland) opened better prospects. In due course shipbuilding and marine engineering, which were among the fastest growing industries from the sixties to the eighties, took a natural place in the northern English and Scottish industrial complexes where iron, and later steel, were produced near tide-water.

Thus resources, first of charcoal, then of coal and ore, have governed the local fortunes of the iron-smelting industry; the Cleveland and west Cumberland ores in their turn became exhausted, and in this century the growth points of iron and steel have shifted again to the Jurassic ores of Lincolnshire and Northamptonshire, to the industrialised districts where scrap accumulates in convenient proximity to coal, and to the ports near to coalfields to which foreign ores can be shipped. In this last connection south Wales has come back into its own since the second world war.

The other mineral resource that has played a major part in shifting the balance of growth between one region and another is, of course, coal itself. Quite apart from its original and dominating role as the source of energy without which a region could not enter the industrial race until, at all events, the railways came, or unless, like London, it had good connections with a coalfield by water, coalmining has been a big enough activity in itself for its distribution to have direct economic significance. The north eastern mines almost certainly declined in relative importance from the late eighteenth century as Lancashire, Yorkshire, Scotland and the West Midlands began to mine more of their own coal for local use, still more in the 1840s when the railways broke Newcastle's monopoly of supply to the south east. They provided only between a fifth and a quarter of total output from then until well into this century. Relative shares, indeed, remained fairly stable generally until near the end of the nineteenth century, when Scotland, south Wales, Yorkshire and the East Midlands began to move ahead. These coalfields all doubled, or nearly doubled, their outputs between the late eighties and 1913, and the effect in all of them except Scotland was important in connection with their increases in shares of the national population total in this last generation before the first world war.

In general, however, the great changes in regional fortunes since the beginning of this century, or even since the middle of the last, have been concerned less with the exhaustion or exploitation of mineral wealth than with changes in the markets for goods. One aspect of this is the changing division of demand between the home market and exports. Up to the seventies the proportion of British manufactures that was sold abroad increased until it reached something like 44 per cent. For much of British industry nearness to the domestic market was not an important consideration, nearness to a port perhaps was. From the late seventies or early eighties to the end of the century this proportion decreased; much the greater part of the increase in manufactured output was for the home market. It is perhaps not fanciful to see some connection between this fact and the increased proportion of growth which, in the later part of the century, was taking place in the South East – though there were plenty of other reasons (such as the growth of the commercial and financial functions of London) why the South East should grow fast at this time.

It is true that, in the first fourteen years of the present century, British growth again became more export-propelled – or perhaps one should say foreign investment-propelled – and export markets absorbed a high proportion of the increase in our manufactured output. This was the Indian summer of our nineteenth-century exporting industries and of the regions that depended most on them, but for what had been the two most dynamic of those regions, the growth rate had already decelerated to the national level.

The suddenness with which the pattern of overseas demand for British goods subsequently changed can be blamed to a large extent upon the first world war and the depression of the 1930s. Both war and depression proved to be powerful stimulators of import substitution in the less industrialised countries on whose markets British exporters tended especially to rely, and the war greatly stimulated the competitive powers of other exporters of manufactures, notably the United States. The warning of increasing competition in an industrialising world had been on the wall for forty years; the British industrial structure, however, had managed to remain quite extraordinarily dependent upon exports, and also especially vulnerable in that it was biased towards markets and products in which our comparative advantage was notably subject to erosion – particularly in the relatively labour-intensive industries such as textiles, coal and shipbuilding. Some of the long established capital-intensive industries such as iron and steel were also vulnerable to competition because of the older vintage of their plant and technology; investment had been low both there and throughout domestic industry partly because historical and institutional factors had directed savings overseas.

These well known weaknesses of the British economy after the first world war applied particularly, by virtue of their specialisations, to the economies of the North, Wales, the North West, Northern Ireland, Scotland, and in a smaller degree Yorkshire and Humberside. Through twenty years in which the whole economy suffered from shortage of effective demand manifested by general unemployment, it was these regions that clearly suffered from it most. This constituted a striking reversal of the position immediately before the first world war, when London had had far the highest (trade union) unemployment rate in the country, and Scotland the lowest. The prewar pattern of unemployment is in some degree paradoxical; London can hardly be said to have suffered from shortage of effective demand or from economic stagnation in 1913 – the south east was in a phase of rapid growth. Perhaps the large concentration in London of industries offering casual employment (notably construction and the docks), the attraction exercised over work-seekers by the largest single labour market, and the rapid rundown of employment in agriculture in southern England were responsible. At all events, there can be no doubt that after the war the unemployment pattern was reversed and its contrasts so sharply accentuated that it certainly demonstrated the different degrees in which demand for labour had fallen off in the various regions.

The greater degree of depression existing in Wales and the northern half of the United Kingdom – as evinced not only by higher unemployment but by a radical relative slowing down of growth in employment and population – was no doubt largely due, as has perhaps been implied already, to the fact that these regions had higher proportions of their occupied population engaged in the particular industries for whose products demand (especially export demand) had fallen; in short, that their structure was at fault. On the north east coast, for instance, two-thirds of insured employment in 1924 was in trades that declined in employment nationally in the succeeding decade, whereas in the London area the corresponding proportion was only one-sixth. We have noted that an initial concentration on declining industries is likely to be gradually remedied by more rapid development of other industries – both because such industries tend to grow relatively to the declining ones wherever they occur, and because they are likely to grow faster in the region in question than they do elsewhere, being better fed there by resources released from the prevalent declining trades. Whether, and how far, such offsetting factors have operated in recent decades will have to be investigated shortly; at a first glance, one may note that an unfavourable structure seems, as one would expect, to have been a brake on growth as long as it existed – the regions with unfavourable structures have done badly since 1918, just as the agricultural regions had low growth rates in the half-century before that date.

One should also note, however, that 'unfavourable' structure has sometimes apparently played a part in inducing a faster growth than elsewhere of new industries which have subsequently become important. The process by which the West Midlands got its second wind as a leading industrial area may be a case in point. In the late nineteenth century it may be said to have had an unfavourable structure, in that several of its industries – cast hollow-ware, buttons, small arms, wrought nails – were in at least relative decline. The steel age seemed largely to have passed it by. The availability of factors of production released from its stagnant industries may have been one reason for its more rapid development than other regions, first of the cycle industry, then of motors. The latter industry – rather like cotton textiles a hundred years earlier – sprang up at first in a number of regions where certain minimum conditions existed; in Scotland, Yorkshire and Lancashire, as well as the West Midlands and the South East. Its growth in the West Midlands was, however, the most rapid, and when subcontracting and separate manufacture of components developed in the twentieth century, economies of scale external to the firm but internal to the region were probably in consequence more readily available there (and perhaps in some degree in the South East) than elsewhere. It is important for a region to be specialised on products that are doing well, but no less important in the long run that their success should fail (if it must fail) at a time of new opportunity.

In the years between the two world wars, demand was so deficient generally and unemployment so widespread that unfavourable structure did not give the regions suffering from it an appreciable compensation for their immediate woes in the form of greater facility for seizing new opportunities. Ample supplies of labour and sufficient incentive to look for promising new lines of production were available virtually everywhere – though confidence and supplies of capital were not. The foundations of the new complexes of metalworking industries had already been laid in the Midlands and the South East, as we have noted; the remaining growth industries of the period were to a very large extent directed towards satisfying the home market, and thus were in some degree attracted by the largest single concentration of purchasing power within it. The radio industry is perhaps one in which this factor played some part, and its geographical concentration was further promoted by the external economies of access to a pool of skilled labour. In any case, it is an extreme example of the concentration of a new industry in a prosperous area. In 1935, over 88 per cent of its labour force was in Greater London alone. Greater London's predominance as a centre of growth extended to manufacturing industry as a whole; it was responsible for 40 per cent of the national total of new factory building between 1932 and 1937.

With the second world war and its aftermath of full employment, some of these conditions changed. Labour shortage in the areas of highest activity produced some tendency for industry to diffuse towards slacker parts of the country. Central government policy (which will have to be reviewed later) began to affect the distribution of industry significantly. The general growth rate rose. In spite of these changes, however, it is clear that the main foci of growth continued to be in the south, the most important change being an extension of the area of rapid growth so that it included parts of East Anglia and the South West. After a brief postwar interlude, the absolute decline of employment in textiles, mining, shipbuilding and agriculture resumed something like its prewar importance for general growth rates of the regions that still, to a substantial degree, specialised in those directions. The vehicles, electronics and consumers' durable goods industries, but above all the centralised service trades and professions, both grew fastest and in varying degrees showed tendencies to concentrate on the Midlands or the South East together with their East Anglian or South Western extensions. Hence, at the most superficial level of analysis, the current reversal (except for Scotland and Northern Ireland) of the trends in relative regional population and employment that marked the classic century of the Industrial Revolution.

CHAPTER 6

STRUCTURE AND GROWTH IN RECENT DECADES

We come now to the more recent periods, for which it is possible to attempt some kind of systematic analysis of growth of employment by industry and region. Let us first look at the results of such an analysis, using methods to which we have already referred, but which we shall describe briefly as it becomes necessary. The Census of Population is the source that first becomes available, with an analysis by industry in the Census of 1921 (for Northern Ireland, 1926). Before that occupation rather than industry was used as a basis of classification and, while much of the occupational classificaton related to specified industries, and Mr Lee has attempted to derive an industrial classification for 1881 and 1891 from it,[1] it seems better to take 1921 as our starting point.

Even so there are great difficulties in making the figures for 1921 comparable with those from later Censuses; not only is extensive regrouping of trades necessary to construct Standard Industrial Classification Orders on anything like their later definitions, but a much larger number of economically active persons appear as 'unclassified' in the 1921 Census than in subsequent ones – about 9 per cent of the total occupied population.

Looking at the statistics of changes in employment between 1921 and 1961, one sees first, of course, the relative growth performances to be explained – the outstandingly good performances of the South East and the West Midlands, the better than average performances of the South West, the East Midlands and (marginally) East Anglia, the poor performances of the other regions, especially Northern Ireland, Scotland, Wales and the North West. The North, perhaps rather surprisingly, did markedly less badly in employment growth than these – in fact, rather less badly than Yorkshire and Humberside, the other intermediate case among the relative losers (see the 'totals' in table 6.1).

Second, there is the change in employment structure, broadly common to all regions, that goes with the changing balance between primary and secondary industry (agriculture, mining and manufacture) on the one hand, and tertiary or service industries on the other. The change in structure arises from changes in the pattern of demand – a general shift towards services – as real income per head grows, coupled with

[1] Lee, *Regional Economic Growth in the United Kingdom since the 1880's*.

Table 6.1. *The long-term multiplier, 1921–61: increases in occupied population at work*[a]

Percentages

	Basic			Regional	Total
	Primary and secondary	Tertiary	Total		
North	−7·0	+1·5	−5·5	+16·3	+10·8
Yorks. and Humberside	−8·4	+1·2	−7·2	+15·1	+7·9
North West	−11·7	+0·7	−11·0	+12·3	+1·3
East Midlands	+2·3	+1·2	+3·5	+23·0	+26·5
West Midlands	+14·0	−2·9	+11·1	+28·8	+39·9
East Anglia	−5·7	+5·5	−0·2	+20·6	+20·4
South East	+12·6	−0·7	+11·9	+29·4	+41·3
South West	−1·8	+6·9	+5·1	+24·2	+29·3
Wales	−15·0	+3·5	−11·5	+11·8	+0·3
Scotland	−12·9	+1·8	−11·1	+12·1	+1·0
Northern Ireland[b]	−18·0	+3·8	−14·2	+9·6	−4·6

SOURCE: Lee, *Regional Economic Growth in the United Kingdom since the 1880's*

[a] As percentages of regional total employment at the beginning of the period.
[b] For the period 1926–61.

different rates of growth of labour productivity in the primary, secondary and tertiary sectors of the economy. The fact that it is broadly common to all regions is due to the large degree of dependence of each region's tertiary industry on final demand within the region, which means that the shift to services in regional consumption has to be reflected in regional employment.

THE LONG-RUN EMPLOYMENT MULTIPLIER

This is the fact that is responsible for the existence of the long-run local employment multiplier as a useful instrument of analysis, and it is worth turning aside for a moment to clarify its nature. Its validity depends on the possibility of distinguishing those productive activities that *must* be contributions to local consumption or capital formation from those that *could* be contributions to consumption or capital formation in another region. The latter may, in fact, contribute to local final absorption; a car assembled in the West Midlands may be sold to a user in that region. But for our present purpose it does not matter whether it is sold there or elsewhere. Given the level of West Midland final demand for cars, West Midland cars can be either sold outside the region or substituted for imports into the West Midlands of cars made elsewhere without altering the regional level of activity. On the other hand, regional demand for houses or for the services of retailers cannot normally be satisfied by importing from outside the region, nor are these goods and services saleable for use outside. Production and final absorption of them in the region must be identical and are related to regional total demand – that is to say, principally to the region's total production of goods and services of all kinds. If this relation is linear it follows that, with constant tastes and technology, changes in a region's total production will be a constant multiple of changes in its production of goods and services capable of being finally absorbed elsewhere – its 'basic' production. With constant technology too, a similar relation will hold between changes in its total and in its 'basic' employment.

As a first approximation, one may take tertiary (service) employment as being regional and the rest basic. Tertiary employment, it is true, is by no means the same proportion of total employment in all regions. In 1921 it varied from 36 per cent of the total in the East Midlands to 65 per cent in the South East. It is, however, worth testing the hypothesis that the relation of change in tertiary (or in total) employment to change in primary and secondary employment is the same, over a given period, between different regions. In order to eliminate the effect merely of difference in regional size, it seems best to do this after expressing the figures for each region as percentages of that region's total employment in the base year – in this case 1921.[1] The test thus consists of plotting, for each region, total employment in 1961 against non-service employment in 1961, both expressed as percentages of the region's total employment in 1921.

This yields the relation shown as a scatter diagram in chart 6.1. Most of the imperfection of the relationship is due to the very large increases in public administration and defence in East Anglia and the South West – increases which certainly cannot be regarded as being geared to the regional markets. They were indeed due mostly to the movement of defence establishments away from London, and should be regarded as changes in basic employment. The next step, therefore, is to make some rough adjustment for changes of this kind in portions of tertiary employment that are really basic rather than regional; that is to say, not necessarily related only to changes in the demand of the region in question.

The simplest and best known device is to assume that, at each of the census dates, employment in each of the service Orders was wholly regional in one region – that in which it was smallest in relation to total employment – and that the excess of it over this proportion of total employment in all other regions could be regarded as basic. All

---

[1] For this purpose, the unclassified, who were particularly numerous in 1921, were divided equi-proportionately between the service and other industries.

Chart 6.1. *Relation between increases in total and non-service employment, 1921–61 (total employment in 1921 = 100)*

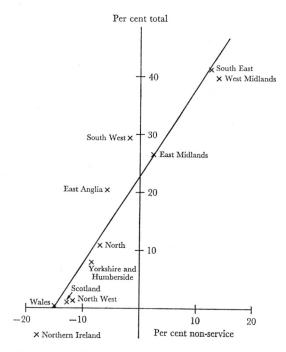

SOURCE: Lee, *Regional Economic Growth in the United Kingdom since the 1880s.*

employment in agriculture, mining and manufacture is still regarded as basic. Since this device consists in defining as regional employment a proportion, r, of total employment that is taken as being the same in all regions, it follows that the ratio of total to basic (non-regional) employment is everywhere the same by definition, and equal to $1/(1-r)$. This is therefore the value of the static multiplier, which would operate on any increase of basic employment if the proportion r remained constant for a sufficient time to let adjustment take place.

Over any considerable number of years, however, the value of r changes with shifts in the composition of final output between inter-regionally transportable and non-transportable items, and perhaps with relative changes in the labour-intensities of the methods by which these two classes of item are produced. In 1921 the proportion of total employment that was regional according to the method of calculation just described was 31 per cent; in 1961 it was 43 per cent. The static long-term multiplier would therefore have been 1·45 according to 1921 data, but 1·75 according to those of 1961. What does this imply about the size of the multiplier that might be deduced by studying the change in employment between 1921 and 1961?

Suppose that, in 1921, the relation between total and basic employment in all regions is described by the equation $T = bB$, where T is total employment, B basic employment and b a constant, identical with the static multiplier, $1/(1-r)$, to which we have recently referred. By 1961, T and B have changed to $T + \Delta T$ and $B + \Delta B$, but the ratio b has changed also to $b + \Delta b$. Then, in 1961 $T + \Delta T = (b + \Delta b)(B + \Delta B)$. Subtracting gives $\Delta T = \Delta b B + (b + \Delta b)\Delta B$, and dividing by T,

$$\Delta T/T = \Delta b/b + (b + \Delta b)\Delta B/T \quad \text{(since } B/T = 1/b\text{)}.$$

If, therefore, we compare data for regions with different growth rates, the value of the multiplier implicit in the comparison is $b + \Delta b$, which is the static multiplier (1·75) arising from the relation between total and basic employment at the *end* of the period. The term $\Delta b/b$, given our assumptions, shows the amount by which total employment (or regional employment) would have grown during the period if basic employment had been constant; its value here is 0·206. But there is a certain ambiguity about this multiplier. The presumption is that it takes some time for regional employment to adjust itself to a change in basic employment, but it is also likely that, by that time, spending habits and therefore the value of the static multiplier will have changed. It is a multiplier doomed always to be out of date.

The figures, subject to these cautions about their interpretation, are given in table 6.1. From this it will be seen that while, rather strikingly, only the South East and the two Midlands regions showed increases in primary and secondary employment over the forty year period, the South West and East Anglia were saved from substantial reductions in total basic employment by basic service expansion – mostly in fact in public administration and defence. Wales also showed a substantial increase in basic service employment; there some increase in public services, as well as some in construction and public utilities seem to have been mainly responsible. The South East and still more the West Midlands showed, on our necessarily rather arbitrary reckoning, some decrease in this kind of employment. But independently of the course of basic employment, that which we have identified as regional expanded uniformly by some 20·6 per cent of the total employment in all industries together in 1921. For reasons derived from changes in demand structure and technology, local service employment seems to grow at a rate of about half of 1 per cent of total employment per year, without the help of any change in the employment total.

For the later and partly overlapping period 1953–66, we have data

Chart 6.2. *Relation between increases in total and non-service employment, 1953–66 (total employment in 1953 = 100)*

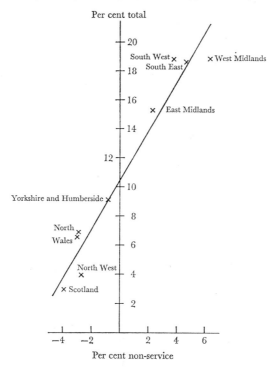

SOURCE: NIESR estimates.

on employees in employment corrected to the 1958 industrial classification for the regions of Great Britain, though it is necessary to combine East Anglia with the South East in order to get continuity. A comparison between increases in total employment and those in primary and secondary (with total regional employment in 1953 as the base) yields the relation shown in chart 6.2. It is interesting, however, to examine the regional increases in the eight service Orders separately.

As one might guess, most of them do not correlate with the corresponding increases in primary and secondary employment very closely; in fact, only the coefficients for transport (0·86) and for miscellaneous services (0·81) are significant, given the small size of the sample that the nine regions afford. Construction yields almost a zero correlation; not surprisingly, since over a fairly short period such as this the *level* of building activity in a region rather than its *rate of increase* might be expected to be related to growth of total regional employment. (It is

Table 6.2. *The long-term multiplier, 1953–66: increases in employees in employment*[a]

Percentages

	Basic			Regional	Total
	Primary and secondary	Tertiary	Total		
North	−2·9	+1·5	−1·4	+8·3	+6·9
Yorks. and Humberside	−0·8	+0·8	—	+9·1	+9·1
North West	−2·7	−0·5	−3·2	+7·2	+4·0
East Midlands	+2·3	+1·2	+3·5	+11·8	+15·3
West Midlands	+6·4	−0·9	+5·5	+13·3	+18·8
South East England	+4·7	+0·7	+5·4	+13·2	+18·6
South West	+3·8	+1·6	+5·4	+13·2	+18·6
Wales	−2·5	+1·0	−1·5	+8·1	+6·6
Scotland	−3·9	+0·3	−3·6	+6·6	+3·0

SOURCE: NIESR estimates.

[a] As percentages of regional total employment at the beginning of the period.

the high rates of growth of building employment in Scotland, Wales and Yorkshire that mainly disrupt the relationship.) Gas, electricity, and water yield another poor relationship, again not surprisingly in view of the extent to which these are interregional services. In public administration and also in professional and scientific services it was the South West and Wales that did well in relation to the growth of their primary and secondary industry, the Midlands regions that did badly; while in insurance, banking and finance, the South East showed a large increase completely out of line with experience elsewhere. For all the Orders except public administration, the change in employment independent of that in primary and secondary industries was significant; it was an increase in all cases except transport.

One could use these regressions as the basis for estimates of those parts of the change in service employment that are to be regarded as basic, but for reasons of comparability it is perhaps better to take the excess over the minimum regional proportion as providing an estimate, as we have done for the period 1921–61. The resulting figures are shown in table 6.2. The comparable relation, identically true by virtue of the way in which basic employment is calculated, is $\Delta T/T = 0.0915 + 1.764 \Delta B/T$. In this period South East England, the South West and the two Midlands regions showed increases in primary plus secondary employment, the rest showed falls, greatest in Scotland. Changes in estimated basic service employment were less dramatic; all regions except the West Midlands and the North West, however, showed increases – fairly substantial in the North, the South West, Wales and the East Midlands. Nearly every region seems to have accumulated some tertiary activity other than that geared to its own domestic market, but no change of this sort was quite on the scale of the decentralisation of the central government (mainly defence) establishments from London at an earlier date.

REGIONAL GROWTH

Having noted these broad tendencies towards parallelism between the movements of employment in two groups of industries within a region, we may now return to a closer scrutiny of the general relations between regional and industrial employment growth and industrial structure, to which we referred in chapter 4. The difference between what the rate of growth of employment in a region would have been with each of its industries growing at that industry's national rate and the rate of growth of employment in the country as a whole is one version of what is generally called the 'structural' or 'composition' component of the difference between the actual growth rates of the region and of the country. It may be expressed as

$$(1) \quad \sum_i G_i(W_{ir} - W_i),$$

where G_i is the national growth rate of industry i, and W_{ir} and W_i are the shares of industry i in total employment in the region and the country respectively.

Similarly, the 'growth component' may be measured as the difference between the rate at which national employment would have grown if all industries had shown the growth rates they showed in the region and the rate at which national employment actually grew, that is

$$(2) \quad \sum_i W_i(G_{ir} - G_i),$$

where G_{ir} is the growth rate of industry i in the region.

The actual difference between the regional and national growth rates is $\sum_i G_{ir} W_{ir} - \sum_i G_i W_i$, which can be written

$$\sum_i G_{ir} W_{ir} - \sum_i G_{ir} W_i + \sum_i G_{ir} W_i - \sum_i G_i W_i \text{ or}$$

$$(3) \quad \sum_i G_{ir}(W_{ir} - W_i) + \sum_i W_i(G_{ir} - G_i).$$

This, minus the sum of the structural and growth components (1) and (2) above, is $\sum_i G_{ir}(W_{ir} - W_i) - \sum_i G_i(W_{ir} - W_i)$, or

$$(4) \quad \sum_i (G_{ir} - G_i)(W_{ir} - W_i).$$

The three components (1), (2) and (4) thus together account for the whole of the difference between regional and national growth. The third of these (4) is clearly connected with the correlation coefficient between the extent to which the region specialises on industries, and the extents to which their respective growth rates are greater in the region than they are nationally; it is zero if this correlation coefficient is zero, positive if it is positive, negative if it is negative. This is an instance of the well known proposition in index-number theory that choice of weighting system is immaterial unless the weights are correlated positively or negatively with the relatives to which the weights are being applied.

It will be evident that we have chosen, in expressions (1) and (2), indices of structural difference and growth-rate difference in which we have used weights (growth rates and employment shares respectively) which are in both cases national rather than regional. As an alternative it is obviously possible to choose regional weights, G_{ir} and W_{ir} respectively. It can be shown that, if we do this, the sum of the structural and growth components corresponding to (1) and (2) will *exceed* the total growth difference between the region and the country (3) by exactly the same amount (4) by which the two components measured with national weights fall below it. An average of the sum of (1) and (2) and the corresponding expressions using regional weights will thus give a value exactly equal to the difference of growth rates under discussion; this device amounts to the use of 'Marshall–Edgeworth' average weights in the indices of structural and growth effects, and eliminates the third term (4).

It is also evident from (3) that, if we measure the structural component using regional growth-rate weights and the growth effect using national employment-structure weights, we again exhaust the growth difference to be explained, leaving no room for a third term. The same is true if we use the other possible mixture of weights – national growth-rate weights for structural differences and regional employment weights for growth-rate differences.

The question that immediately arises, therefore, is why one should not divide the growth difference simply into a structural effect and a growth effect by either using different weights for the two components or taking average (Marshall–Edgeworth) weights. Against the former procedure one can raise the usual index-number objection that whichever of the two sets of weights is chosen is arbitrary and not to be preferred on any rational ground to the alternative choice. The use of average weights is less open to this objection, since it gives central estimates of the growth and structural effects.

The case for avoiding these (or indeed any other) methods of reducing the growth difference to two components, however, seems most rationally to rest on the fact that the third component (4) is one to which a clear and economically valuable meaning can be given. Specialising on the industries at which one is relatively good is not the same thing as specialising on those that are good choices everywhere, nor the same as being better than other regions at production in general. For this reason, it may seem best to choose the nationally weighted ('Laspeyres') indices of structural and growth differences, which give the third term a positive value where specialisation and comparative advantage in growth are positively correlated.

Against the standardisation procedure just described, or any similar one, are to be set at least two considerations. First, there is the essential arbitrariness, to which we have referred, of either national or regional growth rates as bases of the hypothetical cases with which actual performance is to be compared. Second, there is the fact that any standardisation procedure is a mechanical partitioning of actual performance into components, the sizes of which cannot be subjected to any test of statistical significance. The remedy for both these defects is to approach the problem by way of an analysis of variance, in which the growth advantages or disadvantages peculiar to specific industries (in all regions), and those peculiar to specific regions (affecting all industries in them), are first derived by minimising the residual portions of growth not accounted for by these industry or region components, and are then used along with the data on employment structure to yield estimates of the 'composition' and 'growth' (or 'regional') components of the extent to which each region's total growth of employment deviates from the national rate.[1]

The same choice still presents itself in the formulation of these composition and growth components; they may be chosen with either national or regional weights, as estimated from the analysis of variance model. These pairs, which in the standardisation procedure add up identically to the difference between the regional and national growth rates, will, however, no longer do so; they will add identically to the *estimate* of the difference derived from the model, which will differ from the actual difference to the extent that the model does not provide a perfect explanation of the difference. In practice, the difference between the alternative pairs of estimates is very small. The 'residual error' (the actual deviation from the national average growth rate not explained by the systematic part of the model) is accordingly not equivalent to component (4) of the standardisation analysis. It will,

[1] A full account of the problems of analysis is given in unpublished papers by R. Weeden and J. K. Bowers, respectively, 'Regional rates of growth of employment: an analysis of variance treatment' and 'An analysis of regional rates of employment growth'.

Table 6.3. *Regional and national growth rates in total employment: composition and growth components of the differences*

Per cent per annum

	Differences in growth (regional minus national)	Components		
		Composition	Growth	Residual error
North				
1921–61	−0·22	−0·38*	+0·10	+0·06
1953–9	−0·18	−0·16*	+0·03	−0·05
1961–6	−0·04	−0·85*	+0·30*	+0·51
E & W Ridings				
1921–61	−0·31	−0·23*	+0·08	−0·16
1953–9	−0·32	−0·33*	−0·07	+0·08
1961–6	−0·38	−0·60*	+0·14	+0·08
North West				
1921–61	−0·53	−0·06*	−0·55*	+0·08
1953–9	−0·62	−0·32*	−0·28*	−0·02
1961–6	−0·57	−0·30*	−0·27*	—
N Midlands				
1921–61	+0·22	−0·37*	+0·50*	+0·09
1953–9	+0·03	−0·54*	+0·62*	−0·05
1961–6	+0·43	−0·66*	+0·97*	+0·12
(W) Midlands				
1921–61	+0·52	+0·09	+0·54*	−0·11
1953–9	+0·33	+0·11*	+0·10	+0·12
1961–6	+0·22	+0·16*	−0·08	+0·14
South West				
1921–61	+0·28	—	+0·23	+0·05
1953–9	+0·33	−0·10*	+0·42*	+0·01
1961–6	+0·56	−0·06	+0·06	+0·56
SE England				
1921–61	+0·56	+0·40*	+0·15	+0·01
1953–9	+0·53	+0·38*	+0·16*	−0·01
1961–6	+0·24	+0·63*	−0·03	−0·36
East Anglia				
1921–61	+0·06	−0·14*	+0·20	—
Wales				
1921–61	−0·56	−0·55*	−0·29*	+0·28
1953–9	−0·72	−0·26*	−0·79*	+0·33
1961–6	−0·27	−0·55*	−0·17	+0·45
Scotland				
1921–61	−0·83	−0·08*	−0·55*	−0·20
1953–9	−0·78	−0·13*	−0·55*	−0·10
1961–6	−0·46	−0·30*	−0·36*	+0·20
N Ireland				
1926–61	−1·19	−0·49*	−0·41*	−0·29

SOURCE: NIESR estimates.

Notes: (i) Estimates for 1921–61 from data at Industrial Order level, for other periods at level of Minimum List Headings.
(ii) Regions used for 1921–61 are new Standard Regions.
(iii) * indicates significance with $t > 2·5$.

however, be affected by any correlation between an industry's growth rate in a region and the extent to which the region specialises on that industry.[1]

Since all these components arise in this calculation as estimates derived by fitting what is essentially a regression equation to the recorded growth rates of all industries in all regions, standard errors of estimate can be derived for them, and this makes it possible to say which of them are significantly different from zero and whether a composition component (say) is significantly greater than the corresponding growth component – a very great advantage.

Another improvement may also be introduced, which has not yet been mentioned. A large part of the interregional difference of growth rates found within a single industry arises from cases where the amount of employment in the region is very small but is undergoing very rapid percentage growth or decline – the classic case of shipbuilding in the Midlands typifies the kind of thing that is in question. This tends to make the standardisation component large and predominantly negative through the enormous percentage growth rates sometimes shown by industries that are hardly represented in the region at all. The problem cannot be wholly solved, save by arbitrary exclusions or re-groupings of data that would involve sacrificing significant facts along with trivial ones, but it can be mitigated by the method of estimation.

The basic model consists of an equation $G_{ir} = A_i + B_r + V_{ir}$, where G_{ir} is the growth rate of industry i in region r, A and B are two sets of dummy variables, the former for industries the latter for regions, and V_{ir} is an error term which, over all industries and regions together, must sum to zero, and is to have its variance minimised by the estimation procedure. The trick for diminishing the importance attached to shipbuilding in the Midlands is to minimise the variance of V_{ir} when it is measured, not in the obvious way as an error in the percentage growth rate estimated for the industry, but as that error expressed as a proportion of total employment in the region.

We may now proceed to look at the results of applying these analyses to the data for 1921–61, and subsequently to those for some shorter and

---

[1] A term which bears some formal analogy to the standardisation term (4) can be derived from the model, but it turns out to be small in practice and it is not very interesting for our present purpose. It arises at all only because an industry concentrated in regions with favourable growth components, for instance, will show a higher national average growth rate on that account, and positive deviations of its growth rates in particular regions from the national average rate will therefore be smaller than if all industries were similarly distributed between regions. The component in regional growth that arises because there is some degree of correlation between an industry's growth rate in a region and the extent to which the region specialises on it will appear in the residual error of our calculation – that is, the extent to which the analysis of variance estimate of regional growth rate differs from the actual rate.

later sub-periods. Since we have found that the regional industries tend to follow the basic ones in their movements, it might seem natural to confine our further analysis to the latter. Bearing in mind the imperfection of the base multiplier relation however, especially if one confines oneself to the boundary lines provided by the Standard Industrial Classification, it may be more prudent to apply our analysis first to the whole range of industries, then to see what can be done by applying it to the industries of the primary and secondary groups only. The results of the first part of this operation are shown in table 6.3.

In the long period 1921–61 (1926–61 for Northern Ireland), the regions where composition effects were preponderant numerically and of indubitable statistical significance were Wales, Northern Ireland, the North, and Yorkshire and Humberside among the relative losers, the South East among the gainers. The East Midlands showed a large adverse structural component offset by an even larger favourable growth effect. East Anglia and Scotland showed smaller but statistically significant adverse structural effects.

The regions where growth components were predominant and large were the West Midlands and (as already mentioned) the East Midlands on the favourable side, and the North West and Scotland on the unfavourable. It must, however, be remembered in looking at the division between composition and growth effects that the latter tend to gain from the generality of the industrial classification used. Specifically, the fact that the North West's troubles are attributed to 'growth' and not to 'composition' in this particular analysis is due in some considerable measure to the classification of the cotton textile trades with the other textile industries, which on the whole fared much better. The meaningfulness of any analysis of growth into structural and other elements, however it is carried out, depends heavily upon the efficiency of the industrial classification used. Ideally, the products of whatever is classified as a single 'industry' for this purpose should be either homogeneous or, more practicably, mixtures of similar composition in all the areas of production. If they fail to achieve this ideal, the damage to the validity of the analysis may still be small if neither the demands for different components of the 'mix' nor their techniques and costs of production move at significantly different rates in different regions. That is to say, no significant composition effects should in fact take place within a single category of goods or services as classified for the purpose of the analysis, or they will be lost to the 'composition' side of the account and credited to 'growth'. Textiles and transport are the Industrial Orders within which these conditions most signally fail to be realised in the period in question.

Other things being equal, a finer classification is bound to increase the relative importance attributed to the composition component – a presumption which we shall see borne out in more detailed analyses later. With the qualification implied by this (with special reference to the case of the North West), one can say that structure seems to have been about as important as growth components in this period; more particularly, it seems to have been the predominant influence in most of the regions that did badly, and also in one – the South East – that did well.

It should perhaps be emphasised again that the two systematic components we have been explaining do not exhaust the growth differences that we are seeking to explain, or even the part of them that can be called systematic. The magnitude and effects of any tendency for a region to do especially well or badly in the industries in which it specialises emerges in the residual error; perhaps, however, it can best be investigated by a further device to which we shall come later.

The extent to which this analysis of variance model accounts for the actual deviations of regional from national growth in this period is generally fairly satisfactory, though about half the relative decline of Yorkshire and Humberside remains unexplained, while Wales on the other hand did distinctly less badly than the systematic growth and composition elements would have suggested. There is no discernible tendency for favourable composition and poor growth to go together; evidently regions with favourable structures did not, in general, suffer over these forty years from the kind of general brake on their growth that labour shortage might have imposed in a fully employed economy.

So much for the greater part (so far) of the major phase of economic change that may be dated roughly from the first world war. We come now to more recent sub-periods, at which we can look rather more closely.

We have made analyses of growth by industry and region from Ministry of Labour data on employment from 1953 to 1959 and from 1959 to 1966, and also from Census of Population data from 1961 to 1966. The earlier of the analyses from Ministry of Labour data, and that from the Censuses, have been made at both Industrial Order and Minimum List Heading levels of classification. The latter results are given in table 6.3.

The Minimum List Heading analysis of the period 1953–9 carried out by the analysis of variance method shows structural components slightly less important than those of growth on balance; structure is more important in the North, Yorkshire, the North West and South East England, and marginally (not significantly) in the (West) Midlands. Growth (good or bad) is the predominant element in the South West, Wales and Scotland, and very important also in the North Midlands, where, as in the longer period, it rather more than offsets a large unfavourable structural effect. Of the structural components, only those for South East England and the (West) Midlands are favourable. In comparison with an analysis at Industrial Order level, this Minimum List Heading calculation shows a poorer total explanation of the changes, and a greater relative importance of structure – most particularly a greater plausibility in attributing the North West's troubles predominantly, on balance, to that factor rather than to growth. Again, there is no sign of correlation across the regions between their structural and growth components.

It seems to be worth looking separately at the results of applying the analysis to agriculture, mining and manufacture only – the nearest we can get in terms of the Standard Industrial Classification to the basic industries. We have seen that the long-run multiplier tends to superimpose upon the growth of the service trades a movement in sympathy with that of each region's basic industries. A region with a favourable structure of basic industry might be expected therefore to show some tendency towards a favourable growth component in so far as the service trades should be doing better than in regions of less fortunate structure. This tendency might be expected to work against any general slowing of industry growth rates in regions where favourable structure has led to a relative shortage of labour. An analysis of the basic trades alone should display this general effect of factor scarcity on growth without the complications due to the regional consumption multiplier.

In fact in this period omitting the service trades does not make a great deal of difference. The South West's favourable growth component is enlarged and, more strikingly, the (West) Midland region emerges with a considerable negative growth component instead of a positive one, but otherwise the pattern of components is much the same as when all trades are included. There is still no sign of correlation, positive or negative, between growth and composition components (see table 6.4).

In comparison with any of our analyses for 1953–9, however, results for the following period, 1961–6 (or 1959–66 for which an analysis of Ministry of Labour data was carried out), show some notable differences. First, the systematic components explain actual changes much more poorly. Secondly, structure had become more important in relation to growth components; calculated from Minimum List Heading data for all industries it was numerically more important in six out of the nine British regions (the South East and East Anglia being amalgamated for these calculations). In South East England and, negatively, in the North, Yorkshire and Wales, its dominance was very clear and, as in other periods, it was important (though outweighed by a positive growth component) in the North Midlands. The analysis at Industrial Order level, which provides a better total explanation, shows a positive growth

Table 6.4. *Regional and national growth rates in non-service employment: composition and growth components of the differences*

Per cent per annum

	Differences in growth (regional minus national)	Components		
		Composition	Growth	Residual error
North				
1953–9	+0·03	−0·20*	+0·21	+0·02
1961–6	−0·76	−1·50*	+0·01	+0·73
E & W Ridings				
1953–9	−0·45	−0·42*	−0·15	+0·12
1961–6	−0·35	−0·97*	+1·09*	−0·47
North West				
1953–9	−0·80	−0·49*	−0·45*	+0·14
1961–6	−0·59	−0·28*	−0·28	−0·03
N Midlands				
1953–9	−0·23	−0·77*	+0·54*	—
1961–6	+0·51	−0·98*	+1·96*	−0·47
(W) Midlands				
1953–9	+0·30	+0·63*	−0·78*	+0·45
1961–6	+0·40	+0·94*	−0·80*	+0·26
South West				
1953–9	+0·51	−0·30*	+0·98*	−0·17
1961–6	+1·18	−0·44*	+0·51*	+1·11
SE England				
1953–9	+1·00	+0·63*	+0·43*	−0·06
1961–6	+0·17	+1·21*	−0·76*	−0·28
Wales				
1953–9	−1·10	−0·38*	−1·01*	+0·29
1961–6	+0·19	−1·21*	+1·02*	+0·38
Scotland				
1953–9	−0·96	−0·40*	+0·09	−0·65
1961–6	−0·42	−0·77*	+0·26	+0·09

SOURCE: NIESR estimates.

Notes: (i) Estimates for both periods from data for Minimum List Headings, covering agriculture, mining and manufacturing industries only.
(ii) * indicates significance with $t > 2\cdot 5$.

component in the North, almost as big as its companion (negative) structural component, and again switches the emphasis from structure to growth in the North West, but apart from these it tells much the same story, with the emphasis on growth that is to be expected of it. For basic trades alone also, the structural component calculated at Minimum List Heading level was more important on balance than the growth component.

Third, a decided negative correlation emerges in this period between structural and growth components. For all trades together, the correlation (at $r = -0.38$) is not significant, but for the basic trades only (at $r = -0.77$), it is. The clearer emergence of this correlation in the absence of the obscuring effect of the multiplier on the service trades is in accordance with expectation. Whether its existence is due to the theoretically presumable effect of labour shortage in the regions of favourable structure may be doubted, however. Pressure on resources in the prosperous regions was no greater in this period than in the previous one when no correlation was apparent; there is, moreover, another candidate for the honour of having made growth less favourable where structure was more so – namely, the stronger operation of regional policy, which we shall examine in a later chapter.

All these remarks relate to changes in male and female employment together. In fact the courses of change have been different for the two sexes and the main differences deserve note.

First, total growth of female employment was, in both halves of the period, well above average in the North and Wales, as well as in the South West, South East and West Midlands, whereas male employment, of course did badly in the first two regions mentioned. (Up to 1959 female employment also did badly in the East Midlands, where male employment was doing better than average.) Otherwise, the growths of male and female employment diverged from their respective national averages in, at any rate, the same directions.

The second notable point is that, in both the sub-periods between 1953 and 1966 that we have distinguished, the structures of female employment in Wales, the North and the South West emerged favourable to growth, and that in Scotland roughly neutral, whereas the structures of male employment in those regions were all very strongly (or in the South West moderately) adverse. Not surprisingly, it is in the three textile and clothing regions – the North West, Yorkshire and the East Midlands – that structures of female employment were strongly adverse, whereas it is predominantly the partly overlapping group of mining, shipbuilding and agricultural regions that show the strongest adverse structural factor in the change of their male employment.

Broadly then, the growth components of female employment increased in importance after 1959 in comparison with the structural components – the opposite of the tendency to be seen in male employment. The main contributions to this change in the development of female employment were the big improvements of growth components in the East Midlands, Wales and the North. In the latter two regions regional policy may have played some part in this; in the East Midlands the rise of the hosiery and knitwear trades, partly in competition with the woven textiles of other regions, may be largely responsible.

EFFECTS OF STRUCTURE ON GROWTH RATES

The analysis can be taken a stage further by adding the hypothesis that growth of an industry in a region is systematically affected, not only by factors peculiar to the industry as such and the region as such, but also by the industry's 'weight' in the region – the proportion of total regional employment for which it accounts. We have adduced earlier a theoretical presumption that the percentage rate of growth *or of decline* of an industry in a region will tend to be greater when it is lightly than when it is heavily represented there in proportion to total regional employment, but this is a hypothesis rather harder to test and we shall return to it presently. For the moment we propose to see only whether growth rate is systematically affected either favourably or unfavourably by weight. The relevant equation is $G_{ir} = A_i + KW_{ir} + B_r + V_{ir}$, where W_{ir} is industry i's proportion of employment in region r, and K is taken to be the same (in the absence of sufficient degrees of freedom to do otherwise) in all industries and all regions.

When this equation is fitted to the data (at Industrial Order level of aggregation) for 1953–9 and 1959–66, it proves to be the case that K has highly significant negative values for both periods – a larger negative value in the second than in the first. The larger an industry bulks in a region, the slower it grows – or, in general, the faster it declines. Any tendency for slow decline (as well as slow growth) in relation to the unweighted national average for all industries and regions to go with a high weight is swamped here by the general relation.

The tendency can be tested for, imperfectly but probably adequately, in another way. The device employed for this purpose is to assume that the rate at which growth of an industry in a region changes with industry weight is proportional (positively or negatively) to the industry's national growth variable, A_i; that is to say, if the relation turns out to be significant, that either the superiority or the inferiority of growth rate specific to any particular industry vanishes in any region as the industry expands to take up the whole of that region's employment. The relevant equation is $G_{ir} = A_i(1 - W_{ir}) + B_r + V_{ir}$.

This hypothesis proves to fit the facts almost as well as the preceding one, of growth rate varying simply with industry weight. What emerges, however, is that for the best fit all values of A_i are positive and those of B_r negative, so that growth rate declines with increase of employment weight in all industries. If there is any tendency for declining industries to survive better where they are the object of regional specialisation, it must indeed be small in comparison with the general association of faster growth and lower weight in the region.

The presumption for such a tendency was deduced earlier from considerations of factor supply; declining industries should be more favoured by labour supply the less important competing (especially growing) industries are in the region. From considering possible economies of scale one would be led to a different hypothesis, namely that industries grow or survive best in those regions where the highest proportions of employment in the industry are concentrated.

This alternative hypothesis can be tested by fitting to the data the equation $G_{ir} = A_i + KZ_{ir} + B_r + V_{ir}$, where Z_{ir} is the proportion of the total national employment in industry i that is located in region r. Applied to the figures for 1953–9 and 1959–66, this fits the data well (slightly better than its counterpart which includes W_{ir} instead of Z_{ir}), and also gives negative values of K. Industries in general grow fastest where there are least, not most, of them. This can be confirmed by fitting the equation $G_{ir} = A_{ir}(1 - Z_{ir}) + B_r + V_{ir}$, which again produces positive values for the A's, though the fit to the data is rather poorer than with the previous equations. Therefore, looking at things primarily with regard either to the industrial composition of employment in regions, or to the interregional distribution of industries throughout the country, one comes on a general tendency towards dispersion or diversification to which we must return in the next chapter. First, however, we must consider what contribution this further analysis makes to the division of regional deviations from the national growth rate into 'growth' and 'composition' elements.

What is newly taken into systematic account in the first of the equations just discussed is the tendency for industries to grow more slowly or decline more quickly when a region specialises on them. One would expect this to give regions that are heavily specialised in their structure a less favourable estimated composition component and a more favourable growth component, regardless of whether their specialisation was on rapidly growing industries or on declining ones. Unfortunately, because of the assumption that growth rate in a region varies in the same way with industry weight for all industries whatever their size in the country as a whole, the sense of specialisation that is relevant here is rather an odd one; a region is 'specialised' if the distribution of its employment between the Industrial Orders is less nearly equal than that in the country as a whole. By this test only South East England, the West Midlands and Wales have positive degrees of specialisation; all the others have negative ones. The general result is to diminish the overall numerical importance of composition components, and to increase that of growth components, in comparison with the straightforward analysis of variance model. For the period 1953–9 composition emerges as very much the junior partner; for 1959–66 it comes out with only about two-thirds of the numerical importance that can be attached to estimated growth components.

Whether these estimates, depending on such unavoidably rickety assumptions, constitute improvements on those made without regard to a systematic variation of an industry's growth rate with the amount of it in the region is uncertain. The more complex model gives only a marginally better explanation of variations of industry growth rates in regions than the simpler one, and still, through the sum of the systematic components, accounts very imperfectly for the deviations of regional from national rates of total employment growth – especially in the second period, 1959–66, and within that especially for Yorkshire and Humberside, Wales and the South West.

The basic difficulty of estimating composition and growth components is that their values depend upon hypotheses that are in varying degrees untrue – either that an industry shows a 'typical' degree of inferiority or superiority in growth uniformly across all regions, while a region shows a 'typical' degree of superiority or inferiority in all its industries, or that, complicating this, there is some additional connection between industry weights and growth. The latter certainly seems to be true, but it is plain that our simple hypotheses about the nature of this additional connection, while they have some validity, still to some extent misstate systematic connections that exist between growth rates and weights. Structure is a more elusive source of interregional growth differences than appears at first sight. While its part may not be so large as is suggested by the straightforward analysis of variance, there can be no doubt that it is important, and that its importance increased between the fifties and the sixties.

SOME ELEMENTS IN STRUCTURE AND GROWTH COMPONENTS

To the extent that structure can be held responsible for departures from the national growth rate, the elements in it that make the main contributions to this departure may, of course, be identified. For the intercensal period 1961–6, and for standard subregions, some mention of them based upon a standardisation analysis is made in appendix H of the Hunt Report.[1] So far as the planning regions are concerned, it emerges that the uniquely favourable structure of the South East in this period was due not so much to the industries it had as to those that it lacked – to the low representation there of the declining industries of mining, agriculture, textiles and shipbuilding – though its possession of some of the fast growing service trades was also an important element.

[1] Department of Economic Affairs, *The Intermediate Areas*, Cmnd 3998, London, HMSO, 1969.

In the regions where structure was particularly adverse – the North, Wales, the East Midlands, Yorkshire and Humberside and, in a rather lower degree, the North West and Scotland – a high degree of reliance upon some or all of these spectacularly declining industries was a main contributor to the trouble, though again lack of nationally fast growing trades was also important in some cases – the low representation of engineering in Wales and Yorkshire, for instance, and of the fast growing service trades in all these regions except Scotland. On the other hand, the favourable structures of female employment which we have noted in Wales, the North and the South West are mainly due to the small total representations there of the relatively declining, female-employing industries of clothing, textiles and footwear. In causing the divergence between the fortunes of the prosperous South East and Midlands and the less prosperous Wales and Great Britain north of the Trent, the concentration of the former on certain fast growing service trades and the faster growing manufacturing industries has probably so far been the minor factor, though an important one; the major factor is still, after fifty years, the decline of coal, the traditional textile industries, agriculture and shipbuilding.

At the subregional level of analysis, it is plain that the failure of structure to explain more of the divergences between total growth rates than it does is in a very considerable measure due to movements of industry and population. In most cases the conurbations possess favourable industrial structures, largely because they are centres of the fast growing service trades, but since manufacturing and some service industries are in process of moving to sites which often lie outside the conurbations' boundaries a large negative growth component tends to appear. Correspondingly, large positive growth components are often found in the surrounding areas (most notably, the outer metropolitan, and some of the outer South Eastern subregions), where the structures may not be particularly heavily weighted as yet with nationally fast growing industries.

The question arises whether similar influences are important at the regional level, with which we are more particularly concerned. We have detailed knowledge for the years since 1945 of the movements of manufacturing industry, in the forms both of migrations of establishments to new sites and of the more common development of branches at some distance from the 'parent' establishments of the firms responsible. How far do these known movements account for the tendencies of industries to grow at different rates in different regions? If we credit growth of employment in new establishments that somehow take their origin from another region to that region of origin, do we come nearer to finding uniform growth tendencies in different parts of the country, subject only to interregional differences of structure and inter-industry differences of expansion in demand for labour?

At this regional level of analysis, the answer is very much in the negative. First, the only two regions that have directly provided more employment growth elsewhere by outward 'moves' originating in them than they have gained from inward 'moves' originating elsewhere are the West Midlands and South East England. Both of these, though our analysis attributes their good fortune more to structure than to growth, show favourable growth components for the period 1953–66 as a whole. Most regions with large net inflows of 'moves' on the other hand – Scotland, Wales, the North West and the North – show adverse growth components. The net movement of manufacturing industry has tended to mitigate rather than to intensify interregional differences in growth rates abstracted from the direct effects of industrial structure.

Secondly, the direct effects of industrial movement are small in scale in comparison with interregional differences in the growth components of total increase of employment. In the period 1953–66, net 'moves' of manufacturing industry may be held, on a very crude interpretation, to have contributed growths of about 2 per cent in employment in each of the five regions, Scotland, Wales, the North, the North West and the South West, and (supposing that factor supplies would have allowed substantially faster growth there than actually occurred) to have diverted elsewhere a potential 2 per cent growth of the West Midlands and a 1 per cent growth of South East England. An allowance for multiplier effects would less than double these hypothetical gains and losses. The favourable growth component for the East Midlands and the unfavourable ones for Scotland and the North West are several times as large as the contributions of industrial movement so calculated, quite apart from the fact that the contributions work in the wrong direction to account for them in the latter two cases. We shall return to the role of industrial movement in another connection in a later chapter; here we need only note that it looks more like a product or a mitigation of interregional growth differences than a cause of them.

A RECAPITULATION

The results of this survey of growth by region and industry since 1921 and, more intensively, since 1953 should now be compared with the theoretical presumptions that we formulated as a result of the discussion in chapter 4. First, we suggested that structural effects were likely to be quite important in bringing about divergences of regional fortunes, because the possession of industries doing better or worse than others for general reasons of demand or technology seemed most likely to introduce an element analogous to differences in the technical improvement terms which are so powerful in single-product models. That expectation seems to have been at least partly confirmed for the various periods since 1921 that we have examined, subject to some inevitable ambiguities in the concept of structural effects. On the simpler interpretations of them, systematic structural effects seem to have been as important as, or more important than, systematic tendencies for particular regions to do well or badly in all industries together.

Secondly, arguing from the substantial immobility of factors between regions in the short run, we suggested that structural differences would be likely to give rise to countervailing differences in systematic growth components – possession of a high proportion of nationally fast growing industries would produce a factor shortage that would tend to limit all the industry growth rates in that region. Of this we have found no trace except in the period since 1960, when policy may have had more responsibility for it than market forces. It may be concluded, therefore, that the substantial degree of factor mobility between regions, coupled perhaps with some positive inter-industry effects, must have been just about strong enough to offset the effects of the interregional differences in factor scarcity that structural differences might be expected to produce.

Thirdly, we considered the significance of the 'third term' that emerges from a standardisation analysis of growth, the term measuring the extent to which a region's superiority in growth is due to its specialising on industries that do rather better in it than they do elsewhere. On the tacit assumption that such a term would prove to be positive, we discussed its possible interpretations in terms of the progressive pursuit of comparative advantage, economies of scale and various self-sustaining dynamic processes.

Finally, we suggested on theoretical grounds the related and partly contradictory proposition that the percentage changes in employment, both of growing and of declining industries, were likely to be bigger where these industries employed small proportions of the regional labour force than when they employed large ones. That the part of this proposition that relates to growing industries is generally true we have abundantly confirmed, but there is little evidence in favour of the supposition that rate of decline is fastest where the industry bulks smallest in relation to others. The systematic tendency is clearly towards industries growing fastest where there is least of them, both in relation to other employment in the region and in relation to their own total employment in the country as a whole. And this, too, increased from the 1950s to the 1960s. We have so far no empirical evidence for economies of specialisation, or of scale.

CHAPTER 7

DIVERSIFICATION, CONCENTRATION AND LOCATION

In this chapter, we shall try to draw together what evidence we have bearing on economies of regional concentration of particular industries and industry as a whole, and to take up the thorny question, already raised in chapter 1, of the general advantages and disadvantages of various degrees of concentration or dispersion of the industry and population of the country taken together. Perhaps one should preface this discussion by repeating the acknowledgement, also made in chapter 1, that for some activities – the primary industries, smelting, petroleum refining, electricity generation, and in a smaller degree shipbuilding, for instance – particular requirements as to physical environment are still paramount over the proximity or remoteness of other industry and population in general. We shall not discuss here the economic geography of these industries. Important though they are in many ways, their part in determining the location of employment as a whole is now relatively small.

DIVERSIFICATION AND CONCENTRATION

It may be best to start with the facts about recent changes in diversification and concentration approached by a rather more familiar route than that of the last chapter. The simplest means of measurement that lie to hand are the coefficients of specialisation of the regions and the coefficients of localisation of the industries.[1] The former (which we have already met in our descriptive survey of the regional economies in chapter 2) have been calculated for 1953 and 1966, and the results are given in table 7.1, which shows a reduction in specialisation in every region. It is plain that some part of this reduction comes from the relative decline of the old nineteenth-century industries, which were (and still are) very highly localised.

[1] The coefficient of specialisation of region r can best be represented as $\frac{1}{2}\Sigma_i|(e_{ir}/e_r)-(e_i/e)|$ and the coefficient of localisation of industry i as $\frac{1}{2}\Sigma_r|(e_{ir}/e_i)-(e_r/e)|$, where e_{ir} is employment in industry i in region r, e_r total employment in region r, e_i total employment in industry i and e total employment in the country. The coefficient of specialisation is (as explained in chapter 2) the minimum percentage of the labour force in the region in question that would have to be shifted between industries to yield an industrial composition like that of the country; the coefficient of localisation of an industry is, correspondingly, the minimum proportion of its employees that would have to be shifted between regions to give them the same interregional distribution as the whole national labour force.

Table 7.1. *Coefficients of specialisation by region, 1953 and 1966*

Percentages

	1953 Actual (1)	1966 Expected^a (2)	1966 Actual (3)	Signs of differences (2)–(1)	(3)–(1)	(3)–(2)
North	17·17	13·17	13·43	−	−	+
Yorks. and Humberside	14·49	12·40	12·86	−	−	+
North West	12·47	10·34	10·05	−	−	−
East Midlands	17·31	13·66	14·70	−	−	+
West Midlands	23·84	23·83	19·75	−	−	−
South East England	11·77	9·58	9·56	−	−	−
South West	16·59	15·38	12·44	−	−	−
Wales	19·29	17·01	16·74	−	−	−
Scotland	10·13	9·74	9·64	−	−	−

SOURCE: NIESR estimates.

^a The value expected for 1966 if each industry grew between 1953 and 1966 at its national average rate.

One may, therefore, next calculate what would have happened to the coefficients of specialisation by 1966 if each industry had grown in each region at its national rate – that is to say, what changes in specialisation would have come about purely by virtue of the initial interregional distribution of industries and their different national rates of growth or decline, without change in the interregional distribution of any particular industry. Table 7.1 shows that these hypothetical changes would have reduced the specialisation of every region, though in the West Midlands only marginally. It is plain, however, that in the majority of cases the actual reduction in specialisation was greater than could have been accounted for by the hypothetical changes. The exceptions are the North, Yorkshire and the East Midlands, where actual diversification fell short of that to be 'expected'. The remaining regions changed their *shares* of the various industries in ways that diminished their specialisations – reduced their percentages of the national total of these industries that were over-represented in them, or increased their percentages of those that were under-represented, or did both of these things. The general conclusion is that the national relative decline of industries initially highly localised explains much, indeed most, of the reduction in specialisation of regions, but not all of it.

The tendency towards diversification, even beyond that implied by the relative decline nationally of the more localised industries and the relative growth of the less localised, was strongest in the West Midlands and the South West. Elsewhere it was relatively slight, though still notable also in the North West and Wales. Some contributors to the result are obvious – for instance, the diffusion in these years of the motor vehicle industry from the West Midlands, the rapid growth of manufacturing industries from small beginnings in Wales and the South West, and the North West's declining national share of the textile group of industries – but a detailed scrutiny would be required to fill out the picture. Some help can be got by looking at changes in the coefficients of localisation of the separate Industrial Orders – the changes in the proportions of each Order's employees who would have to change their region to make the interregional distribution of the Order's employment similar to that of total employment. These changes for the period 1953–66 are shown in table 7.2.

It will be seen that the industries of declining localisation are well in the majority; they include all the service Orders except transport, as well as a majority of the manufacturing Orders. The only industry-groups that showed increasing localisation were mining (mainly through the relative decline of the smaller coalfields), the capital-intensive industries with a trend towards larger individual plants (metal manufacture, chemicals, some of the food and drink trades), clothing and, as already mentioned, transport – the last largely, no doubt, because of the closure of railway workshops. Sixteen out of the twenty-three Orders showed a reduction of localisation, with another (public administration) showing no change.

There is again a complication, however, in as much as if different industries grow at different rates this in itself will bring about a change in coefficients of localisation, even though each single industry grows at the same rate everywhere. The distribution of each industry between regions will, of course, remain constant in these circumstances, but total employment will grow most in the regions best endowed with rapidly growing industries. *Ceteris paribus*, these industries therefore tend to become distributed more nearly like industry as a whole; their coefficients of localisation tend to fall, while those of relatively declining industries tend to increase.

The changes in the coefficients that would have taken place between 1953 and 1966 if each industry had grown at its national rate in all regions are shown in table 7.2, column (2), which illustrates this general tendency. In particular, of the industries that would have become more concentrated in the hypothetical circumstances just described, all but two (agriculture and transport) were growing ones. What is more interesting, however, is how geographical concentration of industries changed in relation to this 'expectation' based upon an assumption of equal growth everywhere. It will be seen from the table that in

Table 7.2. *Coefficients of localisation by industry, 1953 and 1966*

Percentages

	1953 Actual (1)	1966 Expected[a] (2)	1966 Actual (3)	Signs of differences (2)–(1)	Signs of differences (3)–(1)	Signs of differences (3)–(2)	National growth rate 1953–66
Agriculture, forestry and fishing	14·29	13·42	14·06	−	−	+	−36·6
Mining and quarrying	43·95	47·28	45·94	+	+	−	−34·6
Manufacturing							
Food, drink, tobacco	5·59	6·42	8·75	+	+	+	+10·5
Chemicals, etc.	13·25	14·01	15·64	+	+	+	+12·6
Metal manufacturing	37·63	38·90	39·90	+	+	+	+9·2
Engineering and metal goods	9·00	8·89	8·21	−	−	−	+33·8
Shipbuilding	35·51	36·27	35·33	+	−	−	−29·3
Vehicles	18·55	18·62	17·81	+	−	−	+9·4
Textiles	47·31	48·51	45·82	+	−	−	−21·6
Leather and fur	7·06	7·90	6·91	+	−	−	−17·1
Clothing and footwear	16·32	17·30	16·88	+	+	−	−11·4
Bricks, pottery, glass	19·27	19·35	16·73	+	−	−	+5·1
Timber and furniture	9·67	8·44	9·37	−	−	+	+3·0
Paper, printing, publishing	15·92	14·88	15·18	−	−	+	+29·6
Other	16·88	15·34	12·73	−	−	−	+37·2
Construction	6·13	5·45	4·88	−	−	−	+27·3
Gas, electricity, water	6·20	4·96	3·88	−	−	−	+13·4
Transport and communication	6·25	5·52	7·01	−	+	+	−7·7
Distribution	6·34	5·10	4·52	−	−	−	+26·3
Insurance, banking and finance	21·81	20·35	20·26	−	−	−	+44·1
Professional and scientific services	7·58	6·51	4·99	−	−	−	+56·7
Miscellaneous services	11·73	10·27	10·74	−	−	+	+12·4
Public administration and defence	9·84	8·60	9·84	−	0	+	+6·2

SOURCE: NIESR estimates.

[a] The value expected for 1966 if each industry grew between 1953 and 1966 at its national average rate.

fourteen out of the twenty-three Industrial Orders, the fall in localisation was greater or the increase smaller than 'expected'.

The exceptions – those in which interregional growth-rate differences were such as to promote greater concentration – were a mixed bunch: agriculture and transport among the declining industries; among the growing ones, the relatively capital-intensive, large-plant food, chemical and metal-manufacturing groups, also timber and the slower growing 'miscellaneous services' and public administration categories. The Orders that decreased their concentration most markedly in relation to expectation were the miscellaneous 'other manufactures', textiles, bricks, pottery and glass, professional and scientific services, mining, public utilities, leather and shipbuilding – a fine assortment of growing and declining industries. There is no general systematic tendency for increasing concentration to go with growth, or the reverse, after one has eliminated the automatic negative connection between the two that comes from the way in which concentration is measured. The fastest growing industries all showed increasing geographical dispersion, but so did a majority of the most rapidly declining ones. Increasing localisation seems to have been associated, on balance, with industries in the middle range showing moderate growth or slight decline of employment in relation to the national average.

INDUSTRIAL ADVANTAGES OF SCALE

On the face of it these analyses of changes in the distribution of industry do not go far towards suggesting either a progressive realisation of regional specialisations based upon comparative advantage, or progressive realisation of economies of scale internal to Orders and regions. So far as scale economies are concerned one can check another hypothesis, namely that productivity is benefited by aggregation even if employment growth is not. As always outside the textbook cases of perfectly homogeneous physical outputs, we have to measure productivity by value of net output per head. It is an imperfect measure in so far as markets both for labour and for goods are imperfect, and values of inputs and outputs therefore vary between regions to some extent independently of the corresponding physical quantities. But it is the best we can manage.

If this is accepted, one can test the hypothetical relationship between output per head and aggregation in a number of different versions. First, one can test whether *growth* of output per head is associated with size of aggregation, or whether its *level* is. Positive association of growth of output per head with size of aggregation would suggest that investment is drawn to the large aggregations of an industry, or that they provide an atmosphere in which the progressive improvement of technology, or application of improved technology, can go on better than elsewhere. It would suggest a somewhat unstable pattern of growth, in which large aggregations would presumably have some tendency to grow faster than small ones, despite our failure so far to find direct evidence for this in terms of employment.

Association of higher levels of output per head with large aggregations is perhaps *a priori* more probable; it might mean that there are realised productive advantages, mainly external to the establishment, that flow from location in a large aggregation of the relevant industry.

The definition or recognition of an aggregation presents problems. On the whole, however, the British regions are sufficiently compact for an establishment in any one to be regarded as fairly near to most of the others within it, in as much as even those regions that are geographically extensive tend to have their manufacturing industry concentrated near to an urban belt or core. One is therefore justified in most (though not in all) cases in taking the size of an industry in its own region as a rough indicator of the aggregation of the industry to which the typical establishment has fairly close access. On the same broad grounds, one is probably justified in taking the regional assemblage of all manufacturing industry, or of any specified collection of industries or trades, as indicating the size of the assemblage of the relevant kinds of industry to which the typical establishment of any kind in the region has most convenient access.

What do tests of the various hypotheses that have just been mentioned show? So far as rate of increase of net output per head is concerned, a calculation from the 1948 and 1954 Censuses of Production shows for that period no general association of a large regional assemblage of a particular industry with a high growth rate of *per capita* output.[1] Indeed the correlation is most frequently negative, though nonsignificant. Only for the residual order 'other manufacturing industries' is it significant, but negative. A more generalised test is to calculate the correlation across regions between the unweighted averages of the rates of increase in *per capita* outputs in the separate manufacturing industries, and the totals of manufacturing employment in these regions; this should show whether there is a tendency for manufacturing industry in general to improve its output per head more in the large aggregations, with scope for economies of scale external to the industry as well as to the establishment, than in small ones with less apparent scope for this. No significant correlation emerges.

The question in terms of level of output per head rather than of change in it is, however, as we have noted, perhaps *a priori* the more satisfying, though the most natural expectation is that, if superior output per head goes with superior aggregation so should superior growth of employment, which we have seen not to be the case. However, the relations of an industry's level of output per head in a region to a number of different variables besides the amount of the industry situated in that region can best be investigated at the same time. The method

[1] Board of Trade, *Final Report on the Census of Production for 1948* and *Report on the Census of Production for 1954*, London, HMSO, 1951–2 and 1960–3. No data on net output by Minimum List Heading and region were published from the 1958 Census, and regional tables from the 1963 Census were published only in 1970 after the work described in the following paragraphs had been completed. Hence the reliance on data from as long ago as 1948 and 1954.

we have adopted is as follows. Within each 'trade' (Minimum List Heading) of the Census of Production, we expressed the average output per head as an index based on the unweighted average of the outputs in all regions. The independent variables were similarly expressed. Thus it was possible to combine into a single equation the data on any number of trades; either all the trades in an Industrial Order, for instance, or all the trades covered by the Census. The independent variables introduced were the proportion of the national employment in the trade that was situated in the region concerned (a measure of the scope for regional 'scale' economies external to the establishment but within the trade), the average employment per establishment in the trade in the region (a measure of the scope for internal economies of scale), and a number of regional dummy variables, intended to test whether, after allowing for effects of scale, particular regions possessed general advantages or disadvantages of productivity in the combination of trades under review. Calculations of this kind were made with the data from both the 1948 and 1954 Censuses, with broadly similar results. It will be simplest to describe those of 1954; they are shown in tables 7.3 and 7.4.

First, differences between regions in average plant-size seem rarely to have significant effects on productivity. Such effects were found for chemicals, where they were positive, and for leather and fur, where they were negative (that is small plants did better). There were also positive effects when all the trades in the Census were considered together in one equation. In clothing the effects of plant-size appeared significantly negative when no regional dummies were included, but this appearance was seemingly due to the prevalence of small establishments and high productivity in the South East.

Second, the amount of the trade in the region (its scope for external economies) was positively significant in clothing, in leather and fur, and in wood and cork, as well as in all trades taken together.

Third, the only cases where the dummy variables for particular regions attained anything above the 5 per cent level of significance for the trades in a single Industrial Order were clothing, where (as already mentioned) the South East emerged with significantly high productivity, and wood and cork, where the Midlands regions appeared rather less but still definitely pre-eminent. For all trades together however, a number of regions (or conurbations) showed significant variations. The London conurbation and the West Midland conurbation (both considered separately from the remainder of their regions), the South, the East and the North Midlands stood out above the rest.

These results are not surprising in anything positive that they assert, but their positive assertions are rather meagre. The variables of chief

Table 7.3. *Levels of net output per head (Industrial Orders) explained by scale, size of plant and region, 1954*

	R^2	Constant	Scale (X_1)	Plant-size (X_2)	Regional dummies E, S, LSE GLC (X_3)	Regional dummies N, Sc, Wa. (X_4)	Regional dummies NM, (W)M (X_5)	No. of observations	Significant coefficients
Non-metalliferous mining products	0·133	99·874	−0·031 (0·80)	0·041 (1·04)	2·499 (0·49)	−4·868 (0·93)	−2·260 (0·43)	35	None
Chemicals etc.	0·131	84·256	0·021 (0·54)	0·142 (2·14)	−0·258 (0·03)	3·198 (0·30)	−5·549 (0·52)	71	X_2 (5)
Metal manufactures	0·118	93·231	−0·029 (0·90)	0·081 (1·26)	1·498 (0·19)	−1·592 (0·19)	5·790 (0·77)	30	None
Shipbuilding	0·506	112·657	−0·029 (0·58)	−0·087 (1·65)	−6·315 (0·94)	5·614 (0·69)	..	15	None
Engineering	0·052	96·915	0·012 (0·95)	−0·005 (0·20)	2·731 (0·90)	0·088 (0·02)	5·911 (1·72)	102	None
Vehicles	0·118	89·636	0·003 (0·13)	0·071 (1·60)	2·601 (0·50)	1·560 (0·27)	6·510 (1·16)	53	None
Metal goods	0·068	98·086	0·002 (0·11)	0·006 (0·12)	3·517 (0·70)	−4·908 (0·92)	4·488 (0·86)	77	None
Precision instruments	0·343	99·325	0·040 (1·36)	−0·112 (1·44)	18·054 (1·90)	−0·238 (0·02)	..	24	None
Textiles	0·135	92·519	0·008 (0·39)	0·113 (1·52)	−8·941 (1·32)	−11·676 (1·55)	4·415 (0·60)	79	None
Leather and fur	0·511	117·894	0·102 (4·19)	−0·255 (2·26)	2·921 (0·37)	−10·995 (1·29)	−6·366 (0·59)	33	X_1, X_2 (0·1) (5)
Clothing	0·518	90·293	0·039 (2·67)	−0·029 (0·82)	19·515 (4·32)	−1·456 (0·28)	8·477 (1·66)	47	X_1, X_3 (1) (0·1)
Food, drink, tobacco	0·087	85·916	0·047 (1·56)	0·055 (1·28)	5·844 (0·97)	−1·377 (0·21)	8·723 (1·26)	148	None
Wood and cork manufactures	0·302	86·380	0·074 (4·03)	−0·006 (0·12)	8·220 (1·64)	2·417 (0·43)	13·837 (2·42)	62	X_1, X_5 (0·1) (2)
Paper and printing	0·247	89·914	0·007 (0·34)	0·069 (1·35)	10·488 (1·53)	−8·830 (1·18)	1·493 (0·20)	61	None
Other manufacturing	0·204	91·746	−0·002 (0·10)	0·085 (1·61)	4·731 (0·63)	−13·713 (1·61)	1·446 (0·18)	53	None

SOURCE: NIESR estimates from Census of Production, 1954.

Notes: (i) The dependent variables, net output per head, are expressed as indices, with the unweighted national average for the trade = 100.

(ii) Figures in brackets under coefficients are t-values; those in the last column are significance levels.

Table 7.4. *Levels of net output per head (all census trades) explained by scale, size of plant and region, 1954*

	Coefficient	t-value
Scale (% of trade's national employment in region)	0·015	2·06
Plant-size (average in region as % of average for trade)	0·043	3·17
Regional dummies		
North	−1·58	0·49
E & W Ridings	2·76	0·89
North West	3·32	1·04
North Midlands	7·91	2·50
WM conurbation	7·04	2·24
Rest of (W) Midlands	5·70	1·70
East	6·27	2·00
Greater London	16·06	4·89
Rest of London & SE	4·86	1·36
South	8·33	2·57
South West	0·16	0·05
Scotland	−1·65	0·54
Constant	89·58	

SOURCE: NIESR estimates from Census of Production, 1954.

Notes: (i) Equation based on 890 observations. $R^2 = 0·111$.
(ii) Dummy for Wales is zero by definition.

interest for regional economics are those denoting external economies of scale, and specific, so far unidentified, sources of general superiority or inferiority in particular regions. So far as the former is concerned one can readily believe that older industries predominantly with small establishments, such as clothing, leather and fur, and wood and cork, should show external economies of scale, but would one not expect some evidence of such economies in some other fields in which inter-establishment division of function is carried far, such as engineering, vehicles, metal goods, precision instruments and textiles?

The amount of the trade in the region appears as a positive variable in the equation in all of these cases. In vehicles and metal goods it never comes near to significance, but in the rest it seems to be trying (if the matter may be put anthropomorphically). Indeed, in the precision instrument equation it misses the mark only because high productivity is more closely associated with the South Eastern regions than with agglomeration as such. It is, in any case, probable that the equations are not formulated in the best way for bringing out the benefits of an industrial complex; high productivity in a particular engineering trade is perhaps more likely to be associated with an agglomeration of engineering or other metalworking trades in general than with a large representation of the trade itself in particular. In our formulation the near significance of a positive dummy variable for the South Eastern regions in the case of precision instruments, of the Midlands in the case of vehicles and engineering, of Yorkshire and Lancashire in that of textiles, gives some support to this. Considering the basic imperfection of output per head as a proxy for productivity, and the hazards that arise from the industrial classification – which by no means guarantees that we are comparing like with like – it is striking that some evidence for economies of aggregation should emerge, even though only patchily and not very strongly. (The *average* effect over all manufacturing is that having an extra 10 per cent of a trade's national employment in a region raises its output per head in that region by a seventh of 1 per cent.)

The concept of productivity used in this connection however – *value* of net output per occupied person in the industry in question – requires further scrutiny; this point is of greater importance when one comes to look at the systematic differences between regions that the values of the significant dummy variables suggest. High productivity in this sense may mean dear products associated with either high profit rates, or dear labour, or both. Or it may mean greater capital-intensity than elsewhere, presumably prompted by dearer labour and/or cheaper or more available capital, and resulting in products that may be competitively priced. Or, thirdly, it may spring from some locational advantage, probably reducible to low costs of transport and communication, or perhaps to low site costs, which would permit high earnings and/or high profits per employee to be reconciled with competitively priced products.

None of these possibilities can be entirely ruled out. At least some of the goods produced in regions showing high productivity of labour according to our calculations may be dearer than they would be if produced in other regions – or dearer than similar goods actually produced in other regions – either because their markets are protected by transport costs, or because of market imperfections and entrepreneurial inertia of one sort or another. On the other hand, it is possible to imagine a region which, because of low internal transport costs connected with its production, or because the quality of its labour and/or its management is especially high, has an absolute advantage over other regions in producing practically everything, and enjoys higher physical productivity and higher factor rewards. But what is more likely is a larger margin of comparative advantage in the things the region exports than other regions enjoy in their production for sale outside. This will tend to mean high prices of the less interregionally mobile factors in the region concerned (especially perhaps of labour), and a generally high productivity of labour measured in value terms. The most likely source of a wide margin of comparative advantage for a region's exports in the short run is simply that, in its specialisation, it is 'on to a good thing'; it has a structure which, for the time being, is favourable.

We cannot check all these possibilities from hard data. It is clear that there is a strong positive correlation between our regional dummies (indicating general productivity differences in value terms) and earnings differences, even though reliable regional data on earnings do not begin until some years after 1954, the date of the Census of Production with which we have worked. The 'productivity dummy variable' for London and the South East (compounded from the two relevant ones in our table) indicated a general advantage there of about 9 per cent over an average for Scotland, Wales, the North, the North West, the South West and Yorkshire. London and the South East's advantage over them in average male manual earnings, when the statistics started a few years later, was of the same order of magnitude. There can be no doubt that London and the South East, along with the rest of South East England, and at least the (West) Midlands, which in some degree shared this productivity advantage, were favoured by structure, and perhaps by location and other factors bearing on competitiveness. They were the regions of highest pressure of labour demand. It is not necessary to suppose that they were better than other regions at everything, but they undoubtedly enjoyed advantages in relation to their 'interregional goods', which meant labour shortage, high wages, possibly high capital-intensity in the development of industries already there – perhaps even to some extent choice of capital-intensive industries, though that was largely controlled by other considerations. All these factors helped to raise productivity measured in value terms throughout their range of production.

Another possible source of differences in the equilibrium value of output per head is difference in the cost of living of labour. To some extent this might arise from differences in physical productivity in the basic industries, just as superior national productivity in the manufacture of international goods (in the United States for instance) makes for a high price level of personal services in the country concerned, due to high labour costs from competition with manufacturing without as great a superiority of labour productivity as manufacturing enjoys. But some dearness of living costs can arise from physical and economic conditions of life, most notably in the conurbations – extra costs of travel to work and high prices for residential accommodation. In London, as we have seen in chapter 3, these probably raise the consumers' price index some 10 per cent above the national average, and they arise only very partially from any extra physical productivity that London enjoys, trade by trade, over the rest of the country. The extra travel to work costs stem mainly from the sheer size of the conurbation together with the traffic congestion it generates; the high accommodation costs stem also in part from size, and in part from the competition for housing of an unusually large proportion of highly paid workers in central service occupations, as well as of rentiers who are attracted by metropolitan amenities. The flight of manufacturing industries from the conurbations illustrates the fact that the high value of output per head recorded in them is a matter more of necessity than of virtue. We shall return to these considerations of conurbation-size at the end of this chapter.

COMPARATIVE ADVANTAGE

This evidence tells us something (though less than one would wish) about advantages of agglomeration; something about absolute regional advantage, though that perhaps turns out to be mainly advantage in the region's main exporting industries, including that of having chosen the right ones. Perhaps this is the place to turn aside and see whether similar evidence tells us anything about a tendency of regions to specialise according to comparative advantage, or (what may be hard to distinguish from this) a tendency to realise comparative advantage in the industries on which they happen to have specialised.

In so far as one is looking for a tendency either to realise *progressively increasing* comparative advantage, or gradually, by the pattern of growth, to take advantage of *potential* comparative advantages not already grasped, one is, of course, really looking for signs of increasing regional specialisation; and that, as we have seen, has been at a discount in recent years, even after one has made allowance for the relative decline of the industries in which regional specialisation had been most fully realised. There is probably not much more to be found by continuing this search, except perhaps in much finer detail than would be possible or appropriate here.

What may still be worth looking for is evidence that the industrial structure of regions at a given time – a census date – shows some sign of bias towards those industries in which their output per head is higher in comparison with other industries than is the case in other regions. More specifically, one can seek to account for the bias of an industry's distribution towards a particular region in terms of the extent to which its output per head there remains high, after it has been deflated both for the extent to which that industry has a high output per head in all regions and the extent to which the region in question has a high output per head in all industries. The convenient measure of 'bias' towards a region is the employment location quotient – the share which the

Table 7.5. *Industrial structure and comparative advantage,*[a] *1954*

	Constant	Regression coefficient	R^2	t-value	No. of observations	Significance level
North	−0·3516	5·4959	0·1588	3·34	61	0·2
E & W Ridings	−0·0476	2·0647	0·0488	1·97	78	6·0
North West	−0·1257	3·1765	0·1406	3·50	77	0·1
North Midlands	0·0404	1·5325	0·0172	1·07	68	> 25·0
(West) Midlands	0·0524	1·0090	0·0377	1·71	77	10·0
East	0·0766	1·3358	0·0249	1·31	69	15·0
London & SE	0·1272	0·6387	0·0152	1·15	87	25·0
South	0·0207	1·7251	0·0489	1·73	60	10·0
South West	−0·0988	2·9723	0·0672	2·04	60	5·0
Wales	−0·0529	2·4296	0·1354	3·01	60	1·0
Scotland	0·0196	1·5803	0·0332	1·69	85	10·0

SOURCE: NIESR estimates from Census of Production, 1954.

[a] Regression equations for location quotients on relative net output per head for all manufacturing industries at Minimum List Heading level.

industry claims of total employment in the region divided by the share that it claims of total employment in the country as a whole. These quotients can be correlated with the corresponding indices of output per head divided by indices expressing the (unweighted) average levels of output per head for the relevant industry across all regions, and for the relevant region across all industries.[1]

If this is done at Minimum List Heading level from the 1954 Census of Production, a modest, but varying, amount of success is achieved (table 7.5). In no region does comparative advantage so expressed explain much of the industrial structure – that is to say, the variance of the industrial location quotients – but in three regions it explains more than 13 per cent of it, and in eight the correlation is, at all events, significant at better than 10 per cent level. The North West, the North and Wales turn out to show the closest relationships, the North Midlands and London and the South East the poorest, with the Eastern region and the (West) Midlands also among the less significant. The regression coefficients, which show the sensitivity of regional concentration to its comparative advantage in the region, tell much the same story.

This points the contrast between static virtue and expansionary opportunism. It is the regions with the remains of specialisation in old,

[1] The location quotient for industry i in region r is $(e_{ir}.e)/(e_r.e_i)$, and the measure of comparative advantage, in terms of output per head, $(p_{ir}.\bar{p})/(\bar{p}_r.\bar{p}_i)$, where the e's denote employment, the p's net output per head and the bars unweighted averages.

declining industries that seem nearest to optimality on criteria that take no account of prospective change of demand or of economies of scale. However modest is the evidence that we may have found of the latter complication, it may be presumed, and has indeed been shown to exist in some degree, while the existence of trends in demand is all too obvious. In evaluating regional industrial structures, outputs per head should presumably not be assessed on the prices and physical productivities of the moment, especially if the prices are protected by devices that one would not expect to persist for ever as was the case of coal in the relevant period. One should use values that reflect both the physical effects (if any) of expected changes of scale and the discounted present value of expected prices. This seems to point once again to the part played by relative changes in demand, in conjunction with regional industrial structure, in determining regional fortunes. Let us, however, return from this excursion into the territory of comparative advantage to resume our consideration of locational forces operating on economic activity as a whole.

'POTENTIAL' AND GROWTH

We have seen that most of the individual industries have been dispersing rather than concentrating, and have paid some attention to evidence of the effect of concentration on productivity within industries and on the growth of productivity in manufacturing generally. We have not examined the connection between geographical concentration and growth in economic activity as a whole.

The simplest hypothesis in this connection is that nearness to markets and to other sites of economic activity is always an advantage; that there are economies of scale (external to the establishment), or of proximity and centrality, that can be represented by some device such as an index of 'potential'. This magnitude, loosely analogous to its namesake in gravitational, magnetic or electrostatic theory, can be regarded as an inverse measure of the sum of the transport costs from the place in question to the sites of all the units of production (or income) in the economy. In short it is an index of accessibility. The best known calculations of such an index are those made by Mr Colin Clark.[1]

Superficially, the map of potentials in Great Britain accords with the general impression of variations in prosperity (see chart 7.1). The area

---

[1] Colin Clark, 'Industrial Location and Economic Potential', *Lloyds Bank Review*, no. 82, October 1966, pp. 1–17. Chart 7.1 is based on Mr Clark's map of potential; the regional potentials referred to in the following paragraphs of the text are rough magnitudes derived from this map.

DIVERSIFICATION, CONCENTRATION, LOCATION

Chart 7.1. *'Potential' in Great Britain*

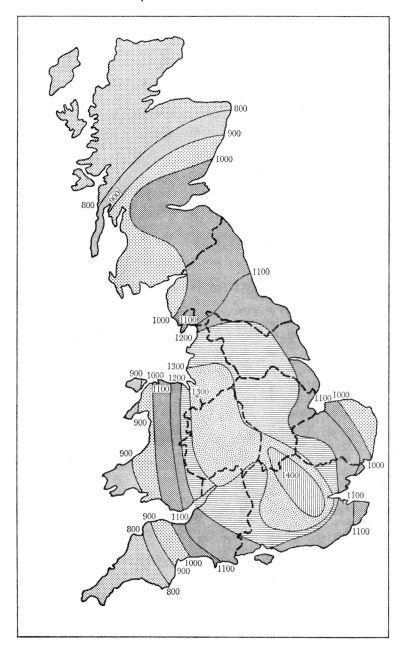

SOURCE: Clark, 'Industrial Location and Economic Potential'.

of highest potential runs from London, through the (West) Midlands, to south Lancashire – the old 'coffin' of the economic geographers – while those of lowest potential are the Highlands, south west Scotland, west Cumberland, west Wales, the South West west of Exeter and the eastern edge of Norfolk. The high-potential areas naturally coincide pretty well with the areas of highest pressure on space (if one is painting with a broad brush and not taking account of highly localised urban congestion elsewhere) and, with one notable reservation, they coincide with the areas of high pressure on labour supply and of high earnings. The reservation concerns south Lancashire, which in prosperity (however measured) and in pressure on labour supply fails markedly to live up to its high potential.

Potential is, however, not well correlated with actual growth in detail. A comparison of the growth rates of total employment in standard subregions from 1961 to 1966 with their estimated potentials yields no relation to all. On inspection one sees the main perverse influences to be the low growth rates of all the conurbation subregions (some of which have very high potential indeed) and the high growth rates of a number of mainly rural subregions of low potential – north eastern East Anglia, the north Wales coast, the two westernmost subregions of the South West, for instance.

Some of this anomaly is associated with the spread of the conurbations beyond their subregional boundaries, but even at regional level (where much of this phenomenon is avoided) correlation between potential and growth of employment is poor. The slow growth of the North West and the fast growth of the South West and East Anglia destroy what without them would be a passable positive relation, with Scotland and the North at one end of the line as the low-potential, low-growth regions, and the South East and the (West) Midlands at the opposite end. This is true whether one considers total employment, employment in primary and secondary industry, or employment in manufacturing alone. East Anglia and the South West, moreover, add emphasis to the anomaly by enjoying rapid growth of employment in their peripheral subregions, where potential is lowest.

There are obviously other important factors affecting growth, notably structure which we considered in the last chapter. It does not seem, however, that the growth components of regional employment growth – the components measuring the extent to which each region's industries in general did better than their counterparts nationally – are well correlated with regional potential, either. If one considers primary and secondary industry, Scotland, the North and Wales still emerge as having low growth components to match their low potential, but the high-potential regions, South East England and the (West) Midlands, had, in fact, relatively low growth components. Their high employment growth was largely accounted for by their structure and the residual components.[1]

One might suppose that the relatively poor growth components of these prosperous regions were due to regional policy, to congestion, or to labour shortage, so that the expansionary pressure generated by their favourable situation was frustrated or diverted into 'moves' to other regions. So far as the 'moves' of manufacturing industry are concerned, their effects can be roughly allowed for. The result of making this allowance, though in the right direction, is, however, far from big enough to produce a significant positive correlation between the part of the growth component due to growth originating in the region and the region's potential. It may be added that the correlation between growth components and potentials of regions was not significantly better in the period of weak regional policy, 1953-9, than in the period of stronger policy, 1961-6. There is nothing here, therefore, to support a suggestion that policy was the main, or perhaps even a major, factor in preventing the regions of highest potential from showing also the highest growth rates industry by industry, though it no doubt played some part in this.

What are we to conclude from the relation of potential to growth? For primary and secondary industry there is no evidence that systematic growth components have been poorer in the regions of low potential than of high. The same is true of total growth excluding systematic composition components. If a rough allowance is made for the effect of 'moves' of manufacturing industry, the adjusted growth (or non-composition) components, which one might call indigenous growth components, still show only a very slight tendency (far from statistically significant) for the four high-potential regions (South East England, the two Midlands regions and the North West) to perform better than the five of lower potential. Perhaps the conclusion is that, as between the existing major industrial concentrations of Great Britain, differences in the average extent to which an establishment in them is accessible to the industry and population of the country as a whole are not very important in promoting or hindering growth, other things being equal. Small and remote industrial areas may be at a disadvantage, but so far as the major ones are concerned, the extra growth at the centre of the United Kingdom economy as compared with its periphery is to be explained largely by differences of structure.

[1] Much the same results are obtained if one plots against potential, not regional growth components, but actual growth minus composition components – i.e. growth components plus the residuals, which largely measure tendencies for the regions in question to specialise on industries that do better in them than elsewhere in the country.

OPTIMAL SIZE OF AGGREGATION

So much for the evidence on the relation between industrial performance and the setting of population and industry in which the establishments in question find themselves. However, we should perhaps return here to the general question of net advantages or disadvantages – to industry and population as a whole – of various sizes of aggregation, and the possibility of a divergence in this matter between what is likely to happen through individuals and firms seeking their own advantage on the one hand, and the optimal arrangements for the general good on the other.

This is a particularly intractable subject, especially through lack of really relevant information and the difficulty of quantifying many of the considerations that arise, even in principle. It will do no harm, however, to set out some basic theory, even if our attempt to give practical content to it afterwards is not very fruitful.

The best approach to the theory of this subject seems to be to think of the ways in which the advantages and the disadvantages separately of living in communities are likely to vary with community size. First the advantages: these may perhaps be thought of as being measured, for the 'average' inhabitant, as the advantage he enjoys through living in communities of the sizes we shall consider, in comparison with those which he would enjoy in (say) a small village taken as the standard comparison. (To compare him with a hermit or with Robinson Crusoe would smell too much of the textbook.)

The sort of way in which one would expect advantage so measured to vary with community size is shown in chart 7.2. Amenities such as shops, public transport connections with elsewhere, libraries, social and cultural meeting places, restaurants, entertainments, probability of meeting people with similar interests and so on will all increase with size of community. We must also add to the advantages of living in an aggregation those that accrue through the pay packet. If external economies make labour more efficient as the aggregation gets bigger, the wage level may be expected to rise. The generality of goods with considerable transport costs may be cheaper in a bigger place, because an increasing number of them will come from points of production or of wholesale distribution that are close at hand. But all the advantages will pretty certainly grow at a decreasing rate, after a point at least.

Disadvantages of living in large communities consist of the inability of the representative inhabitant to live near to his work (except perhaps at high rent cost), of the tendency of traffic congestion to increase with town size (though this factor is heavily dependent on town form and standard of planning), of greater lack of easy access to open country

Chart 7.2. *Gross benefits of aggregation*

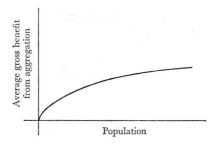

Chart 7.3. *Gross costs of aggregation*

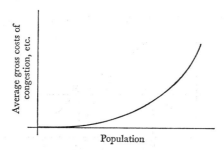

and, with existing standards of planning, to open space of any kind, and of generally higher levels of noise and air pollution than in smaller centres. It is not easy to judge whether the sum of these disadvantages increases at an increasing or a decreasing rate with rise of population when community size is already high, though one would perhaps expect any levelling-off to start only at a very high population level. With small communities too, one may guess that the sum of disadvantages increases only very slowly with rise of population, so that the curve is perhaps rather like that shown in chart 7.3. This shape, however, is highly speculative, and the only thing one can be reasonably sure of is that the curve rises throughout the whole of the range with which one is in practice concerned.

Chart 7.4 shows the net advantage to the representative inhabitant of living in communities of various sizes in comparison with village life; it is simply derived by subtracting the vertical ordinate of chart 7.3 from that of chart 7.2. The figure also shows the curve of marginal net advantage conferred on the community by the addition to it of one further inhabitant. This, of course, cuts the average net advantage curve at its maximum point; where marginal equals average the average is

Chart 7.4. *Net benefits of a single aggregation*

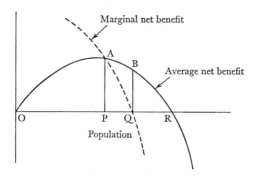

Chart 7.5. *Maximising net benefits of a single aggregation*

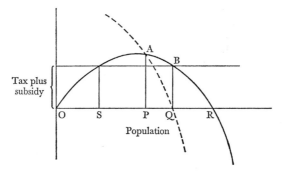

unchanged by the addition of the marginal unit. The marginal net benefit becomes negative at considerably lower population levels than is the case with average net benefit.

The simplest case to discuss is a rural territory with one town the growth of which does not alter the size of the rural population, or at least does not alter the amenities of rural life significantly. In this case, it is plain that 'representative inhabitants' would find a net advantage in going to town until the latter's population was OR and the net advantage of living in town thus the same as that of living in villages. But this population level is well beyond that, OP, at which extra inhabitants begin to lower the average level of benefit of all the inhabitants of the town. It is also beyond the level, OQ, at which an extra inhabitant coming from the 'village' level of welfare would just cease to raise the total benefit, or, in other words, where the improvement QB in his own benefit obtained by moving into town is just offset by the consequential lowering of benefit for all the other townspeople.

In the circumstances described OQ will presumably be the optimal population of the town; it maximises the benefit of townsmen and villagers taken together. The most obvious way of promoting this state of affairs is to impose a tax on townsmen and give the proceeds in subsidy (or remission of other taxation) to villagers to such an extent that the burden on a townsman plus the benefit to a villager equals BQ. Measuring net benefit from the datum-level of villagers, the situation will then be that shown in chart 7.5. At town population levels above OQ, town life will be less attractive than village life, so that people will leave town. If town population is already between OS and OQ, more people will be attracted by the town's net advantages until the level OQ is reached.

It would, of course, suit the townsmen if the town population could be limited to OP where they enjoy their greatest average advantage, but this would lower the welfare of the community as a whole by depriving PQ villagers of the opportunity to benefit themselves more than they would injure existing townsmen. If the town declared its political independence, it could try to maximise the average net benefit of its citizens by simply controlling immigration – either by quota, or by a tax of AP on immigrants (and perhaps their descendants) only. In mediaeval conditions, with negative natural increase of the town population, such measures could be entirely adequate. Even, however, if the town adopted the more broad-minded policy of letting its population rise to the general optimum level of OQ, measures applied solely to immigrants would involve a loss in comparison with the taxation of all townsmen. The latter measure would secure a better distribution of individuals between town and villages, tending to exclude from town all those (whether originally townsmen or villagers) whose personal preference for town life was weakest (less than the tax plus subsidy), whereas measures applied only to immigrants would leave in town many people whose preference for being there was weaker than the desire of some frustrated would-be immigrants for admission.

The discussion so far has been about a rather remote case in which a single town was opposed to a population in small villages whose welfare is supposed not to vary with changes in the numbers in the town. The more realistic situation is one in which one town is set against another. The easiest case to consider is one where the populations of both towns are stationary except in so far as there is migration between them, so that the growth of one is always at the expense of equal shrinkage in the other.

The situation can be represented as in chart 7.6, where the total population of the country is shown by the length OO', that of town (or conurbation) X being measured to the right from O, and that of

Chart 7.6. *Net advantages of two aggregations (unstable equilibrium – case 1)*

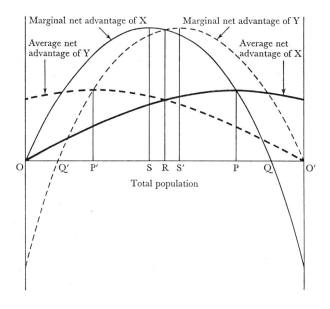

Chart 7.7. *Net advantages of two aggregations (unstable equilibrium – case 2)*

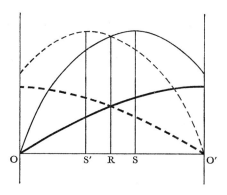

the rival aggregation Y to the left from O'. The vertical ordinate of the thick unbroken line represents the average net advantage of living in X as compared with living in a very small place, and that of the thick broken line the advantage of living in Y, the populations of the two places being measured as just described. The thin lines, unbroken and broken, are the corresponding curves of marginal net advantage accruing to the whole population of X and Y respectively from unit increases in their numbers. We assume for simplicity that the relations between net advantage and size are exactly the same for the two aggregations, so that the diagram is symmetrical about a vertical line through its centre.

It will be plain that if, as in this diagram, the average net benefit curve of X cuts that for Y from below, the point of intersection (where people going from X to Y or Y to X will, on average, experience no difference in benefit) will be a point of unstable equilibrium; whichever conurbation has more population than this point indicates will continue to attract still more. At the same time, since in this diagram the marginal net benefit curve for X cuts that for Y from above, to the right of this point an emigrant from Y to X decreases the total benefit to the two conurbations together (including his own benefit in moving), so does an emigrant from X to Y in population situations to the left of the point of intersection, which accordingly represents the socially optimal distribution. There is a divergence between the outcomes dictated by private benefit and social benefit.

If the total population to be divided between the two aggregations is smaller (OO' shorter as in chart 7.7), the marginal net benefit curve for X may cut that for Y from below, and the point of intersection will represent a minimum point of social benefit; the optimal outcome is for all the population to move into one aggregation or the other, as will indeed happen through the free movement of individuals in search of the highest available private advantage. On the other hand, if the available population is large enough, the average net advantage curve for X will cut that for Y from above (chart 7.8), so that the point of intersection is one of stable equilibrium; people will tend to divide equally between the two aggregations. This will also be the arrangement of greatest social benefit, since the marginal net benefit curve for X also cuts that for Y from above. It is important to note, however, that this outcome – the division of the population between two equal aggregations – can be expected only in the long run, or where the number of nuclei about which population can cluster is somehow limited to two.

A more common situation is that where there is one large aggregation and a number – perhaps a large number – of smaller ones. The simplest case to consider is that where these smaller centres are all of equal size. The average and marginal net benefit curves relating to all these smaller centres together will then resemble those for a single centre, except that their horizontal dimensions will be multiplied by the number of centres, and it is these 'stretched' curves of average and marginal net advantage that are shown plotted to the left from the origin O', and set against the curves for a single centre plotted to the right from origin O, in chart 7.9. It will be seen that the size of the single centre

Chart 7.8. *Net advantages of two aggregations (stable equilibrium)*

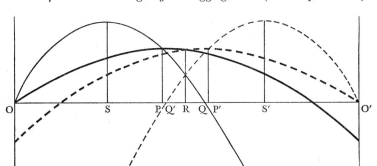

Chart 7.9. *Net advantages of one aggregation and many small centres*

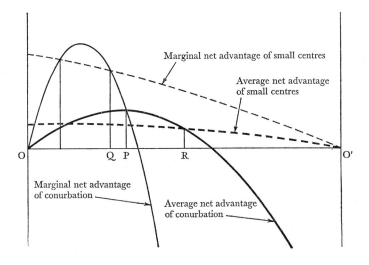

at which average net benefit in it equals that elsewhere is OR – much beyond the optimal size OP for the single centre in isolation, and even further beyond the size OQ which is its optimal size taking account of the interests of the country as a whole.

In the long run, however, it is to be expected that some of the smaller centres will grow at the expense of others, producing centres of more nearly optimal size. A system of centres all of less than optimal size is unstable, because any one that grows bigger than the rest will increase its margin of attractiveness over them and grow at their expense still faster. Centres that become smaller than the rest will, correspondingly, tend to shrink. When, by this process, all centres are of

Chart 7.10. *Net advantages of one aggregation and several others all of optimal size*

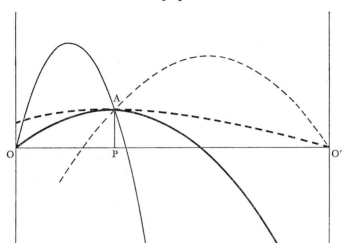

optimal size, the equilibrium is more nearly stable. At least, one can say that if one centre gains at the expense of all (or several) of the others, it is likely to suffer a bigger fall from the equilibrium level of advantage than they do, so that such a gain will be reversed. The general case, where one centre is set off against others, all being of optimal size, is shown in chart 7.10 – the curves plotted to the left from O' again relating to the combination of all centres other than the single one that is selected for representation by the curves plotted to the right from O. The average net benefit curve for the selected centre touches that for the rest combined at their common maximum A, through which both marginal net benefit curves naturally pass also.

But the equilibrium is still not entirely stable. If one centre were to lose to all (or a number) of the others, it would depart further below the equilibrium level of attractiveness than they would, and would thus continue to lose. Since accidents of this kind cannot be ruled out, there seems to be a long-run tendency for systems of communities between which population is mobile to reduce, in our simplified conditions, to the two-community case which we have already examined.[1]

We have so far made the assumption that the net benefit curves for all communities are identical, so that their optimal sizes are the same. This, of course, is not so. First, aggregations with different productive

---

[1] Variations can be worked on this conclusion by assuming various degrees of symmetry between the slopes of the average net benefit curve to left and right of its maximum.

specialisations will enjoy technical economies of scale in production to very different extents, and local shortage of supply of some immovable factor of production will operate to bring decreasing returns to very different extents in different industries and on different sites for the same industry. Second, the tendency of people who like small and large communities respectively to gravitate towards the kinds of community they prefer, or for people in general to prefer what they are used to, may mean that the optimal sizes of large aggregations are increased, those of small aggregations diminished, by virtue of the different tastes of their inhabitants. We must therefore make allowance for the existence of net benefit curves of different shapes.

In so far as these are associated with aggregations that sell different basic products, another consideration enters – the relative prices of these products. Those that can be produced with the greatest economy of factor inputs only in aggregations that are too big or too small for comfort will, in equilibrium, have to be priced high enough to compensate the people concerned for the inconveniences and expenses of big-conurbation living on the one hand or rural isolation on the other, unless these premia exceed the extra cost that would be involved in producing the goods with rather less technical efficiency in a community of a more popular size. But once again full equilibrium would be represented by a situation in which the aggregations, large and small, were all at their respective optimal sizes, with optimal average net benefits all equal – taking account, of course, of the benefits of pay as well as those of environment and amenities. Moreover, it may in this case be a relatively stable equilibrium. Given fixed demand conditions, it will not be easy for portions of (say) an optimal-sized textile complex to be absorbed by a metalworking complex, where they would be deprived of the advantages of the local economies of scale that they previously enjoyed. It is still true, however, that if one textile complex (say) begins to lose population and establishments to a number of others which are already at their optimal sizes, the gainers will begin to feel the disadvantages of being super-optimal in size. This may not mean that they are in any danger of losing establishments to other complexes of a different character, but at least they will be in danger of losing their labour unless they pay it more. The equilibrium of optimal-sized aggregations is still probably rather fragile, even if they differ in function, unless there is only one of each kind.

All this, however, is rather trivial in comparison with the elements introduced into the picture by changes in technology and in the structure of demand. If there were at any time a number of aggregations, some different from others in function, but all of optimal size and presenting equal net advantages (so that there was no tendency to net migration between them), this arrangement would be destroyed by anything that altered the relative market positions of their different products. For some the net benefit curves would be pushed vertically upwards, for others depressed. As is seen from chart 7.5, the effect of this would be to push the former beyond their optimal sizes, and to extinguish the latter, or to diminish them below their optimal sizes in the short run – perhaps to reduce their number in the longer term. Where economies of scale are strong, the possibility of increasing the number (rather than the size) of the aggregations whose market positions have improved will presumably be relatively remote. Nothing will compete with the existing aggregations until they are so far above optimal size as to remove most of the competitive advantage which that size gave them over isolated establishments. The suggestion is that complexes based upon expanding industries tend to exceed their optimal size – indeed very probably their social optimal size.

As it happens, most of the technological and market changes of recent times have tended to favour activities that go with large optimal collections of people – the more centralised service industries, commerce, central government, complex mass-production and assembly industries, as opposed to agriculture, mining and the relatively simple processing trades. It does not necessarily follow from this, however, that the urban aggregations where the expanding industries flourish have necessarily been pushed beyond their theoretical optima. It is certainly the case that many of the technological and associated changes have had the effect of creating new scope for economies of scale, and thus have extended the optima – conceivably faster than they (and other influences) have expanded the aggregations. There are, alas, no easy *a priori* answers to practical questions in this subject.

It is, however, worth seeing if these considerations, supplemented by others that are at our disposal, throw any light at all upon United Kingdom problems, starting with the old question, central to (among others) the Barlow Commission's discussion of location policy,[1] whether the London aggregation is too big.

Two things can be said with reasonable confidence. First, the London aggregation, widely defined so as to include most of the South Eastern region, has, with some help from policy, come more or less into equilibrium with the rest of the country, in that net migration into it has become zero or negative in recent years. Second, the London conurbation is at a disadvantage as a place to live in, its unique urban amenities notwithstanding, as is shown by the existence of 'London weighting' in pay. Moreover, the source of the higher cost of living to which London weighting is related is plain to see; as we have noted in chapter

[1] Royal Commission on the Distribution of Industrial Population, *Report*.

3, it is traceable mostly to extra costs of housing and travel to work, including in the latter the time-cost of travel. These costs are mainly a consequence of the size of the urban area, which raises the value of sites for non-residential (and therefore their cost for residential) purposes, creates traffic congestion over a very wide area, and reduces the ratio that the peripheral zone near to open country bears to the whole. They are raised further by the competition of the wealthy for accommodation near to the social and cultural attractions of central London. It might be argued (and is no doubt true to some extent) that the higher incomes of the London area, due largely to the occupational composition of its population, enable Londoners to afford the luxury of living in relatively attractive surroundings a long way from their work. But the basic fact is that the suburbs are not so much superior in their attractiveness to those of lesser cities as further off from the centre. And the fact that London weighting is paid as a differential reward for particular kinds of work in London over what is offered for the same work elsewhere, without causing heavy net migration to London, must be taken as indicating that the extra costs of London life outweigh its advantages for the average person to an extent that the differential roughly measures.

All this having been said, however, it remains to be asked whether London's size enables it to *produce* goods and services (or some of them) more efficiently to an extent that justifies, or earns, this difference in pay. We have touched on this earlier in the present chapter. We saw that the question need refer only to the basic industries that do not provide necessarily for the London market; those that do provide for that market without serious competition from elsewhere can pass on to their customers any extra costs due to the higher London rates of pay. We are concerned, therefore, with manufacturing industry and the central services. Does the size of London make them more productive than they would otherwise be to an extent that matches the higher London pay rates?

So far as the manufacturing industries are concerned, we have noted that they are moving, to a large extent spontaneously, outwards from London, and indeed the other conurbations as well. Although the reasons for moving have often more to do with space for redevelopment than with labour cost, this flow of the tide away from the areas of highest value of net output per head suggests that the high value is due to high labour cost not entirely matched (or at least not overmatched) by high physical productivity.

The other basic trades of London are central government, finance, wholesale (and to some extent retail) distribution, professional services, and head office activity. To some extent these probably gain in productiveness from their common concentration in one place, though it is hard to believe that better telecommunications and faster personal travel are not undermining the basis of this mutual advantage, and in any case some countries separate out their central governments from the mixture without manifest ill effects. Whether having Westminster, the City and the Port of London more or less together in the middle of a huge conglomeration of miscellaneous light industry benefits their efficiency to an extent outweighing the burden of London weighting and the equivalent which their location imposes upon them seems by now very doubtful. London is the product of a very long period of gradual urbanisation, during which it has had no close rivals as a centre of urban growth. If, in these circumstances, it has reached something like equilibrium with the rest of the country so far as movement of population is concerned, the presumption is very strong that it is far beyond its own optimal size – and a good way beyond the social optimum too – unless with modern developments something very dramatic has happened to the optimal size for an aggregation of population and industry. All that can be said on this is that, on the evidence we have quoted, London seems to be further from the optimum than other aggregations in the country. Since it is bigger than they are the presumption is that it is super-optimal, not that all our aggregations are sub-optimal.

The other big urban aggregations also suffer from congestion – as indeed practically all towns do in which modern traffic tries to fit into a nineteenth-century or older urban fabric. If growth rate is a criterion of suitability for purpose, then one should perhaps take note of the fact that the local authority areas with the fastest growth have recently been those with populations round about the hundred thousand mark. But caution is necessary; these are by no means all independent, free-standing communities, and it may be that this particular size happens to be typical of those areas into which the overspill of the conurbations is flowing – in which case they derive their rapid growth not so much from how big they are, but from where they are.

In any case, we are not primarily concerned here with criteria of intra-regional planning. The London aggregation is a special case because it dominates a whole region – and that by far the largest – and its size and changes thereof can hardly avoid being of major significance for the interregional distribution of population and industry as a whole. If London is too big, then any rational policy for mitigating this state of affairs is likely to include more than re-deployment within the South East; it is likely to affect the balance of the regional growth rates that are thought desirable throughout the country.

CHAPTER 8

DYNAMIC CONSIDERATIONS

In our discussion of regional growth in chapter 4, we have already given some attention to the dynamic mechanisms by which economic growth in a region might be to some extent self-reinforcing. We there glanced at the various kinds of multiplier mechanism, and noted the possibility that these, or some of them, might interact with a tendency to adjust a region's capital stock to changes in the size of its income or its population in such a way as to give rise to a more continuing kind of self-reinforcement. We must now turn back to these matters, beginning with a closer scrutiny of the multiplier mechanism in its several manifestations.

REGIONAL MULTIPLIERS

One of these manifestations, the long-term 'economic base multiplier', has been scrutinised in chapter 6, since its existence is a central fact of economic growth. It arises simply because any extra basic employment in a region (employment in the production of goods and services other than those that are necessarily provided locally for the local population) will bring about a further increase of employment in the necessarily local-market activities. We have examined the operation of this relation over longish periods (forty years and thirteen years) and have found it useful. A unit increase in basic employment seems to go with an increase of about 1·8 units in total employment. Much the same relation presumably holds between additional income produced in basic industry and total additional income – also in the fairly long run. In the short run there is no guarantee that the essentially local service trades will grow in step with the basic trades, either in income or in employment. Indeed, so far as income changes are concerned, an increase in the production of a region's basic industries over a short period may come largely from an increase in production per head of the existing labour force, and the same may be largely true of the consequential increase in production of local goods and services as well. The relation between these two increments in income may be different from that between the corresponding basic and local increases of income or of employment that are to be seen over a period of years.

So far as short-term changes are concerned therefore, we need to look at income separately from employment. We must also be clear (as we have to be with the long-term multipliers) about what is the

DYNAMIC CONSIDERATIONS

purpose of the multiplier. The questions that call for its use are generally of the form – what total increase in income (or employment) in a region may be expected to follow from a stated increase in:

(i) value added (or employment) in its basic industries as a whole, either in direct or indirect response to orders from outside the region, or for capital formation within it, or to replace goods hitherto imported into it;

(ii) value added (or employment) in particular basic industries that are the immediate suppliers of goods for which orders (say from outside the region) have risen;

(iii) orders for goods that emanate immediately from basic industries in the region;

(iv) capital formation within the region.

Each of these four kinds of initial data constitutes a different 'multiplicand' to which the question demands the application of a multiplier. The *form* of the multiplier required is different in each of these cases, except that it is broadly the same for (iv) as for (iii). The *numerical value* of the multiplier in all the cases except (i) will also vary according to the identity of the extra goods that are stated to have been ordered, or the kind of capital formation that is being increased. To make matters worse, if we are evaluating any of these multipliers *ex ante* by considering what happens to the postulated additional payments that are made for regional basic production, we can either ignore or take into account the repercussions that operate through other regions – in principle an infinite converging series of extra demands for the region's production that result from payments leaking out of the region into the rest of the economy or the world and raising its purchasing power. We can, however, consider once for all at a later stage how much difference these repercussions are likely to make.

The simplest multiplicand one can choose (speaking for the moment in terms of income rather than employment) is an additional expenditure on factors of production within the region. The multiplier applicable to this is what may be called the Keynesian income multiplier, derived by adding to the initial extra expenditure the infinite series of secondary expenditures on regional factors of production by regional households whose disposable incomes are increased. It proves to be, broadly speaking, the inverse of the sums of the proportions of extra factor income that, at each 'round', leak into savings, tax payments, or expenditure outside the region, instead of going into additional payments to resident factor owners. If extra employment is proportional to extra income, then this multiplier is identical in form with the economic base multiplier, which we have already considered. How the values of the latter which we have found to hold over longish periods can be reconciled with such values as we may deduce for the Keynesian multiplier in the short run we shall have to discuss later.

If one is told, not the total additional income or employment in all the basic industries of the region that is occasioned by (say) new orders from outside, but only the additional income or employment that these orders will generate in the industry from which the goods that are ordered immediately come (the 'main' industry), then before applying the Keynesian multiplier one must know of any income generated in the region through the production of direct or indirect inputs into that industry. The ratio of total regional income generated in, or employment involved in, the extra production in question to that which is *directly* concerned in the industry from which the goods to fulfil the orders immediately come may perhaps best be called the 'input multiplier'. (It is sometimes referred to as the 'matrix multiplier', but this differs from the original use of that term and is rather confusing.) Identifying the indirect inputs in question is difficult, because they form an infinite converging series of inputs into the 'main' industry, inputs into those inputs, and so on indefinitely. Once the appropriate input multiplier is known, however, one has only to apply it to the income (or employment) created in the 'main' industry to get the multiplicand to which, in turn, it is appropriate to apply the Keynesian multiplier.

Finally, one may be told only the gross value of the extra orders given for additional goods from establishments in the region, or the gross value of additional capital formation within it. In that case the first task is to pick out the net output from the gross value of the orders, or, in the case of capital formation, to pick out the net output required directly from suppliers in the region from both their inputs (which make up the rest of the gross value of their additional orders) and those parts of the additional capital that are not ordered from establishments in the region at all. This gives us the additional income in the 'main' supplying industries of the region to which the input and Keynesian multipliers should both be applied in order to estimate the total effect on regional income. The ratio of the result to the initial increase in export orders from the region, or in capital formation, may be described as the 'export multiplier' or the 'investment multiplier'. Its value will, as we have already mentioned, vary according to the kind of exports or of investment concerned. In cases where a high proportion of the inputs into the 'main' supplying industry, or of the extra capital goods to be installed, come from sources outside the region, it may be small – possibly less than unity.

With these distinctions in mind, we may now consider the probable magnitudes of the various multipliers in British conditions.

THE SIZE OF THE INPUT MULTIPLIER

In trying to evaluate the input multiplier, one comes sharply up against a lack of data. Of the United Kingdom regions, an input–output matrix has been constructed only for Wales,[1] and even that, apart from the data on inter-industry and interregional flows of five industries' products, is based on assumptions about flows of goods that can be shown almost certainly to yield gross underestimates of those flows in most cases – they exclude the very large amount of two-way traffic between regions that is to be found in practice for most classes of of product. It is necessary, therefore, to resort to cruder considerations for some idea of the orders of magnitude in question.

The only simple category of payments made for an additional export of a product from a region, of which one can say that it virtually all goes to residents in the region, is the category of payments to employees in the industry from which the product immediately comes. The proportion which this forms of the ouput of the representative establishment varies from as little as 6 or 7 per cent in oil and sugar refining to nearly 60 per cent in coalmining. It stands between 30 and 40 per cent in most of the mechanical and electrical engineering industries, electronics, shipbuilding and aircraft, round about 30 per cent in clothing and footwear, 20 per cent in motor vehicles and textiles, and generally lower in the chemical and food-processing trades.

To get further, let us take the motor vehicle industry as an example. Payments to employees are there about 22 per cent of the representative establishment's gross output. Some part of the payments for other primary inputs (which are 9 per cent of output) will also no doubt be made within the region. The payments to other establishments in the industry (about 18 per cent of the representative establishment's output) will largely be within the region for an establishment in the West Midlands, as will the 19 per cent spent with the engineering, electrical and rubber industries. For establishments outside the main vehicle-making complex, the intra-regional payments under these headings may be low. A study of the metalworking industries in central Lancashire showed that only about 20 per cent of their intermediate inputs came from the North Western region.[2] Payments to other British industries are likely to be distributed fairly widely over the country; those for imports and those that are indirect tax contributions are certainly leakages from the region.

---

[1] E. Nevin, A. R. Roe and J. I. Round, *The Structure of the Welsh Economy*, Cardiff, University of Wales Press, 1966.

[2] By Economic Consultants Limited, *Study for an Industrial Complex in Central Lancashire*, London, 1969.

Putting down plausible figures for the intra-regional factor contents of payments made to establishments in the region, and carrying the calculation to the point where further additions to regional income become relatively small, one may form the impression that the regional input multiplier in the motor industry is probably between 1·2 and 2, the higher figure applying to the West Midlands, or perhaps to the South East where a complex of ancillary industries exists, the lower one to regions where such industries provide only minimal inputs. It may be recalled that Moore and Peterson in their pioneering study of the Utah economy obtained input multipliers ranging from 1·1 to 2·5 for exports from a variety of industries, apart from one exceptional one of over 8 for non-ferrous metals.[1] With British industries generally, the regional input multiplier could, at the lowest, be very little above unity in most cases and, on the most favourable assumptions with regard to complementarity in the region, seems likely to approach 2 only in industries of high regional concentration (motors in the West Midlands, wool textiles in Yorkshire). In most industries, whether highly capital-intensive ones like oil-refining, or relatively labour-intensive ones such as clothing or electronics, the highest value likely to be found in a region seems to be somewhere in the neighbourhood of $1\frac{1}{2}$.

THE SIZE OF THE KEYNESIAN MULTIPLIER IN THE SHORT RUN

With this rather vague indication of how big the regional input multiplier is likely to be, we may pass on to the short-run Keynesian income multiplier, which operates through the expenditure of households that have received extra factor incomes. The first problem in calculating it is to identify the various 'leakages' from the flow of purchasing power in the region, and to decide to which portions of the flow they can be regarded as functionally related. The flow itself is shown in chart 8.1.

We start with the flow of factor incomes that pay for the production carried on in the region – its gross domestic product at factor cost. To this is related the direct corporate taxation of this income, which we can regard as being deducted from it at this point. From the residue we have to make two further deductions – the income (after corporate tax) produced in the region that is paid to households elsewhere, and the undistributed profits arising from activity in the region that are put to reserve. Changes in both of these may be regarded as related to changes in regional gross domestic product after corporate tax. We must, however, add as an autonomous sum any income paid to house-

---

[1] F. T. Moore and J. W. Peterson, 'Regional Analysis: an interindustry model of Utah', *Review of Economics and Statistics*, vol. 37, no. 4, November 1955, pp. 368–83.

Chart 8.1. *The flow of regional income and expenditure as a basis for estimating regional income multipliers*

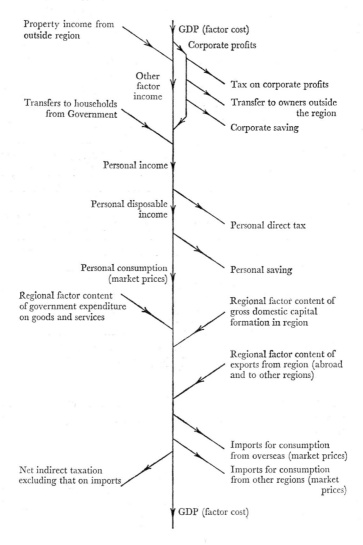

holds in the region from their property elsewhere. We must also add any other transfers to such households from the government or other sources outside the region. Part of this transfer income, consisting of unemployment insurance benefits and other assistance to households, may be regarded as varying in the short run inversely with gross domestic product. To the resulting stream of personal incomes is related the direct personal taxation levied on the households of the region; the deduction of it leaves their disposable personal income.

Personal saving may be plausibly related to this and deducted from it, giving the region's personal consumption expenditure at market prices. To this we may add four flows that can be taken, in the first instance at least, as autonomous: public current expenditure on goods and services in the region, gross domestic capital formation in it, and payments for the two streams of exports from the region – those going abroad and those to other regions of the United Kingdom. Finally, three deductions can be made: first, payments at market prices for the region's two streams of imports, those from abroad and those from other regions, and then its payments of net indirect taxes on its purchases other than imports. This leaves us with the payment made to factors of production for the production carried out in the region, which is the regional gross domestic product at factor cost with which we began.

If this flow is regarded as feeding back to the starting point, it is clear that the resulting circulation will be in equilibrium when it is at such a level that the various inflows into the circuit are exactly matched by the outflows from it – some of the inflows and some of the outflows being related, as we have noted, to the rate of flow at some point in the main circuit. The change in the equilibrium rate of flow when there is a unit change in the rate of payments to factors of production in the region from public expenditure on goods and services, or for capital formation or exports to anywhere outside the region, is the region's simple Keynesian income multiplier. The algebraic formula for it is derived as follows:

Consider the flows of payments in region A shown in chart 8.1, and take the following symbols as representing *changes* in the elements named:

Y – gross domestic product at factor cost
Y_c – corporate income before tax
Y_{ab} – corporate income transferred out of the region (after tax)
Y_{ba} – income (after corporate tax) transferred to households in the region from corporate profits elsewhere
Y_p – personal income
T_{dc} – direct tax on corporate income
S_c – corporate saving
U – transfers to households from the government
T_{dp} – direct tax on households
S_p – household saving
C_a – consumer's expenditure in region A (at market prices)

G_a – regional factor content of government expenditure on goods and services in region A
I_a – regional factor content of gross domestic capital formation in region A
X_a – regional factor content of exports from A to other regions and overseas
M_f – imports into A from overseas (at market prices)
M_b – imports into A from other regions (at market prices)
T_{ia} – net indirect tax (indirect taxes minus subsidies) on goods and services absorbed in A, other than taxes on imports

We assume I_a and for the present purpose X_a and Y_{ba} to be zero. Suppose that the following relations exist (the lower case letters representing constant coefficients):

$$Y_c = y_c Y$$
$$T_{dc} = t_{dc} Y_c = t_{dc} y_c Y$$
$$S_c = s_c y_c Y (1 - t_{dc})$$
$$Y_{ab} = y_{ab} y_c Y (1 - t_{dc})(1 - s_c)$$
$$U = -uY$$
$$T_{dp} = t_{dp} Y_p$$
$$S_p = s_p (1 - t_{dp}) Y_p$$
$$(Y_p = Y - T_{dc} - S_c + U + Y_{ba} - Y_{ab})$$
$$M_b = m_b (1 - s_p)(1 - t_{dp}) Y_p$$
$$M_f = m_f (1 - s_p)(1 - t_{dp}) Y_p$$

(that is to say, imports are related to consumers' expenditure)

$$T_{ia} = t_{ia}(1 - m_b - m_f)(1 - s_p)(1 - t_{dp}) Y_p.$$

We have also the identity:

$$Y = C_a + G_a + I_a + X_a - M_f - M_b - T_{ia},$$

from which, by assuming a unit increase in G_a, with I_a and X_a still equal to zero, we get a value for the simple multiplier of the reciprocal of:

$$1 - (1 - s_p)(1 - t_{dp})(1 - t_{ia})(1 - m_b - m_f)$$
$$\times \{1 - u - y_c[t_{dc} + s_c(1 - t_{dc}) + y_{ab}(1 - t_{dc})(1 - s_c)]\}.$$

What we now want are the values of the coefficients we have used. Most of them can reasonably be obtained from national data. The marginal rate of change of corporate income per unit change in gross domestic product seems, for instance, to be about 0·22, and this can, provisionally at least, be assumed to be true for all regions. The marginal incidence of direct tax on corporate income since 1966 can be accepted as being 0·45. The marginal rate of saving out of corporate income (after tax) is about 0·46. The marginal rate of personal saving out of disposable income is a dubious magnitude to which a very tentative value of 0·10 may be given. The marginal rate of direct personal taxation was calculated by Professor Prest to have been about 0·18 at 1959/60 tax rates (a central estimate), that is to say, just about twice the average incidence of taxes on personal income.[1] A similar relation of marginal to average rate in 1968 would give a marginal rate of 0·26. There is, presumably, some variation between regions in the marginal rate of tax; it will be higher in the richer regions. The average incidence of direct taxation on personal incomes in 1961 varied from 7·2 per cent in Northern Ireland to 11·8 per cent in South East England, the United Kingdom average then being 9·8 per cent. The (overseas) import coefficient applying to consumption may reasonably be assumed to have the national value in all regions – about 0·23 including the indirect taxes that fall on imports.

The remaining coefficients, however, are more difficult. The incidence of indirect taxation on purchases other than imports into the region may depend a good deal on whether highly taxed items such as spirits are of local origin or not. Some intelligent guesswork would no doubt enable plausible adjustments to be made for regional peculiarities, but in the first instance a national value, based on the assumption that United Kingdom goods moving interregionally bear the same rate of tax as those that do not, would probably not give too false a picture. The coefficient in question is probably about 0·12.

The variation of transfers to the personal sector with the level of income is hard to detect empirically because of the strong trends in both variables and the irregular element in the increase of transfers due to discontinuous changes in rates of benefit. The best way of evaluating it is through the short-term variation of unemployment with *real* income and the relation of rates of benefit to average output (or perhaps earnings) of labour. The relation of unemployment to production varies, as we have noted in another chapter, from one region to another. Nationally, it seems reasonable to say that short-term variations in transfers tend to compensate those in income to the extent of something like one-fifth.

The sensitivity to income of property-income transfers to other regions

---

[1] A. R. Prest, 'The Sensitivity of the Yield of Personal Income Tax in the United Kingdom', *Economic Journal*, vol. 72, no. 287, September 1962, pp. 576–96.

cannot be positively known, since we do not know the interregional distribution of the owners of property situated in any given region, especially owners of equities. Our earlier estimates of net transfers of factor incomes into or out of regions are not sufficient to illuminate this: where the effects of an increase in the region's income with other regions' incomes unchanged are concerned, we need to know about gross flows. We can perhaps assume that ownership of rents is substantially intra-regional and, in any case, rent income is not volatile in the short run. Fixed interest ought to be as fixed as its name suggests. It is distributed corporate profits that constitute our problem. If ownership of all individual companies' shares were distributed in the same way geographically as ownership of shares in general, a region where (say) a tenth of the country's shares were owned would lose to other regions nine-tenths of any increase in distributed earnings originating in establishments located within it. In fact, there is probably some tendency towards localisation of ownership, but it is impossible to say to what extent. What seems certain is that there is a fairly high leakage of distributed profits out of any region, especially a small region. Arbitrarily, we might guess that in a 'typical' region, smaller than the South East but bigger than East Anglia or Northern Ireland, about half of the changes in distributed earnings overflow in this way.

The biggest uncertainty of all, however, concerns interregional imports. What proportion of additional consumption in a region is met from the rest of the country? The data on road and rail goods transport do not directly provide the answer because they do not give any basis for distinction between intermediate and final goods. Except in the South East, Northern Ireland and Scotland, our estimates of movements into the region (from home and overseas) are sufficiently large to allow the whole regional absorption of movable goods and interregionally tradeable services to be provided from outside. This, of course, cannot be what happens. Much of the inflow of goods into a region is not for final use or consumption but for processing, or even merely for storage or breaking of bulk before they are sent out again – but *how* much the statistics of movement do not tell us. All one can say for the moment is that these statistics of inflow of goods set a theoretical upper limit in some regions, and in others encourage one to believe that the regional economy is a very open one indeed.

It is easier to specify the parts of consumers' additional expenditure that necessarily or almost necessarily fall, as value added, within the region. Professor Archibald has estimated this proportion conservatively at 0·23;[1] with the associated net indirect taxation this would be about

[1] G. C. Archibald, 'Regional Multiplier Effects in the U.K.', *Oxford Economic Papers* (new series), vol. 19, no. 1, March 1967, pp. 22–45.

0·27. The total proportion of consumers' outlay spent on necessarily local inputs and necessarily external (foreign) ones is therefore about 0·50, leaving the other half in principle for either intra- or extra-regional sources; we may call it the 'mobile United Kingdom content' of consumption. The problem is how to allocate this half.

The highest degree of interregional mobility of mobile goods and services would, presumably, mean that a unit of demand for 'mobile United Kingdom content' would be equally likely to be satisfied by any of the units of supply in the country, so that a region would satisfy its demand from the other regions and from its own production in proportion to their respective volumes of relevant output – for the mobile content as a whole, very roughly in proportion to their gross domestic products. On this assumption, South East England with 37 per cent of the national production of goods and services, would satisfy 37 per cent of its own demand for 'mobile United Kingdom content', leaving 63 per cent ($31\frac{1}{2}$ per cent of its total demand for consumers' goods and services) to be got from other regions. Scotland on a similar calculation would satisfy nearly 46 per cent of its consumers' demand from other United Kingdom regions, in addition to the 23 per cent we have assumed to be satisfied from abroad.

But this is hardly convincing. We have no right to suppose that the 'mobile' content of goods and services consumed in a region is perfectly mobile. The simplest way of improving on this unreasonable supposition is to assume that, even among mobile goods, the probability of a region's consuming a specified, representative unit produced outside it is only some fraction of the probability of its consuming a given, representative, home-produced unit. On some such assumption as this, and with a little broadening of our picture, we can perhaps make the interregional traffic data useful for the present purpose after all. The argument is given in the appendix to this chapter.[1] Crude though the calculations in question are, they serve to give some quantitative content to the effect of the 'openness' of regional economies. One might well conclude from them that the proportion of final demand for 'mobile United Kingdom content' that is satisfied by imports from outside the region does not fall below about 0·4 even in the South East or in the most peripheral regions, Scotland and Northern Ireland, and that in the more central regions smaller than the South East it rises to perhaps three-quarters.

But when all is said and done, what we suppose about the origin of the 'mobile United Kingdom content' of final demand (and in particular of consumers' demand) makes only a limited amount of difference to the size of the regional Keynesian income multipliers, since

[1] See p. 202.

the leakages of purchasing power into foreign imports, saving, taxation and payments to non-resident factor owners are already large, even without the additional leakage into payments for goods and services from other regions. Calculations of the multiplier based on the extreme assumptions – first that 0.4 of the 'mobile United Kingdom content' of consumption comes from outside the region, then that 75 per cent of it does – produce answers only 8 per cent apart.

On the valuations of the coefficients that have just been discussed, the values obtained for the short-run Keynesian income multiplier range from about 1·15 for a small region – allowing the maximum plausible values for imports of 'mobile United Kingdom content' of consumption and outflows of distributed corporate earnings – to about 1·24 for a large region, where the minimum values of these coefficients are used. If the large region in question is the South East (and indeed, what other Standard Region could it be?), then it is proper to allow for a rather higher than average marginal incidence of personal taxation, because incomes are on average higher there. Assuming that marginal rates vary between regions in proportion to average rates, this raises the amount of leakage and lowers the multiplier to about 1·21. Similarly, if in calculating the value for a small region one is thinking of a poor one, the lower marginal rate of personal taxation will give a rather higher value for the multiplier. If one has in mind the region that is, outstandingly, both small and poor – Northern Ireland – then its peripheral position probably tends to lower the extra-regional United Kingdom content of consumption below the value assumed, so that the true value of the multiplier may climb to 1·18 or more. It is, however, sufficiently clear that, unless the various coefficients of leakage have been given quite wrong values, regional multipliers are both low – not very far above unity – and not very different in different regions. Our formula gives for the whole United Kingdom, making allowance for profits paid abroad, a value of only 1·41.

It was noted earlier that, in calculating regional multipliers, the question arises whether it is practically important to allow for interregional repercussions. It is in connection with the Keynesian income multiplier that this becomes relevant. When a unit addition is made to expenditure on factors of production owned in a region, the effect of these repercussions is equivalent to that of the 'multiplicand' being increased over and above this unit by three elements. First, there is the regional factor content of extra consumption in other regions due to the extra profits remitted to them from the region in question. Second, there is the similar impact of extra production (and income) induced in other regions by the increased imports from them of the region in question. Third, other regions will remit increased profits to the region in question, which will increase its demand for its own factors of production. Similar considerations apply in the other regions taken together, and it is not hard to solve the equations expressing these facts so as to obtain the 'Keynesian income multiplier with repercussions'. With leakages at the levels that seem to apply in the short run in the United Kingdom however, the effort of doing so is not well rewarded – the multipliers with repercussions prove to be less than 1 per cent larger than the simple multipliers. This is true both of large regions and of small ones: a very large region spills only small amounts of its additional purchasing power into the rest of the economy, so that not much comes back; while a very small region, though it may spill out much of its extra purchasing power, is too small a target to attract the return of a significant part of it – bearing in mind in both cases, how much of the purchasing power vanishes abroad or into the tax collector's coffers, or is offset by changes in welfare payments, at each round of expenditure. In any region, therefore, it seems a fair deduction that a primary increase in demand for the region's factors of production is supplemented by secondary demand to the extent of only something between 15 and 25 per cent.

THE 'INVESTMENT' AND 'EXPORT' MULTIPLIERS

Putting together what we have so far found, we can get some idea how big 'export' or 'investment' multipliers in regions are likely to be – what change in regional income is likely to follow a unit change in regional exports (of specified kinds) or in regional capital formation. We may again take an increase in exports of motor vehicles as an example. With a unit increase (say £1 million) in such exports, the extra incomes of owners of primary factors of production in the region from their direct contribution to the extra vehicles produced for export in the motor industry will be £0·25–£0·28 million. The operation of the input multiplier will raise this, through the further regional activity in providing intermediate inputs for the motor industry (and extra inputs for the industries providing those inputs, in an endless succession), to anything between £0·30 million and £0·56 million, according to whether the relevant component and subcontracting industries are located mostly outside the region or mostly inside it. The income multiplier operating through consumers' expenditure will raise these figures by anything from a seventh to a quarter, leaving us with a final extreme range of values for our 'motor-car export multiplier' of about 0·35 to 0·70. The former figure might be about right for Wales or East Anglia, the latter for the West Midlands. Or again, unit expenditure on a mixed bag of construction projects (roads, houses, factories, commercial buildings) might directly raise factor incomes in the region by between 0·4 and 0·45 of a unit, which the input multiplier might raise to between 0·5 and 0·6, and the income multiplier, in turn, might bring up to 0·6 or 0·75. A representative addition to capital formation in manufacturing industry (about one-fifth new building and works, 70 per cent plant and machinery, 10 per cent vehicles) could lead to widely varying results, chiefly because anything from a very small proportion to (say) half of the plant and machinery and the vehicles in question might come immediately from the region where the investment takes place. In total, the investment multiplier might turn out to be anything from 0·1 to 0·5.

It seems, therefore, that a unit of additional expenditure, labelled as being 'in' a given region, in the sense that it is either expenditure on goods and services emanating immediately from that region, or expenditure on the formation of new physical assets within it, is likely to generate through the multiplier less than a unit addition to the income of residents in the region – in many cases an addition of only half a unit. It will, of course, generate a good deal of income elsewhere in the country. Take once again our example of additional motor vehicle exports (to an overseas country, if that supposition makes the issue clearer). An extra £1 million spent on British motor vehicles means (according to the 1963 Input–Output Tables[1]) an extra £0·845 million of factor incomes generated in the United Kingdom from the extra production of vehicles – the 'missing' £0·155 million being, of course, the import content of the output in question and indirect taxes on various inputs. The operation of the income multiplier would bring the total increase in United Kingdom factor incomes to about £1·2 million.

Comparing this figure with those that emerged from our regional calculations, we find it implies that, if the extra motor vehicles were bought from the West Midlands, then, since West Midlands income is raised (as we suggested earlier) by about £0·75 million, the income of the rest of the country is raised by some £0·45 million. If, on the other hand, the vehicles were bought from a small region with only a minimal motor industry, that region's income might be raised by something like £0·35 million – the bulk of the total national increase, about £0·85 million, being generated in the rest of the country.

These figures depend upon too many uncertain assumptions to be regarded as at all precise, but it seems unlikely that the order of magnitude is wrong. Even at national level, export (and investment) multipliers are not much above unity. At regional level, they probably do not rise, even in favourable circumstances, much above 60 per cent of

[1] Central Statistical Office, *Input–Output Tables for the United Kingdom 1963*.

the corresponding national values, while in unfavourable circumstances – in relation to purchases of oil-refinery products, for instance, or to the construction of power stations in a region without sources of the relevant machinery and equipment – they could be very small. This is, of course, only to say that the United Kingdom is a highly integrated economy, quite heavily dependent upon imports from overseas, and given to high marginal rates of taxation on incomes and expenditure.

THE LONGER RUN AND THE ECONOMIC BASE MULTIPLIER

We noted earlier in this chapter that the Keynesian income multiplier is, in form, identical with the economic base multiplier. Yet the former, as we have calculated it *ex ante* for the short run from a consideration of changes in money flows, has relatively low values of between 1·15 and 1·25, while the latter, calculated *ex post* from changes in employment over periods of thirteen and forty years, showed values of 1·7 or 1·8. Can these results be reconciled?

In calculating values for the short-term multiplier we have made assumptions that, on the face of them, are not very appropriate for throwing light on the longer-term employment effects of a primary increase in activity. These assumptions were essentially related to short-period changes; it was taken for granted that the primary injection of purchasing power did not lead to any increase in the region's total population, but only to a diminution of its unemployment (registered or unregistered) and an increase in the earnings of the existing owners of factors of production. It was also assumed that, because regional population was unchanged, public spending of the kinds that are geared to numbers rather than to income, such as that on the social services, would not be increased; on the contrary, account was taken of a diminution of social insurance and supplementary benefit expenditure as unemployment fell and the lower incomes were raised.

If one is concerned with the process of regional growth over (say) a decade, different assumptions are in order. It is reasonable for this purpose, as a first approximation at least, to suppose that the proportionate incidence of unemployment and of poverty that gives rise to public relief expenditure is unchanged and, again as a first approximation, that personal incomes do not rise into higher tax brackets in the region to a greater extent than elsewhere. This means that, instead of using marginal rates of tax incidence and of corporate profits with respect to income, one should use average rates, calculated not (in principle) for a particular point of time, but for the whole period of growth that is under study. Public transfers to residents in the region and expenditure on resources in it for welfare and similar purposes must be regarded as increasing with population, which, on these assumptions, means with gross domestic product. On the other hand, more specific account must be taken of the 'leakage' into social insurance contributions, which in our previous multiplier calculation was ignored, though it should in principle have entered marginally to take account of variations with the proportion of the (supposedly static) population that was contributing.

These modifications make a considerable difference. The term describing the 'stabilising' effect of unemployment insurance benefits and the like is replaced by a 'destabilising' one with an estimated value of 0·08 – the average ratio of such benefits plus state pensions and similar personal grants to gross domestic product. Against this, 5 per cent of gross domestic product is taken as the leakage into insurance contributions. The marginal personal income tax rate of 0·23 calculated for the late sixties is replaced by an average rate of 0·09, taken as appropriate for the period 1953–66 to which this calculation is notionally related. The marginal personal saving rate of 0·10 comes down to an average one of 0·05, the corporate rate (out of profits) from 0·45 to 0·37. Finally, there is the additional term for public expenditure on goods and services of the region that is geared to its population (or, in our terms, gross domestic product). This was taken to be the ratio to gross domestic product of average public expenditure on non-defence salaries in regions other than the South East, together with one-third (a rather arbitrary estimate of the regional factors' share) of expenditure on goods other than those for defence and central administration. To this was added a proportion (45 per cent) of public expenditure on housing and other non-defence capital formation, which was thought to be a reasonable estimate of the average proportion of it that would fall on factors of production within the region. The implied assumption that this capital formation is proportional to regional population perhaps requires justification. It disregards the presumption that net capital formation, at least, is governed by considerations of capital stock adjustment, and therefore ought to be related to the *rate of increase* of population rather than to its size. We shall see, however, that in recent British experience signs of the operation of the capital stock adjustment principle are not very obtrusive. In practice, the tendency has been for public capital formation to depart relatively little from proportionality to population.

With these modifications, the numerical value of the long-run income multiplier rises to just under 1·9 if one assumes the degree of dependence on mobile inputs from the rest of the country that we estimated earlier to be appropriate to a large region, to just under 1·6 assuming the degree of external dependence appropriate to a small one. We seem, therefore, to have effected a reconciliation between, at any rate, the broad magnitudes of the long-run income multiplier as calculated, on the one hand *ex ante* from the pattern of money flows, and on the other hand *ex post* from long-term changes in employment.

It thus seems safe to take the long-run value of the regional Keynesian income (or employment) multiplier as lying in the same range as our economic base multipliers. If we may assume that input multipliers and direct regional factor contents of regional exports or capital formation are the same in the long run as in the short,[1] it is possible to amend our values for the export and investment multipliers to apply to the long run. The long-run motor-car export multiplier will thus, according to the region to which it applies, vary between half and unity (in comparison with a range of 0·35 to 0·70 in the short run). The long-run investment multiplier for a representative increase of capital formation in manufacturing industry might be anything between 0·15 and 0·75. These are still not large figures, but they are at any rate half as big again as their short-run counterparts.

CAPITAL STOCK ADJUSTMENT: THE LONG RUN

If the multiplier in its various formulations is not very powerful at regional level, what about capital stock adjustment, the multiplier's partner in most dynamic analyses of income generation? How powerfully the adjustment of a region's capital stock to a change in the level of demand for its product itself supplements that demand will depend on at least three things. First, it obviously depends on the ratio of the desired or normal stock of capital to the level of demand with which it is associated – in short, to the capital–output ratio. Secondly, it depends on the amount of 'slack' or 'tolerance' in this ratio – how much the actual ratio is permitted to vary from whatever is regarded as its normal level within the period with which one is concerned. Thirdly, it depends on the extent to which the augmentation of the region's capital stock requires economic activity within the region at the time when the augmentation is taking place, as opposed to production of the required capital goods in another region, or to later production of additional exports in the region with which we are concerned to finance interest on and repayment of its borrowing for the acquisition of capital in question.

For the country as a whole, the Central Statistical Office puts the replacement value of the total gross capital stock at nearly four times

---

[1] The assumption is not a very safe one. In the long run local sources of components may develop in response to demand, raising the regional input multiplier for instance. But there is no obvious way of quantifying such an effect.

the gross domestic product. From this one might suppose at first sight that, for a region to increase its productive capacity by 1 per cent, it would somehow have to acquire additional capital assets equivalent to nearly 4 per cent of its annual domestic product – an incremental capital–output ratio of something approaching 4. The conditions under which this is a plausible assumption are, however, rather restrictive – unchanging techniques of production and a rise of working population proportional to that of output. In these circumstances a 1 per cent increase of productive capacity would require a 1 per cent increase in working population and in the stock of every kind of productive asset, except in so far as the intensity of utilisation of the assets can be, and is, changed. In practice techniques are very far from constant. Their rate of change stands in a mutual relation with the rate at which equipment is replaced and added to, influencing it and influenced by it, since new techniques are introduced in new equipment, and their discovery or publication may stimulate investment. Both the magnitude and the direction of investment are influenced also by the conditions of factor supply, such as shortage of labour. With changing composition of both output and capital stock, statements about the relations between the two become ambiguous except in terms of historical or replacement cost, of which the former is not very relevant to most interesting questions and the latter clearly depends on the relative rates of technical progress in the capital goods industries and elsewhere.

There is thus no guarantee that the *incremental* capital–output ratio will coincide with the corresponding 'average' ratio – the simple ratio of the capital stock to the annual output. The United Kingdom figures, when both stock and flow are measured at 1963 factor cost, suggest that the incremental ratio was about 3 in the years 1948–61 and has been about 5 since then. Professor Beckerman, after an investigation that showed how elusive an estimate of the marginal capital–output ratio is, and how the component of it relating to manufacturing industry seems to vary with the rate of growth of output, arrives at figures ranging from under 5 to over 7.[1]

Assuming, then, that we know at least the order of magnitude of the incremental capital–output ratio, we may proceed to apply this knowledge to the question about regional growth on which it seems most likely to cast light – how far do differences in sustained rates of growth over considerable periods imply differences in levels of capital formation, which in turn imply interregional differences in levels or pressures of demand? Suppose that a certain region has shown over a considerable period a rate of population growth in excess by 1 per cent a year of the

[1] W. Beckerman and Associates, *The British Economy in 1975*, Cambridge University Press, 1965.

rate in the rest of the country. Unless there is a marked difference between the capital-intensiveness of development in the region and elsewhere, the condition on which this state of affairs can continue is clearly that the whole capital stock should be enlarged to keep pace with the superior population growth, so that *net* capital formation must, taking one year with another, be in excess of that in the rest of the country by something like 5 per cent of the region's income.

Of this 5 per cent only a part will constitute demand for factors of production in the region. We have already faced this question, or one like it, in considering the regional investment multiplier. Although in a building project it is quite possible that the regional contribution might be considerably more than half the total, capital formation involving a high proportion of plant and machinery might derive only to a very small extent from factors owned in the region. A comprehensive addition to capital of all kinds, composed more or less like recent additions to the national capital stock, might typically come as to a third or a half from regionally owned factors of production. The regional part of the 5 per cent may therefore amount to somewhere round about 2 per cent of the region's income. A minor part of the difference in demand between the region and the rest of the country which the additional regional investment generates will be offset by the incidence of the region's extra capital demands on the other regions of the economy. Fast growth in one region may raise demand for capital goods (and inputs into them) by a greater absolute amount, though in most cases a much smaller proportionate amount, in regions other than itself.

The outcome clearly depends a great deal on the 'region' we are talking about. If, at one end of the scale, it is a small region such as East Anglia, the extra internal investment demand induced by a 1 per cent superiority in growth rate may be only about $1\frac{1}{2}$ per cent, raised to about $2\frac{1}{2}$ per cent by the operation of the long-run income multiplier. The percentage change in activity in the rest of the country brought about by the entire East Anglian capital formation will be negligible, so that we may say that the East Anglian demand is raised by something under $2\frac{1}{2}$ per cent in relation to that in the rest of the country because of East Anglia's 1 per cent superiority in growth rate.

If we are talking about the whole of the South East and Midlands (comprising half the British economy), a high proportion – perhaps as much as two-thirds – of the direct and indirect extra investment demand will be internal to the area, but the overflow of the remainder into the rest of the country will constitute a proportionate addition to demand for investment goods there fully half as big as that of the faster growing regions. The direct effect of the south's superior growth will be to raise investment demand in the south by perhaps $3\frac{1}{3}$ per cent of its income, that in the rest of the country by $1\frac{2}{3}$ per cent of *its* income, so that the superiority of demand pressure in the south engendered by its faster growth, even after we have applied to the investment demands the long-term regional income multipliers of the appropriate size, is unlikely to be much greater than 3 per cent of the regional income.

In fact, the superiorities in growth rate both of the South East and the Midlands over the rest of the country, and of East Anglia over the rest of the country including the Midlands and the remainder of the South East, have been in the last decade or two of the order of only half of 1 per cent a year. The figures estimated on the basis of hypothetical 1 per cent superiorities in growth can therefore be halved for application to the actual cases in question. It seems that the differences in internal demand pressure generated by the superior growth rates, either of East Anglia or of the South East and the Midlands as a whole, in the last fifteen or twenty years are likely to have been of the order of 1 or $1\frac{1}{2}$ per cent of the relevant regional incomes.

A difference of $1\frac{1}{2}$ per cent in effective demand is not negligible, but neither is it likely to be overwhelmingly important in determining differences in regional prosperity. In the country as a whole, capital consumption in recent years has been equal to about 9 per cent of gross domestic product, so that quite small differences in regional rates of replacement of fixed assets could offset the differences in investment that we have associated with growth-rate differences. Still more is this true of public current expenditure on goods and services, which has been running at more than 20 per cent of gross domestic product in the country as a whole. Likewise, the magnitude of *net* capital formation (about 12 per cent of gross domestic product), together with the variability of capital–output ratios between industries and hence between regions with different industrial structures, makes it probable that the sort of relation between regional growth rate and the consequent level of demand that we have been discussing will, in practice, tend to be masked by other interregional differences in the parameters of the relation.

When it comes to testing these presumptions we suffer from a sad lack of data. For regional capital formation in total we have only the estimates for 1961 and 1964 that were discussed in chapter 3. These may be combined, and expressed for convenience as *per capita* expenditures, taking the United Kingdom average figure as 100. For regional income trends we may reasonably use population trends as proxies, on the ground that, as between one region and another, the differences in growth of population have made up the major part at least of differences in growth of total real income over any recent period – the divergences in growth of *per capita* income have been relatively small.

When one plots the 1961–4 indices of *per capita* investment against population growth, it seems that they are rather more closely connected with the growth of the decade 1951–61 than with that of the quinquennium 1961–6; in particular, the investment level in the South West was less low in relation to the moderate growth rate of population in the fifties than in relation to the much higher rate in the early sixties. Wales in any case spoils the relation by showing a very high rate of capital formation and a low rate of population growth – a consequence largely of very high investment in steelworks and fairly high road and electricity investment. Northern Ireland stands somewhat out of line in the opposite direction, with low investment (especially in the public sector) and a medium rate of population growth. The remaining regions, however, show a positive correlation between *per capita* capital formation and growth of population, though the amount of evidence they provide is necessarily small. At all events, the South East and the two Midlands regions, with a rate of population increase and of total income increase just over $\frac{1}{2}$ per cent per annum above that of the northern half of Great Britain (Scotland, the North, the North West and Yorkshire), show a rate of capital formation about 10 per cent greater. If we assume that absolute *per capita* rates of replacement are not very different in the two groups of regions in question, the ratio of these two magnitudes (investment difference to growth difference) is consistent with an interregional incremental capital–output ratio of about 4 – the same order of magnitude as the national incremental and average ratios. On the other hand, it is hazardous to say the least to assume equal *per capita* rates of replacement in the regions. Regional stocks of capital per head probably differ; so may regional replacement rates. If it were (rashly) assumed that the rate of capital replacement is proportional to regional product, we should come to the conclusion that *net* capital formation per head in the South East and Midlands in 1961–4 must have been very decidedly *less* than it was in the four northernmost regions of Great Britain, which showed slower population and income growth.

Can more be said about the differing rates of replacement and the differing incremental capital–output ratios of the regions? The rate of replacement of houses has certainly been greater in the north than in the south; in 1955–66 slum clearance disposed of 9 per cent of the housing stock in Scotland and 6 per cent of it in the three northernmost English regions, against 4 or 5 per cent in the Midlands and East Anglia and only 2 per cent in the South East. This presumably arises largely from differences in the age distribution of the housing stock. In 1964–7 the gross reductions (to offset against additions) in floor-area of shops, offices and industrial hereditaments in the three northernmost English regions amounted to some 2·8 per cent of the initial stock, against some 2·2 per cent in the South East England and the Midlands. The replacement element in gross investment is thus, because of the age and nature of the capital stock, almost certainly substantially greater north of the Trent than in the Midlands and the South East.

As for the incremental capital–output ratio, there is a presumption of substantial interregional differences in manufacturing industry arising from differences in the identity of the expanding trades. A very rough calculation based upon indices of industrial production and other sources suggests that, in the decade 1958–68, the incremental capital–output ratio in the Northern region, where expansion of output was mostly in engineering and electrical goods and chemicals, may well have been bigger by about one-third than that in London (the London Electricity Board area), where engineering and electrical goods, printing and publishing, the food trades, and timber and furniture accounted for most of the growth. Estimates of incremental capital–output ratios for single industries are subject to the high degree of uncertainty to which we have made reference, but there is a presumption that overall ratios are higher in the North and Wales than in the South East and at least the West Midlands.

For new buildings and works (as opposed to total capital formation) we have annual figures extending over the years 1964–8. The average *per capita* levels for the whole period show, like total *per capita* investment, a slightly better correlation with the population growths of the fifties than with those of the sixties. (The high figure for East Anglia, however, is more in keeping with its later, faster population growth. Can this be the effect of overspill schemes? At least it looks as if East Anglian capital formation was particularly quick on the draw.)

The general impression is that Scotland, Northern Ireland, and to a smaller extent Wales and the North, had high levels of *per capita* construction in relation to their population growth, the North West, the East Midlands and the South West relatively low levels. The evidence is slight and is influenced by the incidence of 'lumpy' investment in motorways and power-stations, but there is again some hint of greater capital-intensiveness and/or greater replacement outside the South East region, the West Midlands and the South West.

All that can be extracted from the empirical evidence is perhaps two rather weak generalisations. First, that, as between regions, factors such as difference in mean capital–output ratio (because of differences in the composition of investment) and difference in the ripeness of the capital stock for replacement are sufficient to upset any presumption that faster growth of population or income goes with higher *per capita* gross capital formation. Second, there is some indication that, within regions, an acceleration of the rate of growth of population, in so far as it induces a higher rate of capital formation, does so only after a fairly long, and distributed, time-lag.

THE SHORT RUN: STABILITY PROBLEMS

So much for the relation between growth trends and levels of capital formation over periods of several years. It seems that the Hicksian 'super-multiplier' operating through capital formation is far from being a dominant factor in determining the regional level of prosperity. What about the shorter-term stability or instability of regional activity, as determined by the interaction of the ordinary multiplier with capital stock adjustment? Again one can produce *a priori* presumptions that any mechanism of this kind in United Kingdom regions will be elusive.

The capital stock adjustment doctrine is at its strongest in regard to a closed economy, where productive capacity is presumably adjusted to actual or expected *internal* demand. In so far as a region's activity is geared to the satisfaction of demand elsewhere the situation is somewhat different. It is true that existing manufacturing or primary producing establishments selling outside the region may take their cue from the rate of expansion of their output (which is part of the region's total output) in planning additions to their capacity, but in so far as they are planning to move over to products or markets of greater expansionary promise than their existing ones they will have their eyes on recent growth rates other than their own. And new establishments may be planted in a region to produce for expanding markets mostly situated elsewhere without regard to the region's recent expansion rate, or even in part because it presents an easy labour market, which may well result from a poor record of general industrial expansion. There seems, moreover, to be little room for doubt that most manufacturing and primary industry in most regions is geared to produce for extra-regional markets. So far as this kind of production is concerned therefore, one would expect the causal effect of recent demand growth in an industry on its investment plans – and *a fortiori* the effect of aggregate regional income growth on total investment plans – to be a loose one. Over a long period it will no doubt be found that a high growth rate goes with high investment in primary and manufacturing industry taken together, but that may well be because high investment produces or permits fast growth rather than because fast growth induces high investment. It is with the latter direction of causality that we are concerned.

Of course, manufacturing and primary industry investment is very far from being even the major part of total capital formation. In the country as a whole it accounts for only about a quarter of it, and the greater part of the remainder – investment in dwellings, distribution, social services and public utilities – is much more likely to be geared to local demand. There is a general presumption that, in this major field of investment, it will be growth of income – or in much of it perhaps growth of population – that is to be regarded as the cause of capital formation, rather than the reverse. Only perhaps in the case of major new and expanded towns and overspill schemes is the investment decision likely to precede the population trend on a regional scale, rather than following either from projection of existing trends or from a manifest shortage of facilities. Even in this field of infrastructure investment however, the relation between income (or population) growth and capital formation cannot be expected to hold very closely in the short run. These are areas in which the ratio of the stock of capital to annual investment tends to be high; the permissible variation in degree of utilisation is considerable in relation to a year's investment. Moreover, many of the facilities in question – power-stations, major roadworks, sewerage schemes – are 'lumpy', so that a single scheme in any but a very big region may provide for a good many years' growth of demand. (The same is true, of course, of some facilities in manufacturing industry such as steelworks and oil refineries.) Regional investment, therefore, must be expected to show considerable year-to-year irregularities unconnected with variations in growth of income or population. We have already seen that investment seems to follow population growth with a distributed lag.

In addition to these complications we have the effects of replacement, or of variations in it. The amount of the capital stock that falls due (in some sense) for replacement this year depends on the history of capital formation in the region – on what assets happened to be constructed at such a date that they are regarded as having now reached a conventional age limit or a standard of performance that is judged intolerably low. But these criteria are not rigid, and an increased pressure of demand, for instance, is likely to be accommodated to some extent by retaining some assets that would otherwise be retired, rather than by increasing the pace of new construction. This is particularly true of housing, and perhaps of buildings and works generally in the public sector. For a variety of reasons, therefore, it does not seem likely that anything like a capital stock adjustment relation will be very clearly visible with regard to regional capital formation in the short run.

Any attempt to use capital–output ratios for purposes of theoretical analyses, moreover, comes up against another difficulty. The capital–output ratio, being the ratio of a stock to a flow, depends for its numerical value on the time-unit in which the flow is measured. To have direct relevance to such analyses it must be measured for the same time-units as are used for the model in question, which are usually the periods between the supposedly discontinuous acts of investment decision. How long these are it would be very hard to say; no doubt they vary immensely between different kinds of investment.

A different approach perhaps helps a little more. It is possible to write the capital stock adjustment equation in a more general form than that which implies an 'accelerator' relation – a form in which investment is stated simply to vary positively with the previous period's income and negatively with the stock of capital.[1] This, with an unlagged multiplier equation, leads to a second order difference equation, relating not to income but to the stock of capital. We can, however, consider questions of stability and instability as well in relation to capital stock as to income.

The expression on which the stability or instability of this system turns is simply the ratio of the regional component of the income coefficient of investment to what, in a closed system, would be the marginal propensity to save. Now, it is very unlikely that investment plans vary absolutely by anything like as much as the immediately preceding levels of income – after all, investment is only something like a quarter of income in aggregate. And we are concerned only with the *regional component* of this income coefficient of investment, which, as we have seen, is perhaps a half or a third of it. On the other hand, what corresponds in our case to the marginal propensity to save – the total of all the marginal rates of leakage in the regional economy – is a coefficient of something like 0·8. The expression on which the stability of the system turns, therefore, is certainly much below unity and the system is stable. When disturbed by a change in (say) autonomous investment, the regional economy will quickly converge to a new equilibrium position, either with or without highly damped fluctuations. What one can guess about the values of the various coefficients seems to leave it an open question whether there will in fact be fluctuations or not, but so high is the rate of damping that it does not seem to matter.

---

[1] The model in question is to be found in R. C. O. Matthews, *The Trade Cycle*, Cambridge University Press, 1958, p. 55. It postulates $I_t = aY_{t-1} - bK_t$ and $Y_t = I_t/s + Z/s$, where I is net investment, Y is income, K is capital stock, Z is a constant and s, a and b are constant coefficients. It follows from this that $I_t = (a/s)(I_{t-1} + Z) - bK_t$ and, since $I_t = K_{t+1} - K_t$, etc., that $K_{t+1} + (b - a/s - 1)K_t + (a/s)K_{t-1} = (a/s)Z$. This is a difference-equation describing the behaviour of capital stock over time. It is unstable if a/s exceeds unity. Both a and s are pure numbers with no time dimension (in both cases the ratios of two money-flows per unit of time), so that the units in which we measure time do not matter as long as they are the right ones to measure the time-lags postulated for the model. The value of the constant b, which relates investment per unit of time to capital stock, does, on the other hand, depend on the time-unit chosen. This makes it hard to say anything about the cyclical or non-cyclical property of the model, which depends on b.

It will be remembered that we found some slight evidence that, in so far as capital formation is influenced by foregoing changes in income or population, a widely distributed time-lag is involved. On general theoretical grounds it seems likely that this increases the stability of regional economies in the face of autonomous changes in demand.

All the evidence, therefore, seems to suggest that fairly short-term interactions of the multiplier and capital stock adjustment are of little account as destabilising influences. The regional economy is so 'open' that fluctuations (if they are initiated) are very quickly damped, and no self-sustaining divergence from the trend set by 'autonomous' investment and external demand is likely to arise. But what about these creators of a 'trend'? In the first place, they are very much larger than any internally induced capital formation could be, since they include not only those parts of capital formation not influenced by regional income and capital stock, but also direct and indirect external demand (including public demand) for the region's factors of production, which may amount to more than half of all demand for those factors. Variations in demand elsewhere in the economy, therefore, are likely to be very much more important as determinants of the region's activity than any internal influences, whether geared to the preceding course of its growth or not. In so far as there are cycles or other variations in the income of the economy as a whole, any region that comprises much less than half the national economy will be strongly pulled along with them, with little scope for showing peculiarities of its own. Peculiarities in the short-term activity of any minor part of the economy are more likely to spring from current peculiarities in the course of external demand for its products than from its internal dynamic processes; so are long-term trends and the general level of regional activity over a long period. It is the flows of goods and services and the flows of factors of production across regional boundaries that govern regional fortunes in the main.

OTHER DYNAMIC MECHANISMS

Other dynamic mechanisms by which growth differences may reinforce themselves are harder to assess. One of them depends simply on the fact that faster growth means a capital stock of lower average age, which may give a region superior attractiveness to footloose people and footloose industry, both as a physical environment to live in and as an industrial milieu to work in. The Board of Trade's 'Inquiry into Location Attitudes and Experience' shows good amenities and environment to be one of the most widely acknowledged *desiderata* in choice of location, though generally not the most important.[1] That it

[1] Unpublished document, 1971.

is least often quoted by firms going to the old industrial regions of slow growth (Yorkshire, Wales, the North, Lancashire outside Merseyside) and most often in the regions of fastest growth (the South West, East Anglia, the Midlands and the South East) may suggest that the atmosphere that goes with rapid growth is attractive.

A related mechanism works through the fact that the young, enterprising, and more highly trained are the most mobile part of the population, so that they tend to gravitate preferentially to regions of high net inward migration, which they probably thereby help, on balance, to make more attractive to their own kind. The effects of this should not be exaggerated; the distribution of highly educated people does not suggest that this factor is dominant. Scotland, for all its heavy net emigration, keeps more than its 'share' of such people in proportion to total adult population – and still more in relation to what its occupational structure would suggest – so does Wales; while the West Midlands, in spite of their growth, are in the opposite case. Age structure, however, inevitably reflects migration movements, and the growing regions have some advantage of youth in their human as well as their inanimate capital, which presumably further assists their growth.

At a subjective estimate (which is the best that can be done in this connection), this advantage of relatively new physical capital and young population is likely to be a more important engine of 'circular and cumulative causation' in British circumstances than the multiplier–capital stock mechanism.

There is one final mechanism which must be mentioned. In earlier days, when the services that could be provided by local authorities depended to a large extent on their local rate revenues, a powerful destabilising influence resulted. Those areas that were poor and burdened with heavy relief payments were automatically made unattractive to mobile industry and to mobile well-to-do residents, and so became poorer. With the increased importance of central government grants adjusted to need, this mechanism has been very much weakened in the last generation or two, but it is still not negligible. The importance of avoiding any strengthening of it in the course of changes in local government finance requires to be kept firmly in mind.

APPENDIX

Proportions from other regions of the 'mobile United Kingdom content' of regional consumption

One extreme hypothesis (as mentioned in the text) is that the 'mobile United Kingdom content' is perfectly mobile, so that consumers in a given region take it from their own and other regions in proportion to the respective volumes of relevant production – to which we can perhaps approximate by using figures of regional gross domestic product. On this hypothesis, the proportions of 'mobile United Kingdom content' imported into the various regions would be:

N	Y & H	NW	EM	WM	EA	SE	SW	Wa.	Sc.	NI
0·95	0·91	0·88	0·94	0·90	0·97	0·64	0·94	0·96	0·92	0·98

A more plausible hypothesis, however, is that a region is more likely to absorb a unit of output produced within itself than one produced in another region. Suppose the former probability is p times the latter one, then:

$$\frac{\text{regional absorption of imports}}{\text{total regional absorption of mobile goods and services}} = a = \frac{(1-y_r)}{py_r+(1-y_r)},$$

where y_r is the ratio of regional to national gross domestic product.

Now, we have no information relating specifically to goods imported into regions for consumption; our only data relate to all goods. We must therefore broaden the argument to include all mobile goods and hope that the conclusion will throw some light on those passing into final consumption. Specifically, suppose that $a = M_{CIG}/(kY_r)$, where M_{CIG} is imported mobile United Kingdom content of the region's consumption, capital formation and public current expenditure, and k is the ratio of the mobile content of final absorption to Y_r, the regional gross domestic product. If M_X is the imported United Kingdom mobile content of the region's exports, M_f is its total *foreign* imports, T is its total external trade (exports or imports, assuming them to be equal), m_f is the average foreign import propensity and k' is the proportionate mobile content of the region's exports, then:

$$T = M_f + M_{CIG} + M_X = m_f Y_r + akY_r + ak'T.$$

Thus, if we suppose that mobile inputs into regional exports come from outside the region to the same extent, a, as those into regional consumption, investment etc., $T/Y_r = m_f + ak + ak'T/Y_r$, or

$$a = (T/Y_r - m_f)/(k + k'T/Y_r).$$

Of the terms on the right hand side, we already have some sort of estimate of T/Y_r for each region from chapter 2. We can use for m_f the national figure 0·17. In discussing consumption above, we estimated that the *total* mobile content accounted for about 0·73 of it. If we put $k = 0·73$ and take k' as having this value also, we get the following for the ratio of imported to total mobile United Kingdom content of consumption, investment and public absorption:

N	Y & H	NW	EM	WM	EA	SE	SW	Wa.	Sc.	NI
0·61	0·68	0·74	0·77	0·69	0·73	0·40	0·55	0·58	0·45	0·49

Far too many special, and not entirely plausible, assumptions are made here for the figures to be taken as giving more than a very general order of magnitude, but for this purpose they may be regarded as helpful.

CHAPTER 9

THE LABOUR MARKET

THE SIGNIFICANCE OF LABOUR-MARKET DISCREPANCIES

The state of regional labour markets has been a central theme in discussions of regional problems and regional policy for at least three reasons. First, high involuntary unemployment in any region is a cause for concern in itself – a manifest social evil as well as a waste of productive power. The same may be said of situations in which, without being formally registered as unemployed, a high proportion of the population of working age in a region is without gainful employment through lack of opportunity. Second, a greater shortage of labour in some regions than in others is widely regarded as a source of inflation, in the sense that if demand for labour could be diverted from these regions of greater to those of less shortage the average rate of wage and cost inflation in the country as a whole would be reduced. Third, where labour incomes in a region are unusually low, this is regarded at least locally as a cause for complaint. More generally, it may be looked on as indicating that the geographical distribution of factors of production is less than optimal.

It will be convenient to start our discussion of these matters by first surveying and analysing the distribution of, and changes in, regional activity rates and unemployment; then to look briefly at interregional differences in labour earnings and the evidence on the determination and mutual relations of earnings and unemployment within regions; and finally, to consider the efficiency implications of interregional differences in wage levels.

ACTIVITY RATES[1]

The only published activity rates for the United Kingdom and its regions are those calculated by the Department of Employment; they are *employee* activity rates, obtained by dividing the Department's estimate of employees including the unemployed by the Registrar General's estimate of the total population aged 15 and over.

If, however, one is interested only in the position at a single point of time (or at widely separated points) and wishes to follow the calculation up with further investigations, there is some advantage in starting

---

[1] This section is based upon J. K. Bowers, *The Anatomy of Regional Activity Rates*, NIESR Regional Papers I, Cambridge University Press, 1970.

Table 9.1. *Variations in male activity and inactivity rates, 1961: deviations from England and Wales average*

Percentages

	Activity rates					Inactivity rates			
	Employees[a]	Self-employed	Family workers	Forces	Total	Retired	Students	Other[b]	Total
North	+1·4	−1·2	—	−0·3	−0·1	+0·7	−0·5	−0·1	+0·1
E & W Ridings	+2·5	−0·9	—	−1·0	+0·6	—	−0·4	−0·2	−0·6
North West	+2·5	−0·8	—	−1·3	+0·4	−0·1	−0·3	—	−0·4
N Midlands	+1·2	−0·1	+0·1	+0·1	+1·3	−0·4	−0·7	−0·2	−1·3
(W) Midlands	+4·3	−1·0	—	−0·7	+2·6	−2·1	−0·4	−0·1	−2·6
East	−2·5	+0·8	—	+1·5	−0·2	+0·2	−0·1	+0·1	+0·2
London & SE	+0·9	−0·3	−0·2	−0·6	−0·2	−0·5	+0·5	+0·2	+0·2
South	−5·3	—	−0·1	+4·3	−1·1	+0·7	+0·3	+0·1	+1·1
South West	−9·1	+3·2	+0·3	+2·7	−2·9	+2·6	+0·1	+0·2	+2·9
Wales	−3·4	+2·0	—	−0·5	−1·9	+1·4	+0·3	+0·2	+1·9
Scotland	+1·1	+0·1	+0·2	−0·5	+0·9	−0·8	—	−0·1	−0·9
N Ireland	−10·0	+9·0	+1·1	−0·3	−0·2	+0·1	+0·5	−0·4	+0·2

SOURCE: Bowers, *Regional Activity Rates*, tables 1.3 and 1.6 (small adjustments for rounding have been made to the figures originally published).

[a] Ministry of Labour definition. [b] Includes institution inmates.

with corresponding figures worked out from the Census of Population. The results show considerable interregional differences. For males, the 1961 rate varied from 80·9 per cent in the (West) Midlands to 66·6 per cent in Northern Ireland; even within England and Wales it stood as low as 67·5 per cent in the South West. Inspection, however, proves that nearly all these variations in male activity rates arise from differences in the ratios of employees (persons insured against unemployment) to the numbers who are economically active in a wider sense. The self-employed, family workers and members of the forces are not classed as 'employees'; if their numbers ascertained from the Census are added to those of employees, one gets what is perhaps a more meaningful activity rate for our purpose. For males in the year 1961, this rate varied much less: the highest regional figure was 88·7 per cent for the (West) Midlands, the lowest 83·2 per cent for the South West; the standard deviation of 4·47 per cent for the employee activity rate comes down to only 1·39 per cent in this 'total' activity rate.

Interregional variations in incidence of the non-employee categories largely offset those in the proportions of employees. The forces are thickest on the ground in the South and South West; the self-employed and family workers in the South West and, even more, in Northern Ireland (see table 9.1).

The variations in proportions of self-employed perhaps deserve a little further attention, since it is possible that in this category some 'concealed' unemployment may be found. Self-employed without employees (the most variable subdivision) are to be found mostly in agriculture, construction, transport, distribution, and professional and miscellaneous services; most of the variations in their incidence between the English regions are explained by the incidences of these industries, though the variations from the United Kingdom average to be found in Scotland, Wales and Northern Ireland owe more to differences in their frequency within the industries concerned. In particular, agriculture in Northern Ireland and, to a smaller extent, in Wales is carried on more by self-employed persons without employees than in the country as a whole. In Scotland the deviation is in the opposite direction – a relatively small proportion of self-employed, especially in agriculture, distribution and other services. The high proportion o self-employed without employees in agriculture in Northern Ireland and Wales may be taken as reflecting, among other things, a shortage of employment opportunities in those economies.

The interregional variation in proportions of all males aged 15 and over who are *not* economically active, either as employees, as self-employed, or as members of the forces, is thus small. The biggest source of variation is, not surprisingly, the retired, who accounted in the South West for over $2\frac{1}{2}$ per cent more of the total population than they did nationally, and in the (West) Midlands for almost as much less. Most of this interregional variation in the incidence of retirement, moreover, is explained by differences of age composition. The residual variation from the national average still unexplained does not amount to as much as 1 per cent of the adult population in any region, and seems itself to be accounted for largely by unusually high (or low) incidences of pensioners from professions with early retirement ages, or of ex-miners whose employment opportunities (in many cases no doubt for reasons of health) are especially poor.

On the whole then, variation in the proportions of males who are economically active is small, and the part of it reasonably attributable to differences in opportunity or pressure of demand is smaller still. In proportion to regional populations the 'concealed' unemployment among the self-employed in the agriculture of Northern Ireland is probably the most notable instance of this latter category. The story is, however, very different when we come to examine the activity rates of the female population.

There, the employee activity rates calculated from the 1961 Census varied from 40 per cent in London and the South East (and nearly as much in the (West) Midlands and the North West) to 25·6 per cent in

Table 9.2. *Variations in female activity and inactivity rates, 1961: deviations from England and Wales average*

Percentages

	Activity rates				Inactivity rates			
	Employees	Employers and self-employed	Forces and family workers	Total	Retired	Students	Other[a]	Total
North	−6·0	−0·2	−0·1	−6·3	−1·2	−0·2	+7·7	+6·3
E & W Ridings	+0·9	—	—	+0·9	—	−0·3	−0·6	−0·9
North West	+3·9	+0·4	+0·1	+4·4	+0·8	−0·2	−5·0	−4·4
N Midlands	−1·0	—	—	−1·0	−0·8	−0·3	+2·1	+1·0
(W) Midlands	+4·0	—	−0·1	+3·9	−0·6	−0·3	−3·0	−3·9
East	−4·2	−0·2	−0·1	−4·5	−0·4	—	+4·9	+4·5
London & SE	+4·5	−0·2	−0·1	+4·2	+0·6	+0·2	−5·0	−4·2
South	−4·4	—	+0·1	−4·3	+0·2	+0·2	+3·9	+4·3
South West	−7·0	+0·3	+0·1	−6·6	+0·3	+0·2	+6·1	+6·6
Wales	−9·9	+0·5	−0·2	−9·6	−0·9	+0·5	+10·0	+9·6
Scotland	−1·2	−0·4	−0·2	−1·8	−0·5	—	+2·3	+1·8
N Ireland	−2·4	+0·3	−0·3	−2·4	+0·3	+0·8	+1·3	+2·4

SOURCE: Bowers, *Regional Activity Rates*, table 2.1 (small adjustments for rounding have been made to the figures originally published).

[a] Includes institution inmates.

Wales. Since the proportions of women who are self-employed, family workers, or members of the forces are smaller than the corresponding proportions of men, and also show little interregional variation, the total activity rates including these classes of non-employees present a very similar picture. Measured from the total female activity rate for England and Wales (a convenient yardstick), regional rates run from nearly 10 per cent below in Wales to about 4 per cent above in London, the (West) Midlands, and the North West.

The classes of *inactivity* that mostly account for variations in male activity rates do not help much with females. The proportion of women described as 'retired' varies much less between regions than that of men – it is highest in some of the regions with high female activity rates (London and the North West) and in others that are well known retreats of the retired (the South and the South West). The big interrregional variation in the proportion of inactive women is in the class described as 'other inactive' – from 52 per cent in London and the North West to 67 per cent in Wales (see table 9.2).

To take the story further we have to look at separate age and marital status groups. The activity rates of married women and of the rest (single, widowed and divorced) are, of course, very different; so are the rates observed for women of either of these descriptions in different age groups. It is among married women that the variation in activity rates is greatest – ranging from 19 per cent in Wales to 36 per cent in the North West; though those among other women vary considerably as well – from 43·6 per cent in Wales to nearly 56 per cent in the (West) Midlands. It can be shown that differences in age composition go some way to explain the interregional activity rate deviations of single, widowed and divorced women (especially where the deviation from the national average is extreme in either direction), but that such differences do not help at all in explaining deviations in the activity rates of the married.

Taking regional activity rates of all women together, composition by age and marital status in fact explains some, but only a little, of their interregional differences. To what then can we attribute the rest – the main part of these differences?

On the face of it, a good deal of them seems to go with degree of urbanisation; the highest proportions of jobs for women are in conurbations, lower proportions in other towns, and the lowest in the country districts. A better explanation of the differences is given, however, by differences in either occupational or industrial structure, especially the latter. The ratio of women to total employees differs from industry to industry, and the kind of industries a region has goes a long way towards explaining its overall ratio of women to total employment, or of women in employment to total adult women. In fact the ratio of women to total employees *within particular occupations* does not seem to vary in a significant way according to the type of area (conurbation, large town, rural district) in which they live, nor does the corresponding ratio *within particular industries* seem to vary between different kinds of area within which the workplaces are situated. It seems to be not degree of urbanisation as such, but kind of industry (which to some extent goes with degree of urbanisation) that matters so far.

But there are significant differences in the ratio of women to total employees within industries (and for that matter within occupations) between different regions. Industrial structure does not explain everything. The unexplained variations are not random; some regions show consistently high female employee ratios (in relation to the national ratio for the relevant industry) in practically all industries; others show consistently low ones. The regions where the ratios are outstandingly high are the East and West Ridings, the North West, the (West) Midlands and, rather less certainly, London and the South East. Those where they are outstandingly low are the South West, Wales and the East.

It will be noticed that the regions where the female employee ratio is high are, in general, those where the structure is heavily weighted with female-employing industries. It can be shown that interregional differences in the marital status and age composition of the female population also help somewhat to explain these variations in the ratio, but after taking these differences into account the net influence of a female-employing structure on the mean female employee ratio[1] in a region is still positive.

What does this mean? If the propensity of women to go out to work bore the same relation to that of men in all regions, we might, at first sight, expect that industries would distribute themselves so that the relative demands for male and female labour were roughly the same everywhere. But, given that there are other past or present locational forces that prevent this, we might expect that where predominantly female-employing industries have congregated female labour will be relatively scarce, and the female employee ratios of industries will tend to be *below* those of the same industries nationally. This is the opposite of what we find. One possible explanation is that it is differences of supply not of demand that are dominant; that the propensity of women in the North West, for instance, to go out to work is so great in comparison with that in (say) Wales that the North West has adjusted to the situation not only by attracting more than its share of female-employing industries such as textiles and clothing, but by substituting female for male employees in all or most industries.

This does not seem very plausible; it is likely that the explanation is less general and tidy. The old textile areas (the North West, Yorkshire and Humberside) have built up a strong tradition of female employment and their traditionally female-employing industries are in relative or absolute decline, so that the supply of female labour to industry generally is relatively strong. In the (West) Midlands and, with qualifications, London, the shortage of labour generally in relation to demand might be responsible for pulling into employment, in all industries, a high proportion of the elastic, female part of the potential labour force. In the agricultural, mining and heavy industry regions (Wales, the North, the South West and the East), the structure still keeps down demand for female employees, but the decline of employment in their basic industries means that the supply of male labour is relatively strong, and the substitution of female for male labour is inhibited. In short, the breakdown of the old, extreme specialisations of male and female-employing industries, plus persistent labour shortage in the South East, where the structure is biased towards the new, female-employing, light manufacturing and service trades, may be used to account for the

[1] That is to say, the *unweighted* mean of the ratios of female to total employees in all the separate industries.

current association between bias towards female-employing industry and high female employee ratios throughout industry.

Too much stress should not, however, be put upon this association, nor indeed upon variations in the female employee ratio within industries in general. The greater part of the interregional variation in female activity rates is accounted for not by them, but by differences in industrial or occupational structure. The implication is that the propensity of women to go out to work is responsive to differences of opportunity – of industrial demand – over a wide range and in the long run, but that it takes time to change.

Further light can be thrown on this by examining the changes that have come about in female activity rates and employment ratios over a recent period, namely the decade 1954–64 for which Ministry of Labour statistics provide suitable data. The period in question, indeed the whole postwar period, has been one in which demand for female labour has risen ahead of that for male. Not only has female employment risen proportionately faster than male employment, but female unemployment has been lower than male and has declined relatively to it. Female activity rates rose in every region except the North West in the decade in question, and in general they rose most where they were lowest to start with – Wales, with a rise from 25·0 to 28·9 per cent, standing at the top of the list.

The increase, however, was far from uniform between age groups; in fact the activity rates for those aged 15 to 24 everywhere decreased – no doubt from a combination of increasing full-time education and earlier marriage and motherhood – the decrease being sharpest in the high-activity regions. The next age group, 25 to 44, showed an increase in activity rates everywhere except in the North West, the rise (as with the adult female population as a whole) being generally greatest where the starting level was lowest. The 45–59 group showed the most spectacular increases of all, extending across all regions, with much less tendency than was apparent with the two younger groups for regional rates to converge. The smaller increases shown among those over 60 were also fairly uniform across the regions.

The change in relative regional rates – their general levelling-up – was thus entirely due to the age group 25 to 44, which is presumably most concerned with the bringing up of children. The increase of fertility in the decade 1954–64 may have helped (along with the decline of the cotton industry) to reduce the activity rate in this age group in the North West; it must in all regions have tended to strengthen, or to lower, the ceiling towards which the generally buoyant demand for female labour was tending to raise it. It may be also that this is the age group most likely to enter manufacturing industry, which increased its female employment especially fast in some of the regions with low activity rates – the South West, Wales and the North – though it did so in the (West) Midlands as well.

The fairly uniform increase in the activity rates of the older age groups, for whom home duties do not compete with going out to work as actively as they do for younger women, may perhaps be taken as suggesting that neither the increase in demand for female labour nor the rate of breakdown of traditional inhibitions against going out to work showed great differences from one region to another – or that, if there were differences on the demand side, they were pretty well offset by countervailing differences relating to supply. Or it may be that these older women were drawn largely into service trades, where demand increases were more nearly uniform between regions than was the case with manufacturing industry. At all events the differences that remained in 1964 between regional activity rates in these older age groups were considerable; for the 45–59 group the rates varied from under 32 per cent in Wales to nearly 51 per cent in the North West. With continuing pressure of demand, one would expect to see considerably bigger further increases of the rate in the regions where it is still low, just as there were in the decade we have examined among the women aged 25 to 44 – for whom also there remains a good deal of scope for further levelling-up of the rates.

An examination of the female employment ratios in the decade 1953–63 shows that the changes in the percentages of all employees in the industry who were female were markedly different in different industries. The ratios rose substantially in agriculture, distribution, insurance, banking and finance, and public administration, as well as in construction, mining and the public utilities including transport; they fell in textiles, vehicles, timber, paper, chemicals and the miscellaneous services group. Analysis of variance shows, however, that there was no significant tendency for the ratios generally to rise or to fall within industries more in one region than in another. The greater rises of female activity rates in some regions than in others must, therefore, have been due, in the main, either to their having larger complements of the industries in which the ratio rose, or to increases in relation to the rest of the country of those industries where the ratio was high, or to a higher than national proportion of female labour in industries that were growing.

Although, as we have noted, there has been a general tendency in some regions for their female employment ratios to be low across the board, there is no sign that this tendency changed more in some regions than in others between the mid-fifties and the mid-sixties. The suggestion is that the interregional differences in female employment ratios extending across all industries are chronic ones. Some of them may really be structural – for example, the tendency for the ratio of office workers to manual workers to be high in the South East because head offices are concentrated there – others may be associated with rates of change in the supply and demand patterns which have reached rough equality, with a fairly constant set of maladjustments between the patterns corresponding to the social and economic frictions at work.

THE 'RESERVE' OF FEMALE LABOUR

Taking female activity rates as we find them, however, to what extent do they indicate the presence of unused reserves of labour in particular regions which can be regarded as constituting wasted resources? It is easy enough to calculate such 'reserves' on superficially plausible assumptions. One can, for instance, assume that, within each of the four age groups distinguished in the Department of Employment's statistics, it would be possible for all regions to attain the highest female activity rate that any of them attains and compute the amounts by which they fail to do so. A calculation of this kind for 1966 (table 9.3) suggests that raising the age-specific activity rates to those of the region where they are highest (the South East for the two younger age groups, the North West and the West Midlands for the two older ones respectively) would increase female employment in the United Kingdom by some 884,000. This is about 3·4 per cent of the total economically active population (of both sexes), and more than twice the registered unemployment at the census date. The levelling-up we have postulated would raise the active populations of the regions by proportions varying from a negligible one in the South East to 8·9 per cent in the North, 9·0 per cent in East Anglia, 9·9 in the South West, 10·2 in Northern Ireland and 12·8 in Wales.

These are substantial figures, and must be taken as confirming that differences in female activity rates are indeed important. One must not, however, ignore the necessary qualifications. On the one hand, the highest age-specific activity rates so far attained are not to be taken as absolute standards. The 15–24 age group's rate will probably continue to fall generally (for men as well as for women) with the growth of full-time education. The highest rate for the 45–59 group has continued to rise in recent years in spite of a net slackening in the pressure of demand for labour, and there is no saying where, short of the comparable rate for men (still more than half as high again), it will stop. The scope for raising general regional activity rates in the medium or long run is therefore almost certainly different from (probably greater than) that suggested by our calculation, though the absolute differences in scope between regions may not be greatly misrepresented.

Table 9.3. *'Deficiencies' of economically active women[a] below those in the region with the highest age-specific activity rate, 1966*

	Age group								All ages	Percentage of active population[b]
	15–24		25–44		45–59		60+			
	(%)	(000)	(%)	(000)	(%)	(000)	(%)	(000)	(000)	(%)
North	5·5	13	11·3	46	17·0	53	5·6	18	130	8·9
Yorks. and Humberside	5·6	19	4·4	25	6·5	30	2·1	10	84	3·8
North West	2·7	10	0·1	1	—	—	2·2	16	27	0·8
E Midlands	5·3	12	6·7	27	6·1	19	2·5	8	66	4·2
W Midlands	4·4	17	1·8	11	1·1	5	—	—	33	1·3
East Anglia	10·1	11	13·6	25	13·2	19	4·5	8	63	9·0
South East	—	—	—	—	0·6	10	0·3	6	16	0·2
South West	14·6	37	12·5	53	13·2	47	4·9	21	158	9·9
Wales	18·4	35	14·1	45	18·6	50	6·4	17	147	12·8
Scotland	7·8	29	3·2	21	7·5	38	2·4	12	100	4·3
N Ireland	7·9	9	10·8	18	19·0	24	7·2	9	60	10·2
United Kingdom		192		272		295		125	884	3·4

SOURCE: *Sample Census 1966, Great Britain. Economic Activity Tables;* Department of Employment

[a] Employees.   [b] Male and female.

On the other hand, one should not assume that the scope for raising output (or still less welfare) is correctly represented by the scope for raising the overall activity rate in a region. That scope relates as we have seen almost entirely to female employment, and female output per hour is less than male. Moreover, a considerable proportion of the female employment taken into account in these calculations is part-time, and the proportion may increase as female activity rates rise – high demand makes it worth employing part-timers. Finally, one should not ignore, even if one cannot quantify, the loss of services in the home when women go out to work. Some of the extra employment in a high-activity region – on provision of household help, meals, nursery schools and laundry services, for instance – is a substitute for the unpaid services of housewives in regions where employee rates are lower, and there are no doubt some services rendered by housewives in the home, in the care of young children for instance, for which the available substitutes are generally inferior. It is not, therefore, to be assumed that the level of welfare in Wales, for instance, would rise by an eighth if the structure of industry, the pressure of demand and social customs were adjusted to reproduce the activity rates of South East England. That it would rise substantially, however, there seems little room to doubt.

UNEMPLOYMENT[1]

On registered unemployment there seems to be so much information that this aspect of differences in the working of regional labour markets should be relatively easy to analyse. There are, however, difficulties, one of which had better be faced at the outset. How far do the statistics of registered unemployed represent the number of people not at the material time in jobs, who are in the labour market in the sense that they are either actively seeking work or at least hoping for something to turn up? This is not a question that admits of a very precise answer, since it relates to intentions about which even the people holding them may not be very clear or consistent. The point should be borne in mind in considering the best evidence we have, which is the Census of Population.

In the 1966 Census, about 61 per cent of the population of Great Britain aged 15 or over described themselves as economically active. Of these 733,000 or 2·9 per cent were actually out of work on the stated day (18 April), but only 297,000 or 1·2 per cent of the economically active were registered as unemployed at an employment exchange or youth employment office. Nearly 200,000 of those unregistered were sick. Some 259,000 of those out of work on the day in question had not been at work at any time during the preceding twelve months, and only about 50,000 of these had been registered as unemployed for a year or more. There was thus a very considerable penumbra of unregistered persons whose claim to be regarded as 'economically active' was rather a vague one,[2] and our knowledge of its size is also necessarily vague.

The question that concerns us is whether the penumbra bears a different relation to registered unemployment in different regions to such an extent that differences in unemployment rates cannot be taken as reflecting reliably the differences in involuntary worklessness. It is worth looking quickly at the relations between the registered and the unregistered who regarded themselves as 'active' but were without jobs on 18 April 1966, considering separately men, married women and other women.

In Great Britain as a whole the registered and unregistered men who were out of employment were about equal in numbers. In the individual regions there were departures from this equality. In the low-unemploy-

---

[1] This section draws heavily upon P. C. Cheshire, *An Investigation of Regional Unemployment Differences*, NIESR Regional Papers II (forthcoming).

[2] It may be noted that some of those who have been employed at some time during the year and have not subsequently registered as unemployed on ceasing to work are included in the Ministry of Labour's statistics of 'Employees in employment' in the *Ministry of Labour Gazette* (now the *Department of Employment Gazette*).

ment regions the unregistered tended to be more numerous than the registered – the extreme case being the West Midlands where they were nearly twice as numerous. In the high-unemployment regions the unregistered were less numerous – in the North they numbered not much more than half as many as the registered unemployed. As percentages of the economically active population they showed a fairly high correlation with registered unemployment rates but varied less between regions. The suggestion is, therefore, that *relative* differences in unemployment rates may somewhat overstate differences in the incidence of involuntary worklessness, but their absolute differences tend to understate them.

Among women on the other hand, the number who were registered as unemployed was little more than a quarter of the number who regarded themselves as economically active but were without employment on the stated day. The unregistered formed a proportion of the total women aged 15 and over which did not vary much from region to region – as with the men it tended to be a little over 1 per cent – but it was virtually uncorrelated with the proportion of adult women registered as unemployed. One may deduce from this that unemployment rates among women are more imperfect as measures of the comparative incidence of involuntary worklessness in different regions than those among men; they are overshadowed by the penumbra of unregistered unemployed (if the metaphor is not too inappropriate). But it is of the nature of the penumbra that it should not be taken very literally as a measure of involuntary worklessness either, especially as its interregional variations seem to be small.

With this clearing of the ground we may proceed to look with due caution at interregional differences of unemployment as measured by registered unemployment rates. The striking feature of these rates is that their rank order has remained almost unchanged for fifty years, though, as we noted when we had occasion to take an even longer view, that rank order is almost the reverse of that prevailing among trade union unemployment rates before the first world war. By the late 1920s Wales was established as the region with the highest rate, with Northern Ireland running it fairly close. England north of the Trent had then a somewhat higher rate than Scotland, and the Midlands a decidedly higher one than London and the South East. The order was broadly preserved throughout the depression of the 1930s, but by 1937 Northern Ireland had the highest regional rate, and Midland unemployment was little more severe than that of the South East. Since the war, the Welsh rate has improved relatively, as has that of Yorkshire and Lancashire; Scotland has consistently shown the highest rate in Great Britain, but Northern Ireland has retained one in a higher bracket altogether – in some ways more reminiscent of prewar than of postwar British conditions. Ever since the twenties however, it has continued to be broadly true that unemployment rates have risen as one has gone north-westwards from London.

In analysing regional unemployment differences, perhaps the first question to ask is how far these differences are, in the strict sense, 'regional' at all. How far are rates of unemployment specific to industries, so that regional rates are simply averages of these specific industry rates weighted according to amounts of employment that the industries provide in the region? One approach to this question is by analysis of variance of unemployment rates classified by industry and region. Investigations of this kind, carried out for June 1963 and June 1965 for men and women separately, show that differences of unemployment rates between the same industry-groups (Industrial Orders) in different regions, and between different industry-groups in the same region, are both, at first sight, highly significant statistically, but that the mean square difference between regions is greater than that between industries – for men roughly twice as great, for women relatively much greater. Moreover, there seems to be a considerable tendency for the good or bad average records of particular regions or industries to be due to a few industries in the region, or a few regional sections of the industry (as the case may be), rather than to generally good or bad performance. This makes it improbable that most of the interregional difference in average unemployment rates can be explained *directly* by differences of industrial structure; for this to be possible each industry would have to show much the same unemployment rate everywhere, and we see that this is not so.

The contribution of structure in this simple sense to regional unemployment averages can, however, be investigated more directly by calculating how much regional rates would differ from the national rate if each industry showed the same (national average) unemployment rate in every region, or alternatively, if the country as a whole showed the region's unemployment rates in each industry – in short, conducting a standardisation or 'shift-and-share' analysis of the influence of industrial structure on regional unemployment averages.

The result of a number of calculations of this kind for different dates, using different (regional or national) unemployment rates as weights, and different degrees of disaggregation in the classification of industries, is quite unambiguously that structural differences are responsible, in this sense, for very little indeed of the differences between regional unemployment rates. Regions do not have high unemployment because they specialise on high-unemployment industries – indeed, the extent to which there *are* any high-unemployment industries, in the strict sense of industries having high unemployment in all regions, is limited though statistically significant. It is rather more nearly true, though again with limitations, that there are high-unemployment *regions*, in the sense of regions having high unemployment in most industries.

None of these findings is very surprising. If there was only negligible mobility of labour between industries, seasonal and perhaps cyclical unemployment might be expected to be industry-specific, and much the same in a given industry in all regions. Structural unemployment due to the decline of particular industries' demands for manpower leading to redundancy might also share this character if the industries in question reduced their manpower demands at the same rates in all regions. Inter-industry mobility is, however, quite high; according to the Labour Mobility Survey, nearly two-thirds of the employees who change jobs change their industry-group as well.[1]

The smaller variance of unemployment rates between industries than between regions suggests that inter-industry mobility is in fact greater than interregional. This, too, is confirmed by the Labour Mobility Survey; the 'representative British employee' changes his industry-group once in seven or eight years, his region of residence only once in sixty; and even the fact that there are more industry-groups than there are regions (twenty-four against ten) does not seem to account for this difference.

Even within a single region, moreover, the correlation between the rate at which an industry's employment is growing and the unemployment percentage in that industry, though in our investigations always negative, is rarely significant. The unemployed are classified industrially according to their last job, so that a worker leaving a declining industry ceases to be classified as belonging to it as soon as he has been employed – even very briefly – elsewhere. Moreover, a high proportion of the workers becoming redundant in some declining industries (most notably coalmining) leave the labour force altogether. The result, therefore, of a heavy specialisation by a region on declining trades is not so much a larger number of unemployed registered as belonging to those trades as a general shortage of demand for labour, leading to high unemployment rates in all industries in the region. On the face of it unemployment differences are between regions rather than between industries, though a region may have high unemployment because it specialises on industries that are doing badly.

The next question to suggest itself, perhaps, about the interregional differences is whether the high-unemployment regions suffer their unhappy pre-eminence constantly over time, or in the form of rates that are relatively high at seasonal or cyclical peaks. Part of the answer, of

[1] Government Social Survey, *Labour Mobility in Great Britain 1953–63*.

Table 9.4. *Total and partial unemployment rates,[a] 1958–67*

Percentages

	N	C[b]	NW	LSE	E & S	SW	Wa.	Sc.
Male								
Seasonal	0·30	0·14	0·15	0·15	0·23	0·31	0·32	0·31
Cyclical	0·77	0·39	0·57	0·29	0·26	0·31	0·56	0·60
Basic	2·20	0·79	1·52	0·85	0·88	1·25	1·89	2·71
Total	3·27	1·32	2·24	1·29	1·37	1·87	2·77	3·62
Female								
Seasonal	0·18	0·05	0·10	0·07	0·13	0·28	0·26	0·20
Cyclical	0·36	0·15	0·36	0·09	0·10	0·12	0·35	0·36
Basic	1·33	0·55	0·80	0·39	0·45	0·68	1·57	1·87
Total	1·87	0·75	1·26	0·55	0·68	1·08	2·18	2·43

SOURCES: Ministry of Labour, *Statistics on Incomes, Prices, Employment and Production; Ministry of Labour Gazette.*

[a] Proportions of the regional labour forces.
[b] Midlands regions and Yorkshire combined.

course, has already been given in the statement that the rank order of unemployment rates has changed little over time; regions have not changed their ranking in the course of the year or the trade cycle to any considerable extent. A more systematic inquiry is needed, however, to find how far unemployment in each region consists of a standing reserve army and how far of a fluctuating one.

Ideally one should investigate this question industry by industry or occupation by occupation. A community consisting in equal parts of professional footballers and professional cricketers would have a constant amount of unemployment all the year round, which should, nevertheless, be described as 'seasonal'. Such an investigation would, however, be tedious, and would not necessarily give a correct answer since, to an extent that only still further detailed enquiry would reveal, workers in seasonal trades do in fact have second jobs for the off-season. We have therefore limited our enquiry to variations in *total* unemployment in the regions, distinguishing first the average unemployment in excess of a trend drawn through the seasonal minima, then the average excess (excluding seasonal) above a trend drawn through the cyclical minima, and finally the average basic level of these cyclical minimum rates.

The finding (table 9.4) is that, over the decade 1958–67, the 'basic' unemployment was the major component of total unemployment in all regions, both for men and for women. It was, in fact, not very far from being a constant proportion (about two-thirds) of unemployment everywhere. As a proportion of the male labour force it varied from 2·71 per cent in Scotland to 0·85 per cent in London and the South East. (Northern Ireland was not included in this analysis.) Much the same was true of female unemployment.

Seasonal unemployment proves to be rather more independent of the total unemployment rate of the region, though it shows some positive correlation with it; for men it ran from 0·32 per cent in Wales to 0·14 in the Midlands and Yorkshire (which have to be combined because of a change in the delimitation of Ministry of Labour regions). For women it ran from 0·28 per cent in the South West to a negligible 0·05 in the Midlands and Yorkshire. The influences of agriculture and the tourist trade are visible in the variations of this component.

Cyclical unemployment of men averaged over the cycle was decidedly higher in the Northern region than elsewhere in Great Britain, though also quite high in the North West, Wales and Scotland. Among women cyclical unemployment in the decade seemed to have only two levels – relatively high in Wales and north of the Trent, relatively low elsewhere.

Both seasonal and cyclical unemployment show some correlation over regions with basic and total unemployment rates. A certain amount of light is thrown on this correlation in the case of cyclical fluctuations by considering interregional differences in the relations between short-term changes in unemployment and those in employment. A good deal of work has been done on this and related subjects at national level. We investigated for each region the relationship between employment, unemployment, changes in population of working age and, as a residual influence, changes in activity rates in the period 1953–65.

It was plain at the outset that the short-term fluctuations in employment were generally bigger than those in unemployment, but it emerged that this was so to a far greater extent in some regions than in others. In the South East, the South West and the Midlands and Yorkshire, the ratio of the relevant variances was high; in the North, Scotland and Wales it was much lower – in fact its difference from unity was not statistically significant in the latter regions. In the South and the Midlands and Yorkshire – regions of low unemployment – the effective short-term reserve of labour is not, apparently, to be found among the registered unemployed; in the North, Scotland and Wales, to a large extent it is. This conclusion is confirmed more systematically by regression equations that seek to relate short-term variations in employment, corrected to allow for the purely demographic changes in the region, to changes in unemployment. In the North, Scotland and Wales, a change of 100 in the number of registered unemployed tended to go with an opposite change of 150 in employment (excluding the effect of demographic changes), and thus by implication a change of 50 in 'the rest'.[1] In the South East the corresponding changes in (corrected) employment and 'the rest' were 250 and 150; in the Midlands regions and Yorkshire 280 and 180. The North West is in an intermediate position, with changes in 'the rest' a little less important than those in registered unemployment. The South West, however, seems to rely even less on 'the rest' as a reserve than the North, Wales, or Scotland.

Very broadly this picture seems comprehensible. Where there is high pressure of labour demand there is never much registered unemployment because those actively offering themselves for work are snapped up. In relatively slack times workers already employed tend to be 'hoarded'; a boom – a push to get more labour – tends to draw largely on those who are only marginal members of the labour force, and who tend to drop out of it spontaneously in a slump, so that their numbers in employment decline without adding to registered unemployment. In the regions of lower demand pressure these conditions do not apply: redundant labour is laid off more freely – since labour is not expected to be scarce, there is less reason to incur the costs of hoarding it – and those laid off will normally register for benefit. We saw from census data that the unregistered unemployed vary little as a proportion of the labour force from one region to another; in regions of slack demand they are a small proportion of the actual reserve of labour, in regions of high demand a large one. There are some anomalies, notably the very small part played by fluctuations of 'the rest' in the South West which is not a region of outstandingly low demand for labour. There are, however, special factors at work there; more than most it is a region of small towns and partial labour monopsony, which may reduce hoarding and make for prompt registration by the unemployed. At all events it is clear that, in general, the fluctuations of registered unemployment give very much fuller indications of the true variations in involuntary worklessness in some regions than in others; they are more inefficient indicators of it where demand is high, so that they tend to overstate the relative (though perhaps not the absolute) differences in regional incidence of cyclical unemployment.

To distinguish any differences in the character and origins of unemployment in the various regions, however, we need a more searching analysis than one built merely upon temporal patterns of change. It used to be customary, when unemployment was very much more severe than it has been since the war, to distinguish three sources of the un-

[1] 'The rest' here means all those of working age who are neither in employment nor registered unemployed. It comprises those whom we have called the unregistered unemployed (people who claim to be looking or hoping for a job, but are not registered as unemployed), along with people who, in effect, change their minds about their membership or non-membership of the labour force, and a third group who move between employment and self-employment. Interregional migration may also contribute to changes in 'the rest'.

employment existing at any moment – friction, structural maladjustment, and demand-deficiency which in those days was often thought of as being essentially cyclical. It is possible to provide precise definitions corresponding more or less to these distinctions. Let us try to do so.

Frictional unemployment may be said to be present in so far as unemployed people co-exist in a region with unfilled vacancies in the industries (or, in an alternative formulation, the occupations) in which the unemployed are registered. The implication is that these people have in principle jobs waiting for them, but they have not found them yet – either because of the imperfection of the information system, or because the jobs are in the wrong part of the region. It will not escape the reader, however, that there may be other reasons, leaving aside imperfections in the system of industrial or occupational classification used, why these unemployed have not fitted into the existing niches – they may have been judged or found deficient. We could separate out in principle a fourth source of unemployment – unemployability – and we must return to this point.

Meanwhile, we can define structural unemployment as existing to the extent that, while there are vacancies, they are in the wrong industries (or occupations) for the unemployed. Demand-deficiency unemployment is even simpler – it is the excess of unemployed over unfilled vacancies of all kinds in the region.

It can be shown that these 'kinds' of unemployment add up to the total number of unemployed in any region (still including in our frictional category any whom we may subsequently choose to classify separately as unemployable). There is, however, a logical difficulty. If things were so bad in a region that there were no unfilled vacancies, we should have to classify all the unemployment as due to demand-deficiency. But this would be unhelpful, because if effective demand were increased unfilled vacancies would appear, and so, therefore, would structural and frictional unemployment, which we wish to distinguish from the demand-deficiency variety as carrying different policy implications. One can solve the problem by defining demand-deficiency unemployment not simply as the excess of unemployed over vacancies, but as this excess minus the maximum sum of frictional and structural unemployment the region is capable of showing – which turns out to be the level of unemployment at which unemployment and vacancies are equal. This level of unemployment – the zero demand-deficiency level – seems a useful diagnostic magnitude; it measures the extent to which the region's labour market is in a certain sense 'imperfect'. Any level of actual unemployment below it can be put down as entirely structural or frictional. Any excess of actual unemployment above it can be put down to deficiency of demand.

In practice, of course, our statistics do not mean exactly what we should like them to mean for this purpose. In particular the registration of unfilled vacancies is incomplete to an unknown extent. It is believed that only something like a third or a fifth of all the vacancies that occur are filled after being registered at an employment exchange, but it is likely that those filled otherwise tend to be the more easily and quickly dealt with, so that the 'stock' of vacancies standing on the register at any time constitutes a good deal more than a fifth or a third of the vacancies then in existence. Moreover, while it may be that the proportion of all existing vacancies that are registered varies from region to region and time to time, there is no positive evidence that it is grossly unreliable as an index of unsatisfied demand for labour.

As we have seen, registered unemployment too is very imperfect as an indicator of involuntary worklessness. Perhaps, however, we may accept both these statistics with due caution as proxies for the 'true' unemployment and vacancy data which are beyond our reach.

The next practical problem is how to find the zero demand-deficiency level of unemployment for any given region, since unemployment at any time is likely to be at some level quite different from this. A solution is possible if it can be established that there is a functional relation for the region between the levels of unemployment and of vacancies which is stable over time and can be derived from time-series of the two variables. It is in fact the case that there are fairly good empirical relationships between unemployment and vacancies for most regions over considerable periods of time. There are also important shifts which we shall have to consider in due course. But for the moment we may usefully look at the relations that appear over a relatively short period, in which shifts do not seem to disrupt them badly.

The relationships are double logarithmic. Where the ranges of the variables for which we have data include the point of zero demand-deficiency we can be fairly confident in estimating the latter by interpolation; where they do not we must resort to extrapolation of the curve fitted to the data we have and confidence in the result cannot be so high, but the calculation still seems worthwhile.

It seems that the differences between the levels of unemployment (or vacancy) rates at which the two are equal vary relatively little between regions. According to the data for adult males in the period from the third quarter of 1963 to the second of 1966 (a period in which the unemployment–vacancy relation seems to have been unchanged), the difference between the levels where unemployment equalled vacancies for the Midlands and for Scotland was only 0·70 per cent. The average difference in actual unemployment rates over this period was about 2 per cent. Unemployment and vacancy rates since 1966 have been generally too far apart for estimates of the levels at which they would have been equal to have much value, and the basic relations between them have shifted. Broadly the same conclusion, however, emerges from a calculation based on male unemployment and vacancies in 1969–71, when it seems possible that the unemployment–vacancy relations might have become stabilised in new positions further from the origin. Whatever the reasons for the apparent shift in these relationships (a matter that is being keenly disputed at the time of writing), the immediately significant fact for our present purpose is that, while the estimated values of the unemployment rate at which it would equal the vacancy rate have risen in *all* regions, their interregional range has remained much smaller than the corresponding range of actual unemployment rates. It does not seem from this that interregional unemployment differences can be attributed mainly to differences in the degree of imperfection of regional labour markets. Differences in pressure of demand seem to be responsible for most of the variation.

Some attempts were made to analyse zero demand-deficiency unemployment in the regions into its structural and frictional components, using the formal definitions of these categories given earlier. It is a hazardous operation, and all that seem worth reporting about it here are some very tentative general indications. Frictional unemployment seems to vary relatively little between regions and is not necessarily lowest where total unemployment is lowest; there is a suggestion that it is higher in the South East than in some other regions because the rate of labour turnover is high there. It is also probably high in the more sparsely populated areas. Total unemployment was significantly correlated, negatively, with size of labour force across a sample of some 120 towns and development districts.

One would expect the amount of structural unemployment in a region to be related to the rate at which its industrial or occupational structure has been changing. This rate of change can conveniently be measured by the minimum proportion of the labour force that would have to shift between the industrial (or occupational) categories in the period under review to bring about the changes in percentage distribution between the categories that are actually observed. Estimates of these rates of change, calculated for the period 1959–63 from Minimum List Headings, are indeed of some interest in themselves and are shown in table 9.5. It is noteworthy that for male employment there are virtually three rates of change; a high one in the North, Wales and Scotland, a low one (less than half as big) in London and the South East, and an intermediate one common to all the remaining English regions. For female employment the range of variation is smaller, though the average amount of structural change is not very different. The North West, not

Table 9.5. *Structural changes in employment, 1959–63*[a]

Percentages

	Male	Female
North	7·91	6·34
East and West Ridings	5·54	5·94
North West	5·59	7·25
North Midlands	5·65	4·34
(West) Midlands	5·13	5·72
London & South East	3·30	4·68
East and South	5·51	6·31
South West	5·57	6·18
Wales	7·03	5·93
Scotland	6·95	4·78

SOURCE: *Ministry of Labour Gazette*, 'Employees in employment'.

[a] Minimum proportions of the relevant labour force that would have to be transferred between Minimum List Headings to transform the industrial structure of 1959 into that of 1963.

very surprisingly, emerges at the top of this list, with London and the South East and Scotland more surprisingly partners, along with the North Midlands at the other end, and the remaining regions in between.

These indices of change have been correlated with three unemployment variables – estimated structural unemployment, estimated zero demand-deficiency unemployment (structural plus frictional) and actual mean unemployment. In the outcome, the correlations relating to male employment and unemployment all prove to be highly significant. Perversely those between structural change and estimated structural unemployment are less good than those between structural change and either structural plus frictional or mean total unemployment. The data are scanty and it would be unwise to hang firm conclusions on these results, but there is perhaps some suggestion here that the differences in structural unemployment as estimated owe something to differences in adaptability as well as to differences in the extent to which patterns of demand and actual patterns of employment have changed.

The corresponding calculations for female employment and unemployment reveal no significant correlation at all, which is consistent with our other evidence that the unregistered rather than the registered unemployed constitute the effective reserve of female labour.

The discussion so far of the relation between unemployment and unfilled vacancies, and its bearing on the imperfection of regional labour markets, has been based on the assumption – broadly verified for some periods – that the relation is stable over time. On a longer view the assumption proves incorrect. Most conspicuously, the level of unemployment corresponding to any given level of vacancies has been rising quite rapidly since late 1966; there is also some evidence that it was falling in 1960–2. One possibility is that these shifts are connected with variations in the rate of structural change in the economy. If this is so one should be able to explain levels of unemployment in particular years in terms of two variables – the rate of change of industrial structure in the region in question in that year as compared with the previous one, and the level of unfilled vacancies. One should perhaps not assume that the peculiarities of regional labour markets can be neglected, but should also insert into the equation dummy variables relating to the individual regions (or rather all but one of them) to take account, for instance, of frictional problems of particular regions.

An analysis of this sort based on the years 1960–8 shows that a high proportion (80 or 90 per cent) of the variance of regional rates for individual years can be explained without difficulty, though if one inserts a simple linear trend as well as regional dummy variables the rate of structural change is deprived of its significance. So far as the diagnosis of differences in the imperfection of regional labour markets is concerned, however, the chief finding can be easily stated. Given equal values for all the regions of whatever other variables were included in the more successful of the equations tried, and taking the Northern region as the standard of comparison, unemployment tended to be significantly high (by about 0·2 per cent) in Wales, low by about the same amount in the South East, and lower still (by about 0·5 per cent) in the 'Central' region into which the Midlands regions and Yorkshire have to be combined to secure so long a time-series. There are indications at a lower level of statistical cogency that, *ceteris paribus*, unemployment in the North West and the South West ran a little lower than in the North.

This gives us then some indication, based on evidence for nine years, of the extent to which systematic regional peculiarities made regional unemployment rates high or low after the pressure of demand (that is vacancies), the rate of change of regional industrial structure and any general influence summarised by a national time-trend have been taken into account. All it amounts to is a range of 0·7 per cent in the unemployment rate between Wales on the one hand and the 'Central' group of regions on the other, which is less than half the difference of their total unemployment rates, and less than 0·3 per cent out of the 2·6 per cent difference between the unemployment rates of South East England and Scotland. The rest is, by implication, difference in demand pressure or difference in rate of industrial change.

This brings us back to a point which we set aside earlier. The definitions we have adopted of frictional and structural unemployment between them include any persons who are *de facto* unemployable – who because of their personal shortcomings, *not* imperfections of information or geographical distribution, are prevented from filling existing vacancies in their own trades, or probably in others. Interregional differences in the incidence of such people are implicitly included in the estimates of interregional frictional and frictional-plus-structural rates that we have made. The only reason for referring to the subject again is that the Ministry of Labour published in 1966 a survey of the characteristics of the unemployed which, on the face of it, provides an independent estimate of the relative regional incidence of this group.[1]

The survey shows numbers of men judged likely to 'find difficulty in getting work on personal grounds', which at the date in question (October 1964) formed proportions of the regional male labour forces varying from 0·61 per cent in London and the South East to 1·77 per cent in Wales. In two regions (the North and Scotland) the number so classed exceeded our estimates of total structural and frictional unemployment for the period 1961–5. For women the corresponding proportions were lower – in all regions lower than our estimates of 'structural and frictional' unemployment – but they showed again a considerable range from 0·2 per cent in London and the South East to 1·1 per cent in Scotland. The question is whether these differences correspond to differences in the objective qualities of the regional labour forces as a whole.

Let us consider what we should expect if the distribution of personal characteristics were exactly the same in all regions, and the Ministry's assessment was also perfectly objective in the sense of being uninfluenced by local market demand. In a region with high unemployment one would expect employers to be so selective that virtually all the objectively least employable 1 per cent (say) of the population would in fact be out of work. In a region with a severe labour shortage, on the other hand, a considerable proportion of the least employable 1 per cent would at any given time be in employment; they would have been taken on more freely than in the high-unemployment region both because employers were under greater pressure to take *someone* on, and because the probability of their finding someone better in a given time was very much poorer. They would also be more reluctantly dismissed, if only because it would take longer to find someone better. The number of the unemployed found personally deficient will therefore be smaller as a proportion of the total labour force where unemployment is low.

If one considers only the unemployed, however, and thinks what proportion of them one would expect to find objectively deficient, it seems almost certain that it will be higher where unemployment is

[1] *Ministry of Labour Gazette*, April 1966, pp. 156–7 and July 1966, pp. 385–7.

lower. If employers succeed at all in being selective, 3 per cent of a labour force left out of employment must be of higher average quality than 1 per cent left out of a similarly constituted force.

We do indeed find that the number judged difficult to place measured as a proportion of the regional labour force is very highly correlated with the unemployment rate; the correlation coefficient for men is 0·995. This, as we have argued, is not inconsistent with the same proportion of the labour force with objectively similar incapacities for employment being the same in all regions. The proportion of the unemployed judged difficult to place on personal grounds is, however, very nearly constant. The national proportion is 61 per cent; the only considerable departures from this are 56 per cent in Scotland and 73 per cent in the Midlands, by virtue of which a just significant negative correlation is produced. The correlation is in the right direction to be consistent with a constant proportion of objectively unsuitable people in all regional labour forces, but it seems doubtful whether it, and the regression coefficient, are large enough.

It seems likely either that there are rather more such people (proportionately) in the regions of high unemployment, or that the Ministry of Labour's allocation of people to this category was in some degree influenced by the regional demand situation – the Welsh, for instance, being judged to some extent by the difficulty of placing them in Wales, which would be greater than the difficulty of placing the same people in London. It is impossible to decide satisfactorily which of these two possibilities – or what combination of them – corresponds to reality. The second of them seems very likely to have had some force. There is, on the other hand, independent evidence of some variation between regions in the proportion of the labour force with certain characteristics likely to make for difficulty in employing them. The registered disabled, for instance, vary interregionally in their incidence. The incidence shows, moreover, a positive though imperfect correlation with unemployment rates: in April 1964 it was 4·1 per cent of the labour force (male and female) in Wales, 3·3 per cent in Yorkshire, the North and the North West, against 2·8–2·9 per cent (about the national average) in Scotland, the Midlands and the South West, and 2·3 per cent in South East England. But most of the people in question were employed; the unemployment rate among them was nationally about 5·6 times that in the workforce at large, and this ratio was about the same in Wales, where there was the highest incidence of them, as in London and the South East, where there was the lowest.

The best one can conclude from all this is, perhaps, that there is some interregional variation in the proportion of the labour force unsuited to employment by national (not regional) standards, perhaps

Table 9.6. *Proportions of unskilled in unemployed adult males and economically active males, 1961*

Percentages

	Labourers/unemployed adults	Unskilled manual/ economically active workers
North	63·7	12·3
Central[a]	59·1	9·7
North West	57·1	13·4
London & South East	38·6	10·8
East and South	41·0	10·0
South West	41·8	11·0
Wales	64·1	13·3
Scotland	61·6	12·2

SOURCES: *Ministry of Labour Gazette*, 'Employees in employment'; *Census 1961. England and Wales* and *Scotland. Occupation Tables*.

[a] Midlands regions and Yorkshire combined.

most notably a higher incidence of physical disablement in certain mining regions, but that it goes only a very little way towards explaining the interregional variations of total unemployment rates, or even the smaller variations we have found in our estimates of structural and frictional unemployment within which personal unemployability should in principle be included.

There is another important characteristic of the unemployed and the total employee population of the regions about which, however, it is possible to learn something independently – namely degree of skill. Since 1961 the Ministry of Labour (now Department of Employment),[1] has given a regional analysis by occupation of wholly unemployed adults, in which an unskilled class of 'labourers' is distinguished. The proportion of this class among the unemployed may be compared (though the definitions are not necessarily identical) with the proportion of 'unskilled manual workers' in the 1961 Census.[2] The relevant figures for males are shown in table 9.6.

First, it emerges that the proportion of labourers among the male unemployed is very much greater than that of unskilled manual workers in the total active male population – broadly, four times as great. The difference is far greater than could be accounted for by differences in the definitions; the unskilled are clearly much more susceptible to unemployment than those with some formal skill. They are also, in

[1] In their Gazette.
[2] General Register Office, *Census 1961. England and Wales* and *Scotland. Occupation Tables*, London and Edinburgh, HMSO, 1966.

general, a more permanent constituent of the total body of unemployed than the skilled are. Over time in most regions, though very noticeably not in South East England, the proportion of labourers among the unemployed falls as unemployment rises and rises as it falls.

Across regions however, high unemployment goes with a high proportion of unskilled among the unemployed; the proportion of the unemployed classified as labourers is highest in the high-unemployment regions – Wales, the North and Scotland – markedly lowest in London and the South East. To some extent this might be explained by the fact that unskilled manual workers form rather high proportions of the active male population in the high-unemployment regions, but the correlation between these proportions and those of labourers among the unemployed, though positive, is not significant. Differences in the composition (as well as the strength) of demand must come into the picture; it looks as if the relative demand for skilled labour (in comparison with that for unskilled) tends to be highest in at least some of the regions of highest unemployment. In high-unemployment regions, moreover, formerly skilled men may well register for casual or unskilled jobs to a greater extent than elsewhere. All these factors may assist in leaving these regions with apparently less skilled bodies of unemployed than the low-unemployment regions.

More light is thrown on this qualitative difference by a study of the duration of unemployment. A given total of unemployed persisting over time can be made up by either a lot of people suffering short periods of unemployment, or a few people suffering long periods, or any of a range of mixtures of the two. Similarly, the total unemployed population may consist of any of an infinite number of mixtures of people who have been unemployed already for different periods. When unemployment is increasing the proportion of people who have been out of work for a short time is likely to increase, and the reverse when it decreases, but it can be shown that the ratio of those men who have been unemployed for six months or more to the average of the total unemployed at the date in question and a date six months earlier is remarkably constant over time in any given region. Between regions however, it varies widely; over the years 1962–7 it averaged only 21 per cent in London and the South East, but 36 per cent in the North, with not much lower percentages in Scotland, Wales, or indeed the South West. The unemployed in the high-unemployment regions are made up to a greater extent than elsewhere of those who have been out of work a long time. This state of affairs goes with a tendency in the high-unemployment regions for the long-term (six months and over) unemployment rate to vary more sensitively with the total unemployment rate of up to six months earlier. In Scotland in the years 1961–7, a rise of 1 per cent in the total male unemployment rate maintained for six months went with a rise of 0·38 per cent in the long-term rate at the end of that time. In the East and South the corresponding rise in the long-term rate would have been only 0·22 per cent.

This points towards the differences in life history of the unemployed in the various regions. These have been shown more precisely, in the experience of the years 1960–5 taken as a whole, by Mr Fowler.[1] At the point of becoming unemployed, the expectation of remaining on the register varied on his calculation from five weeks in London and the South East to over eleven weeks in the North. These interregional variations do not correspond to variations in the regional unemployment rates, which means that the rate of turnover on the register varies from one region to another inversely with the expectations. There is some broad tendency for the regions of high unemployment to have slow turnover (high initial expectation of staying on the register), but it is only a very rough one. London and the South East is outstandingly the region with the highest rate of turnover, but the two Midlands regions with the same average unemployment rate have turnover rates lower by 18 per cent (West Midlands) and 27 per cent (East Midlands). The West Midlands has a similar rate of turnover to the Eastern, Southern, and Yorkshire and Humberside regions – which have, indeed, fairly similar unemployment rates – but the East Midlands turnover rate is comparable with those of the North West, the South West and Wales. Scotland has a lower turnover rate still, and the North the lowest of all.

In every region the longer a person is unemployed the less likely he is to get work within a stated time – the longer he is likely to continue to be out of work. To a large extent, no doubt, this simply reflects the fact that people of low inherent employability stay out of work a long time. In so far as this is the case, low rate of turnover in a region might mean either that it had an unusually high proportion of people of low employability, or that the pressure of labour demand in it was low, or that labour supply and demand were qualitatively or geographically ill adjusted to each other. It would however seem likely, *a priori*, that long unemployment causes a reduction in the chance of getting a job. To that extent low turnover, whatever its other causes, will have a self-reinforcing quality. It is probable that this is a factor in lowering turnover (and raising the unemployment rate) in the regions where turnover is in fact low – perhaps especially in the North, Wales and Scotland, and in those parts of the East Midlands where structural employment is heavy. But we cannot prove the existence or measure

[1] Central Statistical Office, *Duration of Unemployment on the Register of Wholly Unemployed*, by R. F. Fowler, London, HMSO, 1968.

the strength of such a tendency from the known distribution of periods of unemployment by length in the different regions. We can say only that, as far as it exists, it contributes to the pattern that we find.

What then is the general upshot of our discussion of the different natures and causes of regional unemployment problems? It seems to be that, while there are some qualitative differences in the nature of unemployment and the characteristics of the unemployed in different regions, it is differences in pressure of demand for labour, not differences in the experience or qualities of the supply, that account basically for the greater part of the interregional differences in unemployment rates, and that these differences are for the most part persistent. It remains to see whether they are reflected in the price of labour or its rates of change.

THE PRICE OF LABOUR

We have already, in chapter 3, given some attention to the different levels of earnings in different industries and regions – the most detailed data being those on the earnings of adult male manual workers. We saw that there were significant differences both between average earnings in different industries within regions, and between average earnings within industries in different regions, but that the former were very decidedly the greater – inter-industry variance was nearly three times as great as interregional variance. This is in interesting contrast with our finding that unemployment rates differ more between regions than between industries, and the fact that inter-industry mobility (or at all events actual movement of labour) is very much greater than interregional. Even within the restricted category of adult male manual workers, the very great inter-industry movements of employees did not succeed in reducing inter-industry earnings differences within regions as effectively as the very much smaller interregional movements of labour (or some other influences) succeeded in reducing interregional earnings differences within industries. And this in spite of the fact that intraregional movements presumably did succeed in bringing unemployment rates in different industries within single regions much closer to one another than the rates within corresponding industries in different regions.

Granted, however, that interregional earnings differences are not as large as one would perhaps expect from what is known about unemployment differences and labour mobility, they are, nevertheless, as we have noted, significant as a whole. In particular, earnings in the South East and the Midlands are significantly above the national average, those in Scotland, the South-West and, *a fortiori*, Northern Ireland significantly below. Do those differences reflect, at a point of time, the differences in pressure of demand as indicated by unemployment rates?

It seems best for this purpose to measure earnings in a way that does not reflect directly differences in regional industrial composition – by (say) the unweighted or nationally weighted averages of earnings in the various industries or industry-groups. Such regional averages prove to be correlated with regional unemployment rates negatively (as one would expect), but not significantly so. This is true whether one takes the earnings in industry-groups (Industrial Orders) or in those single industries for which earnings figures are published for all regions. The Midlands and the South East show low unemployment and high earnings, Scotland and Northern Ireland high unemployment and low earnings, but other regions are less well-behaved; in particular, Yorkshire and Humberside, the South West and (so far as the data go) East Anglia show much lower earnings than one would expect from their unemployment levels, and Wales rather higher earnings. Matters are not made very much better by using estimated demand-deficiency unemployment instead of total unemployment in such calculations.

But we must look a little more closely at the implications of the relation between regional earnings levels and the pressure of demand, and also at those of the dynamic relation between demand and the rate of change of earnings. The simplest theory about these matters is one to which we have already referred in chapter 1. Suppose that one region has some constant source of advantage, such as a location that is favourable in current conditions, or high specialisation on an industry particularly favoured by the trends of technology and markets, so that it generates (or attracts) a larger amount of employment-creating investment in relation to the natural increase of its indigenous workforce than other regions do. The immediate result of these conditions coming into being will be a fall in unemployment and a rise in vacancies in the favoured region (in relation to what is happening elsewhere), which one would expect to go with, or to be closely followed by, a relative rise in both weekly and hourly earnings. The demand curve for labour in the region has moved to the right faster than the indigenous supply curve, or has done so more than the demand curves in other regions.

In the longer run however, the relative rise in earnings may be expected to draw in a net inflow of labour from other regions. Moreover, the raised relative cost of labour in the region will offset some of its advantage as a site for employment-creating investment. If its initial locational (or other) source of advantage remains constant (which we can take as our first hypothesis), we should expect the establishment of a new equilibrium situation, in which growth of employment is in excess of the growth of the indigenous labour force by a constant amount corresponding to net inward migration, and earnings levels are in excess of those elsewhere by a constant amount which is the amount required to bring this net immigration about. There would be no long-term divergence of regional earnings unless the favoured region for some reason became continually more favoured in relation to others.

On the other hand (to take a second hypothesis), if regional advantages undergo sharp changes in the short or medium run, we may expect on this reasoning to see more or less corresponding variations in relative earnings levels as the regional demand curve for labour moves against its stationary or slowly moving, short-term supply curve. This result may be complicated by the effects of the induced (and probably delayed) interregional movements of labour, from which some sort of 'cobweb' or 'pig-cycle' could follow.

A third possibility is that, while some differences of regional advantage have arisen, earnings have been slow to reflect them, so that what we see in the short or medium run is a *rate of change* of relative earnings correlated positively with pressure of demand (or negatively with unemployment rate) – the long-term equilibrium of earnings differentials corresponding to the (supposedly constant) pattern of regional advantages not having had time to appear.

What in fact do we see? Statistics of male manual earnings classified by region and industry had existed for less than a decade at the time of writing, so that the evidence is limited. It is, however, summarised in chart 9.1, which shows for each region from 1960 to 1969 a nationally weighted average of the hourly earnings indices of the twenty Industrial Orders, the United Kingdom average for each Order being taken as 100.

The first thing to be said is that there is no evidence at all for the third of the suggestions that have just been made; the rate of change of earnings over a five-year period is almost completely uncorrelated across regions with the levels of regional unemployment rates. The high-unemployment and low-unemployment regions are not gradually adjusting themselves through a change in relative earnings to their different levels of demand pressure, or if they are something else is happening that effectively conceals the process.

The second point is that, over the 1960s, the relative levels of regional earnings measured in this way (so as to eliminate the direct effects of industrial composition differences) changed very little (chart 9.1). Combining the two Midlands regions, and also including East Anglia with the South East, to deal with the change of Ministry of Labour regional boundaries during the period, one finds that the rank order of the regions with regard to male hourly earnings was the same in October 1969 as it had been in 1960 (or 1962), except that Scotland had moved up above the North, the North West and Yorkshire, and the last

Chart 9.1. *Hourly earnings relatives weighted by United Kingdom structure (male manual workers, all industries)*

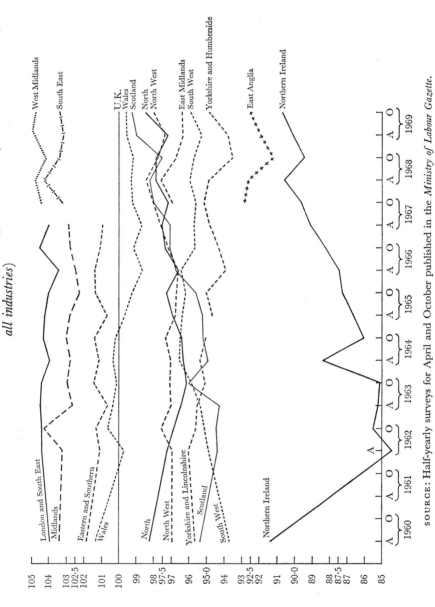

SOURCE: Half-yearly surveys for April and October published in the *Ministry of Labour Gazette*.

mentioned region had fallen below the South West. (At the top of the list South East England may have usurped the first place held originally by the Midlands, but the relative change was very small.)

The third point worthy of note is that there seems to have been some tendency towards convergence of earnings over the period. Of the regions of low earnings, Northern Ireland showed a substantial relative improvement after 1962, though without overtaking any other region in the race. Scotland's very distinct improvement came after 1963, so did a recovery by the North; the South West showed a relative advance up to 1964; the North West showed a slightly improving trend on the whole. Only Yorkshire and Humberside among the regions of less than national average earnings showed a generally downward relative trend. And at the other end of the range, Wales and the Midlands showed downward trends throughout, and perhaps South East England showed signs of developing one from 1966.

Scrutiny of the earnings relatives for the separate industry-groups naturally shows a greater amount of 'changing station' among the regions than is shown by the all-industries average. Some of the instances of this – the dramatic improvement of Northern Ireland in textiles and chemicals, that of the North West and Scotland in vehicles, of the South West in clothing and footwear – reflect known movements of manufacturing industry. The general tendency for improvement in wages to go with a high proportion of new investment – a rapid percentage growth of manufacturing industry in a region – is fairly clear. It is mainly in the highly regionalised industries, of which some regions have only small or specialised sections (such as boat-building in the Midlands), that erratic movements are to be seen. In some of these sampling errors may play a considerable part. But much the same relative stability of regional earnings as is shown by the general averages appears also in those industry-groups that are both large and well represented in most regions.

The marked stability of interregional earnings relatives, at least over this decade, is broadly consistent with our first hypothesis of fairly constant interregional differences of advantage, causing supply of and demand for labour to be brought into equality at different levels of price with the help of steady interregional flows of labour and capital. It certainly does not suggest that our second hypothesis – sharp changes of regional advantage accompanied or followed (perhaps with complications) by corresponding changes in relative earnings – has much to offer. We have already rejected the third hypothesis, which demanded that rates of change of earnings should be positively correlated across regions with some measures of demand pressure. Can we then accept our first hypothesis?

There is clearly a good deal more to be said on the question. For one thing we must not forget that the correlation between earnings levels and unemployment, even non-demand-deficiency unemployment, is not very good – the South West, East Anglia and Yorkshire, in particular, having low earnings in relation to the apparent pressure of demand, and Wales relatively high earnings. There is immediately at least a partial possible explanation of this. The regions whose earnings are 'too high' are those with high proportions of highly paid industries; those whose earnings are 'too low' tend to be in the opposite case. It is true that we have eliminated the direct effects of structure by weighting the industry-indices of earnings similarly in all regions, but we have not thereby necessarily (or even probably) eliminated *all* the effects of structure. In a region with a high proportion of steelworkers and coalminers, other industries may be expected to have to pay more for their male manual labour than in a region with a high proportion of agricultural and textile workers. The supply curve of labour to any given industry may be expected to be affected by the nature of opportunities in other industries, especially in view of the high inter-industry mobility of labour to which we have referred. Wales, along with the Midlands, and in a lower degree the North which also shows rather high male earnings in relation to its unemployment level, are the regions with their male manual employment most heavily biased towards highly paid industries. This argument, however, does not help us much with the Yorkshire region or the South West, which are outstanding anomalies; their industrial composition does not bias them towards low-paid industry-groups.

Another point that arises in connection with the simple static, difference-of-advantage theory of interregional earnings differences is concerned with the highly dynamic nature of the actual labour market in recent times. Wages and earnings have been rising in all regions at rates that are high compared with most interregional differences. It may be possible to think of the differences as being determined by simple differences of demand in relation to regional supply, while the whole set of regional earnings rates is swept upwards on the escalator of national (or world) inflation, but when one considers the nature of the bargaining process by which wages and earnings are changed it is perhaps hard to be satisfied with a picture that takes the escalator for granted, without enquiring either why it moves or what keeps the regional rates on it.

For reasons of this kind quite a different approach to regional earnings changes have been pursued by a number of writers, starting from the 'Phillips curve' doctrine – the doctrine that the rate of change of the price of labour in an economy stands in some inverse, non-linear relation to its rate of unemployment. Why this should be so is explained in different ways by different people.

The first account (or variety of accounts) seems to begin with the proposition that, because of the imperfection of the labour market both in regard to information and in regard to the varying suitability of people for jobs, the unemployment rate does not get down to really low levels unless there is excess demand – employers anxious to take on more employees of at any rate normal competence than are in fact available. In these circumstances, both by competition between employers to divert or 'poach' labour from each other, and by employees' organisations taking advantage of their bargaining power at factory and national levels, wage rates and earnings will be bid up. Since these rates are 'sticky', the speed with which they are raised may be supposed to be a function of the amount of excess demand, and this in turn will be indicated (inversely) by the level of unemployment. Moreover, since the unemployment rate has a lower limit of zero (or in practice some finite level above zero), while there is in principle no limit to the level of excess demand – to the amount of labour employers would like to take on in excess of what is actually available – one may expect that as unemployment falls successively larger accelerations of wage increases will go with further equal small reductions of the unemployment rate. In this version of the story we are not told why there is excess demand, or why (or even whether) it continues to exist after the price of labour has risen to the extent required to extinguish it on the assumption that the supply and demand curves stay in the same place. We simply take very low unemployment as an indication that for some reason there is excess demand for labour, and expect it to be associated with the appropriate rate of increase of wages.

The second kind of account is, on the face of it, rather less a partial-equilibrium, supply-and-demand affair. It postulates a price–wage spiral in which wage earners who would like bigger money incomes ask for higher rates and, in so far as these are granted and costs accordingly raised, employers more or less automatically raise the prices of goods, because the prevalent forms of oligopolistic competition in the kind of industrial economy we are considering leads firms to take movement of costs as a cue for adjusting prices correspondingly. They do this partly because it seems right in itself, partly because it keeps them in step with each other.

The possibility of this process continuing without shortage of purchasing power interfering with it at the macro-economic level could, to some extent, be preserved by the ability of advanced economies to create new sources of credit when pressed to do so, even without official co-operation. Monetary authorities, however, tend to supply money in response to demand, partly to avoid such developments of unofficial credit and, in the last resort, governments favour such a monetary policy as will keep unemployment down to some tolerable level and enable growth to take place. In this view of the world, the 'Phillips' relation emerges perhaps most naturally from the tendency of the price–wage spiral to go faster at high levels of effective demand than at low ones, since employers may be supposed to be more willing both to concede wage increases and to raise prices when their order-books are full, and wage earners may be expected to be more pressing when employment is full, capacity fully used and profits high than they are in slacker times.

It does not seem on reflection, however, that these two accounts are mutually exclusive. The first applies more convincingly to the bidding-up of the price of labour in an unorganised market, the second to the process of collective bargaining especially at national level – in addition, of course, to its inclusion of some sort of account of the macro-economic machinery whereby this kind of inflation can continue indefinitely. A synthesis of the two is not difficult. Perhaps for our present purpose it is not necessary to elaborate it beyond the hints that have already been given. What is more to the point is the question whether a picture of the kind that could be synthesised is valid at regional levels, and how we are to reconcile it with the substantial parallelism of British regional earnings levels which we have found in, at least, the last decade.

It is in fact possible to 'explain' changes in male manual hourly earnings in each region (at six-monthly intervals) for the period 1959–69 in terms of the prevailing level of unemployment, the contemporary rate of change of unemployment and the contemporary rate of change of retail prices, subject to a shift in the relationship in most regions from about October 1966. The 'explanation' accounts for over 80 per cent of the variance of earnings changes in all the regions except Wales and the South West, where it accounts for only 75 and 71 per cent respectively. In these relationships the unemployment level is statistically significant in all regions except the South West and Wales, but it is both numerically largest and statistically most highly significant in the 'Central' region (the Midlands and Yorkshire regions combined), and high also in the South East in comparison with elsewhere. The rate of change of retail prices (the national index) is significant in most regions also, but the variable that is everywhere significant is the rate of change of unemployment.

That rate of change of unemployment appears to explain rate of change of earnings better than level of unemployment does (though the two influences are, of course, not mutually exclusive) has been fairly widely noted, and a number of explanations have been suggested. The one that seems most obvious to the present writer is a simple one. With short-term changes in the level of demand for labour to which changes in the unemployment rate roughly (and inversely) correspond, the demand curve shifts to and fro, and earnings thus move inversely with unemployment if the supply curve of labour does not move in such a way as to prevent it. But the supply curve itself moves upward, not only with rises in the cost of living (represented in the equations by the retail price index), but also, probably less irregularly, at a rate related to the effective bargaining power of labour, which is higher at low levels of unemployment than at high ones – thus introducing a true 'Phillips' influence into events in at least some regions.

It is, however, noteworthy that it proves in some respects easier to explain changes of earnings in terms of unfilled vacancies than of unemployment. In particular, if vacancies are used as a measure of the pressure of demand, the relation of earnings increase to the explanatory variables does not shift significantly after mid-1966, as it does when unemployment is used as an (inverse) measure. We have already noted that the relationship between vacancies and unemployment changed from mid-1966 onwards, and one may infer that when this happened vacancies remained for some reason the more relevant indicator of pressure, until they too seem to have fallen from grace in 1970. Regional vacancies seem to make a significant contribution to the explanation of earnings increases in all regions except (again) Wales and the South West, though in the North West and Scotland there is the curious circumstance that it is the vacancy rate of the *following* period that fits best with any period's earnings increase. (A corresponding phenomenon is even more apparent in some formulations of the relationships using unemployment as a measure of demand pressure.[1]) Change of vacancies makes a significant contribution in some but not all regions, and so does price change. It may thus be claimed that the 'Phillips' type of relation is less overshadowed by other influences if it is formulated in terms of vacancy rates rather than rates of unemployment.

The fact that the rate of increase of earnings in most regions varies over time in a way that can be related to (among other things) the level of either unemployment or vacancies in the region concerned is, prima facie, an interesting one, if only because it promises to make possible a calculation of the effect on wage inflation of varying the distribution of unemployment among regions – a matter that has sometimes been advanced as an important criterion of regional policy. Indeed

---

[1] This lag of unemployment change behind change of effective demand for labour as indicated by other measures has been widely noted. In part at least it arises because the first response to an increase (for instance) in demand for output takes the form of harder work and longer hours rather than more employment.

a calculation has been made of the rates of earnings inflation to be expected nationally, based upon the unemployment–earnings increase equations just referred to, and on interregional distributions of unemployment corresponding to those prevailing both before and after the changes of recent years which have narrowed the interregional gaps.[1] It suggests that the national average rate of earnings increase corresponding to any national unemployment rate should, *ceteris paribus*, be rather smaller with the less widely dispersed than with the former, more widely dispersed regional unemployment rates. The reduction estimated amounts to 0·07 per cent a year, which is only about 1 per cent of the prevailing rate of increase, but the implication of the relationships used in the calculation is that a further redistribution of unemployment, broadly in the direction of interregional equality, would further reduce the rate of inflation corresponding to any given national unemployment total.

It is, however, difficult to be completely satisfied with a calculation of this kind, based as it is on assumptions of rather high degrees of independence between regional labour markets. The 'Phillips' relation operating by itself within each region would hardly give a convincing model of a multi-regional economy, and would certainly be difficult to reconcile with the very substantial degree of parallelism in regional wage movements which we have described. If the 'Phillips curves' (the functional relations between unemployment or vacancies and rates of earnings increase) were identical in all regions, then earnings could not move parallel in different regions unless they had identical unemployment (or vacancy) rates. The existence of persistent unemployment differences between regions coupled with substantial parallelism of wage movements would imply, therefore, that the regions have different Phillips curves and are constrained to occupy those points on them that yield substantially similar rates of earnings increase. What could so constrain them?

One obvious agent is competition in national and world markets; the region where the price of labour goes up faster than elsewhere, for example, will suffer a deterioration in its balance of external payments and a rise in unemployment relative to other regions, which will presumably stop when a competitive relation with the outside world is restored. The other obvious agents are interregional movements of labour and enterprise, as we have already noted in this and other connections; the region that runs ahead in earnings attracts immigration, which eventually raises unemployment to the level where wage inflation

---

[1] See J. K. Bowers, P. C. Cheshire and A. E. Webb, 'The change in the relationship between unemployment and earnings increases: a review of some possible explanations', *National Institute Economic Review*, no. 54, November 1970, pp. 44–63.

is no faster than elsewhere, and also (unless superiority of earnings is matched by superiority of output) deflects enterprise, which again helps to raise unemployment to the equilibrium level. By at least three mechanisms the level of unemployment, and with it that of wage increase, is governed – though not without short-term fluctuations – to an equilibrium level.

This theory is a coherent one, but the implication that regional Phillips curves differ sufficiently to be consistent with the wide and persistent interregional unemployment differences we actually observe is hard to swallow. It would be plausible enough if we had found that interregional unemployment differences were wholly or mainly due to different degrees of labour-market imperfection; but in fact our evidence points to their being associated rather with differences of demand pressure which, on a pure Phillips curve doctrine, one would expect to go with differences in rate of wage increase. And these, for the reasons we have just mentioned, cannot persist, and indeed are seen in general not to.

Moreover, a doctrine that regional rates of wage increase are governed only by regional unemployment (or vacancies) is theoretically implausible. In any system of interconnected markets supply curves are in varying degrees subject to shifts arising from changes in expectations and aspirations induced by new information about what is going on in other parts of the system. To some extent (in the security or commodity markets, for instance) parallelism between prices of the same things in different countries is induced by the mere fact that international transactions are possible, without those transactions necessarily taking place. In regional labour markets matters are somewhat different, but national negotiating machinery introduces a degree of uniformity into basic rates, while the (sometimes major) parts of earnings that are determined by local negotiation cannot be unaffected by knowledge (where it exists) of what is being paid for corresponding work in other regions. The interregional influences may be in part indirect. In industries where there is not much awareness of what is being earned in other regions, demand (and willingness to pay) may be influenced by changes in local differentials between those industries and others in which interregional comparisons are made or in which earnings are mainly governed by national agreements. In one way or another the national situation must influence regional wage formation through one or more of several channels, quite apart from the regional unemployment or vacancy position.

In the regional equations that have been described, the national situation was shown impinging on local earnings increases through the agency of the (national) retail price index, which may well have been acting to some extent as a proxy for wage movements elsewhere as well as in its own right. The quite large and significant constant terms in the equations featuring vacancies – implying constant earnings increases of from 1 to 3 per cent a year even if demand was so slack that there were no vacancies – also suggests an inflationary agency of which explicit account is not taken. The work of Cowling and Metcalf has shown (as also has some of our work relating to a rather longer period) that, for change of earnings in all other regions, change of earnings in the South East is a better explanatory variable than any other that was included.[1] This suggests a direct influence, not operating through regional unemployment or vacancy rates, but working directly on the demand or supply curves – more probably on the latter – for labour in the region.

An influence of this kind, in so far as it emanates from a region of relative labour scarcity, has the effect of making wages in regions of less strong demand tend to rise rather more than they would under the influence of their domestic market situations alone. To some extent this may be expected to deflect enterprise from them, to some extent to diminish net emigration from them, and to some extent to reduce the competitiveness in the outside world of their existing enterprises. All of this would increase unemployment to the point where it, or the accompanying reduction in unfilled vacancies, reduced the regional element in wage increases so that regional earnings moved parallel to those elsewhere, though rather higher in relation to them than they would be in the absence of the direct effect from the more prosperous regions.

To put it in another way, with uniform labour prices in operation throughout the country some regions would suffer from demand-deficiency because their competitive power is for some reason relatively low. In the absence of direct influence between regional labour markets they would adjust to wage levels sufficiently below those of the stronger regions to compensate for their weakness, and would then (assuming that all regions have similar Phillips curves) show the same unemployment rates and the same rates of increase of earnings as their more fortunate neighbours. The direct influence – their continual attempt, in effect, to 'keep up with the Joneses' – prevents them from making the full downward adjustment of relative wages required for this, and they therefore tend to be found at different points on their Phillips curves from their neighbours, with higher unemployment and lower indigenous wage inflation to make up for the wage inflation that they 'import' through national wage agreements and direct emulation of the higher rates of earnings elsewhere.

---

[1] K. Cowling and D. Metcalf, 'Wage–Unemployment Relationships: a regional analysis for the UK 1960–65', *Bulletin of the Oxford Institute of Economics and Statistics*, vol. 29, no. 1, February 1967, pp. 31–9.

This argument brings us back to the first of the hypotheses that we discussed earlier in this section concerning the relative levels of wages and unemployment in the regions. We saw that a broadly negative correlation between regional wage levels and regional unemployment rates, and the substantially parallel movements of regional wages over time, seemed to indicate fairly constant interregional differences in growth of demand for labour in relation to the indigenous supply of it. These we suggested produced different degrees of labour scarcity, which were stabilised in relation to each other by interregional movements of factors of production – notoriously only imperfectly mobile and requiring finite differences of prospects to make them move at all. We did not there consider why differences in regional factor prices fail to build up to the points at which they eliminate differences in unemployment rates, but we have now suggested a reason for this. It is a suggestion, moreover, that bears upon another matter discussed at the beginning of this section – the much smaller size of interregional than of interindustry wage differences despite the vastly greater actual movement of labour between industries than between regions.

Nationally negotiated rates, the attachment to the concept of 'the rate for the job' as a criterion of justice in a field where criteria with an intuitive appeal are hard to come by, the preservation of interindustry differentials (largely a by-product of the preservation of interoccupational differentials) as marks of status and also as premia for recognisable skills and compensations for recognised disutilities, the industrial or occupational rather than regional organisation of trade unions: all these help to explain the higher degree of uniformity within industries, which also works against the full operation of the price mechanism in producing differences between regions.

We noted too that the negative correlation between regional unemployment and regional earnings (after making all possible allowance for the effects of differences in industrial structure and in the imperfection of labour markets) is very poor. We have now a possible explanation of its imperfection. Only if the direct effect of earnings in the high-wage regions on earnings levels elsewhere did not exist, or if it spread out to all the regions of lower economic advantage more or less in proportion to the extent of their disadvantage, would one expect to find earnings levels and unemployment inversely related to a really significant extent. The regions where both earnings and unemployment are low are presumably those in which the pressure of national wage agreements geared to more prosperous areas, and of direct emulation of the earnings achieved in those areas, operates most weakly. It is easy to believe that Yorkshire, the South West and East Anglia – the regions that we found to have low earnings considering the low level of their unemployment – agree with this description. The two latter regions are largely regions of small towns and a degree of labour oligopsony; the Yorkshire region specialises in substantially different trades from the high-wage areas of the West Midlands and the South East, it probably has fewer connections with these regions through common ownership of industry than have most other regions and, apart from coalmining, it is not notable for militant trade unionism.

Very tentatively therefore, we may claim that an interpretation of our labour-market data, based on fairly steady interregional differences in pressures of demand, imperfect interregional mobility of labour and a rather uneven direct diffusion of demand for higher wages from the high-earning regions to the others, is a promising one. We have not yet examined patterns of labour migration in relation to this picture, but that can perhaps best be done when we look at migration comprehensively.

THE LOSS OF INCOME THROUGH MISLOCATION OF FACTORS OF PRODUCTION

To conclude this survey of regional aspects of the labour market, we come to the third of the questions mentioned at the outset – how much does it matter so far as the allocation of the national resources is concerned if factor prices (such as wage levels for comparable work) stand at different levels in different regions, as they in fact do? This is a broad question and must be dealt with here at a rather abstract level in the light of simple theory.

Suppose that there is a labour force of n workers distributed between two regions (called region 1 and region 2) in which the marginal products of labour (capital and other factors being taken as given) vary with labour supply in the ways shown respectively by the lines m_1 (where labour supply is measured to the right from O) and m_2 (where labour supply is measured to the left from O') in chart 9.2.

Then the total product is given by the areas under these two lines – areas which partially overlap in the diagram. The total product will be maximised when there are OA workers in region 1 and AO' in region 2, so that the marginal product is the same in both regions, and is given by w. If there is perfect competition the marginal product will equal the wage rate.

If Δn workers are now transferred from region 2 to region 1, marginal products (and wage rates) will rise to w_2 in the former and fall to w_1 in the latter. Region 1's product will rise by ABEC and region 2's will fall by ABDC, so that the national product falls by CDE, which (if the marginal product functions are near enough to being linear over the relevant range) is $\frac{1}{2}(w_2 - w_1)\Delta n$.

Chart 9.2. *Loss of real income through inequality of marginal products*

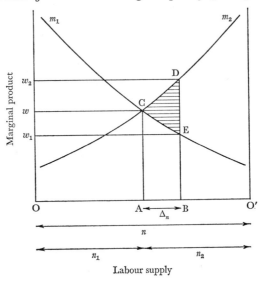

In practice we can observe wage (or earnings) differences such as $w_2 - w_1$, but we not not know the transfers of labour such as Δn that are required to extinguish them. The only obvious way round this difficulty is to express our formula for income loss in terms of the wage difference and the elasticity of marginal product with respect to labour supply, and then make a guess at this elasticity with the help of what is known about production functions.

The elasticity, ϵ, is defined as $-\dfrac{\partial w}{\partial n}\cdot\dfrac{n}{w}$, or approximately $-\dfrac{\Delta w}{\Delta n}\cdot\dfrac{n}{w}$. We might as well take it as having the same numerical value in both regions, so that:

$$\epsilon = -\frac{\Delta w_1}{\Delta n}\cdot\frac{n_1}{w} = \frac{\Delta w_2}{\Delta n}\cdot\frac{n_2}{w} \quad \left(\text{whence } \frac{\Delta w_1}{\Delta w_2} = -\frac{n_2}{n_1}\right)$$

$$(\Delta w_1 = w_1 - w,\ \Delta w_2 = w_2 - w \text{ and } n_1 + n_2 = n).$$

Then $\Delta n = -\dfrac{\Delta w_1}{w}\cdot\dfrac{n_1}{\epsilon}$, or, since $\dfrac{\Delta w_1}{\Delta w_2} = -\dfrac{n_2}{n_1}$ and thus $\dfrac{\Delta w_1}{w_2 - w_1} = -\dfrac{n_2}{n}$,

$$\Delta n = \frac{1}{\epsilon}\cdot\frac{n_2 n_1}{n}\cdot\frac{w_2 - w_1}{w}.$$

Thus the income loss,

$$\frac{1}{2}(w_2 - w_1)\Delta n = \frac{1}{2\epsilon}\cdot\frac{n_2 n_1}{n}\cdot\frac{(w_2 - w_1)^2}{w}.$$

The best available evidence on the labour elasticity of the marginal product of labour is probably that derived from attempts to fit Cobb–Douglas production functions to various kinds of data. The function is of the form $P = kn^a u^b v^c \ldots$ where $u, v, \ldots$ are factors other than labour. The usual finding is that the exponent a has a value of about two-thirds; this is broadly supported by the deduction that, in perfect competition, labour's share of the total product would be a, and the fact that income from employment is regularly about two-thirds of total factor income in the United Kingdom.

It is clear that the labour elasticity of the marginal product of labour, granted a Cobb–Douglas type of production function, is $1 - a$ since:

$$\frac{\partial P}{\partial n} = akn^{a-1}u^b \ldots$$

$$\frac{\partial}{\partial n}\left(\frac{\partial P}{\partial n}\right) = a(a-1)\, kn^{a-2}u^b \ldots = \frac{\partial P}{\partial n} \cdot \frac{a-1}{n}.$$

This suggests $\tfrac{1}{3}$ as a plausible value for ϵ, and a value of

$$\frac{3}{2} \cdot \frac{n_2 n_1}{n} \cdot \frac{(w_2 - w_1)^2}{w}$$

for the income loss due to mislocation of labour between the regions. To get an idea of the orders of magnitude involved, imagine two regions with 10 million employees each and average earnings of £1,000 a year, but with earnings 5 per cent higher in one region than in the other. According to the foregoing argument, the gain in national product from a transfer of labour sufficient to equalise earnings in the two regions would be roughly

$$£\frac{3}{2} \cdot \frac{10 \times 10}{20} \cdot \frac{50^2}{1000} \text{ million} = £18\cdot 8 \text{ million,}$$

the required transfer being

$$\frac{3 \times 10 \times 10}{20} \cdot \frac{50}{1000} \text{ million, or } \tfrac{3}{4} \text{ million employees.}$$

The assumption here is that the interregional difference in marginal productivities of labour is due to a relative mislocation of labour and capital, resulting in production in every single trade being more capital-intensive in one region than in the other. It has been seen that, in these circumstances, relatively little is lost by a departure from equality of marginal products. If capital-intensity remained rigidly the same in both regions, so that the three-quarters of a million workers who (as above) would have to move to equalise wages were unemployed in the labour-rich region and corresponding amounts of capital were redundant in the other one, the loss from unemployment of factors would amount, in the example given, to 3¾ per cent, or over £1,100 million.

On the other hand, an observed difference of 5 per cent between two regions in the price of labour might be due not to mislocation of labour in relation to capital, but to mislocation of both labour and capital in relation to natural resources in the widest sense – to one region having a locational advantage as compared with the other. If this were so, one could in principle repeat the calculation to determine how much labour and capital (combined) would have to move from one region to another to equalise their regional marginal products, and how much the economy would gain thereby. The combined exponent of labour and capital in the assumed Cobb–Douglas production function would be high – perhaps 0.9 or more – and this would mean that the interregional shift of labour, accompanied this time by capital, to equalise products would be bigger than before, perhaps three or four times as big. The gain from such a shift (that is the loss due to mislocation) would also be bigger, perhaps by a factor of four or five. It would, however, still be only a small fraction of the loss that would occur through unemployment of factors if factor proportions were rigid. The general conclusion at this rather crude level of theoretical abstraction seems to be that mislocation is not very important so long as factor proportions are flexible and factors are in fact employed.

To be more specific, so long as all the available labour is employed, the scope for improving total output by shifting it from one region to another may be very modest, because its marginal product in low-productivity areas may be quite a high proportion of that in high-productivity areas, and the difference between the two might be extinguished if only a small fraction of the labour force was moved up from the lower-productivity to the high-productivity region. The main possibilities that might increase the scope for improvement are:

(i) that labour in the low-pay regions is paid substantially more than the value of its marginal product (or, perhaps less plausibly, in the high-pay regions substantially less), so that the scope for improvement by 'moving people up' is greater than it seems;

(ii) that the high-pay regions possess some more durable superiority – such as physical climate, progressive psychological attitudes which infect incomers rather than being diluted by them, or locational advantages not easily offset by increase of congestion – so that a large number of people could be 'moved up' into these regions without extinguishing the premium they enjoy in real earnings.

It is hard to test these possibilities satisfactorily in real life. The analysis described in chapter 7 of interregional variations of net output per head as shown by the 1954 Census of Production showed a range of variation of the regional dummy variables just about equal to that of regional earnings (or more precisely of male manual earnings) standardised for differences in industrial composition. It does not seem from this that interregional variations in *average* productivity at least are seriously out of line with those in earnings. Earnings may cover a slightly smaller percentage range than average products, but not much smaller, and it seems unlikely either that they are very much less widely dispersed than marginal productivity.

As for the existence of really durable advantages in particular regions, this also has already been discussed in general terms in chapter 7. Isolated and peripheral areas are presumably at some disadvantage, which they can partially overcome by specialising on trades where neither transport costs nor local economies of scale are important. Across the whole range of manufacturing trades the scope for economies of aggregation seems to be rather slight – a productivity improvement of a seventh of 1 per cent for every extra 10 per cent of the national total employment of the trade that is concentrated in the region. On the other hand, the higher productivity (in value terms) in Greater London in particular, seems, as we have already noted, to be largely offset by, and is perhaps largely a consequence of, the high cost of living, which in turn is attributable mostly to high rents and costs of travel to work. To the extent that high travel costs are to blame, it clearly does no good to bring people to the high-productivity area; their extra production there is offset by extra transport facilities that have to be provided. To the extent that high house rents are responsible the same conclusion holds in so far as the high rents measure either specially high building costs, or (as they more probably do) the high suitability of the site for some other use, such as factory, office or shop-building. On the other hand, high rents due to the residential desirability of the site (for example, the general advantages of living in London) can hardly be regarded as a reason for wages there to be high – the advantages should make people willing to pay higher than normal rents out of a normal wage. But against this a further factor has to be taken into account; the abnormal proportion of people with property incomes and people in the higher paid occupations to be found in London is certainly a factor raising the rent charges or increasing the travel-to-work costs that fall on other residents there. In the light of all these considerations, it does not seem that the interregional differences in earnings or marginal products of labour within industries reflect very considerable permanent differences of locational suitability. If this is so we cannot regard them as indicating any serious loss of real output to the country through the mislocation of its labour between regions.

CHAPTER 10

FACTOR MOVEMENTS

The movements of factors of production between regions play, as we have already noted, a crucial part in regional studies, differentiating the analysis that is appropriate to them from the theory – and particularly from the classical theory – of international economics. A description of the course of growth can start from rates of increase of factor supplies in various parts of the country and rates of growth of demand for the various kinds of goods and services. Given these elements, it is the relative mobility of the various factors – which of them move about in search of co-operating factors and which wait for co-operating factors to come to them – that determines, in the first analysis, where growth takes place; absolute mobility (or lack of it) puts constraints upon the rate at which growth takes place, and determines the extent to which factors are left idle or misapplied because their flow is impeded by frictions. To complete a rough sketch of regional adjustment we need to add only an allowance for the parts played by the immobility of goods and services (or conversely the attractions of markets), and the various economies and diseconomies of scale.

MOVEMENTS OF CAPITAL

What, for a start, do we know about the general patterns of these movements? It is the movements of capital that are more elusive. The best direct information we have is that contained in the Board of Trade's monograph on 'moves' of manufacturing industry.[1] This, of course, covers only part of the field, in so far as manufacturing industry is responsible directly for less than a quarter of fixed capital formation. Moreover, the direction of the move corresponds to the direction of the associated capital movement only on the assumption that the capital invested in branches or re-located establishments originates from the region which is regarded in the Board of Trade study as the region of origin of the move. This is justified if the capital arises from undistributed profits accumulated by the activity of the 'parent' establishment. It is not justified if the firm responsible for the move has simply gone to the capital market and drawn on the general stock of British

[1] Board of Trade, *The Movement of Manufacturing Industry in the United Kingdom, 1945–65*, London, HMSO, 1968, where 'moves' are defined as new establishments set up either as branches from, or by the removal of, 'parent' establishments some distance away.

Table 10.1. *Movements of manufacturing jobs and capital*

	Net annual inflow of manufacturing 'moves'		Capital imports, 1961 (including errors and omissions)[b]	Net inflow of funds, 1961[c]
	1952–9	1960–5[a]		
	(Thousands)		(£ millions)	
North	+1·5	+2·5	—	+20
Yorks. and Humberside	+0·7	−0·8	−50	−130
North West	+2·3	+7·4	+70	—
East Midlands	+0·7	−0·1	−70	−50
West Midlands	−1·5	−6·3	+100	+5
East Anglia	+0·2	+1·6	} −180	−360
South East	−3·0	−14·3		
South West	+1·0	+2·5	+30	+170
Wales	+0·5	+2·6	+110	+180
Scotland	+2·2	+6·0	−30	+40
Northern Ireland	+0·9	+3·8	+20	+80

SOURCES: Board of Trade, *The Movement of Manufacturing Industry in the United Kingdom 1945–65*; table 3.11.

[a] Adjusted for growth potential still remaining in 1966.
[b] Derived from social accounts, see chapter 3.
[c] Capital imports plus public transfers.

(and perhaps overseas) savings, though in these circumstances the gross inflows of jobs into a region from all quarters may be of some use as a rough indicator of gross inflow of manufacturing capital. The 'moves' really indicate movements of entrepreneurship in manufacturing industry rather than movements of the factor of production capital in either a proper or a comprehensive sense. They are, however, very interesting in themselves, and they probably give also general indications of the direction of capital movements. The net regional balances of 'moves' are shown in table 10.1.

The other, more indirect, indicator of capital movements that is available errs, on the other hand, by being too comprehensive. It comes from the social accounts. The difference between the gross domestic product and the expenditure (or absorption of goods and services) of a region is, of course, apart from errors, its net export of goods and services. To the extent that this difference is not required to cover net transfers of property incomes and occupational pensions, it represents the net provision of funds by the region to the rest of the country and of the world. This provision of funds includes not only private and public net lending but also net transfers of funds through public channels. According to our estimates, notionally for 1961, South East England (in fact almost certainly the South East region, *not* East

Anglia), the East Midlands, and Yorkshire and Humberside were the big net providers of funds; the South West, Wales, Northern Ireland, Scotland and, on a smaller scale, the North were the absorbers; the West Midlands and the North West broke more or less even. The total net flow from the providing to the absorbing regions was equal to about 2 per cent of gross national product.

It seems likely that this pattern had not changed much in its very general shape from year to year, since it contains some fairly stable elements. Even the pattern of manufacturing 'moves', which probably reflects to a large extent one of its less stable components, has some fairly persistent characteristics. The South East and the West Midlands showed net outward moves both in the fifties and the first half of the sixties. The other regions all showed net inward moves in both periods, except for Yorkshire and the East Midlands, which seem to have changed from being net exporters to being net importers of manufacturing jobs. Moreover, the rate of flow of moves increased very markedly between the fifties and the sixties; in particular, the net flows from the South East and the West Midlands and into the Development Area regions (also into East Anglia and the South West) were very much increased.

In general, while the pattern of manufacturing moves and that of net inflow of funds deduced from the social accounts do not tell precisely the same story, they agree in showing the South East as the biggest net source of capital; Scotland, Wales, Northern Ireland, the South West, and probably East Anglia if we could separate it in the social accounts, were the main net absorbers. The contradictions relate to the older manufacturing regions of England; Yorkshire and Humberside seems to be a major source of funds but not of manufacturing moves, the West Midlands of moves but not of funds, the North West a major *recipient* of moves but not of funds. Except in so far as we are dealing with errors of estimation, these contradictions reflect the facts that moves of manufacturing industry, transfers of public and private capital, and transfers through public channels, all respond in different ways to differences of affluence and growth.

MOVEMENTS OF POPULATION AND LABOUR MOBILITY

About population movements much more is, of course, known, though still very much less than one would wish. Censuses of population along with registrations of births and deaths give *net* migration into or out of each region (indeed each local authority area). Between Censuses rougher but still useful estimates of these net movements are provided by births, deaths and the Registrar General's calculations based on registration of electors. The Censuses of 1961 and 1966 give sample

FACTOR MOVEMENTS

Table 10.2. *Gross migration between regions,[a] 1961–6*

Thousands

To:	North	Yorks. and Humberside	North West	East Midlands	West Midlands	East Anglia	South East	South West	Wales	Scotland	Great Britain
From:											
North	—	35·2	18·6	15·5	18·4	4·5	45·3	9·4	4·4	11·4	162·7
Yorks. and Humberside	30·8	—	34·2	40·3	13·7	9·3	48·7	13·9	5·9	7·9	204·7
North West	15·9	32·3	—	17·1	26·1	6·6	71·2	20·2	25·4	9·6	224·4
East Midlands	6·1	31·0	13·5	—	22·5	13·4	46·4	13·2	4·7	4·6	155·4
West Midlands	7·2	12·1	28·0	27·8	—	6·9	67·2	37·7	18·6	7·3	212·8
East Anglia	3·2	6·3	3·9	10·5	6·1	—	44·8	8·3	2·6	3·1	88·8
South East	27·1	40·3	59·6	55·3	54·8	82·5	—	165·0	31·1	32·9	548·6
South West	6·9	9·0	11·9	11·1	19·9	8·1	111·5	—	12·6	6·8	197·8
Wales	3·0	5·4	16·7	4·9	19·4	2·2	36·0	19·1	—	2·9	109·6
Scotland	14·2	16·4	20·3	16·7	15·9	4·8	60·6	11·7	4·5	—	165·1
Great Britain	114·4	188·0	206·7	199·2	196·8	138·3	531·7	298·5	109·8	86·5	2069·9

SOURCE: *Sample Census 1966, England and Wales* and *Scotland, Migration Tables.*

[a] All ages, both sexes.

information about *gross* movements into each area (along with the area of origin) for the periods 1960–1, 1965–6, and 1961–6. The Ministry of Labour statistics of gross interregional migration of employees based on annual samples, which formed the basis of much earlier study, have been convicted of error and discontinued. Besides these relatively comprehensive sources, we have the Labour Mobility Survey of 1953–63[1] and a number of mostly local sample studies. Let us see what general picture emerges from these sources.

First, mobility in the sense of propensity to change address is quite high; households move, on the average, more than once in ten years, making about six million changes of address by individuals annually. Three-quarters of all moves within the country are, however, over distances of less than ten miles, and only about one-eighth of the total, involving in England and Wales about 1½ per cent of the population (three-quarters of a million) each year, are interregional. The Labour Mobility Survey shows most short-distance moves to be motivated by housing considerations, long-range moves to be connected mostly with change of employment, or, to a smaller extent, with retirement.

Table 10.2 shows the gross moves between the regions of Great Britain in the five years 1961–6. What characteristics emerge from it? The first is that inward and outward mobility tend to go together;

[1] Government Social Survey, *Labour Mobility in Great Britain 1953–63.*

Table 10.3. *Internal migration between standard subregions,*[a] *1961–6*

Percentages

	In	Out	Net		In	Out	Net
North				**East Anglia**			
Industrial NE (North)	3·0	5·4	−2·4	South East	10·3	7·2	+3·1
Industrial NE (South)	4·5	5·9	−1·4	North East	9·4	6·0	+3·4
Rural NE (North)	9·4	10·0	−0·6	North West	10·1	9·4	+0·7
Rural NE (South)	13·8	12·3	+1·5	South West	14·5	9·2	+5·3
Cumberland/Westmorland	5·2	6·2	−1·0				
				South East			
Yorkshire and Humberside				Greater London	4·1	10·2	−6·1
North Humberside	5·0	5·7	−0·7	Outer metropolitan (West)	16·5	10·8	+5·7
South Humberside	7·4	6·3	+1·1	Outer metropolitan (North)	14·6	11·0	+3·6
Mid-Yorkshire	14·4	11·1	+3·3	Outer metropolitan (East)	17·8	10·5	+7·3
South Lindsey	15·0	14·1	+0·9	Outer metropolitan (SE)	15·0	9·5	+5·5
South Yorkshire	4·2	6·5	−2·3	Outer metropolitan (South)	17·6	13·6	+4·0
Yorkshire coalfield	6·0	6·3	−0·3	Outer metropolitan (SW)	17·2	13·5	+3·7
West Yorkshire	4·0	5·2	−1·2	Berkshire/Oxfordshire	13·3	9·6	+3·7
				Bedfordshire/Bucks.	14·7	10·4	+4·3
North West				Essex	17·4	8·6	+8·8
S Cheshire (High Peak)	13·5	8·1	+5·4	Kent	15·2	8·6	+6·6
South Lancashire	7·0	5·8	+1·2	Sussex coast	15·4	8·5	+6·9
Manchester	4·2	5·7	−1·5	Solent	11·8	7·6	+4·2
Merseyside	3·7	5·6	−1·9				
Furness	6·1	6·3	−0·2	**South West**			
Fylde	13·8	8·5	+5·3	Central	12·6	10·1	+2·5
Lancaster	12·8	8·1	+4·7	Southern	10·8	7·6	+3·2
Mid-Lancashire	7·3	6·4	+0·9	Western	11·6	8·1	+3·5
NE Lancashire	4·1	6·0	−1·9	Northern	9·4	6·8	+2·6
East Midlands				**Wales**			
Nottinghamshire/Derby	5·5	5·0	+0·5	Central/Eastern valleys	3·1	6·3	−3·2
Leicestershire	7·1	5·7	+1·4	South Wales (West)	4·5	5·1	−0·6
Eastern lowlands	10·7	9·5	+1·2	Coastal belt	8·9	6·8	+2·1
Northamptonshire	8·5	6·1	+2·4	North East Wales	7·2	6·1	+1·1
				NW Wales (North coast)	18·6	10·3	+8·3
West Midlands				NW Wales (other)	8·2	8·2	—
Central	15·1	8·6	+6·5	Central Wales	7·8	9·8	−2·0
Conurbation	3·1	7·0	−3·9	South West Wales	7·4	7·4	—
Coventry belt	8·1	7·2	+0·9				
Rural West	11·2	10·0	+1·2				
North Staffordshire	4·1	4·8	−0·7				

SOURCE: Department of Economic Affairs.

[a] As proportions of subregional populations.

a region where immigration is large in relation to the resident population will tend to show an emigration rate that is also large. This is still more strongly confirmed with a richer variety of evidence by data for the standard subregions, which it is worth turning aside for a moment to consider (see table 10.3), even though our main concern is with the regions taken as a whole.

One might suppose that the common variation of inward and outward migration rates is due to their common association with the effective size of the area – there is clearly more scope for changing address inside a populous area than inside one with a small population – and to some extent this is so. Among the lowest rates of inward and outward movement are those relating to the subregions of the Tyneside, west Yorkshire, Birmingham, Manchester and Merseyside conurbations, which are among the most populous ones, and among the highest are those relating to the North Riding of Yorkshire, South Lindsey, and the north Wales coast. The extent to which the common variation of inward and outward rates is explained by size (or populousness) is, however, small; the highest mobilities of all relate to the populations of the outer metropolitan subregions, some of which are quite large, while some of the smallest are those of Furness and north Staffordshire, both relatively small in population. Mobility is, like being accident-prone, to some degree a characteristic of particular people or particular occupations; an area that collects a high proportion of newcomers may expect to lose more than an average proportion of its residents in any year.

The second characteristic that emerges clearly from a scrutiny of subregional migration rates is that the outward rates vary over a much smaller range than the inward ones. The proportion of the resident population that leaves a subregion annually is nowhere much less than 1 per cent, nowhere more than 3, whereas the ratio of annual arrivals to resident population varies from $\frac{1}{2}$ to nearly 4 per cent. Some of the main reasons for outward movement clearly vary little; perhaps most notable is recruitment into those professions and occupations where career requirements are very likely to take one away from almost any specified home area. On the other hand, a high rate of inflow comes from either rapid development or specialisation on activities that tend to draw their practitioners from the national pool of appropriately trained manpower. Both of these characteristics are in fact strongly localised. The subregions that suffer net loss by internal (British) migration do so, in nearly all cases, not because they have unusually high rates of outward migration, but because they do not draw many people in. In fact, out of eighteen subregions losing by net internal migration, those that in 1961–6 had outward rates above the unweighted national average for all subregions were a splendidly assorted trio: Greater London, rural Northumberland – the subregion rural North East (North) – and central Wales.

A great deal of movement seems likely to be due to opportunities for individuals that arise in a random manner, scattered over the whole economy roughly in proportion to the numbers of jobs in its various regions. To test the hypothesis that this is so, and the further hypothesis that distance is an impediment to either learning of the opportunities or accepting them, gravity models of migration have been constructed, the chief published example for the British economy (or rather England and Wales) being that of Mr Hart.[1] About 44 per cent of the variance of movements between the ten old Standard Regions in 1960-1 is accounted for by assuming flows between two regions to vary with the product of their populations and inversely with a power (about 0·7) of the distance between them. This simple version of the model, of course, produces hypothetical flows that balance between each pair of regions, and for each region as a whole, but that seems not to be the largest source of its imperfection. The actual flows in the two directions between a pair of regions often differ in the same direction, and quite often to nearly equal extents from those predicted by the model. It is not only the case that regions with big inflows (for their size and location) have big outflows as well; it often seems, further, that if the flow in one direction between a pair of regions is big, considering the regions' sizes and the distance between them, the flow in the other direction will be big too.

Distance and population provide imperfect measures of the impediments to movement and the incentives or opportunities for it. More specifically, movements in all directions between the four old southern regions (London and the South East, Eastern, Southern, South Western) are greater than the national model predicts, so are those between some pairs like Yorkshire and the North, the two Midlands regions, the West Midlands and the South West. On the other hand, movements between Yorkshire, the North West and the West Midlands, and certain pairs such as Wales and the North, Wales and Yorkshire, Wales and the North Midlands are low. Various specific explanations, such as the unsatisfactory nature of the boundaries between London and the South East and its two neighbours (boundaries lying very close to London) suggest themselves. Mr Hart obtains some systematic improvement in his model by introducing measures of regional growth – the average growth of the pair of regions in question. Growing regions have big inflows (for obvious reasons) and these, as we have seen, go with relatively big outflows. Perhaps this is attributable to the well known tendency for a sizeable proportion of migrants to return whence they came.

All this still leaves us in a symmetrical world, in which we do not explain *net* migration either along any route or into any region, and it is net migration that holds most – though by no means all – of the

[1] R. A. Hart, 'A Model of Inter-regional Migration in England and Wales', *Regional Studies*, vol. 4, no,3, October 1970, pp. 279–96.

FACTOR MOVEMENTS

Chart 10.1. *Net migration, 1961–6*

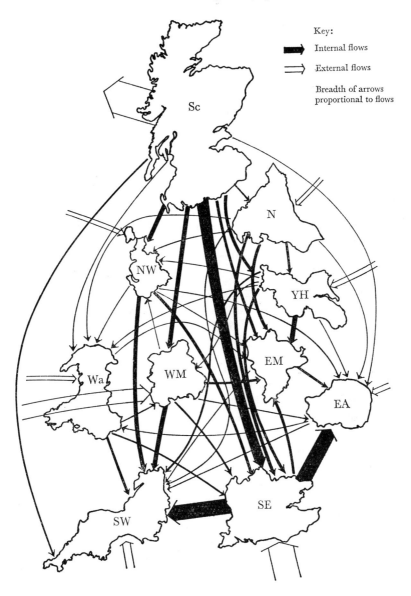

Table 10.4. *Net migration between regions and from overseas,*[a] *1961–6*

Thousands

To:	North	Yorks. and Humberside	North West	East Midlands	West Midlands	East Anglia	South East	South West	Wales	Scotland
From:										
North	—	+4·4	+2·7	+9·4	+11·2	+1·3	+18·3	+2·5	+1·4	−2·9
Yorks. and Humberside	−4·4	—	+1·9	+9·3	+1·6	+3·0	+8·4	+4·9	+0·5	−8·5
North West	−2·7	−1·9	—	+3·6	−1·9	+2·7	+11·6	+8·3	+8·7	−10·7
East Midlands	−9·4	−9·3	−3·6	—	−5·3	+2·9	−8·9	+2·1	−0·2	−12·1
West Midlands	−11·2	−1·6	+1·9	+5·3	—	+0·8	+12·3	+17·8	−0·8	−8·5
East Anglia	−1·3	−3·0	−2·7	−2·9	−0·8	—	−37·7	+0·2	+0·4	−1·7
South East	−18·3	−8·4	−11·6	+8·9	−12·3	+37·7	—	+53·5	−4·9	−27·7
South West	−2·5	−4·9	−8·3	−2·1	−17·8	−0·2	−53·5	—	−6·5	−4·9
Wales	−1·4	−0·5	−8·7	+0·2	+0·8	−0·4	+4·9	+6·5	—	−1·6
Scotland	+2·9	+8·5	+10·7	+12·1	+8·5	+1·7	+27·7	+4·9	+1·6	—
Net immigration										
Internal	−48	−17	−18	+44	−16	+50	−17	+101	—	−79
Overseas	+12	+12	+11	—	+52	+10	+121	+23	+10	−115
Total	−36	−5	−7	+44	+36	+60	+104	+124	+10	−194

SOURCES: *Sample Census 1966, England and Wales* and *Scotland. Migration Tables*; Department of Economic Affairs.

[a] All ages, both sexes.

economic interest. One way of repairing this omission is to look at these net flows by themselves. Table 10.4 and chart 10.1 show the net interregional flows in Great Britain in 1961–6, totalling something over 200,000 in the five years. Not much less than half of this total is accounted for by the flows from the South East to the South West and East Anglia, and another eighth by the flow to the South East from Scotland. The pattern has certain simplicities: Scotland shows net emigration to every other British region, the North to every one except Scotland. There is a general tendency for each region to receive from those to the north of it and to give to those to the south, as if they formed a cascade, until at the bottom the South East's outflow surges into its westerly and north-easterly neighbours, and even splashes into the East Midlands. Another small net flow from the West Midlands to the North West runs counter to this conventional gravity. The South West provides an antithesis to Scotland, with a net inflow from every other region.

Net flows to and from the world outside Great Britain reinforce the broad effects of the internal cascade from north to south. Apart from Scotland (and the East Midlands, which virtually broke even), every region seems to have had a net inflow of population from the outside world in the quinquennium in question. There were, however, only three massive flows of this kind: two, into the South East and the West Midlands, much bigger than those regions's net losses in their exchanges with the other British regions, and the net overseas flow out of Scotland, which was even bigger than that country's losses to England and Wales. At the same time it is noteworthy that there is no significant correlation between the various regions' net gains or losses by internal and by external migration; Scotland loses both internally and externally, the South West and East Anglia both gain (though their external gains are relatively small), but the South East and the West Midlands are joined by the North, Yorkshire and the North West in combining internal losses with external gains. It is clear that any explanation of net migration on simple grounds of total demand for labour and local supply of it would encounter difficulty in dealing with its internal and external components at the same time. Taking the two elements together however, the four regions north of the Trent were losing some 50,000 a year by net migration (more than 40 per cent of their natural increase); the rest of Great Britain collectively was gaining over 75,000.

The pattern of net interregional migration for population of both sexes and all ages together conceals, of course, some important differences between patterns shown by narrower population categories. The two sexes do not differ very much from each other in their net migration flows; the age groups, however, show great differences in their propensities to move, and some important differences in their patterns of movement. Children under 15 move roughly as much in proportion to their numbers as the whole resident population, but the age group 15 to 24 is some 70 per cent more mobile, and the group aged 25 to 44 over 25 per cent more mobile, than the population as a whole. Above 45 mobility falls off sharply; it is only about half as high as for the whole population, and retirement migration serves to make the over-65 group only marginally more mobile than that aged 45 to 64. The immigrants into the various regions show a similar age distribution with some important exceptions: the South East is the great magnet for the young (especially for young women), with those aged 15 to 24 about 20 per cent more numerous among its incomers than they are among interregional movers generally. The South West, East Anglia and Wales (in descending order) are the magnets for the older age groups, in which retirement is an important occasion for movement. Because of movements on retirement the great flows from the South East into the South West and East Anglia dominate the pattern of migration of men of working age less than they dominate that of the total population, but it is still true that it is the population of working age that predominates in those flows.

If one looks at each British region's net balance of migration with the others taken together, the figure for both sexes and all ages can again conceal important differences. The net losses of the North and Scotland and the net gains of the East Midlands were proportionately higher in men of working age than in women, children and retired men. The small net losses of the West Midlands and the North West were relatively light in men of working age in comparison with the other sections of the population, as were the great net gains of the South West and East Anglia. The South East was a net gainer of men of working age from the rest of the country, but a net loser of the remaining population elements taken together (in spite of the net inflow of younger women). Wales was in the opposite situation. The migrations from outside Great Britain, concentrated largely on the South East and, to a less extent, on the West Midlands, the North West and Yorkshire, were, of course, largely immigrations of men of working age. So far as men of working age are concerned, the English regions south of the Trent seem all to have gained substantially by internal and overseas migration together; the other British regions probably all lost, though only from Scotland was the loss indubitable and heavy.

One simple approach to the explanation of total net migration into or out of areas smaller than regions (in fact the counties of England and Wales) between the Censuses of 1951 and 1961 is to be seen in an earlier calculation by Mr Hart undertaken in connection with the present study. It consists in seeking a relation between annual percentage change in population (excluding that by natural increase) and various combinations of explanatory variables. In most of the equations that contain it unemployment rate emerges as a statistically significant influence, with the implication that annual net outward migration rose by between 1 and 2 per thousand of the total population for every 1 percentage point rise in the unemployment rate. Likewise, average employment income per tax case (from Inland Revenue data) is generally significant, implying extra annual immigration of between 3 and 6 per thousand of the population for every extra £100 of average income. The insertion of variables indicating favourable and unfavourable features of the economic structure (proportions of the occupied population in expanding and contracting industries, and in agriculture) improve the general level of explanation, and the signs of their coefficients make sense. It is interesting, however, that if distance from London is introduced it steals the thunder of unemployment rate as an explanatory variable, and that, in an equation where both it and population density per square mile appear (along with others), both unemployment rate and income lose their significance. Distance from London is quite highly correlated with unemployment, and at a simple level of explanation can be regarded as an inverse measure of 'potential' or 'centrality', which may be claimed to be growth-promoting. But much of the statistical explanatory power of both distance from London and population density is accounted for by London overspill, which is responsible largely for the enormous growth of the administrative counties in the outer metropolitan subregion and their neighbours in the outer South East. Relations discovered at county level (quite apart from any inherent ambiguity they may contain) are not very useful at the regional level.

At the regional level of classification, a more elaborate investigation has been made by Mr Weeden, using the migration tables of the 1961 and 1966 Censuses, and working with statistics relating to men of working age. It begins from the gross flows of migrants between all the pairs of British regions, but deduces relations of such forms that parameters describing net internal flows can be derived. The basic relationships used are similar to those of a gravity model; that is to say, it is assumed that the gross flow from one region to another is proportional, *ceteris paribus*, to the product of their population totals. Economic variables, notably unemployment rates in the two regions measured from the national mean, and various income variables are then added. Distance between the two regions in the form in which it is usually introduced into gravity models proves not to be very useful; what is better is a single dummy variable which takes the value of unity when the two regions are geographically contiguous and zero in other cases. This is consistent with the general observation that short-distance moves, largely undertaken for reasons of accommodation, are very frequent, but long-distance moves, usually made for reasons connected with work, are very much less so. The former may involve crossing one regional boundary, especially when it runs through relatively thickly inhabited areas; a 'short' move will not involve crossing two. But where long moves are concerned it is not surprising that most people who are willing to move as far as the next region but one (typically a hundred-mile journey) will show very little more reluctance to move as far as the next but two or three.

No simple device, however, seems to be capable of taking account of the different propensities to move between contiguous regions that arise from the details of their geography and the incidence of urban overspill. Movements (in both directions) between the South East and two of its neighbouring regions – East Anglia and the South West – prove to be heavy, and a better fit is generally obtained for the model as a whole by omitting these four interregional flows (out of the total of ninety).

The model in a variety of slightly different specifications,[1] and when applied to different data (movements in the intervals 1961-6, 1965-6 and 1960-1), generally shows the unemployment rate to have the expected effects to a statistically significant extent. A high rate in the region of origin increases movement from it, a low rate in the region of destination increases movement to it. The implication is that a difference of 1 percentage point between a region's unemployment rate and the average for the rest of the country makes for a difference of between 2 and 5 per thousand of its population in its annual rate of *net* inward or outward migration from or to the rest of Great Britain. The data for 1961-6 and 1965-6 yield results at the lower end of this range; those for 1960-1 give results at the upper end.

The investigation suggests that differences in income per head are less important in determining migration-flows than unemployment differences, or are less representative of whatever labour-market differences do in fact induce movement. Where income variables are included along with unemployment and are statistically significant, they more often than not indicate a tendency for both inward and outward migration to be higher in higher-income regions. This is in accordance with the known tendency for mobility to be higher in the more highly paid occupational groups; it also accords with the observed tendency for regions with a high rate of gross inward migration to show a high gross outward rate as well. In the equations where income variables are included along with unemployment, moreover, the usual tendency is for the income variables to imply *net* interregional movement towards regions of lower average income. This net tendency, however, most often turns out to be below the usually accepted level of statistical significance.

It seems that unemployment difference is superior to income difference as an explanatory variable in this connection. When one looks at the forty-five net interregional flows, one finds that seventeen of them are 'perverse' in the sense of running in the direction of lower average income, but only fourteen in the sense of running towards higher un-

---

[1] One of the more successful forms of the model was $M_{ij} = P_i P_j (A_2 K_{ij} + B_1 X_i + B_2 X_j)$, where M_{ij} is the gross flow of migrants from region i to region j, P_i and P_j are the respective resident populations of the two regions, K_{ij} is the contiguity variable taking the value unity when the two regions are contiguous, zero when they are not, and X_i and X_j are values of specific explanatory variables—unemployment rates in the most successful versions. A_2, B_1 and B_2 are coefficients. This implies a relationship $N_i/P_i = (B_2 - B_1)(X_i - \bar{X})\bar{P}$, where N_i/P_i is the rate of net inward migration into region i per head of its resident population, $\bar{X}$ is the rest of the country's average level of the explanatory variable (e.g. the unemployment rate), and $\bar{P}$ is the rest of the country' resident population. Values of $(B_2 - B_1)/\bar{P}$, which measures the generalised sensitivity of a region's *net* migration to changes in the excess of (for instance) unemployment rate over the rest of the country can thus be calculated from the coefficients of the model.

employment, including eleven that are perverse in both senses. Most of the net flows into the South West and East Anglia (not only those from the South East) are perverse on one or both of these criteria.

One obvious source of perversity is the existence of two occupational sectors in the regional economies – a larger one within which people are relatively immobile between regions, and a smaller one within which they are mobile. The 'gradient' of either earnings or job-opportunities, or both, may run in opposite directions for the two occupational sectors. It may well be that the predominant movement is determined by the gradient applying to the smaller but more mobile sector, but that the gradient derived from statistics relating to each regional labour market as a whole is in the opposite direction. There may be a net movement into a generally low-paying region because relatively high-paying new industries are growing within it. Another complication is the fact that jobs as well as people move in response to market conditions. In so far as firms move in the direction of cheaper labour or higher unemployment rates people are saved the trouble of moving in the opposite direction, though this by itself does not explain perverse movements. They are, however, explained if the inflow of mobile 'key workers' brought in by incoming industry exceeds the outflow of migrants following the remaining, predominant gradient of earnings and/or job-opportunities. But why the predominant movement should be less often perverse with respect to unemployment rates than with respect to earnings is less clear.

Mr Weeden's model was also tried in versions that included growth of employment in the regions as an explanatory variable. The propriety of treating growth as independent in this way is perhaps open to question, but in the event it proves to be unhelpful when included along with unemployment difference, which thus emerges as the variable to which interregional labour movements are most closely related. The fact that availability of labour is the factor in location decisions most frequently mentioned as a 'major' one in the Board of Trade's 'Inquiry into Location Attitudes and Experience'[1] may be regarded as supporting evidence.

Bearing this conclusion in mind, let us try to look at factor movements in rather closer relation to their economic significance.

TYPES OF FACTOR MOVEMENT: 'COLONISATION'

Looking at the whole pattern of interregional factor movements therefore, what can be made of it? These movements may be classified in a very simple way. First, there are movements of both capital and

[1] Unpublished document, 1971.

labour from wherever they originate to specific natural resources that are not mobile. Second, there are the movements of capital and labour towards each other in cases where they do not come into existence in proportions that are, regionally, completely complementary. We must review them briefly in turn.

Among the former of these classes of movement, cases that were of overwhelming historical importance and still dominate much of our national life by their aftermath were the eighteenth and nineteenth-century movements to areas blessed with (or conveniently placed in relation to) mineral resources – mainly coal. Of secondary direct importance for regional studies (but still indirectly important because of their impact on regional populations) were the movements of British and Irish population and British capital to exploit the agricultural and mineral resources of the overseas world. Other writers have shown that in these overseas movements the flows of capital and labour tended to correspond with one another, both in their timing and, to a considerable extent, in their direction. Bright prospects and manifest growth in overseas countries tended to draw in from the United Kingdom (among other sources) both capital and immigrants at the same time; though the two flows did not entirely keep in step – we sometimes financed developments that drew on population mainly from elsewhere. The same sort of process must have operated in the opening-up – the 'colonisation' as one might say – of the coalfields and other areas that developed mainly on the basis of their specific natural advantages.

In the last fifty years this pattern of factor movements has been much less important; no specific natural resource has exerted an overwhelming magnetic attraction. Power-stations and steelworks are still drawn by mineral resources, but both of them are increasingly dependent upon seaborne supplies of their bulkiest input and, like oil refineries, are accordingly attracted to the progressively limited numbers of sites that afford good access for very large maritime bulk carriers. Cement, bricks and some other building-material industries depend on minerals that are moderately localised, and some industries have exceptional demands for water, but none of these requirements – nor the totality of them – is enough to cause a stampede of capital and population in a particular direction. The biggest cause by far of the parallel movements of industry and population in this century has been the least specific of locational requirements – the need for space itself.

Beginning effectively with the City of London in the first half of the last century, residences have been continuously pushed out of city centres by the powerful competition of commercial and industrial land-users, aided by the desire of the residents for suburban or rural surroundings, and by the growing facilities for daily commuting to work in the centre.

At the same time manufacturing industry has been pushed out by the competition of commerce – or rather (what is not quite the same thing) factories have been pushed out by the competition for space of shops and offices, and, within a generally narrower radius, the offices in turn have tended to expel the shops. In the latest phase of this process the more specialised offices, regarded as most dependent upon close contact with the rest of the central office complexes of the cities, or upon the prestige and the convenience for callers that a central site provides, have begun to push out those that are less strictly governed by these considerations. Journeys to work have lengthened, but probably at a decreasing rate, as many workplaces too have been pushed in broadly the same outward directions as residences, and for the most part by the same economic forces stemming from scarcity of land. To some extent in recent years it may have been that industry and commerce have moved outwards partly in search of labour, but for the most part both they and their labour have moved out independently in search of land.

So far as resident populations are concerned, the fringes of the conurbations have been expanding over the past decade or so by about 100,000 a year. Most notably, the population of working age resident in the outer metropolitan subregion grew in the quinquennium 1961–6 by over 11 per cent, while employment at workplaces within it grew by 8 per cent – suggesting a growth of outward commuting population, but a much bigger growth of local employment. In the same period, confirming to some extent the growth of commuting, Greater London's resident population of working age seems to have fallen (though this is not certain), while its employment stayed nearly constant. The same kind of story – population moving outward and jobs moving outward rather more slowly – is broadly repeated in the other conurbations and, to a smaller extent, in cities below the conurbation-size. This is by far the greatest part of the total net movement of population – that is to say, of change in the geographical distribution of the population between local authority areas – that has recently been going on. It accounts for something like a fifth of all changes of address; the great bulk of the remaining four-fifths consisting of the reshuffling of people between existing addresses (mainly over short distances), or of moves to new housing within the same local authority area.

This shift of population and (to a smaller degree) employment to the conurbation fringes is, however, nearly all intra-regional and, to the extent that we are concerned with regional economies as individual units, does not directly concern us. Here and there it involves interregional movement where large towns lie near regional boundaries (as in the case of Sheffield, which has shed some population into both of the neighbouring regions and probably some employment into the neighbouring part of the East Midlands), but basically it is important only in the case of the South East and its neighbours. The London conurbation is so big, and what may legitimately be regarded as its 'fringes' are so deep, that setting an outer limit to them is difficult. Within the region some parts of the outer South East (notably Essex, Kent and the Solent coast) show employment growth faster than that of the outer metropolitan subregion which is the immediate 'fringe'. They also, unlike that fringe, show proportionately faster growth of employment than of working-aged resident population. In neighbouring areas outside the South Eastern region, the same is true of all four subregions of East Anglia (though growth of resident population of working age is particularly rapid only in the two southern ones). The association of rapid population growth with still faster growth of employment also occurs in the northern (Bristol–Cheltenham–Gloucester) subregion of the South West, where it is to a considerable extent the result of London overspill schemes. While the majority of such schemes, whether based on London or not, do not extend beyond the region of their base, some do, and these can best be regarded as pure cases of long-distance 'colonisation'. London's schemes in East Anglia, as far afield as Bury St Edmunds and Peterborough, and its Swindon scheme in the South West, are the leading examples. But the bulk of the more spontaneous movement from the South East to East Anglia, the East Midlands and the South West also has this character.

Among the natural resources that attract both population and industry are pleasant and healthy natural surroundings. The effect of these is hard to separate from that of the man-made environment, though it would be useful if one could distinguish between them, since one of these two components of the total environment can in principle be changed and the other cannot. Together they formed one of the most quoted reasons for choice of location revealed by the Board of Trade's Inquiry into Location,[1] though, as one might expect, rarely as the single outstanding reason. The fact that they were substantially less often quoted by firms that had gone to the older industrial regions than by others may be taken as evidence that industrial blight and old or run-down social capital are substantial deterrents to inward movement of job-opportunities. The tendency of respondents in the Labour Mobility Survey[2] to express a preference (though probably a rather abstract one) for a hypothetical non-industrial area of future residence should probably be interpreted similarly.

The fact that fast growing communities have social capital of a newer vintage on average than have most slow growing ones may thus introduce an element of genuine dynamic instability into the geographical

[1] Ibid.   [2] Government Social Survey, *Labour Mobility in Great Britain 1953–63*.

pattern of development. The fast growing can accelerate their growth to some extent because they are already fast growing and therefore newer and more attractive. Time may take its revenge for this; some towns in East Anglia or the South West are now regarded as attractive because they have hardly anything of the nineteenth century in them. The time may come when some of the Pennine towns are similarly thought attractive because they have hardly anything of the twentieth. But that time is not yet, and meanwhile a predominantly middle-aged built environment diverts growth to a probably significant but not easily measurable extent from the places of later nineteenth to those of later twentieth-century growth, or to the green fields where growth starts from scratch.

It is probable that something of the same kind operates through the age structure of population. Migrants are predominantly young adults as we have noted, and there is some presumption that they prefer destinations where their own age group is well represented, which means places already receiving immigrants. Again time takes its revenge when the growth of such communities has slowed down for any considerable period, but nothing may happen to produce such a check for quite a long time. There is perhaps some presumption too that the occupational and educational structure of the population provides a parallel mechanism – migrants are predominantly the better educated, concentrated in the occupations of higher skill and professional training; hence they are likely to find the growing communities where these qualities are most common the most attractive. But this, though certainly one of the reasons for London's perennial attraction to the young, is not a simple or all-pervading tendency. Growth can still be impressively fast without making much room for the highly educated, as the West Midlands prove; while regions of slow growth, notably Wales and Scotland, can still retain (or apparently, in the case of the latter, reattract) a high proportion of such people, even after one has made allowance for the effect that industrial structure might be expected (on national evidence) to exert on these proportions. Industry is to some extent attracted by skill, though this is far less often mentioned as a locational factor than the availability of labour in general, and, like the environmental influences on movement, it is hard to assess.

Taking all these considerations together, it seems likely that the generally favourable image of the new, bright, growing community as opposed to the old, dull, stagnating one has considerable and cumulative power in directing the more or less parallel movements of capital and labour – the popularity of new towns being an extreme case. Similar considerations also affect to some extent the movements of capital and labour in search of each other to which we now come.

MUTUAL ADJUSTMENT BETWEEN CAPITAL AND LABOUR SUPPLIES AND JOB-MOBILITY

The second class of factor movements, which is of greater interest in relation to regional problems, consists of movements of labour towards regions where that factor is scarcer in relation to capital than in the region of origin, and of capital in the opposite direction.

This is essentially an exchange between north and south. The four regions north of the Trent together with Wales were, in the early sixties, sustaining a net annual loss of about 32,000 a year (including some 13,000 men of working age) to the rest of the country, and also of some 16,000 (about half of them men of working age) to the rest of the world. They were receiving jobs in net manufacturing moves from the rest of the country at the rate (allowing for some subsequent growth) of about 13,000 a year and in addition about 2,000 a year from abroad. Taking account of multiplier effects to which we shall refer later, the accession of jobs due to inflow of firms from the rest of the country was not very different in magnitude from the outflow of occupied persons to it. In the previous decade the inflow of jobs was much smaller, probably less than half the corresponding outflow of occupied persons.

We have seen that it is possible to get some idea of the sensitivity with which net migration seems to respond to unemployment differences and this is valuable, though it must be regarded with great caution, especially since it is derived from cross-section data. But the other data that we really need concern the sensitivity with which the net flow of jobs into or out of a region responds to changes in its excess of unemployment rate over the national average. This, however, is a much more difficult area to explore. In the first place, the interregional flow of jobs however interpreted (whether as the jobs in 'moves', as defined by Mr Howard,[1] or in some other way) is undeniably affected strongly by policy, and policy, or the strength of the instruments by which it was applied, has been changed rather frequently, and in ways the effect of which cannot be estimated *a priori*. If one wants to see what happens in the absence of manifest changes in policy, and with policy at its least obtrusive, the period 1952-9 offers itself as the most promising. It must, however, be presumed that, even then, policy – especially control of industrial building by industrial development certificates – had a considerable effect.

In view of this, the best one can do by cross-section analysis is to set an upper limit to the sensitivity of industrial movement to unemployment differences in the absence of policy; this sensitivity must be less

[1] Board of Trade, *The Movement of Manufacturing Industry in the United Kingdom, 1945-65*.

than any that can be detected for the period 1952-9, when policy was, it is true, trying to push movement in the direction of the high-unemployment areas, but not as strongly as later. The procedure is to plot against regional unemployment rates the rate for the period in question of the net flow of jobs in industrial moves into the region. The numbers of jobs in 'moves' are those calculated by Mr Howard; for this purpose moves originating in a region are treated as outward moves to be subtracted from inward ones to obtain net movement. Moves from overseas are excluded. The net addition of jobs by moves reckoned in this way is then divided by the manufacturing employment in the region to obtain a figure analogous to a net migration rate.

Data of this sort plotted against average regional unemployment rates for the period 1952-9 show a poor but positive correlation – much of it due to the data for Northern Ireland, though the correlation remains positive and the slope of the regression line is not enormously changed in their absence. The regression implies that, for each extra 1 percentage point added to unemployment rate in a region reckoned from the national average, the tendency in this period was for annual net inward moves of manufacturing jobs to be increased by somewhat under 1 per thousand of the manufacturing jobs already in existence there. It is incidentally interesting to observe that the corresponding calculation for the period 1960-5 (after correcting numbers of jobs in moves to allow for the subsequent 'maturing' of the establishments concerned) yields a very much better correlation and a much steeper regression line. The implication is that, in that period of stronger policy, an additional percentage point of unemployment rate in comparison with the national average went with an extra net inflow (or reduced net outflow) of about 4 per thousand jobs in existence. The suggestion this conveys of the extent to which policy effects were strengthened is relevant for our present purpose only in so far as it may render it probable that the not inconsiderable policy measures in operation in the fifties were responsible for a good deal of such systematic tendency as is detectable in that period for jobs to flow towards areas of higher unemployment. The strength of this tendency in the absence of policy, we may conclude, is very weak indeed.

Not much further light is to be thrown on this subject from a study of time-series of industrial movement for the reasons that have been mentioned. Within the years 1952-9 there were big changes in the total amount of industrial movement (including intra-regional moves) largely marching with the trade cycle. But the proportion of the total that had the higher-unemployment regions as its destination remained roughly constant. There were more moves in prosperous years presumably because there was more growth, but in boom and recession alike about a quarter of them (reckoned by their job-content) continued to be moves to (roughly) the present Development Areas, and rather under a half to the West Midlands and the South East, in spite of the absolute gap between the higher and the lower regional unemployment rates being considerably narrower in good years than in bad. The geographical pattern of moves does not seem to be very sensitive to short-run changes in market influences, though in the rather longer term, as we have seen, at least the boldness of the pattern can be greatly altered by policy. We are left with the general conclusion that the pattern that would exist in the absence of regional policy would bias the percentage net rate of acquisition of jobs by moves towards regions of high unemployment only to a fraction of the extent to which the rate of net acquisition of population by migration is biased in the opposite direction.

Armed with this provisional conclusion, we can return to the implied relation between mobility of resources and their equilibrium rates of unemployment, and the impact to be expected on the rates of unemployment of resources from any flow of them additional to those that are brought about by the market. The 'equilibrium' rate of unemployment of labour in a region of deficient demand, it will be recalled, is the rate that has to be built up in the region to produce that net outward flow of people of working age which, along with the inward flow of jobs, will balance the initial discrepancy between the rate of growth of the indigenous potential labour force and that of indigenous jobs for them. We have seen that a rise of 1 percentage point in the regional unemployment rate relative to the rest of the country goes with an increase of about 3 per thousand (estimates vary from 2 to 5) in the net outflow of men of working age in the region. The net inflow of jobs that shows signs of being *induced* by the extra point in the unemployment rate is apparently much smaller; probably less than 1 per thousand already in existence. For every 1 per cent rise in the unemployment rate therefore, we may reasonably expect the gap between the growth of the labour force locally on offer and of jobs locally on offer to fall by 3 or 4 per thousand of the labour force – an extra ten unemployed go with the reduction of the increase in the gap between candidates and jobs by three or four a year. It follows that any extraneous influence – a government-induced extra outflow of men or inflow of jobs – that reduces the gap by three or four a year, will reduce by ten the level of unemployment that is necessary to close the gap. For every man or job extraneously moved per year in the required direction, the equilibrium level of regional unemployment (given the rate in the rest of the country) falls by two or three.

In all this we have ignored a great many complications. First, we have argued as if the whole labour force was male (since our conclusions about labour mobility were derived from a study of males of working age only). Second, we have considered only registered unemployment. Third, we have ignored any implications of the fact that our conclusions about the mobility of jobs were derived only from data on manufacturing industry. Fourth, in our simple model of equilibrium unemployment and factor movement, we have ignored the multiplier and associated phenomena. What corrections do these omissions demand?

The pattern of movement of men of working age is not, in fact, very different from that of the whole economically active population. They constitute some 62 per cent of the labour force; married women (who presumably are mostly married to economically active men and move with their husbands – or whose husbands move with them) are a further 21 per cent. Unretired men over 65 years old, and single, widowed and divorced women in the labour force, are not so numerous that the variations they display from the male migration pattern change the general picture much so far as the flows are concerned. It is the retired whose movements are quite different from those of active men. It is true that unmarried women, or married ones who take the initiative in moving, are likely to respond to the pattern of female unemployment rates which is rather different from that of the male rates used in Mr Weeden's calculations, but the rank correlation at least between male and female regional unemployment rates is high. We can probably take our broad conclusions about the relations of net migration to unemployment differences as applying interchangeably to the male and the total active labour forces.

The basing of the calculations solely on rates of registered unemployment means, of course, that our deductions about the effect of exogenous movement of men or jobs upon the equilibrium rate of unemployment will leave out of account any accompanying effect on the equilibrium number of unregistered unemployed. But this is easily put right in a rough and ready way for any particular region in so far as there is a stable relation between registered and total (including unregistered) unemployment. All we have to do is modify our coefficients relating net movements of people and jobs to differences of registered unemployment so that it relates them to differences of total unemployment instead. It seems from inspection of total unemployment rates (as revealed by the 1966 Census) that a calculation such as Mr Weeden's carried out with them instead of registered rates would have produced coefficients smaller by about a third than those actually obtained. It is also known from calculations described in another chapter that short-term variations in total unemployment in the high-unemployment regions (that is variations in the difference between their estimated labour force and actual employment) are about half as big again as those in registered unemployment. Both these facts suggest that, for every man or job moved exogenously in the right direction, the equilibrium level of *total* unemployment in a high-unemployment region would be reduced by three or four, including the reduction of two or three in the equilibrium number of *registered* unemployed.

The fact that our conclusion about the mobility of jobs was derived from a study of moves in manufacturing industry only raises two questions. Do moves tell the whole story even so far as manufacturing is concerned about the preferential creation of jobs in areas of plentiful labour, which might be regarded as induced by the easy labour supply there? And what about non-manufacturing industry? So far as the former is concerned, do existing establishments in an industry tend to expand more (or new establishments which are not moves to be generated more freely) in a region of abundant labour, either because the abundant labour supply directly favours them, or because the inward moves generated by labour conditions stimulate them through a regional multiplier mechanism? So far as non-manufacturing industry is concerned we can ask exactly the same questions, but are also under the disadvantage of having no information about moves.

For manufacturing (plus a relatively small fringe of other industries), we have the statistics of industrial development certificates, which tell us that, in the years 1956–9, the four British regions of high unemployment received prospects of new employment in approved schemes no more than in proportion to their existing manufacturing employment. We can also examine in relation to unemployment rates the growth components of employment increase in the manufacturing industries of 1953–9 as calculated in chapter 6. These components were *negatively* (though very poorly) correlated with regional unemployment. The weighted average of them for the four high-unemployment regions was certainly higher than it was for the five regions of lower unemployment – a state of affairs that was incidentally reversed (presumably by policy) in the period 1961–6. There is no sign here that our modest estimate of the systematic mobility (in the widest sense) of manufacturing employment towards available labour in the absence of policy is by any means too modest.

Mining and agriculture are pretty clearly not mobile in response to differences in labour conditions; they are the resource-oriented industries *par excellence*. The service industries – that is to say everything except agriculture, mining and manufacture – are mostly, and subject to important exceptions, market-oriented. We have already noted that, as a first approximation, one may seek to explain changes in service employment as being dependent upon changes in employment in the same region in manufacturing, mining and agriculture – the activities that predominantly (though again with some important exceptions) cater for a national or international rather than a regional market. We have seen in chapter 6 that, for every ten extra people in manufacturing, mining and agriculture in a region, seven or eight extra were drawn into service trades, in addition to a steady flow that was drawn into these trades in any case because of the changing general structure of demand and changing relative productivities. This seems to be the direct indication of fairly recent employment changes, and it is broadly consistent with what the independent approach by way of the long-term income multiplier suggests.

The relevant implication of this is that, if we regard changes in mining and agricultural employment as independently caused, a given percentage change in manufacturing employment will tend to go with a smaller, or at least not a larger, *consequential* percentage change in service employment and thus in total employment. The upshot is that a given percentage increase of the number of jobs in manufacturing industry by virtue of net moves of establishments into a region is not likely to induce a greater, but rather a distinctly smaller, proportionate increase in the number of jobs in the region altogether. On all our evidence it still looks as if the interregional flow of total job-opportunities is decidedly less sensitive (at least when regional policy is not active) to interregional differences in unemployment rates than is the flow of candidates for jobs.

Our conclusions about the relation of equilibrium unemployment differences to exogenous changes in migration of people or jobs can probably stand as being, at any rate, of the right order of magnitude – three or four fewer unemployed (including two or three fewer registered unemployed) for every additional job or candidate for work pushed annually in the equilibrating direction. But in considering the magnitude of the long-term employment multiplier, we are approaching the multiplier effects of the factor movements themselves, which are important in their own right and deserve a little further consideration.

A corollary, relating to natural increase of the population of working age, may be added to this. For every rise of 1 percentage point in the natural increase of population of working age, total unemployment may be expected to rise by 3 or 4 per cent of the labour force, and registered unemployment by 2 or 3 per cent of it. The extreme case to which this is most relevant is Northern Ireland, where the natural increase of population in the years 1961–70 was some 1·2 per cent a year, or about twice the average rate for the United Kingdom as a whole. If one assumes that these rates of natural increase also applied approximately to population of working age, the suggestion is that something like 1½ per cent of the Province's labour force owed their unemployment to the excess of the Northern Irish over the United Kingdom rate of natural increase. In other words, between a third and a quarter of its excess unemployment seems to have been attributable to its excess of natural population increase. Within Great Britain the contrasts are smaller. The differences in natural increase between Scotland and the South West would, on this reckoning, account for about 0·5 per cent, out of an actual difference in unemployment rate between them in the early sixties of 1·8 per cent. On the other hand, without the difference that existed between the natural growth rates of Wales and the West Midlands (the lowest and highest respectively of the British regional rates), one might have expected the unemployment difference between these two regions to have been nearly twice as big as it was. The low rates of natural increase in the North West and Yorkshire have, on this showing, played some part, though not a predominant one, in keeping their unemployment rates low. The unemployment differences between the United Kingdom regions have, on balance, probably been increased rather than decreased by differences in natural increase, but predominantly they are attributable to industrial rather than demographic disparities.

THE ROLE OF MULTIPLIERS

We have seen that the creation of a hundred new job-opportunities in the 'basic' industries of a region (those producing what may be called 'interregional' goods, or services which either cater for outside demand or replace things previously bought from outside) will typically raise regional income in the short run not only by the net product generated in those jobs, but by an amount equivalent to the output from something like fifteen or twenty-five further jobs. This secondary increase in regional income may not all come from a further increment in the number of people in employment; some of it may be produced by longer average hours of work or higher output per man-hour, so that the employment multiplier will generally be lower than that applicable to income. On the other hand, if one is considering the effects of a specific act of job-creation in the 'basic' industries (say the bringing into operation of a particular new factory), the employment multiplier effects may be a good deal larger than this implies, because there may be an input multiplier effect as well – a stimulation of the region's 'basic' industries to provide the new factory with some direct or indirect inputs which, in this case, we have not already included in our multiplicand. The short-term employment multiplier applicable to the employment (in say) a new motor-car plant may be very considerably above unity (perhaps 1·5), though that applicable to the whole of the increase in a region's employment in 'basic' industries may exceed unity by only 10 or 15 per cent.

This is all on the assumption that no change in population through migration is induced by the short-run developments in question. But interregional movements of industry produce some changes in the pattern of migration fairly quickly. Most obviously they involve interregional movements of managers and key workers. Luttrell found that these accounted for about $2\frac{1}{2}$ per cent of the employment created after a few years in branch establishments, and nearly 10 per cent of that in establishments that moved bodily.[1] Taking the relative frequency of these two kinds of move revealed by Howard's study,[2] it seems that the average would be 4 or 5 per cent for all moves and 3 or 4 per cent for those into the peripheral areas. The improvement of job-opportunities in a region, no doubt, also quickly effects some reductions in outward migration, though this is harder to substantiate. In the short run however, in which the chief effect of industrial movement is on the balance between demand for and supply of labour, its multiplier effects are probably not much greater than those implied by the income multiplier.

Changes in migration also carry some immediate effects through the income multiplier. These will be least in conditions of generally slack demand when movement does not directly affect employment. Unemployed outgoers obviously do not do so, while employed outgoers bequeath their jobs, in effect, to local unemployed. Incomers either stay unemployed or, more probably, get jobs that would otherwise have gone to local people. In these conditions the primary effect of migration is simply that the number of unemployed is reduced by the number of migrants in the region of origin, increased equally in that of destination. There are no primary effects on production in either region. There are, however, secondary effects, because some expenditure of unemployed people (financed by unemployment benefit, supplementary benefit and savings) is transferred with the migrants. At a guess the average expenditure of an unemployed person might be equal to something between 40 and 60 per cent of the average marginal net product of an employee in employment, and round about 40 per cent of such expenditure might go directly into factor incomes in the person's region of residence. With the help of the further operation of the regional income multiplier, the direct or indirect transfer of one unemployed person between regions might therefore mean the transfer of demand for local factors including the equivalent of anything between (say) 18 and

---

[1] W. F. Luttrell, *Factory Location and Industrial Movement*, National Institute of Economic and Social Research, London, 1962.

[2] Board of Trade, *The Movement of Manufacturing Industry in the United Kingdom, 1945–65*.

30 per cent of an average job. In other words a hundred occupied persons moving in these conditions of slack demand, might carry between eighteen and thirty jobs with them.

If demand is sufficient or more than sufficient for full employment, the effects are naturally different. An outgoing employed migrant, or one who would have entered local employment had he stayed, removes his marginal product from the region immediately. He also removes indirectly, through the multiplier mechanism, demand for local factors equivalent to (say) something between a quarter and third of that product (assuming that his departure is to some extent reflected in public current but not capital spending); but if there is some excess demand for labour, even though only because of his departure, this secondary reduction in demand will be avoided and full employment of the now reduced working population will continue.

Similarly, in the region to which the migrant goes output will be increased by his marginal product, and demand that would normally fall upon that region's factors of production will also increase through the multiplier by a quarter or a third of the migrant's marginal product. If however employment is already 'full', regional income may not be capable of increasing to this extent, demand will be diverted to importable products, or, in the rather longer run, resources will be diverted from exporting from the region to satisfying its internal demand for non-importable goods and services. Indeed, with intra-regional labour mobility any demand in a region would tend to distribute itself between industries so that immigrant labour is drawn into all of them to provide a balanced increase of regional production without secondary imbalances of demand and supply, or (in the absence of the complications following from capital stock adjustment) any secondary induced immigration.

This is equivalent to what we may suppose to happen in the long run over an extended period of regional growth fed by migration. We have seen that over the years 1953–66 growth of employment in a region in those industries that may be supposed to depend necessarily on the local market (the regional trades) has been broadly 80 per cent of that in the industries producing mainly goods and services that are interregionally mobile and competitive (manufacture, mining, agriculture and the 'basic tertiary' industries), plus an independent growth of non-basic employment not related to basic growth. If immigrants make possible an expansion in the basic industries of a region, there will, in the normal course of events, be a corresponding and consequential growth of employment in the regional industries, though clearly the labour in question may be provided either by immigration or from the natural increase of the existing regional population. But an inflow of immigrants into regional industries can equally make possible the maintenance or growth of employment in basic industries, which, according to British experience in the fifties and sixties, would shrink by about half of 1 per cent a year in a region with a fixed total working population – not very far from the actual experience of Scotland. In the long run, migration along with natural increase simply makes possible or limits the growth of employment; in the short run, because people carry some locally effective demand with them, it can be a sufficient cause of some modification in regional rates of employment growth.

Equally, interregional movement of capital and entrepreneurship, in the shape of creation of job-opportunities in a region other than the one where they would have arisen in the absence of this movement, is effective in modifying regional employment growth in so far as it is complemented by the availability of labour, and is a sufficient cause of this modification in so far as it induces complementary labour migration; but it is subject to the overriding condition of balance between basic and non-basic industry in each region. Movement of jobs in manufacturing industry provided that the jobs are filled, will, for this reason, eventually induce the creation of the corresponding 80 per cent of non-basic jobs. (The converse is unlikely to hold to any marked extent; new chain-stores in Scotland will not by themselves make much difference to manufacturing employment there, or to anything else except the rate of bankruptcy among retailers and, temporarily, to the general level of activity mostly in the building and service industries while the new shops are actually being built.) The annual flow of a potential 25,000 jobs in manufacturing moves to the peripheral areas in the years 1960–5, except to the extent that they caused other jobs to vanish or remain unfilled through competition for labour, presumably induced the creation or preservation of jobs in the service sector; probably, though no doubt with varying delays, about 20,000 of them a year.[1] The presumption is that such a total introduction of some 45,000 jobs a year would, again with some delay and other things being equal, make for something approaching a corresponding change in the net migration balance of these areas. But the mill no doubt grinds rather slowly, and one would perhaps hardly expect the service employment in a region to come into adjustment with that in the basic sectors in much less than a decade.

[1] The effect would, of course, be greater in so far as the incoming manufacturing industries induced further employment in existing industries of the peripheral areas through the input multiplier.

COSTS OF MOVEMENT

Finally in this discussion of interregional factor movements, it is necessary to say something about the costs of the movements themselves, as opposed to the costs that are imposed upon the economy (in the shape of unemployment, for instance) because movement does not take place.

Of the costs of movement of people, something has been said in chapter 1. In so far as they fall upon the movers they are largely psychic costs, about which it is very hard to say anything quantitative. In so far as the movement of some people imposes costs upon others who do not move, those costs include both a psychic element, about which again very little of a quantitative kind can be said, and an economic element in the shape of reduced incomes for those engaged in providing local services, which is covered by what has been said in the last section about multiplier effects of migration. The costs of movement of enterprise – of either moving an establishment to another site, or establishing a distant branch instead of an extension to the parent plant – require some further attention.

Movement of manufacturing establishments – both outright removal and inception of branches at a distance from the parent establishment – has been studied a good deal both unofficially by Luttrell,[1] Loasby[2] and others, and officially by the Board of Trade and its successor the Department of Trade and Industry. It is known that removals or new branches display growth curves of both employment and output per head which start very steep and then level off, but may remain appreciably steeper than the growth trends of parent or comparable non-moving establishments for a decade or more. The levels or trend-lines which their productivity and cost figures eventually approach may be either favourable or unfavourable in comparison with those of parent or non-moving establishments, though typically not by more than a few percentage points. There are sometimes identifiable costs of remote control, and of extra transport and communication commitments, on the one hand; on the other, there are sometimes advantages of escaping from traditional practices that were difficult to change and making a fresh start. Most moves have been in directions that have meant lower prices of labour, but perhaps higher training costs.

If there, is on the whole, a permanent loss of efficiency of establishments associated with industrial moves, it seems to be marginal; the settling-in cost is more tangible. To the establishment that moves when

---

[1] Luttrell, *Factory Location and Industrial Movement*.
[2] B. J. Loasby, 'Making Location Policy Work', *Lloyds Bank Review*, no, 83, January 1967, pp. 34–47.

it could have refrained from moving, both output and recurring expenses are probably reduced over the period of adjustment (say five years) before the pre-removal performance is matched, and the excess cost of wages, salaries and overheads over the cost of producing the reduced output actually achieved at the old total cost per unit may turn out to be between six months' and a year's normal net output. To society as a whole the cost may be less than this, in so far as the resources released at the old location find ready employment, while those that are absorbed at the new location would, because of low local demand and their low mobility, have remained in part unused if the establishment had not moved in.

But this is not a realistic comparison. Most industrial moves are connected with expansion of capacity; the greater part of them indeed are inceptions of branches additional to the parent plant. The short-term cost of such moves is the settling-in cost of the new branch minus what the settling-in cost would have been at an extension to the parent plant. There is unfortunately a lack of information about costs and employment growth in extensions. There is a presumption that they are typically more favourable than those in branches at a distance, but in cases where the extension is not merely duplicating operations already carried on in the establishment they may not be very much more favourable. Having some establishments working inefficiently because they are at the 'running-in' stage is an inevitable cost of growth and of economic change, and the extra dislocation caused by combining change of location with growth or change may not be very great. In the light of the evidence it seems likely that the social cost of movement of manufacturing plants (as compared with development *in situ*) is less – perhaps very much less – than six months' normal net output of the establishments that move.

The other cost of high mobility that has been referred to is the possible redundancy of social capital in areas of decreasing population. If the population of an area falls through emigration to other areas faster than housing, social service and public utility installations, roads and the rest fall due for normal retirement or replacement, then, since these assets have to be duplicated in the areas of immigration, there is some extra investment that would not otherwise have been necessary. The first impression is that this is a remote contingency. If one assumes a uniform normal life of (say) seventy years for the assets in question, then those that come to the end of their normal life in any year are those built seventy years earlier. With a uniform proportionate rate of growth of social capital in the past (up to seventy years ago at least), this will be about 2 per cent of the present stock. Population would have to fall at somewhat more than 2 per cent a year for excess capacity to appear, because with rising standards of living the ratio of independent households to population and *per capita* requirements of energy, water and other services rise. No regional or even subregional population seems to be in danger of declining at such rates; ½ per cent a year (in the Greater London conurbation) has recently been the highest standard subregional rate of decline.

On the other hand, social capital does not really have a rigidly determined lifetime. Some items (roads inadequate for modern traffic, branch railways, coal-carbonising gasworks) become due for replacement by physically different kinds of facility because of shifts in demand or technology or both; others, including many residential and some other buildings, present a choice between replacement and renovation. Taste swings back, and some building renovated today may come to be more highly esteemed a generation hence than today's replacements for them would have been. Moreover, while no region or standard subregion as a whole may approach the rate of population decline at which appreciable redundancy of serviceable social capital seems likely to appear, such rates may be reached, through a combination of natural increase with outward movement other than that due to slum clearance or the flight to the suburbs, in particular smaller settlements which are, nevertheless, not insignificant. (Rates of decline which seem at first sight adequate to produce redundancy certainly occur in quite a large number of rural areas, but the social capital involved is mostly not very adaptable to modern requirements, except as weekend homes and retirement residences.)

It is possible, therefore, that it really would be wasteful to let the physical infrastructure of some areas go out of use as fast as it would in the absence of a regional policy – especially as, in that case, the outward migration would be faster than it is now. But, with the present prospect of a substantial increase in the United Kingdom population generally, it is doubtful whether this provides an argument of very wide applicability.

CHAPTER 11

EFFECTS OF POLICY

THE EARLIER PHASES

Some sort of policy designed to reduce maladjustments, which now at least would be regarded as constituting regional problems, has been in operation in the United Kingdom ever since the late 1920s. The story of this policy has been told well by other writers and it would not be appropriate to repeat it here. We do, however, require to assess, so far as we can, the impacts that the various policies seem to have had upon the situations towards which they were directed, and for that purpose we shall have to distinguish the various historical phases of policy, though for reasons that will become obvious it is to the more recent phases that most attention will be given. But the first phase of all deserves some special attention because it was so different from any that has been seen since.

This first phase was dominated by the policy of assisting the movement of labour to work. From 1928 to 1938 the Industrial Transference Board helped selected unemployed adults to move from depressed areas, mostly to fill specific vacancies in other areas. In a substantial minority of cases the people in question had first taken courses at Instructional Centres or Training Centres and, in a substantial minority of cases also, help was given for family removals. Assistance was given also to selected juveniles. The total annual flow of all persons of working age assisted varied from over 40,000 in the boom years 1929 and 1936 to 14,000 in 1932 and 1933 – about 28,000 a year on average. Probably something like half of those who were helped to move stayed at their destinations at least until the end of the scheme.

The numbers involved are at first sight quite impressive. Even in comparison with the half million or so persons accounted for by the *excess* of unemployment rates in the less prosperous regions in comparison with those in the south and midlands, the ten-year total of perhaps 150,000 assisted movers who did not return is considerable. It is, however, very much less than the total of all movements – even of all long-distance movements. The total *net* migration of people of all ages into the prosperous regions in the decade in question must have been not far short of a million, that out of the less prosperous areas about half a million – the difference being accounted for by a large net inflow from overseas. Those who moved of their own accord to find work were certainly more numerous than those transferred under the scheme – probably more than twice as numerous.

In the conditions of that time however, it would have been difficult in all probability to promote very many more moves than the scheme did in fact promote. It was felt to be necessary to help only those who were eminently employable in order to maintain the acceptability of the scheme to employers. Moreover, it was necessary to avoid too blatantly taking the bread out of the mouths of local candidates for jobs in the regions of destination. The latter limitation – the number of vacancies that could not easily be filled locally in the more prosperous areas – is presumably the one that made the numbers transferred so sensitive to the trade cycle. In a time of clear and general labour shortage in the prosperous areas such as the postwar years, the scope for a scheme of this sort would have been very considerably greater, though the proportion of the unemployed who were both highly employable (in conditions of high demand) and willing to move would still have imposed a fairly strict limitation. In 1929 it had been found that, out of 40,000 unemployed men aged between 18 and 45 who were interviewed in depressed areas about the possibility of transfer (with or without a previous course of training), more than half either were judged unsuitable or declared themselves unwilling.

In the light of this, what can be said about the economic effect of the prewar experiment in assisted mobility? Probably it was not very great. The net movement that it brought about must be estimated at something less than the figures that have been quoted, since a proportion of those who were helped to move would no doubt have moved sooner or later of their own accord in the absence of assistance. Despite the care of the Ministry of Labour in, for the most part, encouraging movement only to fill identified vacancies that could be represented as hard to fill equally well locally, it is difficult to believe that in the conditions of that time many of the vacancies so filled would not have been filled a little later, perhaps a little less satisfactorily but still acceptably, from local candidates. One may therefore judge that the amount of employment directly created in the country as a whole through the scheme's contribution to interregional mobility of labour can have been only a fraction of the amount of movement it brought about. To this direct employment the national short-run employment multiplier may have added, in the conditions of that time, some 50 or 60 per cent. But even so the extra employment created in the country over the decade is fairly certainly to be counted in tens of thousands – if indeed it is as big as that – and not in hundreds of thousands. Its impact on a number of unemployed fluctuating between one and three million can hardly have been a major matter.

So far as the depressed areas are concerned the balance of advantage and disadvantage was more complex. Additional movement of unemployed out of them reduced the number of resident unemployed; the local multiplier cannot have diminished the number of jobs by more than a fraction (perhaps a sixth or a seventh) of the number of unemployed whose meagre expenditure was removed. The reduction in resident population must have led to a reduction in local authority receipts of block grant, both through the population factor and through the 'weighting' for unemployment. At the same time, the liabilities for poor relief and for family contributions to the maintenance of the unemployed were presumably reduced, and remittances from relatives in employment elsewhere may have increased. It is impossible without much deeper study to say how this balance would work out. There is a presumption, perhaps, that it would be unfavourable to the populations remaining in the areas in question, at any rate after liability for the able-bodied unemployed was transferred to the central government in the middle thirties.

Certainly the outward transfer of the most employable of that substantial proportion of the local labour force who happened to be unemployed did not arouse local enthusiasm. When, in the next (overlapping) phase of policy after 1934, the emphasis passed to paving the way for a revival of industry in the depressed areas, the transfer scheme was deemed to be inconsistent with it. Such a judgment would be in general too sweeping. Even if the central government had complete control of the movement of industry, it might still have good reason for choosing to adjust matters in a particular area of declining activity by encouraging both outflow of population and inflow of industry, rather than by concentrating on the latter alone. Indeed, if (as is likely) there are rising social costs of increasing the movements of both industry and population, the optimal way of adjusting a situation in which population is growing faster than job-opportunities in a particular part of the country despite the existence of full employment or labour shortage elsewhere will generally be one that includes both kinds of encouragement.

From the point of view of those who live (and intend to stay) in the depressed area, a central government policy of moving industry in is generally much to be preferred to one that includes moving people out; it maintains local markets and employment opportunities, and involves earlier and fuller replacement and modernisation of the local social capital. But if it is not the policy of lowest social cost to the country as a whole it imposes additional costs elsewhere – either costs of moving industry, where those of moving the corresponding amounts of labour would be lower, or costs, largely borne by the unemployed themselves, of remaining without jobs when by being persuaded and assisted to move they could have them.

An argument much used at the time against the transfer policy – operating as it did to increase an already much larger voluntary movement out of the depressed areas – was the 'social capital' argument to which reference was made in the first chapter. It was urged that, with the total population of some of these areas actually falling through net migration (as that of Wales did, for instance), their social capital was coming to be under-utilised, while new assets of the same kind were having to be created in the areas of immigration, and that transfer simply increased this wasteful duplication. In the circumstances of the time this argument was correct so far as it went. The only fault in it was that the concept of waste in an economy with so many unused resources was not an entirely valid one. Without the building of houses, schools and the rest in the south and the midlands for migrants from Wales and the north, the British economy would have been in even poorer shape in the 1930s than it actually was. 'Waste', as Keynes argued, was just the thing it needed.

Indeed, the whole process of drawing policy conclusions from this prewar phase of policy is affected by the existence of severe general unemployment at that time. It can be argued that what was most needed was a full-employment policy of creating additional effective demand with a regional bias, rather than a policy concerned mainly with interregional movements of resources. Against the background of massive general unemployment, massive interregional differences of unemployment and large voluntary movements of labour presumably geared to those differences (as the work of Makower, Marschak and Robinson showed in some detail),[1] specific effects of the transfer policy are not identifiable by inspection. We have deduced that they can have reduced total unemployment only marginally, and may have been slightly adverse (not more) to the prosperity of people remaining in the depressed areas. It is hard to believe that the removal from those areas of some of the more employable of the unemployed (in addition to those, employed or unemployed, who removed themselves) had any serious effect in the short run on their attractiveness to incoming industry, as came to be feared; the supply of mobile industry at the time was too small, and the forces pushing it away from the more prosperous areas too weak, for the question to arise on a serious scale.

The second phase of policy, overlapping with the first, began in 1934 with the Special Areas (Development and Improvement) Act and may be held to have continued until the war. It was characterised by

[1] H. Makower, J. Marschak and H. W. Robinson, 'Studies in Mobility of Labour', *Oxford Economic Papers*, no. 2, May 1939, pp. 70–97 and no, 4, September 1940, pp. 39–42.

the gradual evolution of incentives and assistance designed to promote the growth of industry in the Special Areas; by 1938 these included loans to private industry, provision of industrial premises by non-profit trading estates, contributions to rent, rates and income tax liabilities of new firms, and exemption from the National Defence Contribution. It must be largely credited to these instruments of policy that the proportion of the national total of new factories opened that were situated in the Special Areas (a proportion which had been between 2 and 3 per cent in every year from 1932 to 1936, except in 1935 when it fell below 1 per cent) rose to $4\frac{1}{2}$ per cent in 1937 and, more strikingly, to 17 per cent in 1938. Most of the new establishments in these Areas were small; two-thirds of those receiving assistance up to 1938 were of foreign (largely refugee) origin. It cannot be said that a very visible impact had been made on the less prosperous regions – the excess of unemployment rate over that of the south east was still much higher than in 1929, except in the north east where it was especially sensitive to cyclical recovery in the heavy industries. The efficacy in attracting new enterprise of some or all of the kinds of aid that had been tried may be regarded, however, as having been demonstrated.

The war abolished the problem of the depressed areas for the time being. Not only was effective monetary demand raised to a very high level – one that even with price control, food subsidies, rationing and direction of labour produced a 50 per cent rise in wage rates and retail prices in six years – but the direct controls of manpower and other resources meant that factors of production of all kinds in all regions were brought pretty fully into use. Moreover, the fact that the erstwhile depressed areas were peripheral, in the sense of being a long way from the south east – and from Germany – caused them to be favoured as sites for war production. Some twenty-two million square feet of war factory space were constructed in what, after the war, became the Development Areas. Apart from this the main industries of these Areas, the decline of which had been the main source of their troubles, were in some important cases the very ones that wartime demand particularly stimulated. Shipbuilding (the depressed area industry *par excellence*) is an outstanding case, with the amount of naval work enlarged nearly tenfold between 1938 and 1944, while the production of merchant shipping was maintained at about its 1938 level and repair work greatly increased. Steel production and heavy engineering too were naturally under heavy pressure, and so was coalmining – the fact that its output sank was due to shortage of manpower not of demand.

With the end of the war there was widespread apprehension of a post-war depression, and of the disappearance of the conditions that had temporarily obliterated regional problems as known before 1939. Meanwhile two important documents bearing on regional policy had appeared: the Barlow Report of 1939,[1] and the White Paper on employment policy of 1944,[2] and it was in the light of them that the third phase of policy opened.

This third phase, lasting until the early fifties, was marked by the scheduling under the Distribution of Industry Acts of relatively large Development Areas (larger than the prewar Special Areas),[3] the use of incentives and forms of assistance broadly similar to those developed before the war with the important exception that tax relief was missing, and the use of the power which the Board of Trade received under the Town and Country Planning Act to control industrial building throughout the country by requiring industrial development certificates. It was also, however, marked by certain characteristics apart from those derived from this legislation – characteristics which distinguish it from the succeeding period. The chief of these were the existence of a sense of urgency (the postwar depression, at least for the Development Areas, was thought to be just round the corner), the existence in those areas of a large stock of wartime munitions factories, the general shortage of industrial premises and manpower, and the continued existence in a stringent form of the wartime system of general (not only industrial) building licences.

Thanks to all these conditions, and to the legislation specifically related to regional policy, results were achieved which by any previous standard were spectacular. In 1945–7 more than half the new industrial building in the country was in the Development Areas, which contained less than a fifth of the population. Of the moves by manufacturing industry in the years 1945–50 (new establishments set up either as branches from, or by the removal of, parent establishments some distance away) almost exactly two-thirds of the employment provided in 1966 by those that survived till then was in the peripheral areas of the United Kingdom, roughly corresponding to the Development Areas. Moreover, these moves, or their ultimate results in terms of employment, were substantial in total amount. The Development Area employment for which they were still immediately responsible in 1966 was some 200,000 – a flow of an ultimate 33,000 jobs a year.

It is clear from the work of Luttrell, whose research on the costs of industry in new sites relates to the moves of this period, that it was the search for suitable premises and for labour that led to most of them.[4] It is clear too that the existence of factory space belonging to the Board

[1] Royal Commission on the Distribution of Industrial Population, *Report*.
[2] Ministry of Reconstruction, *Employment Policy*, Cmd 6527, London, HMSO, 1944.
[3] Broadly speaking the Development Areas of 1945 consisted of the more densely populated parts of the 1966 Development Areas shown in chart 11.1 (see p. 291).
[4] Luttrell, *Factory Location and Industrial Movement*.

of Trade, either newly built or converted from wartime use, was the biggest single magnet the Development Areas possessed. By 1955 these factories employed 186,000 people, mainly the result of location decisions taken in the immediate postwar years. As the volume of industrial building increased and the licensing of building became less stringent, the pressure to move relaxed. Board of Trade expenditure on factory building and site works, after running at about £12 million a year for two years, was halved in 1949/50 and subsequently sank further. The filling up of the existing stock of converted war factories, however, was probably the main reason why the postwar rush to the Development Areas died away.

How far that rush was due to the special circumstances to which we have referred, and how much to the new, relatively permanent instruments of regional policy, can in some degree be judged by the extent to which it declined. The Distribution of Industry Act operated only from 1946, the requirement for industrial development certificates only from 1948. In the four years beginning with 1946 some £9·3 million a year was spent under the Act and the annual average number of jobs (remaining in 1966) in moves to the peripheral areas was about 41,000, which was 64 per cent of all jobs in moves throughout the country. In the eight years 1952-9, expenditure under the Act averaged £5·1 million a year and the number of jobs in moves to the peripheral areas was 9,800 a year, or 29 per cent of the jobs in all moves. The results, however judged, had fallen more than in proportion to the expenditure, which was still mostly on sites and factories. It is generally held that this was in some degree due to the greater freedom with which industrial development certificates were given for building in the more prosperous regions from the late forties or early fifties, and this is no doubt correct, but the high success of the early postwar years was certainly due in large part, not to the machinery of the Act or the system of industrial development certificates, but to the temporary circumstances that we have mentioned.

The phase of relatively lax use of the new policy instruments, extending from about 1951 to 1958 or 1959, was, nevertheless, a real and recognisable one. The postwar depression proved not to be just round the corner. The traditional textile industries, it is true, lost their brief postwar euphoria in the Korean slump of 1951-2 (with the result that north east Lancashire and some neighbouring districts of Yorkshire were given Development Area status in 1953), but coalmining and shipbuilding kept up their output past the middle of the decade. The recession of 1958 dramatised the return of the longer-term trends in these industries.

Since then the instruments of policy have been changed more than once. It will be convenient to remind the reader briefly of these changes, and then to select for further discussion the broad effects, in so far as they can be assessed, of the general strengthening of policy that took place underneath various changes of form between the middle fifties and 1970. The consequences of various characteristics of, and changes in, the forms and instruments of policy can then also be considered.

THE RECENT PHASES

In brief then, between 1958 and 1970 policy passed through five stages, all of them short. In 1958 steps were taken, largely in response to criticisms that had been building up in previous years, to render the system of incentives more flexible. Undertakings in areas outside the Development Areas as well as inside them (the so-called DATAC[1] areas) became eligible for financial assistance provided that the local unemployment rate was high. In practice this help tended to become confined to such areas, either inside or outside the Development Areas. Eligibility for assistance was extended beyond the bounds of manufacturing industry to which it had previously been confined. At the same time it was announced that industrial development certificates would be more sparingly made available in the prosperous areas. The immediate effect of all this was that expenditure, both on site works and factories and on financial assistance, rose sharply in 1959, but it took longer for moves into the Development Areas to show any response.

The second step was the Local Employment Act of 1960. First, it consolidated the changes of 1958 by abolishing the Development Areas and substituting smaller Development Districts, which could be scheduled or de-scheduled according to their needs as expressed by their unemployment rates – $4\frac{1}{2}$ per cent being accepted as the critical value. Secondly, incentives were strengthened. Loans and grants continued to be available subject to a demonstration that the development for which they were given would create employment at not too great a price, and the previous condition that the non-availability of other sources of finance had to be proved was removed. Moreover, building grants were made available in Development Districts; they were related to the gap, which was in practice hard to estimate satisfactorily, between the cost of the building and its market value when completed.

From this point of time government expenditure on factory building, loans and grants greatly increased. It had averaged £5·1 million a year in the eight years before 1960/1; in the following three years it averaged £37 million. The great success of this period however, lay in the diversion of major new developments in the motor industry away from

[1] Development Areas: Treasury Advisory Committee.

the Midlands and the South East to Merseyside and Scotland. How far the carrot of financial incentives was responsible for this, and how far the stick of Board of Trade reluctance to grant industrial development certificates for expansion in the main motor-manufacturing regions, is clearly a difficult question – perhaps an unanswerable one. At all events, the number of jobs (surviving in 1966) in the moves into the peripheral areas in these three years averaged some 25,000 a year – two and a half times as many as in the preceding period. These jobs also rose to 58 per cent of the corresponding total in all moves in the country – a proportion not equalled since 1950.

The other chief characteristics of policy in the early sixties however – its flexibility and its gearing to unemployment rates – were not so satisfactory. The disadvantages of continual scheduling and de-scheduling of Districts were soon realised; they bred uncertainty about the help available for expansion in the future. Moreover, the more or less automatic tie of assistance to unemployment rate offended against a principle that was coming to be widely favoured – the principle that development could best be promoted by concentrating aid, with some assurance of its continuance, upon places of good growth potential in or near areas of need, rather than upon the precise places (often singularly unpromising) in which need had arisen. These points were partially recognised in the subsequent White Papers on Scotland and the north east, which assured certain growth areas in those regions of freedom from the risk of being de-scheduled.[1]

The third of the recent steps in policy came in 1963. First, the complicated building-grant provisions of the 1960 Act, which had in practice produced grants at rates varying about an average of 17 per cent, were replaced by a simple 25 per cent grant, though this was still made conditional upon the provision of additional employment. Secondly, investments in plant and machinery in the Development Districts were made eligible for a grant of 10 per cent, also conditional upon employment creation. Thirdly (and quantitatively most important), 'free depreciation' was introduced for investment in plant and machinery by manufacturing industry in the assisted areas; for tax purposes, profits could be written off against depreciation not only to the full extent of that depreciation, but at any rate over time that the firm in question chose. No tax, in short, need be paid until the investment had been written off; the gain was essentially a postponement of tax payment.

The rate of benefit to investment in the Development Districts was now massive by any previous standard and did not undergo any substantial change until the introduction of the Regional Employment

[1] Board of Trade, *Central Scotland. A programme for development and growth*, Cmnd 2188, and *The North East. A programme for regional development and growth*, Cmnd 2206, London, HMSO, 1963.

Premium in 1967. A further policy step was, however, taken in 1966, when a simple cash grant of an additional 20 per cent of investment in plant and machinery (additional, that is to say, to the rate payable in the rest of the country) was substituted for both the 10 per cent grant and the 'free depreciation' provisions of 1963. At the same time, the Development Districts were abolished, and the geographically wider Development Areas that remain in being up to the time of writing were scheduled (see chart 11.1). The arguments adduced for these two changes were, respectively, that the benefits of 'free depreciation' were not understood (and, moreover, did not exist in the case of a firm that was making no profit as is the fate of many firms in their earliest years), and that within widely drawn Development Areas enterprise would choose the most promising spots as growth points, and would not be constrained or tempted to go to depressed places of little intrinsic locational merit.

The final major change, involving a further increase in rates of assistance, came in 1967 with the introduction of the Regional Employment Premium – a simple cash subsidy (initially at thirty shillings a week for each adult male worker and lower rates for others) for each employee in manufacturing industry in the Development Areas. It is perhaps remarkable that, in the history of British policy aimed primarily at assisting areas of high unemployment by the creation of employment, this, after a third of a century, was the first application of a simple subsidy on the employment of labour. The estimated amount of subsidy was £100 million a year; regional policy had moved still further into a range of magnitudes where it might be expected to have an appreciable impact on regional economies, quite apart from its efficacy in persuading enterprises to change their behaviour.

Two further developments in policy must be mentioned, if only because they were the first systematic steps in Britain towards differentiation of rates of assistance between different areas, as opposed to a simple distinction between areas of benefit and areas without it. The first of these was the introduction, also in 1967, of Special Development Areas enjoying additional rates of benefit, and intended to give additional assistance to areas hard hit by the accelerated rate of colliery closure of that time. The second followed – though not very closely – the recommendations of the Report on Intermediate Areas (by the Hunt Committee) in 1969,[1] to which we shall have to refer in detail later. It consisted of the provision, in certain districts outside the Development Areas, of some of the benefits available under the Local Employment Acts.[2]

[1] Department of Economic Affairs, *The Intermediate Areas*.
[2] Both the Special Development Areas and the Intermediate Areas were subsequently added to. Their extent in February 1971 is shown in chart 11.1.

Chart 11.1. *The assisted areas, 1971*

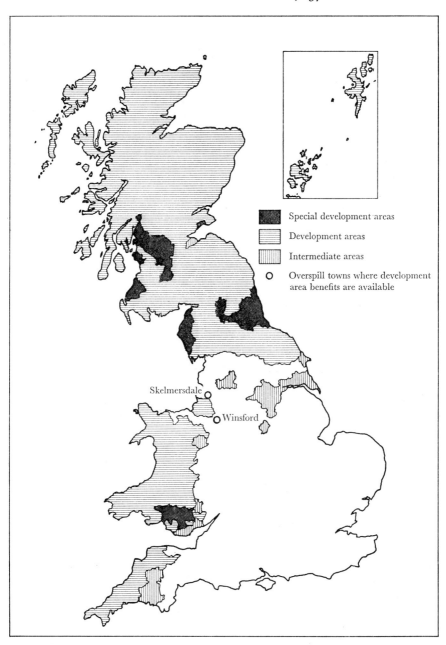

SOURCE: *Trade and Industry*, 24 February 1971

THE EFFECTIVENESS OF RECENT POLICY

We have now looked superficially, and without close attention to detail, at the stages in the development of policy between 1958 and 1970. This bird's eye view may serve to give meaning to some attempt to assess the impact of the measures in question on the economy since the middle fifties, where we left our very rough assessment of earlier measures.

First, it may be useful to look at a variable that should be relatively sensitive to policy: the distribution of moves of manufacturing establishments by destination between the peripheral (mainly Development) areas and elsewhere. The proportions of such moves that were to peripheral areas in each of the years 1945–65 are shown in chart 11.2. (These are, of course, rather different from the proportions of the total 1966 employment in such moves, which has been quoted for certain sub-periods above; there are enormous differences between different moves in the employment they entail, and there is also a tendency for moves to the peripheral areas to involve, on average, more jobs in each than the generally shorter moves to other destinations.)

It is plain that the proportion of moves that were to sites in the peripheral areas fell from a very high postwar level to a minimum of less than a quarter at the end of the fifties, and then rose again. We need, however, a rather more systematic test of the statistical significance of changes in the proportion, and of the temporal relation of any significant changes to alterations in policy. Since individual moves may be regarded as independent events, the significance of these changes can be tested in much the same way as that of differences in (say) the proportions of different samples of the population who have brown eyes. One possible procedure is to examine the moves of every pair of successive years throughout the period to see between which years (considered in isolation from other years before and after) there were significant changes of proportion. If this is done the only breaks significant at the 5 per cent level are those of 1946–7 and 1949–50 – both *falls* in the proportion of moving establishments that went to the peripheral areas. It is not easy to connect these changes with acts of specifically regional policy; as we have suggested earlier, they are more likely to be connected with the running-out of the stock of wartime factories available for occupation in the peripheral areas and the easing of building controls. In the later years, which raise more immediately interesting questions about the efficacy of regional policy, a rise in the proportion very nearly significant at the 5 per cent level comes between 1963 and 1964.

It is, however, also useful to test in a similar way for significant differences between the runs of contiguous years which should have been

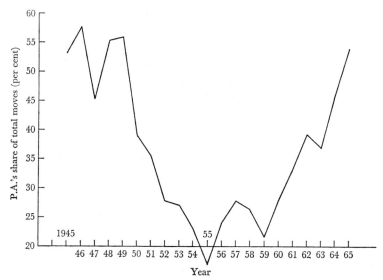

Chart 11.2. *Moves to peripheral areas, 1945–65*

SOURCE: Board of Trade, *The Movement of Manufacturing Industry in the United Kingdom, 1945–65*

affected by distinct phases of policy. Thus it is reasonable to suppose that the years from (say) 1952 to 1958 were all ruled by the postwar legislation, administered with no very great sense of urgency and uncomplicated by the transient postwar circumstances of demobilisation and scarcity. Certainly there is no significant change of the peripheral proportion within pairs of years in this period. A second phase might be identified as 1959–60 (the years governed by the Act of 1958), a third as 1961–3 (under the Act of 1960), a fourth as 1964–5 (after the Act and the budgetary changes of 1963).

If this is done we find that there is no significant difference between the peripheral proportions of moves in 1952–8 and in 1959–60. In spite of the more rigorous administration of industrial development certificates which was specifically announced in mid-1958 and the increase in expenditure, the 1958 changes seem to have been of little effect in the short run, though the possibility of some delayed effect cannot be ruled out. By contrast however, there can be no doubt of the significance of the increase in the proportion of peripheral moves between 1959–60 and 1961–3 (it reaches the 0·1 per cent level), and the significance of the further change between 1961–3 and 1964–5 is even greater. The legislative and perhaps administrative changes of

1960 and 1963 can fairly safely be regarded as effective; each of them seems to have shifted about an eighth of all moves into the peripheral areas.

It may be argued, however, that the timing of these phases is wrong; that legislative and administrative changes would take longer to influence actual moves by industry than we have implied, especially when the construction of a purpose-built factory has to be planned and completed before a move can take place. Suppose then that the changes of 1958 are assumed to take effect only in 1960, those of 1960 in 1962 and those of 1963 in 1965. The proportions of moves going to peripheral areas prove to have increased significantly (at 1 per cent level or better) at all three of the new dividing points (1959–60, 1961–2 and 1964–5), though none of them seems to mark so definite a shift as did 1960–1 or 1962–3. The conclusion that really emerges is that, from the late fifties until the middle sixties, there was a massive diversion of moves to the peripheral areas, which went on more or less continually, reached its maximum rate about 1963, and is almost certainly to be associated with the series of administrative and legislative changes of the time – each of which probably produced some effect quite quickly and further effects cumulatively over a period of two or three years.

It is unfortunate that statistics of moves for more recent years are not available on a comparable basis to enable the efficacy of the 1966 Act and the introduction of the Regional Employment Premium in 1967 to be tested in the same way. Another indicator to which one may look for signs of the effects of policy is the proportion of national total industrial development certificate approvals for schemes of over 5,000 square feet that relates to the post-1966 Development Areas. This proportion rose significantly from 14·9 per cent in 1956–9 to 22·0 per cent in 1966–9. In a complete series of annual statistics the most significant break seems to be that between 1962 and 1963; the share of approvals going to the Development Areas was 15·5 per cent in 1960–2 and 19·6 per cent in 1963–5. Smoothed quarterly statistics of numbers of approvals in the Development Areas are shown plotted against the corresponding totals for Great Britain in chart 11.3.

Changes in the distribution of new floor-space authorised by industrial development certificates, and of the estimated additional employment associated with it, are rather harder both to ascertain and to interpret. The published data require a number of adjustments for changes in definition, which we have tried to make with the very kind assistance of the Department of Trade and Industry. As for the meaning of the results, one has first to admit that the employment figures must be treated with caution because of an apparent (and probably varying) tendency for the estimates to be biased upwards in the Development

EFFECTS OF POLICY

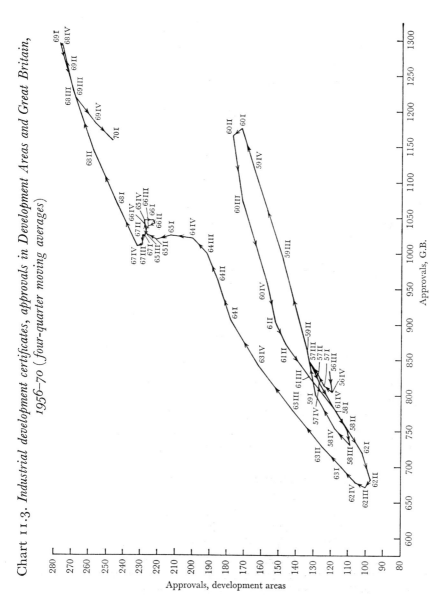

Chart 11.3. *Industrial development certificates, approvals in Development Areas and Great Britain, 1956–70 (four-quarter moving averages)*

SOURCE: Department of Trade and Industry

Areas and downwards elsewhere, at least in those areas where certificates are hardest to get. The floor-area statistics are, of course, more reliable, subject to the success of the definitional adjustments just mentioned. There is some evidence, however, that the proportion of total industrial building that comes within the scope of the industrial development certificate requirements is appreciably higher in the Development Areas than elsewhere, and this discrepancy too may vary over time with the rigor of the control and with other factors.

Subject to these cautions one can say that the proportion of total new floor-space authorised by industrial development certificates that lay within the post-1966 Development Areas rose from 19·0 per cent in 1956–9 to 25·0 per cent in 1962–5 and 31·8 per cent in 1966–9. The corresponding proportion of estimated additional employment rose from 22·6 per cent in 1956–9 to 47·6 per cent and 49·1 per cent in the two later periods respectively. There is no obvious way of testing the statistical significance of these changes, since individual square feet of factory space and individual jobs are not independent of each other, as individual building projects are in general. But the shift of proportion over the whole decade was clearly substantial in any terms. For the adjusted floor-area and estimated employment statistics, Development Area totals are shown plotted against Great Britain totals in charts 11.4 and 11.5 respectively.

In noting this one should also remember what has happened to the absolute amounts of industrial movement and industrial building in the country as a whole and in the Development Areas in particular. Numbers of moves are shown in chart 11.6. Mr Howard has tentatively corrected the amount of employment in transferred establishments or new branches, as recorded in 1966, to allow for the probable growth of the more recent ones that had not yet achieved maturity.[1] On this reckoning the employment at 'maturity' in the average year's moves of the period 1945–51 was 53,000, while the corresponding figures for an average year's moves in the two succeeding periods, 1952–9 and 1960–5, were 35,000 and 46,000 respectively. The employment-creating potential of moves in fact varied over time in much the same way as the proportion of all moves that were to Development Areas. The prima facie conclusion is that the circumstances, including policy, that made for a large volume of moves in total also made for a high proportion of moves to the Development Areas. Perhaps this is not surprising; the net tendency of regional policy must have been to increase movement in general, while prosperity, which also encourages movement, tends to go with shortage of labour that should make the Development Areas' labour reserves relatively more attractive to enterprise.

[1] Board of Trade, *The Movement of Manufacturing Industry in the United Kingdom, 1945–65*.

Chart 11.4. *Industrial development certificates, floor areas approved in Development Areas and Great Britain, 1956–70 (four-quarter moving averages)*

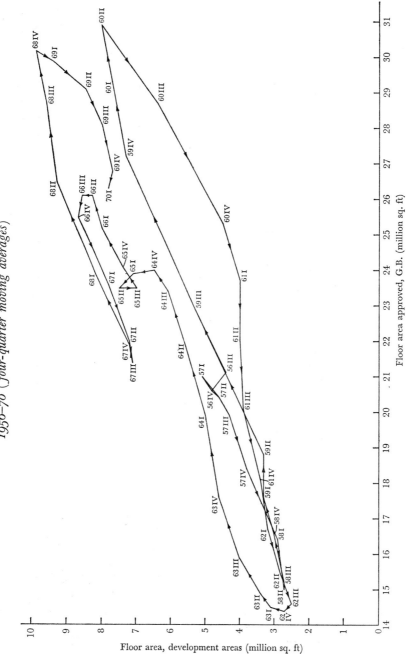

SOURCE: Department of Trade and Industry

Chart 11.5. *Industrial development certificates, estimated additional employment in Development Areas and Great Britain, 1956–70 (four-quarter moving averages)*

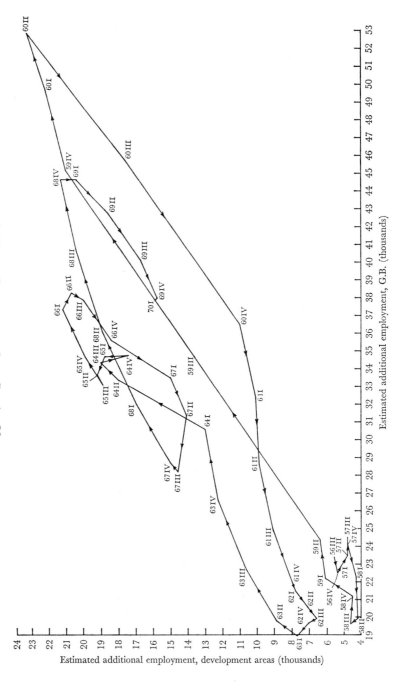

SOURCE: Department of Trade and Industry

Chart 11.6. *Numbers of moves in the United Kingdom, 1945–65*

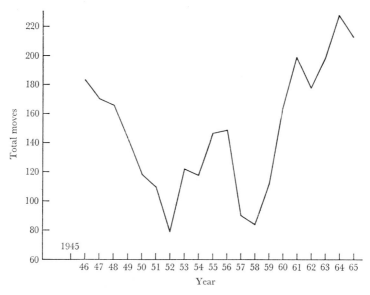

SOURCE: Board of Trade, *The Movement of Manufacturing Industry in the United Kingdom, 1945–65*

The absolute amount of employment reckoned at 'maturity' in moves to the Development Areas rose from about 10,000 a year in the fifties to 25,000 a year in the first half of the sixties. During the latter period it undoubtedly grew; at a rough estimate based on the increase in annual numbers of moves, it must have been running at about 30,000–35,000 a year in the two years 1964–5 after the effects of the 1963 measures had begun to be felt. On this evidence there can at any rate be little doubt that the flow of job-opportunities in manufacturing industries to the Development Areas from elsewhere had trebled or more than trebled since the relatively slack period of the fifties.

There is another, perhaps rather neater way of approaching changes in the flow of jobs contained in moves, to which we have already referred in the chapter on factor movements. It involves examining the *net* flow of such jobs into or out of each region and relating it to the regional unemployment level, which can best be expressed for this purpose as the difference between the region's unemployment rate and the national average. The object of policy is presumably, in the simplest terms, to promote the flow of jobs from regions of low unemployment to those of high; the mechanism of the market may be expected also to promote such a flow. If net flows into or out of each region are expressed as percentages of the existing manufacturing jobs in it, we may hope to find a positive correlation between the net rate of job-inflow and the unemployment rate. A shift in this relation should provide some indication, and some measure, of the effects of a change of policy or of other external forces.

In fact, the data for 1952–9 yield a poor correlation (in view of the small number of degrees of freedom) of 0·61, and a regression coefficient of 0·06 – the extra annual inflow of jobs per hundred already existing in the region for an extra 1 per cent of unemployment above the national average – or 0·10 if Northern Ireland is omitted. Those for 1960–5 give a correlation coefficient of 0·93 (0·78 without Northern Ireland) and a regression coefficient of 0·38 (0·41 if Northern Ireland is left out). The suggestion is then that something changed between the two periods to make the flow of jobs in moves some four or six times as sensitive to unemployment differences, and it is hard to see what but the strengthening of regional policy could have been responsible, for at any rate the greater part of this change, especially as the average national unemployment rate was rather higher in the second period than the first, which would lead one to expect a rather lower level of mobility.

As for industrial building, the total approved annually measured by floor-space corrected for changes of definition has shown a generally upward trend from the late fifties to the late sixties, broken only by the great boom year 1960. There was an 8 per cent rise between 1956–9 and 1960–3, and a further 14 per cent increase between the latter period and 1964–7. Since the proportion that was in the (present) Development Areas also rose as we have already noted, the additional area associated with industrial development certificates in them increased more steeply, more than doubling between 1956–9 and 1965–8.

Total additional employment estimated to arise in Great Britain in new schemes approved rose somewhat more than floor-space; so did that situated in the Development Areas. The annual average in the latter rose from not much more than 20,000 a year in the later fifties to over 70,000 a decade later. Thus, if one credits the whole of this increase to change of policy, that change can be held responsible for an extra 50,000 jobs a year in manufacturing and related industries in the Development Areas. If, more modestly, one takes the increase in the national total for granted and credits only the change in geographical distribution to the strengthening of regional policy, then the Development Areas can be said to owe about 38,000 jobs a year in industrial development approvals to the policy changes between the later fifties and the later sixties.

On the other hand, there is no good reason for regarding a constant proportion between regional building performances as a norm. A scatter diagram suggests that changes in building in the four high-unemployment regions of Great Britain tend on average to be about half of those in the national total, but that they happen slightly earlier both in recovery and in recession, and that there are a number of shifts in the regression line. Very broadly, job-creation in new schemes in the Development Areas in the early sixties seems to have been running about 16,000 a year higher, and in the mid-sixties about 40,000 a year higher, than one would have expected from the national total at the relevant time if no shifts from the position of the late fifties had occurred. In the cycle of the late sixties there seems from this evidence to have been a downward shift equivalent to perhaps 10,000 jobs a year.

There is thus a fairly wide range of estimates that can be made of the effects of (presumably) policy on the volume of additional employment in new industrial buildings approved in the high-unemployment areas. Even if one makes some allowance for over-optimism in estimating the additional employment in the schemes approved in those areas, and for the extent to which approved schemes fail to be carried out, the shift between the later fifties and the later sixties may be put, very broadly, at 30,000 jobs a year or more. Given time for adjustment, such a creation of jobs in (mainly) basic industry might be expected, with the help of the long-run multiplier, to imply a total creation in all industry together of perhaps 50,000 jobs annually – and the number could be considerably greater than this.

Over the past decade or so, however, the expansion of total industrial building has not been sufficient to make the increase in the proportional and absolute share of the Development Areas consistent with absolute increases in all regions. The losers were the South East and the West Midlands, in both of which the estimated employment from new buildings approved fell by some 37–8 per cent between 1956–9 and 1964–7. In relation to total industrial building approved in the country, their loss was, of course, greater; their share fell from over 43 per cent of the total to just over 18 per cent of it. This loss in percentage share of total approvals was a little greater than the gain in percentage share by the Development Areas; the rest of the country's share rose a little from about 38 to 42 per cent of the total for Great Britain. Absolutely, of course, approvals (or rather the estimated employment associated with them) in this large residue of the country outside both the Development Areas and the two most prosperous regions rose very considerably – in fact by nearly 50 per cent.

These considerations lead on to two further questions about the effects of policy, in so far as policy can be held responsible for the changes we have described. First, how far did the restraint of building in the South East and the West Midlands cause national growth to be lost? (In so far as the growth was merely diverted to the Development Areas or elsewhere by incentives, it was clearly not immediately 'lost' to the country as a whole, though it might be true that subsequent growth would be reduced if the Development Area environment proved unsuitable.) Secondly, how far was it the case that regional policy had an adverse effect upon areas outside the prosperous regions and outside the Development Areas, notably by diverting to the latter growth of industry that these intermediate areas would otherwise have enjoyed? This was, of course, one of the central questions with which the Hunt Committee was faced. Let us glance at each of these two matters in turn.

First, the fact already mentioned that total industrial building in the country has followed an upward trend and, more specifically, has increased as regional policy has been pursued more vigorously, is itself prima facie evidence against any major discouraging effect of that policy. Any curtailment of building in the prosperous regions was more than compensated for by extra building elsewhere, at least some of it perhaps consisting of schemes that were in some way diverted from the prosperous areas. The Board of Trade data on industrial moves throw some light upon this.[1] Between the second and third periods distinguished in the Board of Trade study (1952–9 and 1960–5), the employment content measured in 1966 of net outward moves from the South East and the West Midlands to other parts of the country rose from 4,000 or 5,000 a year to about 16,000. Between 1956–9 and 1960–5 the estimated extra employment associated with industrial development certificates in the South East and the West Midlands fell by some 7,000 a year. The two sets of figures are hard to make comparable; because of subsequent growth, the 1966 employment content of moves made some years before may have to be adjusted (not necessarily downwards) to get the estimated employment figure that might have been associated with an industrial development certificate at the time of the move. Moreover, the majority of moves (though probably not the greater part of them reckoned by employment content) do not require an industrial development certificate – they are moves into existing industrial buildings or into new buildings of sizes below the limit. On the other hand, the industrial development certificate figures quoted relate to a rather wider range of industry than that to which the statistics of moves relate (the latter refer to manufacturing industry only) and also include an appreciable proportion of schemes that were dropped after a certificate had been granted.

Making what allowance one can for these difficulties, it seems fair

[1] *The Movements of Manufacturing Industry in the United Kingdom*, 1945–65.

to conclude, however, that the increase in net moves out of the prosperous regions between the two periods in question – the increase in the excess of outward moves originating in them over the inward moves (largely of foreign origin) they received – was of something like the right order of magnitude to match the fall in industrial building within them. Their fertility in producing building schemes that were carried into effect, either within them or elsewhere in the country, cannot have diminished much between these two periods and may have increased.

This conclusion is supported by Board of Trade information about the operation of the industrial development certificate control[1] – the chief potentially restrictive (as opposed to diversionary) instrument of policy. From 1958 to 1963, applications in the West Midlands and London and the South East estimated to contain a seventh or an eighth of the employment associated with all applications from those regions were in fact refused. Subsequent investigation showed, however, that four-fifths of the firms whose applications were thus refused eventually managed some kind of expansion. The total reduction of expansion as a result of formal refusal must therefore have been quite small – perhaps of the order of 5 per cent of the employment content of all applications.

It is, however, often suggested that the main restrictive effect of the control operates not through formal refusals, but through discouragement at the stage of informal enquiry so that in an important number of instances no actual application follows. A questionnaire survey by the Confederation of British Industry suggests, on the basis of replies from about a fifth or a sixth of the manufacturing firms in the South East (measured by employment) that in the years 1963–8, about 9 per cent of the schemes that had been *thought of* for buildings outside the Development Areas were modified, 6 per cent abandoned and 5 per cent deferred because of industrial development certificate requirements, in addition to 8 per cent for which a certificate was refused.[2] This, however, is no more than the rate of mortality often found among projects for which industrial development certificates have already been obtained, and the above evidence that the prosperous areas continued to be fertile in developments – an increasing proportion of them for execution in other areas – still stands.

On the broad question of the effect of policy on the 'intermediate' regions, the changes in distribution of building that we have noted again throw some light. We have seen that these regions (the North West, Yorkshire, the East Midlands, East Anglia and the South West,

[1] Made available to the Hunt Committee.
[2] 'Survey of experience of firms applying for industrial development certificates in the South East and North West regions' (unpublished evidence presented to the Hunt Committee).

excluding the Development Areas within them) in fact increased slightly their proportionate share of the increasing national volume of industrial building between the late fifties and the middle sixties. This does not suggest, prima facie, that as a whole they suffered from the changes of the time, of which the strengthened regional policy was a part. Some parts of them, however, were more vulnerable than others. For a number of reasons one would expect this to be particularly true of those districts that bordered on Development Areas. First, branches set up at a distance by firms from the prosperous regions might well show a strong tendency to go to Development Areas rather than to neighbouring districts that do not offer Development Area incentives and are nearly as far from the home bases of the establishments in question. Secondly, one might expect some short-range 'boundary-hopping' into the Development Areas, since short-distance moves may in some circumstances present relatively few difficulties. Thirdly, the various financial advantages enjoyed by enterprises in Development Areas might be expected to draw in labour from the bordering areas and thus make life more difficult for establishments in the latter.

The evidence for any of these 'shadow' effects is rather thin and varies a good deal from one border area to another. In the middle or late sixties Yorkshire, for instance, was doing rather badly on the whole so far as its general prosperity was concerned, but this could be attributed to the fortunes of its coal and textile industries rather than to the competing attractions of the North – the latter had not drawn much mobile industry directly out of it since the early postwar period. Yorkshire's share of the national total of incoming moves had, however, fallen. Lancashire outside the Development Areas was generally doing better, except for north east Lancashire which (until 1969) lacked the preferential status it had had in the fifties. The relatively large inflow of industry into Merseyside did not seem to be at the expense of the rest of the region to any detectable extent, and the flow of local enterprises over the boundary into the Merseyside Development Area, though it showed a rising trend, was small. In south east Wales there was apprehension of a worsening situation, which led in 1969 to the designation of an Intermediate Area there, but evidence is lacking on how far the trouble was due to the proximity of the Welsh Development Area, as opposed to absence of the advantages which that Area possessed. Devon outside the south western Development Area could show as clear evidence as any subregion that the preferred status of the Development Area had diverted incoming industry from it, and it too (or part of it) subsequently received Intermediate Area status – though the case for this could perhaps be more firmly based on the promise of Plymouth as a growth centre for the South West than on any shadow effect from across the Tamar. Edinburgh and Leith, entirely surrounded by Development Area, might well have expected to suffer particularly from shadow effects, but the situation was much complicated by the commercial prosperity of Edinburgh, on the one hand, and, on the other, by its tendency (like all commercial and administrative capitals) to drive out its manufacturing industry – in this case mainly to Development Area environs.

The simplest generalisation one can make about the shadow effects on the most vulnerable areas is thus, that in a number of instances there does seem to be such an effect so far as inward moves from the rest of the country are concerned, but that there is not much evidence of boundary-hopping, and that total industrial building can hardly be said to have suffered noticeably from the shadow of a neighbouring Development Area in most cases. In some instances, of which Lancashire outside the Development Areas may be one, there may well be an appreciable spread of prosperity from a Development Area that is showing a high absolute rate of growth – a spread that operates through subcontracting by establishments in the Development Area, or through the expenditure of households some of whose members travel to work in it. To the extent that these effects depend on proximity, they may tend to cancel the adverse effects of the proximity of a Development Area to which we have referred.

THE INSTRUMENTS OF POLICY

Financial incentives

All this relates to the apparent effectiveness or otherwise of regional policy in its various recent phases, without any attempt to consider the separate impacts of the different instruments of policy which (unhappily for the investigator) were used in combination with one another, and not generally varied one at a time, as in a well conducted experiment.

Policy instruments have been of many kinds and it is not intended to survey them all here. We must, however, distinguish three main types. First, there are straightforward financial inducements to locate (or to expand) in assisted areas – grants, loans and tax concessions. Second, there are what may be called the 'real' forms of assistance, from provision of factories or site services to environmental improvements including public transport and communications facilities, housing and the like, which are not directed solely towards incoming or expanding industry but improve the general attractiveness or convenience of the district in question. Third, there is the negative control of industrial building through the issue of industrial development certificates, which can hardly be separated from the advocacy of consideration for Development Area sites that accompanies it. We may look at the main financial inducements first.

Before 1963 there were no automatic plant and machinery grants, and building grants, as we have noted, probably averaged about 17 per cent of factory building costs in the Development Districts. With the accompanying Special Grants these must have amounted to 6 or 7 per cent of all fixed capital costs, though it must be remembered that they were conditional and not automatic benefits offered to all comers. The element of assistance in the loans and the provision of factories for rent or sale is much harder to assess, but it probably makes sense to say that the total aid was equivalent to appreciably less than a 10 per cent subvention on all investment.

The measures of 1963 included an automatic 10 per cent plant and machinery grant, a conditional 25 per cent building grant and 'free depreciation'. It has been calculated, using a 7 per cent discount rate, that the total effect of these benefits would be to lower investment costs in a Development District (as compared with elsewhere) by something like 20 per cent,[1] to which one should still, no doubt, add something for the element of assistance contained in Board of Trade factory building for rent or sale (which was increased) and in loans. Certainly one can say that the rate of assistance was more than doubled – perhaps even trebled – in 1963, and that the automatic element in the assistance was increased. In the light of this it is perhaps not difficult to account for the substantial switch of moves that followed. The timing of the change in the location of industrial building, however, is such as to suggest that some other influence was at work a few months before the legislation of 1963.

The 1966 Act, by substituting a 20 per cent premium on investment grants for the 10 per cent grant plus free depreciation, made only a negligible difference to the total subvention on capital cost calculated for a typical combination of building costs, plant costs and working capital. The hope was that the new form of help would be more effective. First, there had been evidence that the great majority of firms, including large ones, ignore tax when computing profitability;[2] free depreciation had not been taken into account by many firms whose accounting methods were unsophisticated. Secondly, an investment grant was available to firms that had no immediate prospects of profit on which to postpone taxation by availing themselves of free depreciation – a category into which newly established firms might well fall.

[1] P. A. Bird and A. P. Thirlwall, 'The incentive to invest in the new Development Areas', *District Bank Review*, no. 162, June 1967, pp. 24–45.
[2] See Inland Revenue, *Report of the Committee on Turnover Taxation*, Cmnd 2300, London, HMSO, 1964, para. 282; also, R. R. Neild, 'Replacement Policy', *National Institute Economic Review*, no. 30, November 1964, p. 36.

Thirdly, the contribution of a cash investment grant to liquidity was immediate (subject only to a short delay in payment) and thought to be attractive especially to beginners.

Our best evidence on the impact of government incentives on recipients comes from the 'Inquiry into Location Motives and Experience'.[1] It is clear from this that for very nearly all the firms that set up establishments on sites new to them in the assisted areas in the mid-sixties these incentives were a factor in choice of location – mostly a major one according to their own statements. The more automatic benefits (investment grants, plant and machinery grants, free depreciation) were quoted collectively as major factors by two-thirds of the firms established in these areas, building grants by just under half. It is unfortunate that specific references to the individual pre-1966 and post-1966 automatic benefits are not separately tabulated. It is, however, stated that the firms that made their decisions in 1966 or 1967 (that is after the 1966 Act) were somewhat stronger in declaring themselves to be influenced by government incentives as a whole than those that made them in 1965 or earlier; 88 per cent of them mentioned these incentives as a major factor and 11 per cent as a minor one, against 78 per cent and 14 per cent respectively of their predecessors. Since the main change in the package of incentives was the substitution of investment grants for the mixture of plant and machinery grants and free depreciation, this would accord with the evidence mentioned above that depreciation benefits tend either to be underestimated by virtue of the method of assessing them, or to lose attractiveness because the proportion of firms that would not benefit from them fully is significant. With all due reservations about the reliability of motives recollected in tranquility, there is much to suggest that the instruments introduced in 1966 had a stronger appeal than those they replaced.

In spite of this the evidence before us suggests that the new package of incentives was more effective than the older one in increasing the proportionate *number* of industrial development certificates granted in Development Areas to only a moderate extent; the percentage rose from 18·8 in 1962–5 to 22·0 in 1966–9. The proportion of the total floor-space of approved schemes that lay in these Areas grew rather more impressively from 25·0 per cent in the former of these two periods to 31·8 in the latter. But again, the change of late 1966, which may perhaps be attributed to the Act, was preceded by a rather bigger change in early 1965, which does not immediately follow any change in financial incentives and may perhaps have been due rather to administrative changes.

The introduction of the Regional Employment Premium in 1967 was,

[1] Board of Trade, unpublished.

financially, a relatively massive change, and its effects (or the absence of them) require more consideration.

The Regional Employment Premium, together with the Selective Employment Premium which was added to it until 1969, subsidised employment in manufacturing industry in the Development Areas to the extent of some £125 million a year, or something like 9 per cent of the labour cost of the establishments concerned – $7\frac{1}{2}$ per cent if only the Regional Employment Premium, as originally introduced, is taken into account. An unpublished official estimate of the Premium's likely effects made available to the Hunt Committee assumed that about a fifth of the subsidy would leak into wage increases, and that the rest would provide for relative price reductions (after allowing for some effects of increased output) of about 3 per cent. Combining with this a rather arbitrary value of 2 for the elasticity of substitution between manufactures of the Development Areas and those of the rest of the country and the outside world, it was tentatively concluded that manufacturing output in the Areas might be raised by about 8 per cent directly, and perhaps a further 2 per cent through multiplier effects. This, it was thought, might involve an employment increase of about 5 per cent and a reduction of the Areas' combined unemployment rate – after allowing for some reduction of their net emigration – of something over 1 per cent of their occupied population. The disparity in unemployment rates between the Areas and the rest of the country might, it was thought, be roughly halved over a period of years – a conclusion that was tentatively stated in the Green Paper on the Development Areas.[1]

An estimate by the present writer and his colleagues at the National Institute envisaged three extreme possibilities: a total leak of the Premium into wage increases, its addition to profits (perhaps to be re-invested in the Development Areas) and a lowering of prices.[2] On an arbitrary assumption of an equal mixture of the three, it was suggested that after three to five years employment in the Areas might have been raised by 60,000 – 80,000, the net effects in the rest of the country (initially adverse) by then being negligible.

In the event the investment effects of the Regional Employment Premium were not conspicuous. In the diversion of both numbers and floor-space of approved schemes to the Development Areas it is possible to argue that it may have had a small and rapid effect, but this seems on the face of it to have faded out, or been countered by some unidentified influence tending to shift investment away from those Areas

---

[1] Department of Economic Affairs, *The Development Areas: a proposal for a regional employment premium*, London, HMSO, 1967.

[2] A. J. Brown, 'The Green Paper on the Development Areas', *National Institute Economic Review*, no. 40, May 1967, pp. 26–33.

from mid-1968 onwards. It can, however, be maintained quite reasonably that the period that has elapsed at the time of writing (the Premium already being under sentence of death) is hardly sufficient for the full investment effects suggested in the above forecasts to have developed. Are there any visible effects in other directions?

First, on the leak into wages some help can be obtained from the chart of averages of hourly earnings in different regions, nationally weighted as to industries so as to eliminate direct effects of different regional industrial compositions, which was given in chapter 9.[1] It is plain from this that the trends of the indices for the regions wholly or mainly consisting of Development Areas in fact improved in relation to the United Kingdom average in recent years. Generally however, the most decisive improvement comes rather too early to be attributed to the Regional Employment Premium. In Wales the previous adverse trend seems to end in 1966, though one can argue that continuous improvement begins only from October 1967. In Scotland the tide turned in 1963, though since 1967 the upward trend has been steeper than it was from 1963 until then. Northern Ireland shows a dramatic change of trend in 1962 or 1963, with no clear break of the upward trend since, except perhaps an incipient deterioration dating from October 1968. For the North also it is hard to detect any change in the favourable trend that began in 1964. As with investment therefore, relative improvement of earnings in the most heavily assisted regions seems to date mainly from a time well before the Regional Employment Premium, though some further effect of the latter in Scotland and Wales is not excluded. In any case, the improvement of earnings in these regions in relation to the United Kingdom average in the two years from October 1967 was only of the order of 1 per cent. There is little sign of leakage here.

The effect on employment is hard to detect by simple inspection. The June proportion of total United Kingdom employees in employment who were in the North, Scotland, Wales and Northern Ireland had fallen quickly between 1958 and 1963 from 21·6 to 20·6 per cent, had then recovered marginally and held firm until 1965, but then began to slip again. From 1967 to 1969 at least it held firm once more.

To test whether these changes include any systematic component that can be attributed to the Regional Employment Premium, it seems useful to apply the analysis of variance treatment that was employed in our general discussion of regional growth (chapter 6). The question is whether growth rates in manufacturing industries (which alone were directly affected by the Regional Employment Premium) improved significantly more between 1965-7 and 1967-9 in the Development

[1] Chart 9.1, p. 235.

Area regions than they did in others. The treatment amounts, it will be recalled, to fitting to the data the relationship $G_{ir} = A_i + B_r + V_{ir}$. That is to say, the improvement of growth rate, G_{ir}, of employment in industry i in region r is explained as far as possible as the sum of a component A_i specific to the industry and another B_r specific to the region, leaving a residue V_{ir} with a mean of zero. Two versions of this model are tried: in the first the procedure involves minimising the variance of the term V_{ir} measured in the ordinary way, but the trouble with this is that industries with very small representations in a region can show very large and erratic proportional growth rates (or changes in growth rate between our two periods), and this distorts the estimates for what are, in substance, trivial reasons. A second version is therefore introduced in which the variance minimised is that of residual growth rate, expressed in terms not of the initial employment in the industry, but of the initial employment in all the industries in the regions. This provides a much better fit ($R^2 = 0.63$).

The results emerge in the form of dummy variables, each showing for its particular region how much better the general improvement in growth was there than in some other region taken as a basis of comparison (in this calculation South East England), in so far as that improvement was specific to the region rather than either random or specific to particular industries. The regional coefficients, expressed as percentages, are:

N	Y & H	NW	EM	WM	SW	Wa	Sc.
—	−2·0	+0·5	−4·6	−0.3	−0·8	+0·5	+3·0

It will be seen that all four of the regions without major Development Areas showed less improvement than South East England (which has a coefficient of zero by definition), and all the major Development Area regions except the North (which happened to have a zero coefficient) showed more. This is a broad indication that something, which may have been the Regional Employment Premium, improved the relative fortunes of the Development Areas, though it must be admitted that only two regions – the East Midlands on the losing side and Scotland on the gaining one – show a statistically significant change of fortune (Yorkshire and Humberside comes relatively near to doing so). It is clear too that the two-year periods over which the test is applied are so short that purely cyclical factors probably influence the results more than one would wish. With the available data however, this is probably the best one can do, and the outcome does, at any rate, suggest some systematic effect of the Regional Employment Premium on growth of employment.

To quantify this effect in a general way one has only to apply the coefficients to the numbers employed in manufacturing in the respective regions. The result of doing so is that, relative to the course of events in the South East, the four high-unemployment regions showed improvements of about 31,000, the remaining regions deteriorations of about 55,000. The literal, though naive, interpretation is that something (possibly the Regional Employment Premium) shifted the bias of growth in favour of the high-unemployment regions to the extent, over the period in question, of about 86,000. The resemblance of this to the NIESR forecast must be regarded as mainly coincidental;[1] the forecast was intended in any case to apply to a rather longer period. The high concentration of the supposed effects on two regions is also disturbing. The first version of the model it may be noted, though providing not so good a fit, gives a rather more even distribution of the effects between regions, with a net bias in favour of the four high-unemployment ones of about 150,000. With all allowance for the limitations of this test, it looks as if, from about the time of the introduction of the Regional Employment Premium, there was an improvement in the relative fortunes of the assisted regions that has been largely overlaid and concealed from simple observation by structural changes – the downturn in shipbuilding, the pick-up in vehicles and textiles.

Perhaps this is all that can usefully be said on the basis of present knowledge about the effectiveness of the separate financial incentives of recent years in shifting the balance of development towards the Development Areas. There is, however, another matter of importance connected with the influence that the form of the incentives exerted upon the form of the development. Throughout the history of regional policy in the United Kingdom the great majority of the incentives to enterprise to establish (or expand) in assisted areas have been subventions of capital costs, or aids in the provision of capital – none, except the prewar tax-remission measures, and latterly the Regional Employment Premium, assistance in training and some other minor items have been unrelated to capital costs. The incentives would seem, therefore, likely to have borne more effectively upon capital-intensive industries than upon labour-intensive ones. This might be expected to be especially true of investment grants, the payment of which (unlike most assistance under the Local Employment Acts) was not conditional upon the provision of a minimum amount of employment in relation to the help given.

Data prepared for the Hunt Committee on the first twenty-one months of operation of investment grants made possible a calculation the results of which are published in that Committee's report.[2] The

[1] In 'The Green Paper on the Development Areas', loc. cit.
[2] Department of Economic Affairs, *The Intermediate Areas*, appendix J.

calculation took the form of a regression analysis, in which the proportion of the investment in an industry that went to establishments in Development Areas was related both to the proportion of the industry's existing employment that was situated in these Areas and to the capital-intensiveness of the industry (stock of plant and machinery per unit of net output). Both of these variables prove to be significant; the constant term is not significantly different from zero.

The meaning of the relation can be illustrated by considering two industries, both with 18 per cent of their employment initially in the Development Areas – this being the average for all industries in the calculation – but one industry having a fairly low capital–output ratio of unity like mechanical or electrical engineering, the other a fairly high one of two like ferrous metals or paper. The former industry could be expected to have about 27 per cent of its 1966/7 investment in the Development Areas, the latter one to have 38 per cent of its investment there. The ratio of an industry's percentage rate of growth in the Development Areas to its percentage rate of growth elsewhere thus seems to have been higher the more capital-intensive the industry was. The calculation also brings out incidentally that the percentage rate of growth was likely to be higher in the Development Areas than outside them for all industries except those of very low capital-intensiveness, or those that were very largely concentrated in the Development Areas already.

In this period therefore, the capital-intensive industries, which were already to a considerable extent concentrated in the Development Areas, were rapidly becoming more so, and it is hard to believe that this tendency was not being materially promoted by the form of the incentive. To benefit from choice of a Development Area site to the extent of a fifth of the net capital cost may not mean very much in a labour-intensive industry, where the interest and depreciation on capital amount to less than a tenth of annual net output (perhaps a thirtieth of annual gross output), but it means a great deal more if one multiplies these figures by two, three, four, or more, as may be appropriate for capital-intensive industries.

What are the economic implications of this bias in the incentives? On the face of it there seems to be some objection to giving extra incentives to capital-intensive industry to develop in regions where there is a surplus of labour. In so far as the incentive payments are geared to capital costs, the consequential fact that capital-intensive industry is most responsive to them means that the cost to the exchequer per job created in the Development Areas is correspondingly high. Apart from this, one may ask whether there is any advantage or disadvantage to the Development Areas in having their industrial structure biased increasingly towards the more capital-intensive kinds of manufacturing industry.

It is sometimes argued that the more capital-intensive industries are the more progressive, faster growing, or higher-wage trades, so that the preferential acquisition of them is good for the Development Areas, provided that the costliness of the movement to the public purse does not correspondingly restrict the extent to which it can be promoted. There is in fact a good deal of general misunderstanding on these matters. It is true that there is a general tendency for all industry to become more capital-intensive, and it may well be (though it is not necessarily the case) that, within any trade, the more capital-intensive establishments are the more progressive, faster growing and better paying ones. But among the twenty-two industries for which data were used in the calculation just described, there was in fact a *negative* (though statistically non-significant) rank correlation between capital-intensiveness and percentage growth of employment in the years 1961–9. (The most highly capital-intensive, mineral oil-refining, reduced its employment by 13 per cent; timber, scientific instruments and unspecified metal goods, printing, and the miscellaneous 'other manufacturing' group, which were the fastest growers, are all labour-intensive. The shrinking textile industry is relatively capital-intensive.) To some extent, of course, shrinkage of employment goes with rapid growth of productivity and output as in oil-refining, but, broadly speaking, it is the course of employment not of physical output that matters to the region where the industry is situated; a rising gross surplus is likely to be locally irrelevant in so far as it accrues mainly to factor owners resident elsewhere.

Nor can one establish a clear relation among either industries or regions between high earnings and high capital-intensity. It is true that the capital-intensive industries of oil-refining, ferrous metals, and paper and board are among those in which male manual earnings are highest, but so are motor vehicles and aircraft, a number of the metal trades, tobacco and printing, which lie decidedly nearer to the labour-intensive end of the spectrum. If one takes the ratio of gross surplus (net output excluding wages and salaries) to wages and salaries as a rough index of capital-intensity, one finds among the census industries virtually no correlation between this index and average earnings per employee. A similar calculation relating to manufacturing industry in regions also reveals an absence of correlation; the West Midlands in particular cancel any slight tendency for a positive correlation to emerge by combining by far the lowest capital-intensity (thus measured) of any United Kingdom region with the highest earnings per employee of any except Wales and the South East. No obvious benefit to the assisted areas or the economy as a whole stems from the very expensive gearing of incentives predominantly or exclusively to capital cost.

'Real' assistance

The second class of instruments of policy that we have distinguished consists of 'real' assistance, ranging from specific provision of sites and buildings to environmental services. In so far as there is an element of subsidy in the terms on which buildings are made available to industry this should be included in our consideration of financial incentives, but it is impossible to make this distinction in practice and we shall have to slur over it – as indeed over much else. We have seen that, in the immediate postwar circumstances of factory shortage and tight building control, the availability of (mainly government-owned) factories in the Development Areas was a means of exercising a particularly effective control of industrial movement, but this was an abnormal situation. Government factories have continued to play a considerable part in location policy; it has been a relatively declining one, but was still important in the mid-sixties. The Board of Trade's Survey of 1964–7 showed that about a fifth of the firms established in the assisted areas at that time ranked availability of a government factory (usually for rent) as a major factor in their decision to move.[1]

Improvement of transport facilities can also be important. It is noteworthy that the Board of Trade's Survey showed more than half the newcomers to sites in the East Midlands and almost a third of those to the North West as placing proximity to a motorway among the major factors affecting their choice of site, these being the two regions perhaps most affected by the earlier motorways. That more than a fifth of the newcomers to sites in Scotland and Northern Ireland regarded proximity to an airport as a major factor is not surprising in view of the remarks of the Toothill Committee on this subject.[2] Proximity to a seaport was thought to be of major importance by about a seventh of all moving firms, including higher proportions of those in Northern Ireland, the North West and East Anglia. Presumably the implication of these results is that anything up to the stated proportions of the firms that have gone to the regions in question might not have done so in the absence of the transport facilities mentioned. The proportions of the new establishments in any region that mentioned these and other infrastructure advantages as major locational considerations, however, were much smaller than the proportions of new establishments in the Development Areas that mentioned the main financial incentives as major factors. Most advantages connected with amenity and environment were mentioned as minor rather than major locational considerations.

---

[1] 'Inquiry into Location Attitudes and Experience' (unpublished).
[2] Scottish Council (Development and Industry), *Report on the Scottish Economy 1960–61*, Edinburgh, 1962.

The moral seems to be that a minority of mobile industry is strongly attracted by outstandingly good (mainly road) communications, and probably at the same time by a central situation; hence the special virtue of motorway sites in the East Midlands. But the absolute number of moves to which this applies is small. Of those firms that actually go to Development Areas, another substantial minority find airports, seaports and in some cases motorways potentially decisive, and a further substantial minority is strongly attracted by availability of government factories. Remedying deficiencies of communications and other infrastructure however, unless they were grosser than one is likely to find in any at all thickly populated area, does not seem likely on this evidence to attract as much mobile industry as was attracted by the financial inducements of the middle sixties. Pleasant environment seems to be on the whole a minor factor; indeed anyone who thinks it a major obstacle to prosperity should look at the Black Country. The attractions of brass are stronger than the repulsions of muck, even though the belief in a natural harmony between the two is waning. But, for industry that is reconciled to severance from its base and is truly footloose, environmental attractions are clearly far from negligible.

It seems then that infrastructure improvement is important industrially as a permissive rather than as a sufficient condition of growth. To rely on extra good infrastructure as an attraction to growth would (as the present writer argued in a Note of Dissent from the Hunt Report)[1] probably be expensive in real resources in comparison with a normal standard of infrastructure plus some financial incentives. This by no means implies that new and well planned infrastructure (in new and expanded towns for instance) does not exercise an appreciable attraction in itself; it does so largely by its very newness. But the financial incentives of recent times have apparently been capable of exerting an even stronger attraction.

Industrial development certificates

Finally, behind all these questions about the inducements used as instruments of policy in recent years, there stands another one about the part played by industrial development certificates. What were the relative roles of the stick and the carrot? It is not an easy question to answer, since each variation in the strength of the incentives either was, or is likely to have been, accompanied by variations in the same direction in the stringency of industrial development certificate controls, so that any succeeding changes in industrial movement or the location of growth generally owed something to both. The declared tightening of industrial development certificate policy in the summer of 1958 seems

[1] Department of Economic Affairs, *The Intermediate Areas*.

to have produced very little immediate effect in the absence of any substantial strengthening of incentives, whereas the incentive changes of 1963 were quickly followed by shifts in the direction of industrial movement and the distribution of industrial building. The large moves of 1960 however, have to be taken into account in assessing the 1958 measures, and one does not know whether there was a further tightening of industrial development certificate administration before 1963, nor what part it may have played. The empirical evidence we have quoted above suggests that there may have been such a tightening then, and that there may have been another in late 1964 or early 1965, perhaps consequent upon the change of government. The Board of Trade's inquiries into the motives and experience of all firms that formed establishments on sites new to them, and at some distance from their previous sites, between 1963 and 1968, show on the other hand a much greater prominence given to the availability of inducements than to difficulty or fears of difficulty in getting industrial development certificates for expansion elsewhere.[1] The Confederation of British Industry's inquiry (with a much lower total response rate) gives a higher relative importance to control by industrial development certificates.[2]

The best generalisation one can make is, perhaps, that industrial development certificates and incentives have acted together to produce effects greater than the sum of those that would have been produced by each of the two instruments operated as they were, in the absence of the other. Without control, and the possibility that a certificate for expansion in the more prosperous areas might be refused, it seems fairly certain that many firms would not have been led by the incentives on offer to examine the possibilities of a Development Area site. Among these would be many that, in the event, were attracted by what their examination showed them. Without Development Area incentives, far more of the firms faced with the probability of refusal (or an actual refusal) of a certificate for a scheme outside the Development Areas would no doubt have postponed or abandoned their expansion, or modified it to something smaller for which a certificate was not required. The forces that oppose movement do indeed resemble the frictions to which they are so often compared, and to overcome friction the *combination* of forces making for movement has to exceed a critical value. One can say from observation only, for instance, that the combination of juicier carrot and bigger stick that prevailed in the early sixties in comparison with that of the fifties seems to have diverted something like a quarter of the factory building in schemes of over 5,000 square feet in the South East and the West Midlands to other parts of the

[1] 'Inquiry into Location Attitudes and Experience' (unpublished).
[2] Unpublished evidence presented to the Hunt Committee.

country, while the net effects of carrot and stick in the country as a whole did not prevent a substantial growth in the total amount of such building.

CONCLUSION

In conclusion it is perhaps worth trying a direct assessment of the changes in the balance of *total* employment growth between the assisted and other areas that may be ascribed, with due caution, to the measures of the late fifties and early sixties. For this we may use a technique rather similar to the one used above for estimating the employment effects of the Regional Employment Premium, but drawing upon the analysis of the relevant periods that was used in chapter 6. We examined there the growth rates of the regions in the periods 1953–9 and 1961–6 measured from the national average, and saw how structural and growth (or regional) components could be extracted from them. For each region it is possible to see how the growth or regional component of its change in employment, so measured and put on to an annual basis, varied between the two periods. Thus, the systematic growth or regional element in the expansion of total employment in Wales was 0·79 per cent a year below the national average in 1953–9, but only 0·17 per cent a year below it in 1961–6; it had improved in relation to the national average by 0·62 per cent a year. The calculation can be done with our data for manufacturing, mining and agriculture, as well as with those covering all industries.

So far as manufacturing, mining and agriculture are concerned, it seems that the four high-unemployment regions improved their regional growth of employment (freed as far as possible from structural elements) in relation to the rest of the country by about 28,000 a year between the two periods. Wales and Scotland did well, South East England did badly, much more than offsetting an improved performance by the South West, the North Midlands and Yorkshire. It will be seen that this relative improvement of employment growth by the main assisted regions is within the same range of magnitude as the increase in manufacturing jobs in approved schemes in those regions that we have tentatively attributed to policy changes. The comparison between the two, of course, cannot be straightforward, because changes in mining and agricultural employment are included in one estimate and not in the other, but the modest degree of correspondence may at least give us courage to believe that we are not hunting a chimera.

One direction for further exploration is the change between these two periods in the systematic, non-structural, relative growth of the assisted regions in *total* employment. The answer proves to be very little above that which we have got for manufacturing, mining and agriculture alone – in fact 29,000 a year. This may seem to yield very little room for the multiplier – implausibly, when one considers that we already know that there is a fairly good relationship across regions between increases in 'basic' and in 'service' employment, with the latter equal to about 70 per cent of the former. There is, however, no contradiction here; the model from which the growth components of regional employment change are deduced fit the data far from perfectly.

There is a variant of the same approach that is also worth mentioning. Instead of looking at the systematic growth components of employment change, that is those that arise essentially as regional dummy variables in a regression analysis, it is possible to examine the residuals that are left over after the systematic structural components have been extracted – that is to say, all the actual growth of employment in the region, whether consistent with a generally good or bad regional performance, or associated with the idiosyncratic behaviour of particular bits of its economy, except that which can be accounted for by its industrial structure.

If this is done for manufacture, mining and agriculture, the improvement of growth in the four regions in relation to the rest between 1953–9 and 1961–6 works out at some 46,000 a year. If it is done for *all* industries, the corresponding improvement can be estimated at 70,000 a year. The implicit long-term multiplier (at a little over 1·5) is at all events of a more convincing order of magnitude.

All that can be said about these estimates is that, in a loose kind of way, they hang together. From the analysis of variance growth models for the periods 1953–9 and 1961–6, it can be deduced that *something* other than structure and changes in the characteristic performance of industries as such caused the four high-unemployment regions to improve their total employment growth rate in relation to the rest of the country by about 70,000 a year, including an improvement extending across all industries that accounts for 29,000 a year – the corresponding figures for the basic industries being 46,000 and 28,000 respectively. We know that, between these two periods, potential employment in moves to the assisted regions increased by about 15,000 a year, and the number of new jobs in industrial development certificates approved in them increased, in relation to the number in the rest of the country, by some 30,000 a year or more, which would eventually bring with them something like an extra 20,000 a year in local service industries. It seems likely from our previous discussion that most of the change of pattern in moves and approvals was due to the strengthening of policy. If this is granted, it is very hard to suppose that the improvement in the relative performance of the assisted regions (after eliminating structural factors) was not largely the result of strengthened policy also.

CHAPTER 12

THE SETTING FOR POLICY

In the first chapter we considered in very general terms what theoretical grounds there might be for regional policy. Subsequently we have examined various aspects of the structure and working of the United Kingdom economy that seem to be relevant to those grounds. We must now look again at the theoretical considerations in the light of our analysis of United Kingdom conditions.

The case for any regional policy arises from situations that seem to call for some public attempt to influence the interregional distribution of economic activity or its rate of growth. More specifically, these situations can be grouped as follows:

(i) Population and industry are judged to be in the wrong places in relation to natural resources and the natural features of the country and its surroundings, or their distribution is changing in what is judged to be a wrong direction, or, if it is changing in the right direction, it is thought to be doing so too slowly.

(ii) Population and industry together are judged to be badly distributed, or their distribution is thought to be changing in the wrong direction, or not fast enough in the right one, in relation to *themselves* – for instance they are (or are becoming) too congested or too scattered.

(iii) Labour and capital – people and jobs – are to a significant extent in the wrong places in relation to *each other*. This is likely to be an important and persistent problem only if the rate of increase of demand for labour and the rate of natural increase of population of working age are geographically out of adjustment with each other – the former greater than the latter in one part of the country, the latter greater than the former in another. This leads to inequality of personal incomes between regions. It also causes labour shortage in one region, labour surplus in another, either or both of which tend to produce net migration of labour in one direction, net movements of enterprises in the other, to such an extent that an equilibrium is reached with these flows more or less steady and with broadly constant differences of incomes and unemployment rates, which could, in principle, persist indefinitely. Interregional income differences are symptoms of maldistribution of resources; regional labour shortage (or capital surplus) and labour surplus (or capital shortage) involve manifest waste, and may in some conditions produce a stronger inflationary tendency than would exist if demand and supply were better adjusted geographically to each other. Differences in income levels and in unemployment (or vacancy) rates both, if sufficiently marked, arouse resentment on grounds of equity.

(iv) The market forces brought into play by the sort of maladjustment described in (iiii) may, in some conditions, work perversely, so that both capital and labour tend to be drawn cumulatively into one region, and the economies of the others waste away without a corresponding gain in aggregate income or welfare.

(v) If population or jobs are moving, the psychic and other costs of movement, including possible waste through duplication of social capital, may be serious.

We shall now consider, so far as we can, what reality these grounds possess in current United Kingdom conditions.

THE MISLOCATION OF POPULATION AND INDUSTRY

Location in relation to natural resources and means of access is still important for some industries; apart from the obvious cases of agriculture and mining, this is true of iron and steel, oil-refining, power generation, processing of agricultural products, cement and brickmaking, shipbuilding, and some others, where the bulk or weight of materials dealt with is large in relation to the value added, and the bulk or weight of the outputs is much less than that of the inputs, and/or where economical handling of either inputs or outputs demands conditions of access that are available only at rather special sites. But it is doubtful whether these restrictions apply at all powerfully to establishments employing more than (say) a tenth of the British labour force. Particular steelworks, shipyards, or refineries can be convicted of being 'in the wrong place' in relation to the natural environment in as much as they cannot take delivery of iron ore or crude oil directly from very large bulk carriers, or cannot launch ships of the large sizes now increasingly in demand, but the charge cannot be brought home against most industry situated in any of the dozen or so major industrial concentrations of the United Kingdom. The most that can be said against the physical siting of any of these concentrations on grounds of suitability for productive activities is that they are disqualified or significantly handicapped as candidates for pursuing a minority of the range of possible activities. The situation is very different from that of the early nineteenth century, when coal burned *in situ* was the important source of power, transport of it (and of everything else) was expensive and, even apart from this, the industries that were tied down by natural resource requirements constituted a much larger proportion of total activity than they do now. Again, some parts of the country are at a natural disadvantage as sites for the *development* of industry – of some kinds more than others – because they are deficient in reasonably flat, firm, unflooded land. But this is more important as a restriction at the local than at the regional level. There is certainly no whole region, though there are certainly a number of towns and urban districts, where shortage of possible sites for any but the most demanding kinds of establishment imposes more than a very distant restriction on the industrial development of which it is capable in principle.

If the constraints imposed by physical geography on location of production at the regional level of discourse are weak except in regard to a minority of productive activities, what about the constraints they impose on the rational location of population? As the ties of employment to (for instance) coalfields, and on a smaller scale the ties of residence to employment, are relaxed and as incomes and expectations rise, preferences for particular kinds of environment to live in may be expected to play larger parts in determining the distribution of population. The quality of the natural environment may also affect one's judgment on the optimal distribution apart from overt preferences. Sticking still to the natural features of the environment, climate and scenery, one may ask first what interregional significance they have.

Scenery is, of course, a matter of taste about which one cannot prescribe standards; empirically it is evident only that most people (but not all) tend to prefer what they are used to, and that preferences differ – though this does not mean that all types of countryside are equally attractive to strangers. Landscape blighted by industrial or mining activity apparently plays a not entirely unimportant part in discouraging the inflow of key people, and therefore of industry, into some areas where the economic attractions are not so outstanding as to swamp all other considerations. The 'colonisation' of the South West and East Anglia by population and industry is almost certainly helped by the pleasantness of their countryside and coasts, well known through holiday traffic, though in the outer fringes of these regions, as in the more spectacularly beautiful areas elsewhere in the country, the decline of agricultural employment dominates the local economic situation. Visual attractiveness of the country is, however, as much a matter of human activity as of natural endowment, and its implications for rational planning of the location of population or for spontaneous changes in location, are generally stronger on the intra-regional than on the interregional scale.

With climate we are on rather firmer ground in that interregional differences are measurable. The superior sunshine record of South Eastern England and the south coast, and the mildness of the South

West, certainly play some part in attracting net inflow of population. This shows up most sensitively in the movements of people of retiring age (who are attracted also to more northern coastal districts both eastern and western), but its influence may be presumed to be wider than that. What would be still more to the point as a planning criterion if we could detect it, is the influence of climate – or natural environment generally – on health.

This, however, is difficult. There are large differences between the regions both in standardised mortality rates and in the incidence of incapacity for work, but the greater part of these seems to be accounted for by differences in occupational structure.

Bearing in mind the considerable number of social and economic factors that affect health, and the scope for interactions between them, the general impression is that the differences attributable to the natural environment are small compared with those due to what man has made of man – though perhaps the southern regions have some advantages that can be ascribed to climate alone. But again, within regions, especially those that are the wettest and least sunny on average, there are big local differences. No region lacks a good deal of lowland area with a very tolerable climate.

It is hard, therefore, to make out a case that, in relation to the natural environment, the concentrations of population and industry are to any great extent 'in the wrong place'. This may be true of specific establishments or local groups of establishments in a few industries. It is also true that there are more people on the coalfields generally than would be justified by the requirements of modern technology and the inherent advantages of those areas for habitation. But it is only in special cases – the higher industrial valleys of the Pennines, the mining valleys of south Wales – that the combined effects of poor climate, constricted sites and, in some cases, a certain degree of inaccessibility make for a low degree of suitability for the maintenance and expansion of industry in modern circumstances, and in all the important cases the areas in question border on others to which these disadvantages do not apply. It cannot be said of any of the major concentrations of industry and population in this small country, taken as a whole, that Nature is decisively against it.

THE CONCENTRATION AND DISPERSION OF INDUSTRY AND POPULATION

But if Nature is not against them, what about Man – in the sense of the relation to them of other concentrations of population and the lines of communication between them? We have considered this from several angles. Perhaps the most comprehensive view is the one that we saw through the device of 'potential', a general measure of the accessibility of each place from all units of population in the country. There is some tendency for prosperity to be high where potential is high, but industrial structure enters as an important independent variable, making south Lancashire and the Potteries, for instance, relatively unprosperous despite their high potential. Growth, moreover, does not seem to be usefully correlated with potential, especially if we eliminate the effects of structural differences; and this remains true even if we consider growth *originating* in a region, that is to say, growth of employment plus outward moves and minus inward moves of industry. The South West and East Anglia (including their outer fringes) show rapid growth despite low potential, while much of the growth of the South East and the West Midlands seems to be attributable to structural rather than locational advantages.

Another view of the question is the one we got from considering the connection between specifically industrial agglomeration and net output per head. Establishments in some industries, we saw, seem to gain an advantage from inclusion in a large regional assemblage of their own kind; but the number of industries in which this effect is statistically significant is small, and the effect over the whole range of industry is not very strong – an extra 10 per cent of a trade's national employment in a particular region seems to go with a raising of its net output per head in that region by about a seventh of 1 per cent. There is scope for much further study of this subject, and the best cases of the benefits of agglomeration of *related* trades in a single industrial complex would have to be sought by detailed study, such as that devoted by Economic Consultants Limited to the possibility of a deliberately planned industrial complex in central Lancashire.[1] But even studies of that kind seem to quantify the advantages of agglomeration only with great difficulty, and our broad statistical enquiry suggests that, over manufacturing industry as a whole, they are not, to say the least, both widespread and strong.

This impression is strengthened in a general way by the closely related tendencies for regions to become less specialised (not only because the most highly localised industries happen to be in relative decline), for most industries to become less localised, and for industries in general to grow most rapidly in the regions that specialise upon them to the smallest extent. We saw also that the strongest evidence of specialisation according to comparative advantage seemed to be associated with reliance upon the old, declining industries rather than the new, growing ones. Clearly, we are far from a condition of static equilibrium in which the existing distribution of industry might be appealed to for evidence as to what,

[1] Economic Consultants Ltd, *Study for an Industrial Complex in Central Lancashire.*

even purely from industry's point of view, is the optimal distribution. And, so far as manufacturing industry is concerned at least, a move towards a new pattern of regional specialisation at all comparable to that of the nineteenth century is not visible. Dispersion and diversification rather are the rule. Perhaps this means only that, in this small and compact country with relatively good communications, the productive advantages of agglomeration on anything as small as the regional scale are important only for rather a small proportion of industry. The Americans, after all, have begun to describe as a single 'megalopolis' an area about as big and about as populous as that between the south coast and the midland valley of Scotland.

Our more general considerations of the economic and social advantages and disadvantages of agglomeration were mostly at a painfully abstract level. We saw, however, some evidence in favour of the often held but largely unproved proposition that the London conglomeration, in the widest definition, is too big. A good deal, indeed, of the high value of net output per head in its industries seems to be traceable to dear labour, which in turn is made dear by the costs of congestion associated with aggregation-size – high costs of housing and travel to work.

Although the other agglomerations of population and industry are much smaller, it by no means follows that they are of less than optimal size. Their functions are different from that of London: they do not bring together national institutions like the central government and the money market which can be supposed to benefit by living together. Their urban cores suffer heavy traffic congestion. Probably all the continuously built-up areas with populations much above half a million are super-optimal in size in the sense that additions to them without drastic re-planning would involve reductions in total utility in comparison with the levels that would be attained if the additional population went (or stayed) somewhere else. But because the scale of their problems is so much smaller than that of London, and in part also because higher proportions of their fabrics are ripe for replacement, the prospect of re-shaping in a way that would raise the optimum is less remote.

What emerges from this argument on the regional scale is perhaps not very impressive. One cannot (as has sometimes been done) regard the whole of South Eastern England (and perhaps the West Midlands as well) as a 'congested area' in contrast with the rest of the country. But it is probably true that the great agglomeration centred on London is well above optimal size, and that the scope for improving matters by development and re-deployment within the South East, having regard to the large prospective natural increase of population in the coming generation, is, in the strict sense of the word, limited. While other regions have their congestion problems, the scale of them is so much smaller that any shift in the balance of population and industry in their direction (or at least the direction of most of them) would make matters easier.

MALADJUSTMENT BETWEEN THE GROWTH PATTERNS OF POPULATION AND JOBS

From rather shadowy considerations relating to the location of population and industry taken together, we come to the much more tangible maladjustment that has lain at the root of regional problems in this country in the last fifty years – maladjustment of location between people and jobs. This is not, as might seem at first sight, simply a matter that could in principle be settled by estimating the deficiency of jobs in one part of the country, of labour in another, and making a once-for-all transfer of a number of either people or jobs to put it right. The root of the matter is that, largely because of interregional differences in the structure of industry, and the different rates of growth of different industries' demands for manpower, demands for labour grow in some regions faster than the natural increase of the local population of working age, in other regions more slowly. Consequently, labour surpluses build up in some regions, labour shortages in others. The surpluses, either through unemployment and diminished job-opportunity, or through relatively low earnings, encourage net outward migration of labour in search of jobs or of better earnings, and net inward movement of enterprises seeking available (or cheap) labour. The labour shortages have the opposite effects. Surpluses and shortages build up until the combined interregional flows of labour and of jobs are sufficient to offset the discrepancies between growth of locally arising jobs and increase of local candidates for work.

The situation can then continue with only slow changes, due mainly to the changes in industrial structure carrying with them changes in growth of demand for labour. Faster growing industries gradually replace or overshadow slower growing ones everywhere, but more rapidly in the regions where the existing structure of industry is unfavourable to growth, and new industry, predominantly faster growing, is coming in from elsewhere. This change of structure, however, takes a long time. Coalmining has been a principal declining industry in (most notably) South Wales and the North, cotton textiles in the North West, shipbuilding in Scotland and the North, for fifty years with intermissions, and there is still enough of them left for their continued decline to be of some regional importance. Agriculture has been exerting an appreciable downward influence on the growth rate of demand for labour in the less industrialised regions most of the time for nearly a century. Until these adjustments have reached the point at which growth of labour demand matches growth of local labour supply, there is continuous pressure for migration of labour and/or movement of enterprises, and since neither labour nor enterprises move with perfect freedom, there remain long-lasting interregional differences in the state of the labour market – differences of either unemployment (and unfilled vacancy) rates, or rates of earnings, or both. Measures to move either labour or enterprises in the appropriate directions have the effect of reducing the amount of mislocation of labour and capital so long as they are in operation. If they are applied and then discontinued before the structural transformations are complete the evidences of mislocation will reappear. The process of structural transformation itself can, in principle, be speeded up by measures to shift labour or capital, in as much as these measures enable rising industries to increase their labour forces more easily and cheaply, and to get larger shares of the world markets than would otherwise be possible – though this can, of course, only be achieved at the cost of killing off declining industries more quickly. Generally the process of transformation cannot be pushed much in advance of the shift in national or world market forces, which is usually quite slow. Regional policy aimed at dealing with the effects on specialised regional economies of shifts in demand or technology is therefore likely to be necessarily a matter of long-term treatment rather than rapid cure.

In the shorter run, in view of what seem to be the degrees of sensitivity to unemployment differences of migration of jobs and of people seeking them, it may very tentatively be suggested that every addition through increased mobility of one per annum to the flow of jobs to high-unemployment areas or of job-seekers in the opposite direction, may well increase the equilibrium level of employment by something like four and decrease the number of registered unemployed by two or three.

WAGE AND INCOME DIFFERENCES

We have noted that income differences between regions have a double significance. In the first place, differences in rewards for the same work in different regions imply some imperfection in the distribution of labour or of jobs, in that there seems to be scope for increasing workers' products by moving them about. Secondly, in so far as interregional inequality adds to the total sum of inter-personal inequality of incomes, it presumably reduces the want-satisfying power of the aggregate income of the country, if we may take the latter as given.

Interregional differences in the United Kingdom are small in comparison with those in most other countries. The average productivity (in value terms) of the labour force at work is about 27 per cent lower in Northern Ireland and 14 per cent lower in Scotland than it is in the South East, where it is highest. Some of these differences are directly due to occupational structure; male manual earnings in a fixed sample of industries are, for instance, only a little more than 20 per cent lower in Northern Ireland and 10 per cent lower in Scotland than they are in the South East. As for real *per capita* consumption, including some allowance for benefits received in kind from public expenditure it is probably about 16 per cent lower in the poorest British region than in the richest, though Northern Ireland would lie outside this range.

Interregional differences in earnings in a given trade or occupation are prima facie evidence of mislocation of resources in as much as people could, in principle and with some reservations, provide an increase in the national product if they were moved to another place where earnings are higher – or a plant could provide an increase if it were diverted to a place where its profits would be higher. How much scope there is for such improvement depends on how quickly the differences in earnings of labour or of capital are (or would be) extinguished by the movements in search of those higher earnings. If the lower earnings of labour in one part of the country are due to labour being more plentiful there, all industries accordingly being carried on in a more labour-intensive way there than elsewhere, it can be shown that, provided that the earnings of labour correspond to its marginal product, the loss of national income due to this circumstance is likely to be small. It is probably only a small fraction of the loss that would be incurred if, despite the relatively easy labour situation, production was carried on by methods no more labour-intensive than in other parts of the country where labour was scarcer, so that the labour-rich regions had some of their labour unemployed. So long, in other words, as all the available labour is employed, the scope for improving total output by shifting it from one region to another may be very modest, because its marginal product in low-productivity areas may be quite a high proportion of that in high-productivity areas, and because it might require the movement of only a small fraction of the labour force from the lower-productivity to the higher-productivity region to extinguish it.

We examined the two main conditions in which this conclusion might be falsified – serious discrepancy between pay and marginal product, and the existence of substantial advantages in some regions of kinds that moving more people into them would not quickly extinguish. Tentatively we decided that neither of these conditions exists on such a scale as to make our conclusion void. The existing interregional differences in income are probably not to be taken as evidence of much scope for raising real productivity by 'moving people up' to the regions where earnings are now highest.

Differences in the levels of unemployment, open and concealed, are, however, quite another matter. In the decade 1958–67, on average about 2 per cent more of the occupied male population was registered as unemployed in Scotland and the North than was so registered in the Midlands and the South East. In addition, to judge from the 1966 Census, there was probably a further difference in the same direction of something like 1 per cent of active male population actually out of work though not registered. As for the female population, while interregional differences in rates of registered and unregistered unemployment are smaller, it can be calculated that if it were possible to bring the activity rate in each age group everywhere up to the highest value observed in any region the effect on the labour force would be substantial. The active population (male and female together) would be increased by proportions that would vary from negligible ones in the South East and the West Midlands to about 9 per cent in the North, East Anglia, and the South West, and still more in Wales. It cannot, however, be suggested that female labour reserves of the implied sizes are in any real sense 'on offer' in the short run; it would take high demand over longish periods and probably some changes in industrial structure to draw them at all fully into the labour force.

So far as the registered unemployed are concerned, interregional differences in rates seem to be due in only minor degrees to differences in the imperfection of the labour market, which permit the simultaneous existence of unemployed people and unfilled vacancies. The evidence is that interregional differences in the incidence of unemployability are still more minor. The major parts of differences in unemployment seem to be due to differences in the pressure of demand for labour.

It follows from this that the regional wage rates are not all equilibrium rates, in the sense of those required to bring the region's competitiveness with the rest of the world to the point where all its labour on offer (except for that made idle by frictional and structural factors, or by physical and mental incapacity) is employed. Keynesian theory, of course, throws doubt upon the existence in the short run of any effective tendency for equilibrium wage levels, in this sense, to be automatically established. However, the simpler versions of Keynesian theory refer primarily to closed economies, whereas regional economies are very open indeed – much more so, according to our evidence, than even the most open national economies. If differences in pressure on regional labour markets make any difference to rates of regional wage inflation, one would expect regional unemployment (and vacancy) rates to settle at relative levels that, in anything but the short run, ensure roughly parallel wage movements – otherwise differences in competitive power would accumulate. We have argued earlier that the evidence suggests that the spread of wage increases from the regions of high demand – through national agreements and otherwise – tends to keep wages in other regions higher than they would otherwise be, and so to raise the level of unemployment that is necessary to keep their cost levels from getting out of line. Since we have found no convincing evidence that marginal products of labour are lower relatively to wages where wages are low than they are in the high-wage regions, it may well be that industry, on the whole, adjusts its methods and employment so that wages and marginal products are roughly in line – certainly, significant tendencies for one region to be generally more profitable than another, industry by industry, do not seem to have been found. On the evidence available one cannot be sure of this. The implication of persistent differences in unemployment levels however, is that the system of wage determination purchases greater interregional equality at the cost of greater interregional unemployment differences. Given that there are floors below which unemployment levels in the trend-setting high-wage regions cannot in practice be depressed, this means that this feature of the system involves buying greater equality of earnings at the cost of greater *national* unemployment totals.

What the rate of exchange between wage difference and unemployment difference is would be hard to say, the answer depends upon several contingencies. *If* wage difference were fully reflected in price difference, then, judging from the rather ambiguous and oblique evidence of international trade statistics, it might take an additional relative difference of the order of 10 per cent between the South East and the Midlands on the one hand, and Wales, Scotland and the North on the other, to eliminate the difference between them of about $1\frac{3}{4}$ per cent in demand-deficiency unemployment which was typical of the late 1960s. It seems likely that, supposing that such a wage difference could be produced, it would take some years to achieve the implied degree of effectiveness, and it is quite possible that its effectiveness would go on increasing slowly beyond this point thereafter. Prices, however, are to some extent standardised nationally, and for various reasons tend not to reflect cost differences fully. In so far as profit margins not prices are affected by wage differences, the effect on employment depends upon the rate at which production is shifted to the lower-cost regions. On this there is very little ground for judgment. Light might have been thrown on the whole of this subject by the experiment of the Regional Employment Premium if it had been continued longer in conditions conducive to its effectiveness.

But despite uncertainty about the rate at which wage equality can be exchanged for unemployment equality in practice, it seems clear, prima facie, that in terms of welfare unemployment is relatively dear. It was argued in chapter 10 (as we have just noted) that the loss of real income from having labour and capital unevenly distributed in relation to each other, so that the rates of return on both varied in opposite directions between different regions, would be very small so long as industrial methods were flexible enough to employ all the labour and capital – for a 10 per cent difference in earnings between the two halves of the country, it might well be only a fraction of 1 per cent. We have argued in chapter 3 that the loss of welfare from the more unequal distribution of this income between people that a 10 per cent interregional difference in earnings would involve can hardly be serious so long as the welfare of different people can be treated as independent of each other, and as dependent purely on their incomes. It would, fairly certainly, be negligible in comparison with that implicit in the existing inter-personal inequality of incomes in the country as a whole. It would, moreover, be considerably reduced by the action of progressive taxation and social service expenditure.

On the other hand, the excesses of unemployment rates in other regions over those in the South East where unemployment was lowest have accounted for about a third of total unemployment in the United Kingdom during the last decade. Adding in some allowances for parallel differences in unregistered unemployment, and for the loss of production through labour shortage leading to under-use of plant in regions of high demand, one can say that the mislocations of demand for and supply of labour in relation to each other have been responsible for losses of production and real income of the order, very broadly, of 1 per cent. In so far as differences in pressure of demand (responsible for the greater part of the interregional differences in unemployment rates) are also effective in slowing down the gradual drawing into employment of the potential reserves of female labour, which are largest in the regions of low pressure, this assessment must be increased.

Having said this one has to admit that the underlying assumptions involved in translating statements about income into terms of welfare must be questioned. On one side of the scale, it is not clear that the welfare implications of differences in rates of pay between people doing similar jobs in different regions can be treated as simply as we have implied. If those on the low side of the gap become aware of it, they are apt to build up senses of grievance, not only on their own behalf, but on that of their similarly placed neighbours. Mixed with local patriotism (and more particularly with Scottish or Welsh nationalism) this can amount to a good deal more than the simple personal welfare counterpart of a 10 or 20 per cent difference in real income.

On the other side, unemployment differences also amount to a good deal more than simply differences in potential real income (and the corresponding economic welfare) lost. Both the diffuse sense of personal insecurity in a community where the risk of redundancy is felt to be high, and the acute senses of rejection and frustration that afflict many of (especially) the long-term unemployed and their families, may well be more important on many people's scales of values. There is no way of striking the balance in terms of the strictly measurable; one can only say as a matter of personal judgment that, in so far as higher unemployment is, at the margin, an alternative to greater interregional earnings differences and greater interregional differences in labour productivity, it is still, in the most comprehensively assessed welfare terms, a dear alternative.

Aside from questions concerned directly with efficiency in the use of resources, there is the possible impact of uneven distribution of demand on the rate of wage and cost inflation. The most usual approach to this has been by way of the 'Phillips curve' – the inverse relation claimed to have been established empirically between the level of unemployment and the rate of increase of the money price of labour. For the country as a whole it now seems that this relation (if indeed it still exists at all) has shifted since 1967 in the inflationary direction – higher rates of wage increase than hitherto for any given unemployment level.

But what also appears from our investigations and others, is that there is in addition a direct spread of wage inflation from the pace-making regions (the South East and perhaps the Midlands) to the others; a spread largely responsible for the evident fact that, while pressures of demand for labour vary considerably from region to region, regional wage levels on the whole move parallel to each other in anything but the very short run. If this is so the slackening of demand in the high-wage regions might be expected to have a nationwide effect that would not be wholly offset by the transfer of some of that demand to other regions that are not looked to as models for emulation. This effect of a more even distribution of demand in slowing the pace of inflation is additional to that which has often been anticipated (and for which there seems to be some slight evidence) from the greater sensitivity of wage inflation to changes of unemployment in regions where the latter is low than in those where it is high. At all events, there seems to be a reasonable presumption that a more even spreading of pressure of demand between regions would do something to reduce the speed of wage inflation, though it is difficult to quantify this effect.

THE PERVERSE WORKING OF MARKET FORCES

The next of the possible grounds for a positive regional policy that were enumerated at the beginning of this survey is that market forces by themselves yield what Myrdal called a process of 'circular and cumulative causation',[1] whereby success feeds on itself without thereby yielding an optimal result. The qualification is, of course, vital. We have already touched on the possibility that there may be permanent economies of aggregation arising from various kinds of economy of scale. If it were the case that market forces of this kind tended to draw the great bulk of the economic activity of the country into (say) the South East, there would be two possibly adequate grounds for objection to it. First, there might be accompanying disadvantages such as congestion, which are not priced in the market and which have already been referred to. Second, it might be argued that, while aggregation is a good thing, the particular aggregation based upon London is the wrong one in modern conditions, and has achieved the superiority of size that makes it the dominant growth point for reasons that are no longer valid. We have found no reason for believing that this is so – it would, moreover, be rather late in the day to find that our biggest conurbation ought really to be on the Tyne or the Solway rather than the Thames. What we are concerned with here is neither of these two contingencies, nor indeed any permanent competitive advantage that an aggregation of population and industry has because it is bigger than others, but a temporary attractive power that it has because, and only so long as, it is growing faster. This could, in principle, make growth geographically unstable and its results in terms of production and welfare arbitrary.

We have examined the chief economic mechanism by which this could happen – the interaction of the multiplier and capital stock adjustment at the regional level. It appears that the regions are extremely 'open', in that round about four-fifths of the expenditure by a resident in one of them is likely to 'leak' out of that region in payments to residents elsewhere or to the public sector. Even payments connected with capital formation in one region are likely to be made largely to residents in others. Increases in rates of growth of income and population in any region are, moreover, likely to induce increases in its rate of capital formation only gradually. In these circumstances, an autonomous increase in regional income is not likely to initiate a self-reinforcing chain of further increases; its effect on the region's growth may be expected rather to be not much greater than, and to last not much longer than, the autonomous increase itself. In the last decade or two, the richer half of the United Kingdom has grown in income and

[1] G. Myrdal, *Economic Theory and Underdeveloped Regions*, London, Duckworth, 1957.

population about half of 1 per cent per annum faster than the poorer half. This extra growth might be expected to be responsible for additional capital formation and, through that, for additional total demand for regional resources in the richer half of the country as compared with the poorer half, amounting to something like $1\frac{1}{2}$ per cent of the richer half's income. This is by no means a negligible difference, but it is small in comparison with many sources of demand that have varying regional impacts, such as public expenditure on goods and services, or the rate of replacement of existing capital stock. It is also small enough to be cancelled out by interregional differences in the capital–output ratios in the different regions arising from their different industrial structures. Indeed the evidence suggests that the ratio of gross investment to income may have been higher in the slower growing than in the faster growing half of the country – the former specialises on more capital-intensive industry and has an older stock of buildings and infrastructure generally, which have been falling due for replacement at a faster rate. The faster replacement in the older industrial areas, despite their being on the whole the poorer ones, is a very important stabilising factor in development. Its existence depends largely, of course, on the high degree of central control in financing of social capital expenditure; a very notable feature of the United Kingdom economy. The tendency for faster growth to have a self-reinforcing character through the interaction of the multiplier and capital stock adjustment seems, therefore, in this instance to have been offset by other factors. The suggestion is that, in British conditions, it need not be taken too seriously.

We have looked also at some less tangible dynamic mechanisms of self-reinforcement in growth differences; the attractions of the younger social capital and the younger population that characterise areas of immigration. Perhaps they are more important than the more strictly economic mechanisms that have just been discussed; it is hard to say, though there is evidence that they exercise an appreciable effect on the movement of footloose industry. One mechanism formerly of some power has, however, been greatly weakened. The vicious circle of poverty, low local revenue and poor local services, leading to low attractiveness to footloose industry and footloose residents, has much less destabilising power than in the circumstances of heavy dependence of local services on local taxation that applied here fifty years ago, and that applies in many countries still. Financial centralisation is a great stabiliser of regional economies.

IS REGIONAL POLICY NECESSARY?

In the light of all these considerations, what can be said about the desirability, or necessity, of some kind of regional policy in the United Kingdom? It is clear from the start that the interregional disparities of economic opportunity and well-being are smaller here than in most countries (obviously smaller than in Italy for instance); that we do not face a tendency towards concentration of growth in a metropolitan area to the extent that (say) France does; that rural depopulation, which is the main component of regional problems in many countries, is not a major worry here, since there is no region where rural pursuits any longer occupy much of the population; that there are no whole regions and few standard subregions that are declining in population significantly through net outward migration. Is there a problem requiring attention?

Before attempting an answer, one should note two further facts. First, we undoubtedly did have a regional problem of real severity, even by international standards, between the two world wars, when over 10 per cent more of the insured population was unemployed in Wales and the northern half of the country than in southern England, more than half the increase of population was concentrated in London and the Home Counties alone, and Wales suffered a substantial absolute fall in population through net emigration. We have had some kind of regional policy since the mid-thirties, without which the disparities of regional growth, of demand pressure and of unemployment would presumably have been bigger, at least since the war, than they have actually been. Are the forces that produced the interwar regional problem approaching exhaustion (or have they vanished and been replaced by others), and what part has policy played in containing whatever forces of this kind have recently been in action?

The most obvious of the systematic forces making for difference in regional growth rates has been differences in regional industrial composition, allied with differences in the growth rates of industries, generally attributable to the conditions of their national or world markets. The other systematic element that can be identified in regional growth differences – though less easily attributed to a satisfying proximate cause – is the tendency of some regions to show significantly fast growth in all their industries, and of others to show significantly slow growth in relation to national growth rates of the industries in question. These elements are not as easy to disentangle and interpret as might at first sight appear, and there are others – notably the tendency of some regions to show significantly fast or significantly slow growth (in relation to the national performance of the industries in question) in the particular industries on which they most specialise. A reasonable estimate can be made however, of the extent to which a region's growth has been fast or slow in relation to the national growth by virtue of its having been fortunate or unfortunate in its industrial composition. For the forty-year period 1921–61, these 'composition elements' in growth differences seem to have been about as important as, or rather more important than, the systematic tendencies of regions to do well or badly across the whole range of industries.

For the purpose of answering the question whether the forces making for regional differences in growth are decaying, one can first look at the changes in this 'composition component' over time. In the forty years 1921–61, employment in Wales was growing $\frac{1}{2}$ per cent a year slower than the United Kingdom total by virtue of this element, in the North and the East Midlands $\frac{1}{3}$ per cent slower, in Yorkshire and Humberside $\frac{1}{4}$ per cent slower, and in South East England over $\frac{1}{3}$ per cent a year faster. Scotland, the North West and the West Midlands showed composition components that were surprisingly small, partly because of the peculiarities of the industrial classification used. In the five-year period 1961–6, the composition components of the regions stood in a fairly similar order (though the North not Wales had the most unfavourable one) but they were on the whole larger. The North was falling behind for composition reasons at nearly 1 per cent a year, the South-East gaining at $\frac{2}{3}$ per cent. One should add that in the earlier six years, 1953–9, when it had been widely felt that regional problems were not pressing and regional policy had been on the whole rather gently applied, the interregional range of composition components had been rather smaller, though not so very much smaller than in the whole period 1921–61. In the whole thirteen years 1953–66, the range of composition components was still somewhat greater than in the partly overlapping forty-year period ending in 1961.

In spite, therefore, of the obvious fact that composition components of growth differences are self-extinguishing, as the declining industries that give a region a bad composition shrink relative to others, and in spite of the manifestly much reduced national and regional importance of the well known culprits, coalmining, cotton textiles, railways and shipbuilding, composition seems to have increased its importance – or at least to show no sign of decreasing it. The reason, of course, is partly that some new declining or slow growing industries have appeared, but much more that some fast growers have been getting more important (largely in the service sector of the economy) and that they are quite strongly localised in the regions that are least handicapped by the traditional declining trades of the last fifty years.

Indeed, the interregional disparities in actual growth rates of employment have shown signs of increasing rather than decreasing. They rose from 1921–61 to 1959–66, and were higher in the latter period than in 1953–9. The only item on the other side of the ledger is a fall between 1953–9 and 1959–66 in the divergence that can be estimated to be attributable to growth components – the tendency for some regions to show larger rates of growth than others industry by industry. And this is the element that one would expect to be influenced directly and immediately by regional policy.

One cannot, of course, say what would have happened to the distribution of employment growth in the absence of any regional policy at all, even on rather heroic *ceteris paribus* assumptions, because there has been no recent period when some regional policy was not operating. It is, however, clear that after the immediate postwar period in which Development Areas were strongly favoured by largely temporary postwar factors, there was a time from the early to late fifties when positive incentives to locate in these areas were not very strong and checks on expansion elsewhere were comparatively mildly administered. After this policy and its administration were gradually strengthened until at least the middle sixties; one may hope to estimate how much difference the strengthening of policy made.

We have seen that there is a considerable degree of agreement between evidence of industrial development approvals and evidence about industry by industry rates of employment growth that, between the later fifties and the early sixties, some influence, which is most likely to have been the great strengthening of regional policy at that time, caused an increase in the rate of increase of manufacturing jobs in the Development Areas by a number that is probably in excess of 30,000 a year. This would be likely to mean, through the long-term multiplier, an eventual additional rate of increase of jobs in industry as a whole by something like 50,000 a year.

In view of what can be tentatively gathered about the responsiveness of labour migration and movement of industry to unemployment differences, a reasonable conclusion from this is that, when this rate of job-creation had been in operation for a few years, registered and unregistered unemployment in the four regions would settle down to an equilibrium level which, for any given level of unemployment in the rest of the country, would be 150,000 to 200,000 lower than it would have been in the absence of the regional policy changes that have taken place since the late fifties. In other words, without this strengthening of policy the indication is that registered unemployment in the high-unemployment regions would in recent years have stood 1 to $1\frac{1}{2}$ percentage points higher than it actually has been, and net emigration from them would have been something like twice as great as it actually was, involving a loss virtually equal in total to all their natural increase – for Scotland much more, for the others less.

The conclusion then is that without the strengthening of regional policy that began in the late fifties, and *a fortiori* without any regional policy at all, we should have been confronted in the sixties with strongly augmented versions of our traditional regional problems. There would probably have been a doubling of the net inflow of British migrants into the prosperous southern half of the country that is largely centred on its biggest and most congested agglomeration; a sizeable absolute fall in the population of one major and highly selfconscious region; a much increased disparity in regional growth rates in general, which might well have been sufficient to override the existing bias towards higher replacement and capital-intensiveness in the north, and to augment itself significantly through various mechanisms of cumulative and circular causation; and probably almost a $\frac{1}{2}$ per cent addition to the national unemployment rate, without any slackening of demand pressure in the prosperous regions where wage inflation seems mostly to be generated. There is no indication that the tendencies towards disparities of regional growth or the forces behind them have been slackening or are likely to do so. Indeed, entry into the European Economic Community would seem likely to increase the differences, as it probably has within the Community already. When the central growth area is one stretching from Lombardy to Paris and Hamburg, Scotland, Wales and Northern Ireland will presumably suffer more from positions peripheral to their market area than they do now. If, therefore, regional disparities very substantially stronger than any we have experienced since the war are to be avoided, some sort of regional policy is certainly necessary.

How necessary or desirable is it to avoid these additional disparities? The costs of some of them can be given rough orders of magnitude – others cannot. The loss of output from having 150,000–200,000 fewer people in work because of a relative mislocation of people and jobs would be £150–£200 million a year, plus probably half as much again if plant was as much under-used in the regions of labour shortage as labour was in those of job shortage. Beyond this there is a further loss of production, possibly considerably greater but not easily calculable, that would result from a slower drawing into employment of women in the regions where their participation rates are low. The increase in congestion costs (or costs of the means of avoiding them) that would result from a higher concentration of growth in the southern half of England might also be large, but it too defies precise estimation.

These costs probably do not amount altogether to more than a few per cent of gross national product, but the impact on national life of the regional problem from which they sprang would be greater than this economic calculation alone would suggest. Regional problems consist most vitally of senses of grievance and resentment in selfconscious communities. The experience of most countries, including the United Kingdom, provides plenty of examples of the social and political importance of these.

WHAT POLICY?

It follows from the earlier part of this discussion that there is no radical change in the interregional distribution of population that is self-evidently required as an overriding long-term object of policy, except to the extent that the great size of London's present and prospective congestion problem puts a strain on the resources of space and natural amenities in the South East and creates a presumption in favour of discouraging the further relative increase of that region's population. We are not in the position of France, where there is a shortage of foci of growth alternative to Paris – of métropoles d'équilibre. The nineteenth century presented us with such foci in the shape, mainly, of the other six conurbations; the trouble is that, beside (like London) requiring much physical redevelopment and local dispersion into overspill centres, most of them have been suffering, and will inevitably go on suffering for some time to come, from unfavourable industrial structures and, to some extent, from attitudes not conducive to new growth. They are far too big and too conscious of their identity to be abandoned or run down (at least against a background of growing national population), as might some remoter and smaller communities that grew up on mining or agriculture; the problem is to help them to get a second wind, as the West Midlands did in the late nineteenth century.

The problem arises at two levels of urgency. First, in all the main Development Areas (and until recently very little outside them) lack of growth in demand for labour goes with substantial unemployment, registered and unregistered, despite substantial net outward migration. This is the classic situation in which there is manifest waste of resources. It can be dealt with either by stimulating the Area's demand for labour, or (as in the interwar Industrial Transference scheme) by stimulating outward migration. Which one does – or in what proportions one mixes the two – should depend partly on relative cost and partly on locational strategy. If it is accepted that, on grounds of the latter, the relative growth of the south should be discouraged rather than encouraged, then assistance to migration – which is on balance from north to south – should be used with discretion where encouragement to job-movement is a feasible alternative. It must be remembered too that net outward migration harms an area's prospects, partly through multiplier and capital stock effects, partly because it is selective. Moving people out to some extent makes it harder to move (or tempt) industry in.

This is not to say that there is no place for encouragement of labour migration beyond the very small extent of existing schemes. Ideally it should be possible to take a firm view that certain areas – notably the remoter agricultural and mining (or ex-mining) villages or small towns, where the pattern of settlement, as well as inaccessibility, climate, or other physical circumstances are against modern development – can best be run down, in which case it would be rational to give all possible encouragement and help to people to move to places where there is a prospect of growth. The same may be true of isolated places based on smelting, and similar establishments which become obsolete and are wrongly sited for modernisation, and it would, of course, be wholly rational to assist movement connected with overspill schemes. The major aggregations of industry and population that suffer from heavy and persistent unemployment, however, seem, prima facie, more suitable for encouragement to expand than to contract – contraction at least in relation to the national total being their tendency if nothing is done.

At the second level of urgency come the 'grey areas' dealt with by the Hunt Report,[1] where employment growth is slow or in some cases negative, but net outward migration, usually assisted by a low rate of natural increase, is sufficient to prevent heavy overt unemployment – though in some cases there has been a fall or an abnormally low increase in activity rates. At first sight it seems possible to take the view that in such cases no action is very insistently called for. Apart from the cases where activity rates are depressed (so that there is in effect concealed unemployment) and those, if they exist, where shrinkage of local communities is such that there is some waste of social capital, and apart too from psychic and social costs of migration, there is no clear waste of resources. Local interests, of course, complain, and the places in question often take on a dispirited air, but it can be argued that this is balanced in the national account by the extra growth and euphoria that are enabled to exist in the areas of immigration.

But on further inspection there is more to be said. First, there is the question of locational strategy. Once more, if we want in the long run to take some of the pressure of congestion away from the South East, can we afford to ignore potential growth centres, already highly developed, in, for instance, Yorkshire and non-Merseyside Lancashire? Not all of the subregional areas concerned, of course, have good potentialities for the growth of newly injected enterprise, but some of them, by any available criterion, have. Secondly, there are as we have noted some self-reinforcing elements in the marked relative decline of an area

---

[1] Department of Economic Affairs, *The Intermediate Areas*.

coupled with substantial net outward migration, and even if these do not operate as dramatically as has sometimes been claimed, they carry the threat that the 'grey areas' (or some of them) may degenerate spontaneously into high-unemployment areas. Any self-reinforcing disease is easier to treat when it is still mild.

These considerations seem to point in a general way towards assistance to growth in at least the major areas of high unemployment, and also (presumably on a lower scale) to at least some areas of slow growth where overt unemployment is not especially high. The present policy is one – but by no means the only possible one – that may be said to conform to this broad prescription. The next question is how selectively and how flexibly the policy should be pursued. The Act of 1960 provided assistance that was selective in the sense that it was given to, and only to, small areas of manifest need (in the sense of high unemployment), and flexible in that it was given only so long as unemployment continued high. By fairly general consent these features had unfortunate aspects, and they were, in practice, soon modified. Assistance does not have its full effect as an incentive unless there is some certainty that it will continue. It is true that uncertainty matters less when the assistance is limited to investment than when it affects current costs, but even with investment assistance firms like to be sure that it will be available not only for an initial outlay but also for future extensions. It was even clearer from experience in the early sixties that unemployment is not a suitable criterion for eligibility if small areas are the units for decision. The best help for a particular small area of high unemployment may be development not within it but in a neighbouring area, preferably within daily travelling range.

These questions of selectivity and flexibility turn on the validity of the argument for growth points – a relatively small number of limited areas on which help is concentrated (preferably guaranteed for a substantial time), in the belief that assistance is most economical when concentrated on areas of high initial potential, and/or that concentrations of industry create economies external to the establishment that will be lost if no impulse towards concentration is given. The case for concentrating help on such points was popular here in the early sixties, and has been incorporated in policy in France and Italy – in the latter especially with the addition of a determined attempt to create a complex of linked industries at one of the chosen sites. The case for such a complex has also been stated by consultants in connection with the central Lancashire new town.[1]

The appropriate degree and form of concentration on growth points naturally depends on the general context of problems and policy.

[1] Economic Consultants Ltd, op. cit.

Wherever it is plain that the existing pattern of settlement is inappropriate – as in southern Italy and much of France, where development consists to a great extent of industrialising and urbanising rural economies – the State, if it has any important economic functions, is bound to take a view about the desirable physical shape of development, if only because it is called upon to provide much infrastructure in advance. This is true also of new town development and, in a lesser degree, of industrial estate and advance factory provision in this country. Having committed itself to provision of expensive facilities on particular sites, it is rational for the State to direct its further assistance towards seeing that those facilities are used. Whether the case for a particular kind of industrial complex can be established in a country as compact and highly industrialised as Britain is rather a different matter; the case for it would be stronger in Scotland or Northern Ireland, where the factor of remoteness from other centres is at its strongest, than in central Lancashire. In any case, Italian experience suggests that the implementation of a fully fledged industrial complex policy is difficult unless the State is prepared to fill with enterprises of its own any important gaps that remain in the structure of the complex that it can recruit from private industry.

New towns and industrial estates are powerful instruments of development consistent with the general philosophy of growth centres, but in British conditions it seems unlikely that they are best fitted to be the only, or even the main, instruments of salvation. In any case they often need the instruments of industrial development certificates and official persuasion, and may need positive incentives to draw industry to them. More important, however, is the fact that re-vitalising an already industrialised and urbanised economy which already has much adequate or good infrastructure is a very different operation from urbanising a rural population or re-deploying one that is scattered in mining communities. The older industrial regions contain great numbers of sites for development or redevelopment where many of the external economies of established industrial areas are already available. What they need, besides help in refurbishing the less attractive features of their built environment, is inducements to bring new enterprise in. It is perhaps reasonable to suppose that such new enterprise is adequately able to choose the particular sites that suit it within such areas if information about existing and prospective facilities is made available to it. If this is so, then the present 'broad brush' policy of scheduling relatively large areas for assistance is justified.

What this implies is that, in British conditions, there is a large part to be played by incentives or other pressure to get industry to move to, or expand in, established industrial areas where existing industry is going downhill, though this is not to the exclusion of more specific measures of the new town or industrial estate kind where radical redeployment of population is called for. What kinds of incentives or pressure are most suitable?

Provision of infrastructure is one form of incentive – or an alternative to the provision of incentives if the latter are defined more narrowly. Inadequacy of any of a number of facilities – housing, public utility services, road communications – can obviously act as a bottleneck impeding development, but use of infrastructure improvement to induce enterprise to favour a particular site implies that the quality of the service is raised somewhat above what the expected demand would justify according to the criteria applied elsewhere, or is provided further in advance. The presumption is that such a policy – building motorways further ahead of full demand for their capacity than elsewhere, for instance – is expensive in real resources in comparison with (say) financial inducements. Motorways consume real resources, whereas financial inducements are money transfers which have an effect of only the second order of magnitude upon the total amount left for consumption and investment. The development-inducing power of infrastructure improvements (as distinct from their cost-saving power) remains very difficult to ascertain, or even to detect in many cases. The conclusion from this is that, while removal of infrastructure bottlenecks is important, infrastructure provision in advance of the normal standards is not in most cases an economical substitute for other locational incentives or pressures.

It has been argued earlier in this discussion that there is evidence that policy – mostly implemented by financial incentives and industrial development restrictions – has brought about large changes in the direction and volume of interregional industrial movement and the interregional distribution of industrial building. Unfortunately the different instruments of policy have seldom been introduced or varied one at a time, and matters have been further confused by the frequency of changes coupled with uncertainty about the length of time some measures take to become effective, so that conclusions about the effectiveness of particular instruments are hard to reach.

There is, however, a presumption that the combination of industrial development certificates with positive incentives to industry in the assisted areas has had effects bigger than the sum of the effects that the restrictions and the incentives would have had by themselves. Firms have been obliged to examine alternatives that they would otherwise have ignored. The combination must be regarded as a well-tried and effective one that should be retained in some form. The best shape for the incentive element in it is less certain. It seems clear that there was a big increase in the effectiveness of policy after 1963, when incentives were both increased and made more automatic. Part of this was probably due to administrative action, but there is evidence that incentives were important. There was some further improvement (taking account of adverse changes in the level of prosperity) after the 1966 Act, which, while it did not raise the level of incentives in general, made the advantages clearer.

Apart from more specific (and in recent practice smaller) kinds of assistance, the choice with regard to financial incentives lies between capital and current assistance, and also between cash grants and remission of tax liabilities. With regard to the former choice, the balance in this country (and largely in others) has been heavily on the side of capital. In so far as assistance has been discretionary (as under the Local Employment Acts), it has been possible to keep what was given in some relation to the employment-creating effects of the investment, but with the more automatic systems, which had substantial advantages because of their automatic nature, the effect has been to give relative encouragement to capital-intensive industry in the assisted areas. In 1966-7 in particular, this effect can be shown to have been very strong; this makes poor economic sense and renders the system unduly expensive. The simplest way to avoid it is to balance assistance geared to capital with that geared to expenditure on labour, so that the latter is encouraged in assisted areas at least as much as the former. Even the Regional Employment Premium has not done that; it has subsidised employment only about half as much proportionately as capital costs were subsidised. The form of help that would be perfectly neutral in this connection is one geared to value added; remissions of Value-Added Tax when it is introduced would have much to commend them provided that the tax liability of multi-plant firms could be, for this purpose, allocated between establishments in assisted areas and those outside – perhaps on the basis of employment if no better method were practicable.

On the other hand, there seems to be evidence that remissions of tax are less powerful as incentives than cash grants. One reason for believing this is the habit of the majority of firms, even large ones, of calculating rates of return on investment without taking account of tax – at least according to evidence gathered by the Richardson Committee[1] and by a National Institute study in 1964.[2] Another is the manifest liquidity advantages (at least so far as capital assistance is concerned) of cash benefits as near as possible to the dates of heavy expenditure. A third is the popularity of investment grants according to common observa-

---

[1] Inland Revenue, *Report of the Committee on Turnover Taxation*.
[2] Neild, 'Replacement Policy'.

tion. Where, in addition, the tax remitted is that on profits, there is the added disadvantage that the concession fails to benefit infant establishments, which are unlikely to be making profits for some years, unless (a quite irrelevant circumstance) they are financially integrated with other establishments that are making profits. Continuing subsidies however, are harder to reconcile with the Treaty of Rome than tax concessions.

Another suggestion of recent experience is that the prospect of continuing cash payments is less effective in stimulating investment than a lump-sum benefit. It is hard to detect any effect on the proportion of total factory building that takes place in the Development Areas that can be attributed to the introduction of the Regional Employment Premium in 1967. There is some evidence that the assisted regions showed better improvements in growth of employment in manufacturing, industry by industry, than the others between 1965–7 and 1967–9, though the only dramatic changes were the improvement in Scotland and the deterioration in the East Midlands. The Regional Employment Premium, however, was designed to have the same kind of effect as a devaluation, and we know from national experience that devaluations take a long time to become effective. The conclusion to be drawn is perhaps that, while continuing benefits (either by way of tax remission or subsidy) have a long-term function in what should be a long-term policy, they are slower in getting differential growth started than those lump-sum benefits which, if discounting were properly done, would be their equivalents.

A final general question about the form of incentives is whether continuing benefits should relate (like the Regional Employment Premium) to all enterprises of the classes to be assisted, new and old, or only to newly established ones. The latter course is obviously cheaper, but it raises great problems both of administration and of equity – firms closing down and re-starting, competing establishments of which one started just before and one just after the date of operation of the scheme. It seems that, in practice, any benefit confined to new or 'incoming' enterprises must be temporary, even if, like the operational grants in Special Development Areas, it lasts for a considerable time.

CHANGES AFTER 1970

The analysis in this book has taken as its material experience up to the year 1970. In that year the instruments of regional policy changed. There was a reversion to accelerated depreciation as the main incentive to investment in Development Areas (an incentive of considerably smaller discounted cash value than the investment grant differential of the preceding five years); additional Special Development Areas were scheduled and additional grants for new establishments in these areas, related to their employment, were introduced; and the Regional Employment Premium was put under notice of termination. Subsequently in March 1972, accelerated depreciation ceased to operate as a differential regional incentive, and investment grants were reintroduced in an altered form on industrial building work as well as plant and machinery. Additional assistance was given to mobility of labour in (and from) the assisted areas. At the same time industrial development certificate requirements were substantially relaxed. It was not immediately clear whether the total force of regional policy instruments was stronger than in the sixties.

What had altered drastically was the general level of unemployment, which in February 1972 reached 3·9 per cent in the country as a whole. As in previous recessions of activity the ratio of the highest regional levels to the lowest decreased, but the absolute difference between them rose. The gap between the male unemployment rates of Scotland and the North on the one hand and the South East on the other reached more than 5 per cent of the labour force, between two and three times the average difference of the fifties and sixties as a whole. At the same time unemployment in the North West and Yorkshire and Humberside rose relatively to a level more nearly central between the extremes, that in the West Midlands also rose in relation to the South East and South West, and Wales showed a considerable relative improvement.

What difference do these changes make to the picture of the regional problem that this book (and, in summary, the present chapter) have tried to present? Essentially, perhaps not very much. In conditions of deficient effective demand in the economy as a whole, the Development Areas always suffer relatively for a number of reasons. Their structures are such as to make them rather more sensitive cyclically than the rest of the country. There is probably some tendency for branch establishments to bear more of the burden of any cut-back in production than the parent establishments do. The inflow of industry from the rest of the country is certainly sensitive to fluctuations in the general level of demand. There is no reason to suppose that recovery of demand will not have its usual effect on the interregional differential, which is no bigger than one would expect in relation to the general level of unemployment.

There has been apprehension that the high unemployment of 1971-2 is in substantial part due to the increase of a frictional element, attributed to increased ability or willingness of labour to bear unemployment (by virtue of earnings-related benefits and redundancy payments), or of a structural element due to an increased degree of mis-match between demand and supply consequent upon accelerated technical or structural change. Some fear that one or both of these elements will persist into more prosperous times. If the former element – change in attitude to unemployment – did so, there is no obvious reason why it should affect regions very differently; one would simply expect a higher national level of registered unemployment to be normal, with interregional absolute differentials not much altered. If, on the other hand, technical or structural change (especially the latter) has increased in pace more than temporarily, one would expect the equilibrium differentials between regional unemployment rates to continue at a higher level than in the past because of increased interregional differences in growth of demand. In this case, therefore, the need for regional policy would be greater than in the period covered by this study. But though (as we have argued) the structural element in interregional growth differences showed a rising trend in the last twenty years, the recent unemployment returns do not themselves give any reason for supposing that it has suddenly taken a great leap forward. If it proves to have done so, the call will be for stronger measures of regional policy than in the past.

CONCLUSION

But the purpose of this book is not to prescribe measures of policy for hypothetical situations. It has been intended primarily as an analysis of the regional problem and the setting within which regional policy in the United Kingdom has to be considered.

What are its salient findings? The root of the United Kingdom's regional problem is a mis-match between regional rates of natural increase of population and regional rates of growth of employment opportunity, allied with the necessarily imperfect mobility of enterprises and people, and with the sense of attachment that people feel to communities and places. The mis-match is traceable mostly to the different degrees in which regions have specialised on the industries that happen now to be growing, in some cases augmented by differences in accessibility or centrality and by the self-reinforcing effects of success (or its opposite) on environment, morale and attractiveness to footloose enterprise. It is mitigated, quite powerfully, by the extremely close commercial connections of the regions – far beyond anything yet demonstrated by State members of common markets – and by the powerful pooling and stabilising machinery of progressive taxation and centralised public expenditure. It has been mitigated also, powerfully since the beginning of the sixties, by deliberate regional policy, despite a tendency in the last twenty years for the structural elements in the underlying mis-match to get stronger.

The fruits of the mis-match are unemployment, open and concealed; income differences; unevenness of demand pressure, which is inflationary in so far as it is the region of highest pressure that sets the pace of cost increase for the rest; the demoralisation or exasperation of some regional communities by lack of prosperity, and diseconomies of aggregation – or the circumscribing of the planners' options for avoiding them – in others. The United Kingdom has not suffered from these evils in an acute degree, except when some of them have been exacerbated by general lack of effective demand in the economy as a whole. Some of them are more serious than others, and some can in principle be exchanged for others. We have for instance some choice (probably hard to put into practice) between regional unemployment and interregional inequality of incomes. But the main choice is the old one between moving people and moving jobs. The latter are far the less responsive, in the absence of policy, to the forces of mutual adjustment inherent in the market mechanism, and while large movements of both jobs and people carry dangers of unacceptable cost, partly psychic, social and political, it is those of the movements of people that lie nearer to the surface.

It is between the costs of these two kinds of movement and the obvious and heavy costs of non-movement that policy has to pick a delicate way. The one thing that can be predicted with confidence is that, in one form or another, the forces that create the need for such policy will continue to operate. Probably they will grow. They are aspects of change, and the rate of change of most things in the economic world is increasing. Our problem in very much its present form has persisted through major phases both of contraction and of expansion in world trade and specialisation; there is every reason to suppose that, in a form not very different, and probably more markedly, it will continue to be evident in a larger economic community, especially one that encourages international movement but does not yet possess the built-in stabilisers that centralised public finance provides between the United Kingdom regions.

In the last analysis, the need for regional policy is not simply a regrettable aspect of a temporary economic sickness – a view that the British have been disposed to take of their economic problems for at least fifty years. It is a normal part of the life of any economic community that likes (or even tolerates) change, but has the humanity to recognise that the economy was made for man and not man for the economy.

LIST OF WORKS CITED

I. BOOKS, ARTICLES AND OTHER SOURCES

ARCHIBALD, G. C. 'Regional Multiplier Effects in the UK', *Oxford Economic Papers* (new series), vol. 19, no. 1, March 1967, pp. 22–45.
BECKERMAN, W. and Associates. *The British Economy in 1975*, Cambridge University Press, 1965.
BIRD, P. A. and THIRLWALL, A. P. 'The Incentive to Invest in the new Development Areas', *District Bank Review*, no. 162, June 1967, pp. 27–45.
BORTS, G. H. and STEIN, J. L. *Economic Growth in a Free Market*, New York, Columbia University Press, 1964.
BOWERS, J. K. *The Anatomy of Regional Activity Rates*, NIESR Regional Papers I, Cambridge University Press, 1970.
— 'An analysis of regional rates of employment growth' (unpublished).
BOWERS, J. K., CHESHIRE, P. C. and WEBB, A. E. 'The change in the relationship between unemployment and earnings increases: a review of some possible explanations', *National Institute Economic Review*, no. 54, November 1970, pp. 44–63.
British Railways Board. *Rail Wagon Load Survey 1964* (unpublished).
BROWN, A. J. 'The Green Paper on the Development Areas', *National Institute Economic Review*, no. 40, May 1967, pp. 26–33.
CAIRNCROSS, A. K. *Home and Foreign Investment, 1870–1913*, Cambridge University Press, 1953.
CHESHIRE, P. C. *An Investigation of Regional Unemployment Differences*, NIESR Regional Papers II (forthcoming).
CLARK, Colin. 'Industrial Location and Economic Potential', *Lloyds Bank Review*, no. 82, October 1966, pp. 1–17.
Confederation of British Industry. 'Survey of experience of firms applying for industrial development certificates in the South East and North West regions' (unpublished evidence presented to the Hunt Committee).
COWLING, K. and METCALF, D. 'Wage–Unemployment Relationships: a regional analysis for the UK 1960–65', *Bulletin of the Oxford Institute of Economics and Statistics*, vol. 29, no. 1, February 1967, pp. 31–9.
DEANE, Phyllis and COLE, W. A. *British Economic Growth 1688–1959*, Cambridge University Press, 1962.
Economic Consultants Ltd. *Study for an Industrial Complex in Central Lancashire*, London, 1969.
FLINN, M. W. *British Population Growth 1700–1850*, London, Macmillan, 1970.
HAMMOND, Edwin. *An Analysis of Regional Economic and Social Statistics*, Durham University Press, 1968.
HART, R. A. 'A Model of Inter-regional Migration in England and Wales', *Regional Studies*, vol. 4, no. 3, October 1970, pp. 279–96.
LEE, C. H. *Regional Economic Growth in the United Kingdom since the 1880's*, Maidenhead, McGraw Hill, 1971.
LOASBY, B. J. 'Making Location Policy Work', *Lloyds Bank Review*, no. 83, January 1967, pp. 34–47.
LUTTRELL, W. F. *Factory Location and Industrial Movement*, London, National Institute of Economic and Social Research, 1962.
MAKOWER, H., MARSCHAK, J. and ROBINSON, H. W. 'Studies in Mobility of Labour', *Oxford Economic Papers*, no. 2, May 1939, pp. 70–97 and no. 4, September 1940, pp. 39–62.
MATTHEWS, R. C. O. *The Trade Cycle*, Cambridge University Press, 1958.
MEADE, J. E. *A Neo-Classical Theory of Economic Growth*, London, Allen and Unwin, 1961.
MITCHELL, B. R. and DEANE, Phyllis. *Abstract of British Historical Statistics*, Cambridge University Press, 1962.
MOORE, F. T. and PETERSON, J. W. 'Regional Analysis: an interindustry model of Utah', *Review of Economics and Statistics*, vol. 37, no. 4, November 1955, pp. 368–83.

LIST OF WORKS CITED 349

Myrdal, G. *Economic Theory and Underdeveloped Regions*, London, Duckworth, 1957.
Neild, R. R. 'Replacement Policy', *National Institute Economic Review*, no. 30, November 1964, pp. 30–43.
Nevin, E., Roe, A. R. and Round, J. I. *The Structure of the Welsh Economy*, Cardiff, University of Wales Press, 1966.
Prest, A. R. 'The Sensitivity of the Yield of Personal Income Tax in the United Kingdom', *Economic Journal*, vol. 72, no. 287, September 1962, pp. 576–96.
Richardson, H. W. *Regional Economics*, London, Weidenfeld and Nicolson, 1969.
— *Elements of Regional Economics*, London, Penguin Books, 1969.
Scottish Council (Development and Industry). *Report on the Scottish Economy 1960–61*, Edinburgh, 1962.
Smith, Wilfred. *An Economic Geography of Great Britain*, London, Methuen, 1949.
Weeden, R. 'Regional rates of growth of employment: an analysis of variance treatment' (unpublished).
Welham, P. J. *Monetary Circulation in the United Kingdom*, Oxford, Blackwell, 1969.
Welton, T. A. *England's Recent Progress*, London, Chapman and Hall, 1911.
Woodward, V. H. *Regional Social Accounts for the United Kingdom*, NIESR Regional Papers I, Cambridge University Press, 1970.

II. OFFICIAL PUBLICATIONS

Ministry of Agriculture. *Household Food Consumption and Expenditure: Annual Report of the National Food Survey Committee, 1964*, London, HMSO, 1965.
Central Statistical Office. *National Income and Expenditure 1964*, London, HMSO, 1964.
— *Duration of Unemployment on the Register of Wholly Unemployed*, by R. F. Fowler, Studies in Official Statistics, Research Series, no. 1, London, HMSO, 1968.
— *Input–Output Tables for the United Kingdom 1963*, London, HMSO, 1970.
Department of Economic Affairs. *The Development Areas: a proposal for a regional employment premium*, London, HMSO, 1967.
— *The Intermediate Areas*, Cmnd 3998, London, HMSO, 1969 [the 'Hunt Report'].
Department of the Environment. *Survey of the Transport of Goods by Road 1967–1968. Report and Tables, Great Britain*, London, HMSO, 1972.
General Register Office. *Census 1961. England and Wales. Occupation Tables*, London, HMSO, 1966.
— *Census 1961. Scotland. Occupation Tables*, Edinburgh, HMSO, 1966.
— *Sample Census 1966. Great Britain. Economic Activity Tables*, London, HMSO, 1968.
— *Sample Census 1966. England and Wales. Migration Tables*, London, HMSO, 1968–9.
— *Sample Census 1966. Scotland. Migration Tables*, Edinburgh, HMSO, 1968–9.
Government Social Survey. *Labour Mobility in Great Britain 1953–63*, by A. I. Harris and R. Clausen, London, 1966.
Inland Revenue. *Report of the Committee on Turnover Taxation*, Cmnd 2300, London, HMSO, 1964.
— *112th Report of the Commissioners of Inland Revenue, 1968/9*, Cmnd 4262, London, HMSO, 1970.
Ministry of Labour. *Family Expenditure Survey 1966*, London, HMSO, 1967.
— *Ministry of Labour Gazette* (monthly) [now *Department of Employment Gazette*].
— *Statistics on Incomes, Prices, Employment and Productivity* (monthly).
Ministry of Power. *Statistical Digest 1966*, London, HMSO, 1967.
Ministry of Reconstruction. *Employment Policy*, Cmd 6527, London, HMSO, 1944.
Royal Commission on the Distribution of Industrial Population. *Report*, Cmd 6153, London, HMSO, 1939 [the 'Barlow Peport'].
Royal Commission on Local Government in England. *Local Government Reform*, Cmnd 4039, London, HMSO, 1969 [the 'Redcliffe Maud Report'].
Ministry of Social Security. *Report of an Inquiry into the Incidence of Incapacity for Work*, Part II: *Incidence of Incapacity for Work in Different Areas and Occupations*, London, HMSO, 1966.
Board of Trade. *Final Report on the Census of Production for 1948*, London, HMSO, 1951–2.

Board of Trade. *Report on the Census of Production for 1954*, London, HMSO, 1960–3.
— *Central Scotland. A programme for development and growth*, Cmnd 2188, London, HMSO, 1963.
— *The North East. A programme for regional development and growth*, Cmnd 2206, London, HMSO, 1963.
— *The Movement of Manufacturing Industry in the United Kingdom, 1945–65*, London, HMSO, 1968.
Department of Trade and Industry. *Inquiry into Location Attitudes and Experience* (unpublished 1971).
— *Trade and Industry* (weekly).
Ministry of Transport. *Survey of Road Goods Transport 1962. Final Commodity Analysis*, London, HMSO, 1964.

United Nations Statistical Office. *Yearbook of National Accounts Statistics 1967*, New York, 1968.

INDEX

Activity rates, 57; female, 208–14; male, 205–8
aggregation, costs and benefits, 164–75, 324
agriculture, 43, 116, 325–6
Archibald, G. C., 185

Barlow Commission, 4, 23, 173
Barlow Report, 4, 286
Beckerman, W., 193
Bird, P. A., 306n
Borts, G. H., 86, 97
Bowers, J. K, 133n, 205n; and Cheshire, P. C. and Webb, A. E., 241n
Brown, A. J., 308n
building controls, 286–7, 292; see also industrial development certificates
building grants, 288, 289, 306

Cairncross, A. K. (now Sir Alec), 110, 111
capital: growth, 86, 99; mobility, 250–2; stock adjustment, 21–2, 26, 96, 176, 192–202, 339
capital–output ratios, 192, 193, 196–7, 199
Census of Distribution, 53
Census of Population, 39, 40, 42, 44–6, 48, 124, 137, 206, 207, 215, 229, 253, 258, 271, 328
Census of Production, 52, 152–5, 157, 159, 248
Cheshire, P. C., 215n; and Bowers, J. K. and Webb, A. E., 241n
Clark, Colin, 160, 161
Clausen, R., 13
coalmining, 116, 118, 119, 285, 287
coefficients of concentration, 38
coefficients of localisation, 147, 149–50
coefficients of specialisation, 38–40, 147–8
Cole, W. A., 103n
communication costs, 7
Confederation of British Industry, 303, 316
congestion, 4, 8, 9–10, 49–50, 158, 163, 175, 324–5, 339
conurbation regions, 33–7
Cowling, K., 243

Deane, Phyllis: and Cole, W. A., 103n; and Mitchell, B. R., 103n, 104
depressed areas, 120–2, 281, 283–5
Development Areas, 66, 285–8, 290–1, 294–316, 338, 344; see also Special Development Areas

Development Districts, 288–90
Distribution of Industry Acts, 286, 287

Earnings, 59–60, 326–7; and unemployment 232–45, 328–31; and vacancies, 240–1; see also labour
Economic Consultants Ltd, 179n, 323, 340n
Economic Planning Boards, 29
education, 47–8, 202
employment: and industrial structure, 124–45, 335–6; by sex, 140; location quotient, 158–9
environment, 5–6, 8–11, 37–8, 164–5, 201–2, 266, 314–15, 321–2; and health, 50–1, 322; see also congestion
European Economic Community, 337

Fertility rates, 111–16
Flinn, M. W., 103n
Fowler, R. F., 231

Grants, 305–7, 345; see also building grants; investment grants
grey areas, 339, 340; see also Hunt Report; Intermediate Areas

Hammond, Edwin, 103n, 104, 115
Harris, A. I., 13
Harrod–Domar, analysis, 85–6, 96–8
Hart, R. A., 256, 260
health differences, 50, 110, 322; see also environment
Hicksian 'super-multiplier', 198
housing, 49; prices, 79–80, 158, 174, 249
Howard, R. S., 268, 275, 296
Hunt Committee, 290, 302, 303n, 311, 316n
Hunt Report, 143, 339; note of dissent from, 315; see also grey areas; Intermediate Areas

Industrial development certificates, 286–9, 293, 300–3, 305, 307, 315–17, 342, 345
Industrial Transference scheme, 281, 338
inflation, 22, 24, 26; see also Phillips curve
Inland Revenue: Reports, 82, 83; Surveys, 47
Intermediate Areas, 290–1; see also grey areas; Hunt Report
investment grants, 290, 306–7, 343–5

[351]

INDEX

Labour: demand, 17–20, 23–6, 109–16, 244, 325, see also employment; mobility, 13, 16, 17–20, 22, 23–6, 144, 233–4, 252–63, see also migration; price of, 232–45, see also earnings
Labour Mobility Survey, 13, 79, 218, 253, 266
Lee, C. H., 103n, 104, 124, 125, 127
Loasby, B. J., 278
Local Employment Acts, 29, 288, 290, 311, 343
location of industry, 2, 4–5, 17, 20–2, 23–5, 325–6
London, 23, 27, 35, 36, 45, 49, 79, 80, 106, 109–11, 113–14, 116, 120, 122, 126, 131, 153–5, 157–8, 162, 197, 260–1; see also congestion
Luttrell, W. F., 275, 278, 286

Makower, H., 284
Marschak, J., 284
Matthews, R. C. O., 200n
Meade, J. E., 86
Merseyside Development Area, 304
metal industries, 117–18
Metcalf, D., 243
migration, 12–16, 21–2, 169, 202, 252–77, 281–3, 325–6, 334, 338; by age and sex 259–60, 267, 271, gravity models of, 256; see also labour
Mitchell, B. R., 103n, 104
mobile United Kingdom content of consumption, 185–7, 202–4
mobility of resources, 2–3, 17, 91–2, 146, 250–80
Moore, F. T., 180
mortality rates, 50, 110–15
'moves' of manufacturing industry, 144–5, 163, 174, 250–2, 272–9, 292–300
Myrdal, G., 332

Neild, R. R., 306n, 343n
Nevin, E., 179n.

Peterson, J. W., 180
Phillips curve, 237–43, 331
Pigou, A. C., 1
population: age structure, 54–7, 89; growth, 103–16, 273–4; location, 5, 108–9; mobility see migration
'potential', 160–3, 323
Prest, A. R., 184
price differences, 19, 22, 78–81, 99–101, 245–8
productivity, 56–9, 101–2, 125, 151–8, 160

Rail Wagon Load Survey, 69
Redcliffe-Maud Commission, 29, 33, 34, 35, 36
Regional Economic Planning Councils, 29
Regional Employment Premium, 64, 289–90, 294, 307–11, 317, 329, 343–5
retraining, 281
Richardson Committee, 343
Richardson, H. W., 86n, 97n
Road Goods Surveys, 69
Robinson, H. W., 284
Roe, A. R., 179n
Round, J. I., 179n

Selective Employment Premium, 308
Smith, Wilfred, 103n
Special Areas, 284–6
Special Areas (Development and Improvement) Act, 284
Special Development Areas, 29, 290–1, 345; see also Development Areas
specialisation, 38–44, 90–5, 99–102, 132, 142, 146, 151, 158–60
Standard Regions, 29–30
Steele, David, 76n
Stein, J. L., 86, 97

Tax inducements, 285, 289, 305–7, 343–4
textile industries, 116–17, 136, 140, 287, 325
Thirlwall, A. P., 306n
Toothill Committee, 314
Town and Country Planning Act, 286; see also industrial development certificates
transport costs, 5, 156, 160, 249
travel costs, 9–10, 80, 157–8, 174, 249

Unemployability, 222, 227–9
unemployment: and distance from London, 260–1; and industrial structure, 217–18; and vacancies, 222–6; cyclical, 218–21; demand-deficiency, 222–4, 233; duration of, 230–2; female, 216, 225, 328; frictional, 222, 345; seasonal, 220; structural, 222, 345–6; unregistered, 215–16, 221

Value-Added Tax, 343

Webb, A. E., 241n
Weeden, R., 133n, 271
Welham, P. J., 70n
Welsh Development Area, 304
Welton, T. A., 110
Woodward, V. H., 52n, 53, 55, 56, 58, 60, 62, 63, 64, 66, 68, 77

PUBLICATIONS OF THE
NATIONAL INSTITUTE OF ECONOMIC
AND SOCIAL RESEARCH

published by

THE CAMBRIDGE UNIVERSITY PRESS

Books published for the Institute by the Cambridge University Press are available through the ordinary booksellers. They appear in the five series below:

ECONOMIC & SOCIAL STUDIES

*I   *Studies in the National Income, 1924–1938*
     Edited by A. L. BOWLEY. Reprinted with corrections, 1944. pp. 256.
*II   *The Burden of British Taxation*
     By G. FINDLAY SHIRRAS and L. ROSTAS. 1942. pp. 140.
*III   *Trade Regulations and Commercial Policy of the United Kingdom*
     By THE RESEARCH STAFF OF THE NATIONAL INSTITUTE OF ECONOMIC AND SOCIAL RESEARCH. 1943. pp. 275.
*IV   *National Health Insurance: A Critical Study*
     By HERMAN LEVY. 1944. pp. 356.
*V   *The Development of the Soviet Economic System: An Essay on the Experience of Planning in the U.S.S.R.*
     By ALEXANDER BAYKOV. 1946. pp. 530.
     (Out of print in this series, but reprinted 1970 in Cambridge University Press Library Edition, £5.00 net.)
*VI   *Studies in Financial Organization.*
     By T. BALOGH. 1948. pp. 328.
*VII   *Investment, Location, and Size of Plant: A Realistic Inquiry into the Structure of British and American Industries*
     By P. SARGANT FLORENCE, assisted by W. BALDAMUS. 1948. pp. 230.
*VIII   *A Statistical Analysis of Advertising Expenditure and of the Revenue of the Press*
     By NICHOLAS KALDOR and RODNEY SILVERMAN. 1948. pp. 200.
*IX   *The Distribution of Consumer Goods*
     By JAMES B. JEFFERYS, assisted by MARGARET MACCOLL and G. L. LEVETT. 1950. pp. 430.
*X   *Lessons of the British War Economy*
     Edited by D. N. CHESTER. 1951. pp. 260.
*XI   *Colonial Social Accounting*
     By PHYLLIS DEANE. 1953. pp. 360.
*XII   *Migration and Economic Growth*
     By BRINLEY THOMAS. 1954. pp. 384.
*XIII   *Retail Trading in Britain, 1850–1950*
     By JAMES B. JEFFERYS. 1954. pp. 490.
*XIV   *British Economic Statistics*
     By CHARLES CARTER and A. D. ROY. 1954. pp. 192.
*XV   *The Structure of British Industry: A Symposium*
     Edited by DUNCAN BURN. 1958. Vol. I. pp. 403. Vol. II. pp. 499.
*XVI   *Concentration in British Industry*
     By RICHARD EVELY and I. M. D. LITTLE. 1960. pp. 357.
*XVII   *Studies in Company Finance*
     Edited by BRIAN TEW and R. F. HENDERSON. 1959. pp. 301.

* At present out of print.

*XVIII   *British Industrialists: Steel and Hosiery, 1850–1950*
         By CHARLOTTE ERICKSON. 1959. pp. 276.
XIX   *The Antitrust Laws of the U.S.A.: A Study of Competition Enforced by Law*
         By A. D. NEALE. 2nd edition, 1970. pp. 544. £4.00 net.
XX   *A Study of United Kingdom Imports*
         By M. FG. SCOTT. 1963. pp. 270. £3.00 net.
XXI   *Industrial Growth and World Trade*
         By ALFRED MAIZELS. Reprinted with corrections, 1971. pp. 563. £4.20 net.
XXII   *The Management of the British Economy, 1945–60*
         By J. C. R. DOW. 1964. pp. 443. £3.00 net.
XXIII   *The British Economy in 1975*
         By W. BECKERMAN AND ASSOCIATES. 1965. pp. 631. £4.00 net.
XXIV   *Occupation and Pay in Great Britain, 1906–60*
         By GUY ROUTH. 1965. pp. 182. £1.75 net.
XXV   *Exports and Economic Growth of Developing Countries*
         By A. MAIZELS, assisted by L. F. CAMPBELL-BOROSS and P. B. W. RAYMENT. 1968. pp. 445. £3.00 net.
XXVI   *Urban Development in Britain: Standards, Costs and Resources, 1964–2004*
         By P. A. STONE. Vol. 1: *Population Trends and Housing*. 1970. pp. 436. £3.00 net.

OCCASIONAL PAPERS

*I   *The New Population Statistics*
         By R. R. KUCZYNSKI. 1942. pp. 31.
*II   *The Population of Bristol*
         By H. A. SHANNON and E. GREBENIK. 1943. pp. 92.
*III   *Standards of Local Expenditure*
         By J. R. HICKS and U. K. HICKS. 1943. pp. 61.
*IV   *War-time Pattern of Saving and Spending*
         By CHARLES MADGE. 1943. pp. 139.
*V   *Standardized Accounting in Germany*
         By H. W. SINGER. Reprinted 1944. pp. 68.
*VI   *Ten Years of Controlled Trade in South-Eastern Europe*
         By N. MOMTCHILOFF. 1944. pp. 90.
*VII   *The Problem of Valuation for Rating*
         By J. R. HICKS, U. K. HICKS and C. E. V. LESER. 1944. pp. 90.
*VIII   *The Incidence of Local Rates in Great Britain*
         By J. R. HICKS and U. K. HICKS. 1945. pp. 64.
*IX   *Contributions to the Study of Oscillatory Time-Series*
         By M. G. KENDALL. 1946. pp. 76.
*X   *A System of National Book-keeping Illustrated by the Experience of the Netherlands Economy*
         By J. B. D. DERKSEN. 1946. pp. 34.
*XI   *Productivity, Prices and Distribution in Selected British Industries*
         By L. ROSTAS. 1948. pp. 199.
*XII   *The Measurement of Colonial National Incomes: An Experiment*
         By PHYLLIS DEANE. 1948. pp. 173.
*XIII   *Comparative Productivity in British and American Industry*
         By L. ROSTAS. 1948. pp. 263.
*XIV   *The Cost of Industrial Movement*
         By W. F. LUTTRELL. 1952. pp. 104.
XV   *Costs in Alternative Locations: The Clothing Industry*
         By D. C. HAGUE and P. K. NEWMAN. 1952. pp. 73. £1.05 net.
*XVI   *Social Accounts of Local Authorities*
         By J. E. G. UTTING. 1953. pp. 81.
*XVII   *British Post-war Migration*
         By JULIUS ISAAC. 1954. pp. 294.
*XVIII   *The Cost of the National Health Service in England and Wales*
         By BRIAN ABEL-SMITH and RICHARD M. TITMUSS. 1956. pp. 176.

* At present out of print.

*XIX *Post-war Investment, Location and Size of Plant*
       By P. SARGANT FLORENCE. 1962. pp. 51.
*XX   *Investment and Growth Policies in British Industrial Firms*
       By TIBOR BARNA. 1962. pp. 71.
XXI   *Pricing and Employment in the Trade Cycle: A Study of British Manufacturing Industry, 1950–61*
       By R. R. NEILD. 1963. pp. 73. 75p net.
XXII *Health and Welfare Services in Britain in 1975*
       By DEBORAH PAIGE and KIT JONES. 1966. pp. 142. £1.05 net.
XXIII *Lancashire Textiles: A Case Study of Industrial Change*
       By CAROLINE MILES. 1968. pp. 124. £1.05 net.
XXIV *The Economic Impact of Commonwealth Immigration*
       By K. JONES and A. D. SMITH. 1970. pp. 186. £1.75 net.
XV   *The Analysis and Forecasting of the British Economy*
       By M. J. C. SURREY. 1971. pp. 120. £1·20 net.

STUDIES IN THE NATIONAL INCOME AND EXPENDITURE OF THE UNITED KINGDOM

Published under the joint auspices of the National Institute and the Department of Applied Economics, Cambridge.

*1 *The Measurement of Consumers' Expenditure and Behaviour in the United Kingdom, 1920–1938* vol. I
     By RICHARD STONE, assisted by D. A. ROWE and by W. J. CORLETT, RENEE HURSTFIELD, MURIEL POTTER. 1954. pp. 448.
2   *The Measurement of Consumers' Expenditure and Behaviour in the United Kingdom, 1920–1938* vol. II
     By RICHARD STONE and D. A. ROWE. 1966. pp. 152. £6.00 net.
3   *Consumer's Expenditure in the United Kingdom, 1900–1919*
     By A. R. PREST, assisted by A. A. ADAMS. 1954. pp. 196. £3.15 net.
4   *Domestic Capital Formation in the United Kingdom, 1920–1938*
     By C. H. FEINSTEIN. 1965. pp. 284. £6.00 net.
5   *Wages and Salaries in the United Kingdom, 1920–1938*
     By AGATHA CHAPMAN, assisted by ROSE KNIGHT. 1953. pp. 254. £4.00 net.
6   *National Income, Expenditure and Output of the United Kingdom, 1855–1965*
     By C. H. FEINSTEIN. 1972. pp. 384. £10.00 net.

NIESR STUDENTS' EDITION

1 *Growth and Trade* (abridged from *Industrial Growth and World Trade*)
    By A. MAIZELS. 1970. pp. 312. £1.05 net.
2 *The Antitrust Laws of the U.S.A.* (2nd edition, unabridged)
    By A. D. NEALE. 1970. pp. 544. £1.40 net.
3 *The Management of the British Economy, 1945–60* (unabridged)
    By J. C. R. DOW. 1970. pp. 464. £1.10 net.

REGIONAL PAPERS

1 *The Anatomy of Regional Activity Rates* by JOHN BOWERS, and *Regional Social Accounts for the United Kingdom* by V. H. WOODWARD. 1970. pp. 192. £1.25 net.

* At present out of print.

THE NATIONAL INSTITUTE OF ECONOMIC AND SOCIAL RESEARCH

publishes regularly

THE NATIONAL INSTITUTE ECONOMIC REVIEW

A quarterly analysis of the general economic situation in the United Kingdom and the world overseas, with forecasts eighteen months ahead. The first issue each year is devoted entirely to the current situation and prospects both in the short and medium term. Other issues contain also special articles on subjects of interest to academic and business economists.

Annual subscriptions, £6.00, and single issues for the current year, £1·75 each, are available directly from NIESR, 2 Dean Trench Street, Smith Square, London, SW1P 3HE.

Subscriptions at the special reduced price of £2 p.a. are available to students in the United Kingdom and the Irish Republic on application to the Secretary of the Institute.

Back numbers, including reprints of those which have gone out of stock, are distributed by Wm. Dawson and Sons Ltd., Cannon House, Park Farm Road, Folkestone.

The Institute has also published

FACTORY LOCATION AND INDUSTRIAL MOVEMENT

By W. F. LUTTRELL. 1962. Vols. I and II. pp. 1080. £5.25 net.

THE IVTH FRENCH PLAN

By FRANCOIS PERROUX, translated by Bruno Leblanc. 1965. pp. 72. 50p net.

These also are available directly from the Institute.